Attor
Baseball

Attorneys in the Baseball Hall of Fame

A Collection of Biographical Essays

Edited by
LOUIS H. SCHIFF *and*
ROBERT M. JARVIS

McFarland & Company, Inc., Publishers
Jefferson, North Carolina

ISBN (print) 978-1-4766-9245-6
ISBN (ebook) 978-1-4766-5596-3

LIBRARY OF CONGRESS CATALOGING DATA ARE AVAILABLE

Library of Congress Control Number 2025022847

On the cover: Commissioner of Baseball Kenesaw Mountain Landis
throws out the first pitch at the 1922 World Series
(National Baseball Hall of Fame and Museum, Cooperstown, New York)

Printed in the United States of America

*McFarland & Company, Inc., Publishers
Box 611, Jefferson, North Carolina 28640
www.mcfarlandpub.com*

Acknowledgments

We are very grateful for the assistance and support we have received from the publisher's staff, particularly senior editor Gary T. Mitchem; from John W. Horne, Jr., the coordinator of rights and reproductions at the National Baseball Hall of Fame and Museum; and from our families and friends. In addition, we wish to thank Professor Edmund P. Edmonds (University of Notre Dame) for his proofreading efforts.

As will become apparent, we largely have followed the abbreviation and citation rules found in *The Bluebook: A Uniform System of Legal Citation* (21st ed., 2020) (published by the *Harvard Law Review*). The book's research is current through July 1, 2024.

In closing, allow us to also thank you, the reader. We very much appreciate you picking up our book and hope you will find it both entertaining and informative.

Table of Contents

Introduction

For a major leaguer, there is no greater honor than being elected to the Baseball Hall of Fame in Cooperstown, New York. Since its creation in 1936, the Hall has inducted 346 individuals. Of this number, only 11 have been lawyers. This book celebrates this unique group. In contrast to previous works, it emphasizes their legal careers rather than their baseball careers. In doing so, it provides readers with a fresh perspective. Due to its painstaking research, it also corrects various errors that have found their way into the public record.

The Editors lead matters off by looking at Kenesaw Mountain Landis (1866–1944; inducted 1944). After earning his law degree at Northwestern University (1891), Landis worked as a sole practitioner in Chicago. In 1905, he was appointed to the federal bench. In 1915, he heard but refused to rule on the Federal League's antitrust lawsuit against major league baseball. Following the 1919 Black Sox scandal, Landis became baseball's first commissioner (1920–44).

Savanna L. Nolan, a law librarian at the University of Georgia, next profiles Hugh Ambrose "Hughie" Jennings (1869–1928; inducted 1945). Recognized as one of the game's greatest shortstops, Jennings studied law at Cornell University (1901–04) but did not graduate. Nevertheless, he became a member of both the Maryland and Pennsylvania bars. In 1907, Jennings and his younger brother William opened a law firm in Scranton, Pennsylvania.

Geoffrey Christopher Rapp, a law professor at the University of Toledo, discusses James Henry "Jim" O'Rourke (1850–1919; inducted 1945), better known as "Orator O'Rourke" due to his distinct speaking style. In 1887, O'Rourke earned a law degree at Yale University. He later became a respected trusts and estates lawyer in Bridgeport, Connecticut (his hometown), where he also regularly represented the poor.

Stephanie Hunter McMahon, a law professor at the University of Cincinnati, studies Miller James "Hug" Huggins (1878–1929; inducted 1964). After earning a law degree at the University of Cincinnati (1902), Huggins

1

The entrance to the National Baseball Hall of Fame and Museum in Coopers-town, New York (established 1936) (National Baseball Hall of Fame and Museum).

devoted himself full-time to baseball, first as a player and then as a manager. Huggins's greatest success came while piloting the New York Yankees (1918–29; six pennants and three World Series).

Walter T. Champion, Jr., a law professor at Texas Southern University, describes John Montgomery "Monte" Ward (1860–1925; inducted 1964). While earning a law degree at Columbia University, Ward organized baseball's first players' union (1885). Later, he formed the sport's first player-run league (1890). After retiring from the game, Ward became a wealthy corporate attorney in New York City as well as a champion amateur golfer.

Richard D. Friedman, a law professor at the University of Michigan, analyzes Wesley Branch Rickey (1881–1965; inducted 1967). After earning a J.D. at the University of Michigan (1911) and briefly practicing law in Boise, Idaho, Rickey became one of baseball's leading executives. In 1945, while running the Brooklyn Dodgers, Rickey signed Jack R. "Jackie" Robinson to a minor league contract. Two years later, Robinson broke baseball's color line.

Edmund P. Edmonds, an emeritus law professor at the University of Notre Dame, chronicles Leland Stanford "Larry" MacPhail, Sr. (1890–1975; inducted 1978). A 1910 law graduate of George Washington University, MacPhail briefly practiced law in Chicago before becoming a businessman. Today, he is both hailed as the father of night baseball and condemned for authoring the 1946 "MacPhail Report," which called for upholding baseball's color line.

Ronald J. Rychlak, a law professor at the University of Mississippi, covers Albert Benjamin "Happy" Chandler, Sr. (1898–1991; inducted 1982). After earning a law degree from the University of Kentucky (1924) and working as a sole practitioner in Versailles, Kentucky (1924–29), Chandler enjoyed astounding success in politics. As a result, in 1945 he was named baseball's second commissioner. After resigning as commissioner in 1951, he reentered politics.

Elizabeth Manriquez, a law librarian at the University of Wisconsin, reports on Bowie Kent Kuhn (1926–2007; inducted 2008). After earning his LL.B. at the University of Virginia (1950), Kuhn joined the Wall Street law firm of Willkie, Farr & Gallagher, where his clients included the National League. In 1969, Kuhn was appointed baseball's fifth commissioner. Following the end of his tenure (1984), Kuhn resumed practicing law.

Editor Robert M. Jarvis, a law professor at Nova Southeastern University, examines Walter Francis O'Malley (1903–79; inducted 2008). A 1930 law graduate of Fordham University, O'Malley became the Brooklyn Dodgers' team lawyer in 1943. After gaining control of the club in 1950, O'Malley in 1957 moved the franchise to Los Angeles, thereby bringing major league baseball to the West Coast.

Lastly, Editor Louis H. Schiff, a retired Florida county court judge and an adjunct professor at the Mitchell Hamline School of Law, scrutinizes Anthony "Tony" La Russa, Jr. (born 1944; inducted 2014). When his playing career was derailed by injuries, La Russa decided to study law at Florida State University. After earning his J.D. in 1978, he became the major leagues' second winningest manager, which put an end to his plans to become a trial lawyer.

The essays are accompanied by two appendices. The first is a table providing each inductee's "vital statistics" (much like the back of a baseball card). The second rounds out the book by turning the spotlight on baseball's non–Hall of Fame lawyers.

CHAPTER 1

Kenesaw Mountain Landis (1944)

Louis H. Schiff *and* Robert M. Jarvis

Kenesaw Mountain Landis (November 20, 1866–November 25, 1944) was a lawyer, a federal judge, and, for 24 years, the first commissioner of Major League Baseball.[1] Although physically diminutive (5'6" and 130 pounds), Landis more than made up for his lack of size by his personality (intimidating), visage (commanding), and unusually long name (a nod to his father's Civil War service).[2]

Squire Landis

Landis was born in Millville, Ohio (30 miles north of Cincinnati), to Mary A. (née Kumler) (1832–1912)[3] and Dr. Abraham H. Landis (1821–96).[4] The couple had married in Millville on September 17, 1850,[5] and had seven children (two girls and five boys), of whom Landis was the sixth: Katherine J. (1851–1921)[6]; Frances Q. (1853–1939)[7]; Walter K. (1856–1917)[8]; Charles B. (1858–1922)[9]; Dr. John H. (1860–1918)[10]; Landis (1866–1944)[11]; and Frederick D. (1872–1934).[12]

In 1875, the Landis family moved to Logansport, Indiana, where Landis's childhood continued, as before, to be an ordinary one.[13] Landis was a poor student and dropped out of school at the age of 14. By this time, however, he had managed to acquire the sobriquet "Squire" because of his "judicial manner."[14]

Initial Practice, Law School, Marriage, and Children

In 1887, Landis, having learned shorthand and having briefly worked as a court reporter in northern Indiana, moved to Indianapolis and got a job in the Indiana Secretary of State's office.[15] Later that year, just before his 21st birthday, he filed the paperwork necessary to become a lawyer (during this time Indiana allowed any registered voter "of good moral character" to become a lawyer).[16] In 1888, having received his law license, Landis quit his government job and opened a law office in Marion, Indiana.[17] His practice failed to take off, however, leading Landis to conclude that he needed a formal legal education if he was going to make it as a lawyer.[18]

In 1889, Landis relocated to Ohio and enrolled in the law school at Cincinnati College.[19] Today, many sources incorrectly claim that Landis went to the city's YMCA law school, but these sources are wrong—the school would not open for another four years.[20]

Following his freshman year, Landis moved to Chicago, Illinois. The catalyst for this change was Walter Q. Gresham (1832–95), a Chicago federal appeals court judge Landis had met in Indianapolis who encouraged Landis to set his sights higher.[21] Landis later described Gresham as "the best friend I ever had."[22]

In Chicago, Landis enrolled in the law school at Northwestern University ("NU") and graduated in June 1891 (despite barely passing his Pleading and Real Property courses).[23] In a preview of things to come, Landis was asked to address his fellow graduates. He used this opportunity to deliver a speech titled "The Conservative Man."[24] During his talk, Landis warned the audience about "radical men, extremists, [and] agitators"; promoted the view that German and Italian immigrants were dangerous; and embraced the Republicans' political agenda.[25]

Armed with his newly minted LL.B., and with no need to take the Illinois bar exam due to the state's "diploma privilege," which exempted the graduates of local law schools from the bar exam,[26] Landis hung out a shingle in Chicago[27]; he also became a teaching assistant at NU.[28] These activities did not last long, however, for in March 1893 Landis agreed to accompany Gresham to Washington, D.C., after President (Stephen) Grover Cleveland appointed Gresham U.S. Secretary of State.[29]

Landis's stay in Washington turned out to be a short one, for Gresham died in May 1895.[30] It was long enough, however, for Landis to meet Winifred Reed (1872–1947).[31] Winifred was from Ottawa, Illinois, and the pair married there on July 25, 1895.[32] The couple soon had two children: Reed G. (1896–1975), an advertising executive,[33] and Susanne (later Phillips) (1898–1977).[34]

Following a brief honeymoon "among the northern lakes,"[35] Landis returned to Chicago and set about to restart his law practice. "My prospects are bright indeed," Landis wrote a friend, "and I think the outlook is such that if I behave myself and attend diligently to business the future is reasonably secure."[36] Despite this upbeat assessment, Landis's ship had not yet come in. Thus, to earn extra money, he agreed to serve as a special Assistant U.S. District Attorney and helped investigate alleged monopolistic practices in the Chicago beef industry.[37] He also accepted court appointments to defend indigent prisoners.[38]

Uhl, Jones & Landis

In 1897, Landis formed a partnership with two more seasoned lawyers he had met in Washington: Frank H. Jones (1854–1931) and Edwin F. Uhl (1841–1901).[39] Although the firm, dubbed Uhl, Jones & Landis, soon dissolved,[40] Landis finally was coming into his own: he was defending transit companies from personal injury claims[41]; he was involving himself in Republican politics[42]; and he was active in numerous clubs and professional organizations.[43] In 1898, when Landis was asked to address the Chicago Bar Association ("CBA"), Mitchell D. Follansbee, the CBA's president, introduced Landis by saying that among Chicago's younger lawyers, "few … are more generally or more favorably known[.]"[44] In 1900, Landis even made it back to Washington, where he argued (but lost) a case in front of the U.S. Supreme Court.[45]

By now, the ever-ambitious Landis was angling for an appointment to the federal bench. Thus, with the help of his brothers Charles and Frederick, both of whom were members of Congress (Charles from Indiana's 9th district and Frederick from Indiana's 11th district), Landis began letting everyone know that the U.S. District Court for the Northern District of Illinois needed an additional seat (and that he was just the man to fill it). To help Landis overcome his lack of courtroom experience, Charles told reporters that Landis is "the genius of our family. [I]n years I am his senior, but in brains Old Ken tops the whole family. He's the most natural lawyer I ever saw...."[46]

In 1905, Landis's efforts bore fruit when a new seat was created and Landis was appointed to it by President Theodore Roosevelt, Jr.[47] At his swearing-in ceremony, Landis expressed his gratitude to the lawyers in attendance: "I doubt if any member of this bar is under a greater load of obligation for friendship and courtesy and high consideration than I am to you." He then added that his "one ambition" in his new role was "to merit your confidence and respect," and that he planned to do so by being "patient and industrious."[48]

On the Bench

During his 17 years on the bench, Landis presided over numerous lawsuits.[49] Two, however, would catch the attention of baseball's leaders and eventually lead to Landis being named the sport's first commissioner: *United States v. Standard Oil Company* and *Federal League of Professional Base Ball Clubs v. National League of Professional Base Ball Clubs.*

United States v. Standard Oil Company

In 1906, the Roosevelt administration set its sights on John D. Rockefeller, Sr.'s Standard Oil Company, Inc. ("SOC"). By now, James R. Garfield, the federal government's Commissioner of Corporations (and a son of the late President James A. Garfield), had amassed substantial evidence detailing SOC's practice of secretly obtaining rebates and other preferences from railroads, which allowed the company to undersell its competitors. As a result, U.S. Attorney General William H. Moody announced that the Justice Department planned to bring SOC to heel.[50] In the summer of 1906, two federal grand juries in Chicago returned 10 indictments against SOC for violating the Elkins Act,[51] a federal statute that made any company that offered, gave, or received an illegal rebate subject to a fine of up to $20,000 per incident. Treating each SOC rail car that traveled under a rebated rate as a criminal act, the grand juries charged SOC with 6,428 violations.[52]

Even before the indictments were handed down, Landis began maneuvering to get assigned to the case. In early 1906, he wrote a letter to Roosevelt complaining that a lawsuit challenging the beef industry's monopoly had failed to secure a conviction; had he been on the case, Landis claimed, the outcome would have been different. His letter also mentioned SOC and his desire to hear its case.[53] The letter had the desired effect, and on January 3, 1907, Landis issued his first ruling in the case, which dismissed SOC's argument that the Elkins Act had been repealed by the 1906 Hepburn Act (a bill expanding the powers of the Interstate Commerce Commission).[54]

Two months later, the trial began. On April 13, 1907, the jury returned guilty verdicts on 1,462 counts.[55] On August 3, 1907, Landis ordered SOC to pay the maximum allowable fine under the circumstances: $29,240,000 (the equivalent today of $971 million).[56] When Landis finished reading his 8,684-word opinion, which likened SOC's executives to counterfeiters and thieves,[57] the crowded courtroom burst into applause.[58]

Landis instantly became the "most talked of man in the country,"[59] and many people urged him to run for high political office.[60] Landis's travel and vacation plans became fodder for the national press.[61] His refusal to comment on the fine earned him headlines.[62] His baseball-watching habits made the newspapers.[63] Through it all, Landis played the role of the reluctant celebrity: "I wish that I could be forgotten for the next six months—absolutely ignored, as if I did not exist."[64] "If you have to write anything I wish you would make it as short as possible," he told a Chicago reporter who located him while he was visiting New York.[65] There also were reports that SOC had hired two private investigators to follow Landis to find evidence to support its appeal. When asked for a comment, Landis replied: "I guess I can stand inspection."[66]

U.S. District Judge Kenesaw M. Landis (1907) (Shutterstock, Inc./Morris Everett, Jr. Collection).

Landis's moment in the sun soon passed (at least for a little while): in July 1908, the U.S. Court of Appeals for the Seventh Circuit unanimously overturned his ruling,[67] while in March 1909, Judge Albert B. Anderson of the District of Indiana, sitting by designation, granted a directed verdict for SOC during the government's retrial of the case.[68]

Federal League of Professional Base Ball Clubs v. National League of Professional Base Ball Clubs

In January 1915, a new lawsuit landed on Landis's desk. Titled *Federal League of Professional Base Ball Clubs v. National League of Professional Base Ball Clubs*, the 92-page complaint alleged that baseball's two major leagues (the American League and the National League), together with their 16 teams and the sport's three-man "National Commission" (consisting of American League president Byron B. "Ban" Johnson, National League president John K. Tener, and Cincinnati Reds president August "Garry" Herrmann), were an illegal monopoly that was attempting to destroy the recently-established (1913) Federal League, which was seeking to become the country's third major league.[69]

Although the Federal League had steered the case to Landis due to his rulings in *Standard Oil*, the defendants claimed to be just as pleased with his selection. "It is gratifying to know that this suit will be heard by Judge Landis," Ban Johnson told reporters. "Judge Landis is one of the best informed legal authorities as to baseball affairs in this country. He is eminently fair.... We will come out with flying colors."[70]

The Federal League filed its petition for a preliminary injunction on January 5, 1915; in response, Landis ordered hearings to begin in two weeks—an accelerated schedule that suggested he was eager to resolve the case before the start of the 1915 baseball season. A seat in Landis's courtroom once again became the hottest ticket in town. To accommodate all the interested observers, the *Chicago Daily Tribune* suggested (tongue-in-cheek) that the trial be held in one of the city's ballparks and proceeded to cover the case like a baseball game—"the greatest contest in the history of the national sport"—complete with a lineup card showing the opposing sides and their lawyers with Landis listed as the game's umpire.[71]

On the first day of the hearings, an estimated 600 spectators filled Landis's courtroom, with many more turned away.[72] "The Judge," according to one account, "smirked, smiled, growled, grinned, and made wry faces as the witnesses—the high, low, and jacks of the game—paraded before him."[73] At one point Landis interrupted Keene H. Addington, Sr., one of the Federal League's lawyers, to press him on whether the case belonged in federal court, a question the media interpreted as revealing Landis's skepticism toward the Federal League's lawsuit.[74]

After four days of testimony, Landis declared, "I have gone just about far enough in this case," and pointedly asked the Federal League's legal team what it wanted from him: "Do you want me to stop the teams from going on spring training trips? Do you want me to break up the clubs or what do you want me to do?"[75] Later, however, when George Wharton Pepper, the chief lawyer for the major leagues, spoke about his own love of the game, Landis rebuked him and told him "to keep ... love and affection out of this lawsuit."[76] He then offered an observation that would be featured prominently in contemporary accounts and later histories of the case: "I think you gentleman around here all understand that a blow at this thing called baseball—both sides understand this perfectly—will be regarded by this court as a blow at a national institution."[77]

Landis's words were seen as putting him squarely on the side of the major leagues. Indeed, Pepper took Landis's statement as an opportunity to sit down, believing that Landis had made his argument for him. Based on these comments, *The Sporting News*, a staunch supporter of baseball's establishment, advised its readers that Landis "is a dyed-in-the-wool fan, has played baseball himself, and the game is safe in his hands."[78]

Having put the case on an accelerated schedule, it generally was assumed that Landis would move quickly to rule on the Federal League's preliminary injunction request and then schedule a full trial. But Landis never issued a ruling, and the case never went to trial. Month after month, through the entire 1915 baseball season, Landis sat on his hands.

By December 1915, the Federal League, having had enough, reached a settlement with the American and National Leagues. The situation had not been profitable for anyone (except the players, who had seen their salaries temporarily skyrocket as a bidding war broke out for their services), and all sides were eager to find a resolution. To make peace, the major leagues bought out four of the Federal League's clubs (the Brooklyn Tip-Tops, Buffalo Blues, Newark Peppers, and Pittsburgh Rebels) and allowed two of the Federal League's owners (Philip D.C. "Phil" Ball of the St. Louis Terriers and Charles H. Weeghman of the Chicago Whales) to purchase major league clubs (respectively, the St. Louis Browns of the American League and the Chicago Cubs of the National League).[79] Agreement in hand, the litigants returned to Landis's courtroom in February 1916 and requested that the case be dismissed.[80]

As matters turned out, the major leagues had not heard the last of the Federal League. While the Federal League's other owners were content to settle, the owners of the Federal League's eighth team—the Baltimore Terrapins—were not.[81] As a result, in 1922 their antitrust lawsuit (filed in Washington, D.C., in 1917) reached the U.S. Supreme Court, where Justice Oliver Wendell Holmes, Jr., famously decided that baseball did not constitute interstate commerce and therefore was not subject to the nation's antitrust laws.[82]

The 1919 Black Sox Scandal

In 1920, baseball's owners were shocked when they discovered that eight players on the heavily favored Chicago White Sox had taken bribes in exchange for agreeing to throw the 1919 World Series to the underdog Cincinnati Redlegs (now Reds).[83] Recognizing that dramatic action was needed to restore the public's faith in baseball, the owners agreed, after much debate, to replace the National Commission, the sport's governing body since 1903, with Landis as a single commissioner with unlimited powers:

> The National League [initially] unified behind the "Lasker Plan," proposed by a Chicago advertising executive [named Albert D. Lasker] who held a small

stake in the Cubs. The Lasker Plan would replace the National Commission with a three-man board of eminent citizens with no prior connection to baseball. This board would have total authority over every aspect of Organized Baseball: players, managers, umpires and even club owners. The October 21, 1920 *Sporting News* identified the front-runners for this three-man board as Judge Landis, General John J. Pershing, and Senator Hiram Johnson of California. A majority of American League teams rejected the Lasker Plan, citing the folly of putting their entire industry under the control of men with no experience in the field, but the three anti-[Ban] Johnson owners embraced it as a means to free themselves from Johnson's yoke.

On November 8, 1920, the Red Sox, Yankees and White Sox declared war on Ban Johnson and their AL colleagues. They joined the eight NL clubs to announce the formation of a new 12-team league [with the twelfth team being an expansion team in either Cleveland or Detroit], with Judge Landis to serve as chairman of the new governing tribunal. The new National-American League promised to allow the minor leagues to nominate one of the two remaining members of the new Commission. Forced to choose between loyalty to Ban Johnson and a potentially ruinous civil war, the "Loyal Five" AL owners [representing the Cleveland Indians, Detroit Tigers, Philadelphia Athletics, St. Louis Browns, and Washington Senators] cast Johnson aside, voting on November 12th to accept Landis as Commissioner. Landis accepted the job later that day, then spent the next two months dictating his own job description to the owners. [As a result, it was agreed]:

- The Commissioner may investigate, "either upon complaint or upon his own initiative, any act, transaction or practice charged, alleged or suspected to be detrimental to the best interests of the national game of baseball," with the authority to fine clubs up to $5,000 per offense, and to suspend or permanently banish any player, employee or league or team official.
- All clubs accept the Commissioner's authority to impose discipline, "and severally waive such right of recourse to the courts as would otherwise have existed in their favor."
- The Commissioner is elected for a seven-year term, with his replacement to be "chosen by a vote of the majority of the clubs composing the two major leagues." Paralleling the constitutional protection for federal judges, "no diminution of the compensation or powers of the present or any succeeding Commissioner shall be made during his term."
- "In the event of failure to elect a successor within three months after the vacancy has arisen, either major league may request the President of the United States to designate a Commissioner, and the person when thus designated shall thereupon become Commissioner with the same effect as if named herein."[84]

Landis also demanded that he be well paid in his new position. As a result, while his judge's salary was just $7,500, his baseball salary was set at $42,500.[85]

In February 1921, Landis, in his first official act as commissioner, rented an office at 333 North Michigan Avenue.[86] Located just a few blocks from his courtroom, the sign on the door read simply "Baseball."[87] Landis also hired Leslie M. O'Connor, a 31-year-old local lawyer, to be his secretary at a salary of $7,500 a year.[88]

Off the Bench

Although most people expected Landis to give up his judgeship, Landis had no intention of doing so. Recognizing that the infighting among the various team owners might make his new job untenable, Landis wanted to keep his options open. Upon learning of his plan, Landis's allies expressed their support[89]; the publication *Law Notes* went so far as to write: "There are many unpaid positions on committees and directorates which a public-spirited judge assumes from time to time, for which in fact his judicial prestige is one of his qualifications, and few if any of these involve more or real public usefulness than that which Judge Landis has accepted."[90]

The rest of the legal community viewed matters far differently. The *Michigan Law Review*, for example, accused Landis of "prostituting his high office for the sake of a commercialized, professional sport" and urged him to resign his judgeship.[91] Chicago attorney Thomas J. Sutherland sent a letter of protest to members of Congress that attacked Landis for his "attempt to mulct the Government and … [engage in a] vicious infidelity to public service."[92]

Landis, however, insisted he had done nothing wrong. "I looked into things well before accepting this baseball work. And you know baseball is a national institution. I feel that I did right in accepting the place offered to me."[93] Landis also promised to resign from the bench if either the House or the Senate passed a majority resolution "expressing … disapproval of this thing."[94]

Dragged into the fight, the U.S. Department of Justice concluded that Landis had broken no laws.[95] One newspaper, after pointing out that Congress could try to impeach Landis, noted that "the very idea of such action is unthinkable, with the tremendous hold Judge Landis has upon the respect and admiration of the entire country."[96] Nevertheless, the pressure on Landis continued to mount.

On February 2, 1921, Representative Benjamin F. Welty (D-OH) introduced a resolution calling for a Congressional investigation into Landis.[97] When U.S. Attorney General A. Mitchell Palmer notified Welty that Landis was breaking no law in holding two posts, Welty promptly introduced a bill making it illegal for a judge to receive payment for non-judicial work.[98]

On February 15, 1921, Welty formally moved for Landis's impeachment.[99] Although the House Judiciary Committee's members expressed skepticism that Landis's behavior was impeachable, many agreed that Landis was in the wrong.[100] In March 1921, the Committee issued a report finding that Landis had committed a "serious impropriety" that was "inconsistent with the full and adequate performance" of his judicial duties.[101] The report also recommended that the House investigate further.[102] Landis responded by reiterating his offer to resign from the bench if either chamber passed a resolution condemning his behavior.[103]

Meanwhile, another impeachment campaign—this one led by Senator Nathaniel B. Dial (D-SC)—was sparked by Landis's handling of a bank embezzlement case. Landis had taken pity on Francis J. Carey, a bank teller at the National City Bank in Ottawa, Illinois, who had pled guilty to stealing $96,000. Landis criticized the bank for paying the 19-year-old just $90 a month and sent Carey home to his mother while Landis decided on a just punishment.[104] On February 12, 1921, Dial, who happened to be the president of the Enterprise National Bank in Laurens, South Carolina, denounced Landis for espousing "the most Bolshevik doctrine I ever heard"[105] and insisted that "any man who utters that kind of statement is not worthy of public confidence and should be impeached."[106]

This time, Landis fought back, attacking Dial as a backwater politician who underpaid the employees in his South Carolina businesses. "No doubt he has little girls as young as 11 years working for him," Landis charged.[107] In a speech on the Senate floor, Dial declared that Landis's response showed "that he is not constituted by temperament to exercise the duties of a judge." Adding that he would not "bandy[] epithets with a self-advertised crank and a freak," Dial promised to use his influence to oust Landis from office.[108]

In September 1921, at the annual meeting of the American Bar Association ("ABA") in Cincinnati, Landis became a topic of heated discussion.[109] Landis's critics were scathing in condemning his actions. One accused him of having "ethically failed by yielding to the temptations of avarice and private gain" and "drag[ging] the ermine in the mire."[110] At the end of the debate, the ABA's delegates approved the following resolution by a voice vote:

> *Resolved,* That the conduct of Kenesaw M. Landis in engaging in private employment and accepting private emolument while holding the position of a federal judge and receiving a salary from the federal government, meets with our unqualified condemnation, as conduct unworthy of the office of judge, derogatory to the dignity of the Bench, and undermining public confidence in the independence of the judiciary.[111]

The ABA's resolution gave Landis's critics in Congress an opportunity to revive their stalled effort to impeach him and pass legislation prohibiting judges from taking second jobs.[112] Landis, however, insisted that he would not quit. By now, however, the jig was up. After holding out for a few more months, Landis on February 18, 1922, sent his letter of resignation to President Warren G. Harding. Later, Landis told reporters: "There isn't time enough to do everything. I've worked hard. I've been getting up at 5 o'clock in the morning. I've had to go without lunch for two weeks."[113]

Landis's last day on the bench was February 28, 1922. He disposed of 12 cases, most having to do with Prohibition violations, and dispensed punishments ranging from a one cent fine to one year in jail. "He conducted his final court in his characteristic fashion," one newspaper reporter wrote, "taking cases away from lawyers to conduct them personally, laughing, joking, storming and fuming. In the words of a court attendant, he was '1,000 per cent Landis.'"[114] When he was done, Landis stepped down from the bench and walked to his chambers without a word. When a different reporter asked if he had anything further to say, Landis replied: "Not much. Just let the curtain fall. At present I have no activities in mind except my baseball job."[115]

In 1924, the ABA adopted the country's first code of judicial conduct—titled the Canons of Judicial Ethics ("CJE")—a direct outgrowth of the Landis affair.[116] In their final report, the CJE's drafters included a lightly veiled reference to the fight to oust Landis:

> The situation ran along until three years ago, when a very forceful illustration occurred in the action of this Association itself at Cincinnati, when it proceeded to pass a resolution in disapproval of the conduct of an individual judge. It was then suggested that it would be much fairer and much better if the Association, instead of picking out individual cases for condemnation, should express its opinion of what the members of the American Bar Association expect from those who sit upon the Bench, to the end that its Canons of Professional Ethics should be as specific with respect to the conduct of judges as with respect to the conduct of members of the Bar.[117]

The drafters also included a specific canon (Canon 24) that would have prevented Landis from accepting organized baseball's offer: "24. Inconsistent Obligations. [A judge] should not accept inconsistent duties; nor incur obligations, pecuniary or otherwise, which will in any way interfere or appear to interfere with his devotion to the expeditious and proper administration of his official functions."[118]

Conclusion

Landis served as baseball's commissioner until his death from a heart attack in 1944 at the age of 78.[119] A short time later, newspapers reported that he had left his entire $100,000 estate, the equivalent today of $1.76 million, to his wife Winifred.[120]

During his time as commissioner, Landis used his power, which, per his contract, was absolute, as he saw fit.[121] Decades later, Ford C. Frick, baseball's third commissioner, explained that

> there was no gray zone of doubt—only the black or white of legal guilt or innocence. [Landis] ruled the game as if baseball were a courtroom, and players and officials were culprits awaiting sentence for their misdoings. Yet with it all, he was a kindly man, with a sense of sympathy and compassion that bubbled to the surface at the most unexpected times and places.[122]

While serving as commissioner, Landis's power was challenged only once. In *Milwaukee American Association v. Landis*,[123] Phil Ball, the owner of the St. Louis Browns, who secretly was stashing players on minor league teams he owned (including the American Association's Milwaukee Brewers), sued Landis after Landis declared stashed outfielder Herschel E. Bennett a free agent.[124] In court, Ball argued that Landis had abused his position as commissioner, but U.S. District Judge Walter C. Lindley of the Eastern District of Illinois (sitting by designation), dismissed the lawsuit:

> Apparently it was the intent of the parties to make the commissioner an arbiter, whose decisions made in good faith, upon evidence, upon all questions relating to the purpose of the organization and all conduct detrimental thereto, should be absolutely binding. So great was the parties' confidence in the man selected for the position [Landis] and so great the trust placed in him that certain of the agreements [will] continue only so long as he should remain commissioner.... The court is of the opinion that the commissioner acted clearly within his authority; that Bennett should be freed from his obligations of any contract with [Ball's teams]; that the prayer for injunction should be denied, and the bill dismissed for want of equity at the costs of plaintiffs.[125]

In November 1944, one month before his death, baseball's Most Valuable Player awards, given out since 1931, were renamed in honor of Landis. In October 2020, Landis's name was removed from them due to his refusal to integrate baseball.[126]

In December 1944, two weeks after his death, Landis unanimously was voted into Baseball's Hall of Fame.[127] Making no mention of either his legal or judicial career, Landis's Hall of Fame plaque reads simply: "Baseball's first Commissioner. Elected, 1920—Died in Office, 1944. His integrity and leadership established baseball in the respect, esteem and affection of the American people."[128]

NOTES

1. For works about Landis, see, e.g., RANDY MCNUTT, KENESAW MOUNTAIN LANDIS: THE MAN WHO BANNED SHOELESS JOE (2017); DAVID PIETRUSZA, JUDGE AND JURY: THE LIFE AND TIMES OF JUDGE KENESAW MOUNTAIN LANDIS (1998); J.G. TAYLOR SPINK, JUDGE LANDIS AND 25 YEARS OF BASEBALL (1947); Dan Busby, *Kenesaw Mountain Landis*, SABR, https://sabr.org/bioproj/person/kenesaw-landis/ (last visited July 1, 2024); John Henderson, "The Most Interesting Man in America": Folk Logic and First Principles in the Early Career of Judge Kenesaw Mountain Landis (unpublished Ph.D. dissertation, University of Florida, 1995), https://archive.org/details/mostinterestingm00hend/. *See also* LARRY MOFFI, THE CONSCIENCE OF THE GAME: BASEBALL'S COMMISSIONERS FROM LANDIS TO SELIG (2006); JEROME HOLTZMAN, THE COMMISSIONERS: BASEBALL'S MIDLIFE CRISIS 15–42 (1998). When he was 50, Landis took his first flight and instantly became hooked. He remained an aviation enthusiast for the rest of his life. *See* Elizabeth Borja, *The Many Flights of the Czar of Baseball*, NATIONAL AIR AND SPACE MUSEUM ARCHIVES, Mar. 28, 2019, https://airandspace.si.edu/stories/editorial/many-flights-czar-baseball.

2. From June 18, 1864, to July 2, 1864, the Battle of Kenesaw Mountain was fought near present-day Atlanta, Georgia. The engagement pitted Union General William T. Sherman against Confederate General Joseph E. Johnston. A total of 5,350 soldiers were killed in what now is recognized as one of the South's last military victories. During the battle, Landis's father, a Union physician, was injured when a Confederate bullet struck his left leg, leaving him with a lifelong limp. Today, the names of both the battle and the mountain are spelled with two "n's," but in the 19th century the more common spelling was with one "n." For a further discussion, see DANIEL J. VERMILYA, THE BATTLE OF KENNESAW MOUNTAIN (2014).

3. For an obituary of Mary, see *Mrs. Mary Landis Dead: Mother of Men Well Known in the Public Service*, BOS. SUN. GLOBE, Oct. 27, 1912, at 5. *See also Mary Kumler Landis*, FIND-A-GRAVE.COM, https://www.findagrave.com/memorial/34816327/mary_landis (last visited July 1, 2024).

4. For an obituary of Abraham, see *Indiana State News*, ARGOS REFLECTOR (IN), Nov. 19, 1896, at 3. *See also Dr Abraham Hoch Landis*, FIND-A-GRAVE.COM, https://www.findagrave.com/memorial/34816313/abraham_hoch_landis (last visited July 1, 2024).

5. *See Mary A. Kumler in the Ohio, U.S., County Marriage Records, 1774–1993*, ANCESTRY.COM, https://www.ancestry.com/discoveryui-content/view/901543691:61378 (last visited July 1, 2024); *Abraham H. Landis in the Ohio, U.S., County Marriage Records, 1774–1993*, ANCESTRY.COM, https://www.ancestry.com/discoveryui-content/view/1543691:61378 (last visited July 1, 2024).

6. For an obituary of Katherine, see *Sister of Judge Landis Dies in Logansport, Ind.*, CHI. DAILY TRIB., Nov. 24, 1921, at 1. *See also Katherine J Landis*, FIND-A-GRAVE.COM, https://www.findagrave.com/memorial/34816323/katherine_j_landis (last visited July 1, 2024).

7. For an obituary of Frances, see *Illness Fatal to Sister of Judge Landis*, INDIANAPOLIS NEWS, Mar. 13, 1939, at 5. *See also Frances Q Landis*, FIND-A-GRAVE.COM, https://www.findagrave.com/memorial/34816317/frances_q_landis (last visited July 1, 2024).

8. For an obituary of Walter, see *W.K. Landis, Brother of Noted U.S. Judge, Dead at Logansport*, INDIANAPOLIS STAR, Nov. 6, 1917, at 1. *See also Walter Kumler Landis*, FIND-A-GRAVE.COM, https://www.findagrave.com/memorial/34816328/walter_kumler_landis (last visited July 1, 2024). Walter was appointed postmaster of Puerto Rico in 1898 but lost his job in 1912 after he campaigned against President William Howard Taft. *See Taft Removes Landis: San Juan Postmaster Who Aided Roosevelt Accused of Neglect*, N.Y. TIMES, Aug. 13, 1912, at 6.

9. For an obituary of Charles, see *Former Congressman Charles Landis Dies: Oldest [sic] of Nationally Known Brothers Expires in Asheville Hospital—Represented Ninth Indiana District in Congress from 1897 to 1909—Gained Wealth in Dupont Company*, J. & COURIER (Lafayette, IN), Apr. 24, 1922, at 1. *See also Charles Beary Landis*, FIND-A-GRAVE.COM, https://www.findagrave.com/memorial/7116683/charles_beary_landis (last visited July 1, 2024).

10. For an obituary of John, see *Cincinnati Health Officer: Dr. John Howard Landis Dies at Hospital in That City*, MANSFIELD NEWS (OH), Aug. 23, 1918, at 2. *See also Dr John Howard Landis*, FIND-A-GRAVE.COM, https://www.findagrave.com/memorial/78979222/john_howard_landis (last visited July 1, 2024).

11. For an obituary of Landis, see *Judge Landis Dies; Baseball Czar, 78: Commissioner for 24 Years—Barred Eight Players for 'Throwing' 1919 Series—Freed 'Slave' Athletes—On Bench, Fined Standard Oil $29,240,000—Presided in Haywood, Berger Cases*, N.Y. TIMES, Nov. 26, 1944, at 56. *See also Kenesaw Mountain Landis*, FIND-A-GRAVE.COM, https://www.findagrave.com/memorial/600/kenesaw_mountain_landis (last visited July 1, 2024).

12. For an obituary of Frederick, see *Landis, Only [Congressional] Republican Victor in Indiana, Dead of Pneumonia: Famed Writer and Editor Taken at Logansport After Illness of Nearly a Month, Special Election to be Called—Family at His Bedside at End; [Governor] McNutt Heaps High Praise on Old Friend, Refuses to Give Date of Voting Until Funeral is Over*, INDIANAPOLIS TIMES, Nov. 15, 1934, at 1. *See also Frederick Daniel Landis*, FIND-A-GRAVE.COM, https://www.findagrave.com/memorial/7116679/frederick_daniel_landis (last visited July 1, 2024).

13. *See* Henderson, *supra* note 1, at 27 (describing Landis's childhood as consisting of school, chores, and, "in warmer weather, … pick-up baseball games and the latest fads, whether … race walking or roller skating … [as well as] fishing"). As Henderson explains, *id.* at 16, Abraham decided in 1868 to move the family to Logansport, an area he considered rich in opportunities, but was unable, for financial reasons, to do so until 1875.

14. *See Friend of Judge Landis*, SUN (Balt.), Aug. 23, 1907, at 11.

15. *See Federal Judges for Chicago*, 37 CHI. LEGAL NEWS 256, 257 (Mar. 25, 1905).

16. *See* Henderson, *supra* note 1, at 59, 62–63 n.17. Indiana began requiring prospective lawyers to attend law school, and pass a bar examination, in 1932 (the last state to do so). *See* Randall T. Shepard, *Building Indiana's Legal Profession*, 34 IND. L. REV. 529, 529 (2001).

17. *See* Henderson, *supra* note 1, at 60, 67.

18. *See* PIETRUSZA, *supra* note 1, at 11–12.

19. *See* Henderson, *supra* note 1, at 67–69.

20. The city's second law school, at the local YMCA, opened in 1893. *See id.* at 339. The city's third law school, at the University of Cincinnati, opened in 1896. *See id.* at 261. The claim that Landis attended the YMCA law school originated in a story by reporter Tom Swope of the *Cincinnati Post* published two days after Landis's death. *See* Tom Swope, *"Tom Swope, I'll Never Forgive You!" … Landis was Having Fun*, CIN. POST, Nov. 27, 1944, at 7 (quoting Landis as supposedly saying, "I never went to college myself. Mighty few persons know that but it's a fact. I started my law course at the YMCA Law School in Cincinnati and finished it at a similar school here in Chicago"). Swope's misreporting gained currency when it was included in Landis's first biography. *See* SPINK, *supra* note 1, at 8.

21. *See* Henderson, *supra* note 1, at 77.

22. *Id.* at 75.

23. *See Fitted for Their Profession: Graduation Exercises of the Law Department of Northwestern University*, CHI. TRIB., June 18, 1891, at 5 [hereinafter *Fitted*] (listing Landis as among the school's 60 graduating seniors); PIETRUSZA, *supra* note 1, at 12 (discussing Landis's academic troubles).

24. *See Fitted*, *supra* note 23.

25. *See* Henderson, *supra* note 1, at 72–73.

26. Landis was admitted to the Illinois bar prior to his graduation from NU. *See* Attorney Registration and Disciplinary Commission of the Supreme Court of Illinois, *Lawyer Search*, https://www.iardc.org/Lawyer/Search (last visited July 1, 2024) (indicating that Landis was admitted on June 9, 1891). As explained elsewhere, the diploma privilege existed in Illinois from 1880 to 1897. *See* Robert Sprecher, *Admission to Practice Law in Illinois*, 46 ILL. L. REV. 811, 841 (1952). Landis therefore is at least somewhat unique: although admitted in two jurisdictions (Illinois and Indiana), he never took a bar exam.

27. *See Locals*, LOGANSPORT DAILY REP. (IN), Sept. 11, 1891, at 3 ("In a neat card of invitation

received at this office Mr. Kenesaw M. Landis announces the opening of his office for the general practice of law, at 506 'Oxford Building,' 84 and 86 La Salle Street, Chicago, Ill."). By the following year, Landis had moved his office to the nearby Tacoma Building at La Salle and Madison Streets. *See* Martindale's American Law Directory—Biennial—1892–93, at 733 (25th ed. 1892). Landis's biggest case during this period was *Atkinson v. The Fair. See The Courts—U.S. Circuit—New Suits*, Daily Inter Ocean (Chi.), Sept. 22, 1892, at 11 (reporting on the filing, by "Kenesaw M. Landis, atty.," of a federal lawsuit titled "Atkinson vs. The Fair," seeking "$25,000"). In *Atkinson*, Landis represented a train conductor named Stephen A. Atkinson who had been wrongfully arrested for shoplifting while trying to return a defective tin kettle. *See Damages Sought from The Fair*, Chi. Daily Trib., Sept. 22, 1892, pt. 2, at 9. As there is no further public reporting about the case, it is assumed the parties settled. (The Fair was a popular discount department store that opened in Chicago in 1875 and was bought out in 1957 by Montgomery Ward & Company. *See* William Clark, *Merger Joins Retail Pioneers: Ward, Fair Hold Rich Heritage*, Chi. Daily Trib., June 27, 1957, pt. 3, at 9.)

28. *See Chicago Law Colleges*, 23 Chi. Legal News 432, 432 (Aug. 29, 1891) (listing Landis as a teaching assistant for the 1891–92 school year); *The Northwestern Law College*, 25 Chi. Legal News 28, 32 (Sept. 24, 1892) (listing Landis as a teaching assistant for the 1892–93 school year).

29. *See Mr. Gresham's Secretary: Kenesaw M. Landis, of Chicago, Appointed*, Daily Inter Ocean (Chi.), Mar. 16, 1893, at 3. *See also Gresham's Secretary: Mr. Landis, an Indiana Lawyer, Who Has Practiced in Chicago*, Daily Inter Ocean (Chi.), Dec. 24, 1893, at 8.

30. *See W.Q. Gresham Dead: Secretary of State Passes Away in Washington; Dies at 1:15 O'clock A.M.—All the Family at the Deathbed Except Otto, the Son; Story of the Last Hours—His Illness, Begun a Month Ago, Takes a Sharp Turn; Talk About the Succession*, Chi. Daily Trib., May 28, 1895, at 1. *See also Walter Quintin Gresham*, Find-a-Grave.com, https://www.findagrave.com/memorial/5885398/walter-quintin-gresham (last visited July 1, 2024). For a further look at Gresham's career, see Charles W. Calhoun, Gilded Age Cato: The Life of Walter Q. Gresham (1988).

31. For an obituary of Winifred, see *Judge Landis' Widow, 75, Dies; Rites Private*, Chi. Daily Trib., Aug. 28, 1947, at 22. *See also Winifred Reed Landis*, Find-a-Grave.com, https://www.findagrave.com/memorial/7008612/winifred_landis (last visited July 1, 2024).

32. *See Landis Marries at Ottawa: Gresham's Secretary Makes Miss Winifred Reed His Wife; Large Numbers of Chicago People Attend the Ceremony*, Chi. Chron., July 26, 1895, at 8 (explaining that the ceremony took place at the First Presbyterian Church of Ottawa). This article describes Landis as the senior partner of the law firm of Landis & Gresham, but no evidence has been found to support this claim.

33. For an obituary of Reed, see *Landis*, Chi. Trib., May 31, 1975, § 1, at 12. *See also Colonel Reed Gresham Landis*, Find-a-Grave.com, https://www.findagrave.com/memorial/74072140/reed_gresham_landis (last visited July 1, 2024). As these sources report, Reed was an ace fighter pilot in World War I and was credited with shooting down 12 German planes. *See also Capt. Reed Landis Back in Business: Hero of Thrilling Battles in the Air Discards Uniform and Re-enters Industrial World with Same Enthusiasm That He Tackled the Hun—To the Doughboy He Gives Major Credit for Winning the War*, Dayton Daily News, Mar. 5, 1919, at 19.

34. For an obituary of Susanne, see *Phillips*, Tampa Trib., Oct. 19, 1977, at 7D. Susanne does not have a *Find-a-Grave* webpage.

35. *Kenesaw M. Landis is to be Married; His Bride to be [is] Miss Winifred Reed of Ottawa, Ill.*, Chi. Trib., July 13, 1895, at 4 (explaining that "A trip to Europe had been planned, but important law business in Chicago prevents").

36. Henderson, *supra* note 1, at 123.

37. *See Landis to Aid [U.S. Attorney John C.] Black: Alleged Beef Combine Work*, Sun. Chron. (Chi.), Dec. 29, 1895, at 7. As matters turned out, Landis did not find any wrongdoing. *See Efforts to Prove Beef Trust Fail: Government Officials Admit They Have Been Unable to Secure Positive Evidence of Its Existence*, Chi. Trib., Dec. 9, 1896, at 4 ("The

Landis Commission spent months last year in its inquiry and nothing substantial was discovered").

38. *See, e.g., Found Guilty of Robbery: John Gate's Trial*, CHI. CHRON., Feb. 5, 1896, at 7 ("John Gate, accused of breaking into the post office at Courtland, Ill., was found guilty yesterday. Sentence was deferred. Kenesaw M. Landis, who has been appointed by Judge [Peter S.] Grosscup to defend the prisoner, practically gave up the fight for acquittal when he detected that his client had been telling falsehoods in regard to the attempted robbery").

39. *See [Ex-President] Cleveland's Men in Chicago: E.F. Uhl, F.H. Jones and K.M. Landis Form a Law Partnership*, CHI. CHRON., Sept. 15, 1897, at 5. For an obituary of Jones, see *Frank H. Jones, Banker, Lawyer, Dies at Age of 77: Served as Assistant Postmaster General*, CHI. DAILY TRIB., Oct. 3, 1931, at 3. *See also Frank Hatch Jones*, FIND-A-GRAVE.COM, https://www.findagrave.com/memorial/56917201/frank-hatch-jones (last visited July 1, 2024). For an obituary of Uhl, see *Edwin F. Uhl Dead: Former Assistant Secretary of State and Ambassador to Germany*, DAILY INTER OCEAN (Chi.), May 18, 1901, at 3. *See also Edwin Fuller Uhl*, FIND-A-GRAVE.COM, https://www.findagrave.com/memorial/16458874/edwin-fuller-uhl (last visited July 1, 2024).

40. *See* Ben Ezra Kendall, *Landis 50 Today, But Feels Only 25, He Asserts: Famous Jurist Drops Stern Judge Role in His Home Affairs*, CHI. DAILY TRIB., Nov. 20, 1916, at 13 (explaining that the firm broke up after Landis got into an argument with Uhl).

41. *See* Henderson, *supra* note 1, at 143–45.

42. *See* SPINK, *supra* note 1, at 25–27.

43. *See* Henderson, *supra* note 1, at 134.

44. *Mr. Landis' Remarks*, 30 CHI. LEGAL NEWS 286, 286 (Apr. 23, 1898).

45. *See* Arnold v. Hatch, 177 U.S. 276 (1900). Landis represented the receiver of the insolvent First National Bank of South Bend, Washington, who was trying to levy a farm in McHenry County, Illinois, owned by Lewis Hatch. The debt, however, had been incurred by Lewis's son Frank W., leading the Court to hold that the receiver could not reach Lewis's property. *See id.* at 281 ("[T]he receiver was unable to produce evidence manifestly inconsistent with the agreement as sworn to by both father and son, and their testimony authorized the jury to find the ownership of the property to be in the former"). For the case's earlier proceedings, see Hatch v. Heim, 86 F. 436 (7th Cir. 1898), and Arnold v. Hatch, 89 F. 1013 (7th Cir. 1898).

46. *Kenesaw Landis Gained His Point with [President] Cleveland*, WASH. POST, Apr. 2, 1905, pt. 4, at 2.

47. *See* 33 Stat. 992 (Mar. 5, 1905) (creating seat); *Chicago Judges are Appointed: C.C. Kohlsaat, Sol Bethea, and Kenesaw M. Landis Secure the Prizes: Charges are Explained; President Decides the Violations of Law by [Kohlsaat] Merely Technical*, CHI. TRIB., Mar. 19, 1905, at 6.

48. *Federal Judges Sworn In*, 37 CHI. LEGAL NEWS 265, 265 (Apr. 1, 1905).

49. *See, e.g.*, Winter v. Bostwick, 212 F. 884 (7th Cir. 1913) (sitting by designation) (rejecting an attempted recission of a mining contract); Knudsen-Ferguson Fruit Co. v. Chicago, St. P. M. & O. Ry. Co., 149 F. 973 (7th Cir. 1906) (sitting by designation), *cert. denied*, 204 U.S. 670 (1907) (finding that a railroad's charge for refrigeration was collected without duress); Ex parte Tinkoff, 254 F. 222 (N.D. Ill.), *aff'd*, 254 F. 225 (7th Cir. 1918) (denying the requests of three individuals to be exempted from military service); United States v. Associated Bill Posters, 235 F. 540 (N.D. Ill. 1916), *appeal dismissed*, 258 U.S. 633 (1922) (holding that the defendants, who were active in the national billboard industry, had engaged in anti-competitive activities); Investment Registry, Ltd. v. Chicago & M. Elec. R. Co., 206 F. 488 (N.D. Ill.), *aff'd*, 212 F. 594 (7th Cir. 1913) (invalidating the transfer of a railroad's property and ordering a new sale to be held); United States v. Thomson & Taylor Spice Co., 198 F. 565 (N.D. Ill. 1912) (ruling that coffee grown in Abyssinia (*i.e.*, Ethiopia), but labeled as coming from Mocha (*i.e.*, Yemen}, was illegally misbranded); United States. v. 1,950 Boxes of Macaroni, 181 F. 427 (N.D. Ill. 1910) (ordering the destruction of macaroni contaminated by coal tar dye); United States v. Atchison, T. & S.F. Ry. Co., 166 F. 160 (N.D. Ill. 1908) (determining that the defendant railroads were guilty of violating "the 28-hour law," an animal protection statute); In re Spitzer, 160 F. 137 (C.C.N.D. Ill. 1908)

(refusing a Hungarian national's request to become a naturalized citizen because he had started his application before he was an adult); United States v. Indiana Harbor R. Co., 157 F. 565 (N.D. Ill. 1906) (agreeing with the government that the defendant had failed to comply with a railroad safety law); United States v. Chicago & A. Ry. Co., 148 F. 646 (N.D. Ill. 1906), *aff'd*, 156 F. 558 (7th Cir. 1907), *aff'd*, 212 U.S. 563 (1909) (declining a request for a directed verdict in a railroad rebate case); Holmes v. Dowie, 148 F. 634 (C.C.N.D. Ill. 1906) (requiring an election to be held to determine the next leader of the Christian Catholic Apostolic Church); Interstate Com. Comm'n v. Reichmann, 145 F. 235 (C.C.N.D. Ill. 1906) (directing a witness to answer questions about possibly illegal railroad rebate practices); Carrara Paint Agency Co. v. Carrara Paint Co., 137 F. 319 (C.C.N.D. Ill. 1905) (rebuffing a defendant's request to place a limit on the number of witnesses the plaintiff could depose). *See also* Berger v. United States, 255 U.S. 22 (1921), *on remand*, 275 F. 1021 (7th Cir. 1921) (determining that Landis should have recused himself after his impartiality was challenged by five individuals accused of violating the Espionage Act of 1917); *I.W.W. Leaders Get 20-Year Terms: Haywood and 14 of His Chief Aides Also Fined $20,000 for Anti-War Activities; Eight Others Sentenced—Receive Terms of from Ten Years to Ten Days—Judge Landis Pleased with Verdict*, N.Y. Times, Aug. 31, 1918, at 1 (reporting on Landis's sentencing of 95 "Wobblies" for their opposition to World War I); *Landis Awards "Matters Baby" to Girl Mother: Margaret Ryan, However, Lets Widow Hold Infant for a While Before Parting; Court Denounces Plot*, Chi. Daily Trib., July 29, 1916, at 1 (describing Landis's decision in a case involving a stolen child).

50. *See War on Standard Oil Begun by Moody: Criminal Prosecutions of Oil Trust Officers Under the Elkins Act—Jail Sentences Will be Sought if Conviction Results; More Probing Ordered*, Wash. Post, June 23, 1906, at 1.

51. 32 Stat. 847 (Feb. 19, 1903).

52. *See Standard Oil Indicted in 10 Bills, 6,428 Counts: Charged with Accepting Rebates from Railroads: Fines May be $128,560,000; The Standard Company Paid About One-Third the Legal Rebates—Long Fight Expected*, N.Y. Times, Aug. 28, 1906, at 1.

53. *See* Henderson, *supra* note 1, at 207, 226 n.23.

54. *See* United States v. Standard Oil Co., 148 F. 719 (N.D. Ill. 1907). For the text of the Hepburn Act, see 34 Stat. 584 (June 29, 1906).

55. *See Standard Oil Found Guilty: Could be Fined $29,260,000 Under Chicago Jury's Rebate Verdict; Only One Ballot Taken—Judge Landis Charged That Company was Supposed to Know Rates—Strong Precedent Made; Many Other Cases Brought Against Standard Oil Can Now be Pressed by the Government*, N.Y. Times, Apr. 14, 1907, at 1 (incorrectly reporting that the jury had found SOC guilty on 1,463 counts). Following the trial, Landis announced that he planned to get to the bottom of SOC's byzantine corporate structure prior to passing sentence to be able to hold it fully accountable. *See Judge Landis Determined: John D. [Rockefeller] May Have to Appear and Tell Some Things He Knows*, Det. Free Press, June 29, 1907, at 4 ("I want to know whether the Standard Oil Co. of New Jersey owns the Standard Oil Co. of Indiana, the defendant in this case. I want this information and I intend to have it if such a thing is possible").

56. *See* United States v. Standard Oil Co. of Indiana, 155 F. 305, 321 (N.D. Ill. 1907). *See also* S. Morgan Friedman, *The Inflation Calculator*, https://westegg.com/inflation/ (last visited July 1, 2024) (converting 1907 dollars to 2023 dollars).

57. *See Standard Oil*, 155 F. at 319.

58. *See Forces New War on Standard Oil After [Maximum] Fine: Judge Landis Calls Special Grand Jury for Conspiracy Case [and] Jail May Result—Penalty Put at $29,240,000—Scathing Rebuke by Court Who Places Corporation on Same Level as Counterfeiter—Sixty Days to Prepare Appeal*, Chi. Sun. Trib., Aug. 4, 1907, at 1.

59. *See Landis in Gotham and Undetected: Judge Roams About Standard Oil Lair Two Days Before Reporters Find Him*, Chi. Daily Trib., Sept. 6, 1907, at 4 [hereinafter *Landis in Gotham*].

60. *See* Henderson, *supra* note 1, at 218–19.

61. *See Cleveland Advised Landis: Judge Consulted Ex-President About Fishing Outfit for Jaunt to Michigan*, Wash. Post, Sept. 7, 1907, at 3.

62. *See Landis Silent on Oil; Sits on Bench in Indiana: Judge of United States Court Tries Case Here, but Declines to Discuss Rockefeller,* INDIANAPOLIS STAR, Aug. 7, 1907, at 14 [hereinafter *Landis Silent*].

63. *See Cubs Trim Reds; Score is 2 to 1—Overall and Weimer are in Fine Form and Contest Lasts Ten Innings: Judge Landis Looks On. Shows Judicial Temperament by Applauding the Good Work of Each Team,* CHI. DAILY TRIB., Sept. 19, 1907, at 6. Despite this headline, Landis was a well-known fan of both the Chicago Cubs and the Chicago White Sox. *See* SPINK, *supra* note 1, at 27–29.

64. *Landis Silent, supra* note 62.

65. *See Landis in Gotham, supra* note 59.

66. *Judge Landis Shadowed: By Agents of the Standard Oil Company, It Is Said,* CIN. ENQUIRER, Aug. 13, 1907, at 2.

67. *See* Standard Oil Co. of Indiana v. United States, 164 F. 376 (7th Cir. 1908), *cert. denied,* 212 U.S. 579 (1909).

68. *See* United States v. Standard Oil Co. of Indiana, 170 F. 988 (N.D. Ill. 1909). For a further look at the case, see, e.g., BRUCE BRINGHURST, ANTITRUST AND THE OIL MONOPOLY: THE STANDARD OIL CASES, 1890–1911, at 138–40 (1979). For a profile of Anderson (1857–1938), see *Judge Albert Anderson Dies at Age of 81: Lake County Attorneys Recall His Work in Hammond,* TIMES (Hammond, IN), Apr. 28, 1938, at 1. *See also Albert Barnes Anderson,* FIND-A-GRAVE.COM, https://www.findagrave.com/memorial/98286312/albert_barnes_anderson (last visited July 1, 2024).

69. The complaint, together with the other materials generated by the case, has been digitized and placed online by the Society for American Baseball Research. *See 1915 Federal League Lawsuit Case Files,* SABR, https://sabr.org/research/article/1915-federal-league-lawsuit-case-files/ (last visited July 1, 2024).

70. *Case to Landis; Johnson Happy,* CHI. DAILY TRIB., Jan. 7, 1915, at 9.

71. *See* James Crusinberry, *Moguls Mold Shells for Big Legal Battle: Baseball Chiefs Busy Preparing Affidavits of Many Sorts and Sizes,* CHI. DAILY TRIB., Jan. 16, 1915, at 9; James Crusinberry, *Organized Ball and Feds in Big Legal 'Game' Today: Rival "Teams" Set for Clash in Big Series; Confident and Eager, Both Sides Go Before "Umpire" Landis—Stars on Firing Line,* CHI. DAILY TRIB., Jan. 20, 1915, at 9.

72. *See* James Crusinberry, *Federal League Opens Court Battle Against O.B. [Organized Baseball]; Reserve Rule Attacked by Feds' Lawyer: Bases Claim of Monopoly on Form of Contract Given Players—Fight Goes on Today,* CHI. DAILY TRIB., Jan. 21, 1915, at 9.

73. SPINK, *supra* note 1, at 40.

74. *See* James Crusinberry, *O.B. Attorney Goes to Plate in Feds' Suit: Judge Landis Causes Stir by Questioning Right to Hear Case; Blow at Trust Claim,* CHI. DAILY TRIB., Jan. 22, 1915, at 14. For a profile of Addington (1874–1922), see *Keene Addington Dies After a 3 Week Illness: Was Mayor of Lake Forest for Two Terms; Achieved Many Reforms—Nervous Breakdown,* WAUKEGAN DAILY SUN (IL), Oct. 19, 1922, at 3. *See also Keene Hardwood Addington,* FIND-A-GRAVE.COM, https://www.findagrave.com/memorial/27925221/keene-harwood-addington (last visited July 1, 2024).

75. SPINK, *supra* note 1, at 41.

76. *See Sentiment Barred by Judge Landis: Who Also Objects to Ball Players Being Called Laborers; Big Baseball Suit in Chicago is Nearing an End—List of Salaries Received by Some of the Former Stars of Organized Baseball,* CIN. ENQUIRER, Jan. 23, 1915, at 8. For a profile of Pepper (1867–1961), see *George Wharton Pepper Dies; Noted Attorney, Ex-Senator,* PHILADELPHIA DAILY NEWS, May 25, 1961, at 8. *See also George Wharton Pepper,* FIND-A-GRAVE. COM, https://www.findagrave.com/memorial/6860309/george-wharton-pepper (last visited July 1, 2024).

77. SPINK, *supra* note 1, at 41.

78. *Judge Kenesaw M. Landis,* SPORTING NEWS, Jan. 28, 1915, at 2.

79. The Federal League's seventh team—the Kansas City Packers—was in bankruptcy and therefore did not figure in the settlement. For a further look at the Federal League, see, e.g., DANIEL R. LEVITT, THE BATTLE THAT FORGED MODERN BASEBALL: THE FEDERAL LEAGUE CHALLENGE AND ITS LEGACY (2012); ROBERT PEYTON WIGGINS, THE FEDERAL

League of Base Ball Clubs: The History of an Outlaw Major League, 1914–1915 (2008).

80. *See Dismissal of Suit Ends Baseball Tiff: Judge K.M. Landis Takes Final Step in Ending Long Drawn-Out Fight Between Organized Baseball and Federals*, Phil. Inquirer, Feb. 8, 1916, at 14.

81. As has been explained elsewhere:

> In their negotiations with the major leagues, the owners of the Terrapins asked for the right to buy an existing major league team and move it to Baltimore. Convinced that Baltimore was too small, too poor, and too black to support a franchise, the major league owners rejected this proposal and instead sought to buy out the Terrapins. Although they eventually were offered $75,000, the club's owners considered this amount to be an insult. As a result, in 1917 they filed their own anti-trust lawsuit in the Supreme Court of the District of Columbia (now the U.S. District Court for the District of Columbia).

Louis H. Schiff & Robert M. Jarvis, Baseball and the Law: Cases and Materials 52 (2016).

82. *See* Federal Baseball Club of Balt., Inc. v. National League of Prof'l Baseball Clubs, 259 U.S. 200 (1922). Although widely criticized, the decision has managed to hold on. For a further discussion, see, e.g., Samuel A. Alito, Jr., *The Origin of the Baseball Antitrust Exemption: Federal Baseball Club of Baltimore, Inc. v. National League of Professional Baseball Clubs*, 34 J. Sup. Ct. Hist. 183 (2009). *See also* Multiple Authors, *1922—Federal Baseball Club of Baltimore, Inc. v. National League of Professional Baseball Clubs*, SABR, https://sabr.org/supreme-court/1922 (last visited July 1, 2024).

83. Numerous works have been written about the scandal, including, most famously, Eliot Asinof, Eight Men Out: The Black Sox and the 1919 World Series (1961). The bribes were bankrolled by Arnold "The Brain" Rothstein, a New York City crime boss, who made a fortune betting on the Redlegs. *See* David Pietrusza, Rothstein: The Life, Times, and Murder of the Criminal Genius Who Fixed the 1919 World Series (2003). Rothstein was gunned down in 1928 after he refused to pay the $320,000 (the current equivalent of $5.8 million) he had lost in a three-day poker game (ironically, Rothstein refused to pay because he claimed the game was fixed). *Id. See also* Friedman, *supra* note 56 (converting 1928 dollars to 2023 dollars).

84. Doug Pappas, *75th Anniversary of the Commissioner's Office*, 1 Outside the Lines (newsletter of the SABR Business of Baseball Committee) 1, 2 (Fall 1995).

85. *See Judge Landis, the New Czar of Baseballdom*, 67 Literary Dig. 46, 46 (Dec. 4, 1920) ("The Judge will remain on the bench of the Federal Court, where his salary is $7,500 a year. He stipulated that this sum should be subtracted from the $50,000 offered by the baseball men, and so his salary as chairman of America's national pastime will be $42,500 a year").

86. *See Judge Landis Opens Office: Baseball Headquarters in a Michigan Avenue Building*, K.C. Star, Feb. 2, 1921, at 12.

87. *See* David Quentin Voigt, Baseball: An Illustrated History 147 (1987).

88. *See* James Crusinberry, *Judge Landis Picks Lawyer as Secretary*, Chi. Daily Trib., Feb. 5, 1921, at 11. For a profile of O'Connor (1889–1966), a 1916 graduate of the Kent College of Law in Chicago, see *Leslie M. O'Connor, Aide to Landis for 24 Years*, Sporting News, Feb. 5, 1966, at 32 (explaining that when O'Connor initially refused Landis's offer, saying that he (O'Connor) did not know anything about baseball, Landis replied: "That's all right, neither do I—we'll learn it together"). *See also Leslie M. O'Connor*, Find-a-Grave.com, https://www.findagrave.com/memorial/186173089/leslie-m-o'connor (last visited July 1, 2024). O'Connor served as Landis's secretary for the entirety of Landis's commissionership.

89. *See, e.g.*, Harry W. Standidge, *Landis' Post Called Tribute to Bench by Ex-Head of State Bar*, Chi. Daily Trib., Jan. 16, 1921, pt. 2, at 1.

90. *"Side Lines" for Judges*, 24:9 Law Notes 162 (Dec. 1920).

91. *See Baseball and the Judiciary*, 19 Mich. L. Rev. 190, 191 (1920).

92. *Chicago Lawyer Attacks Landis: Petition to Congress Protests Against Judge Becoming Baseball Head*, N.Y. Times, Jan. 16, 1921, at 10.

93. *Landis' B.B. Job Draws Protest to Washington*, CHI. DAILY TRIB., Jan. 15, 1921, at 10.

94. *The Landis Case*, 7:3 A.B.A. J. 87, 88 (Feb. 1921) (quoting Landis's remarks to the Missouri Bar Association in St. Louis on December 4, 1920).

95. *See Landis Can Keep Both Jobs, Government Officials Decide: Department of Justice Investigators Rule that Supreme Dictator is Within His Rights in Accepting Leadership of Baseball Organizations*, SUN (Balt.), Jan. 18, 1921, at 12.

96. *Id.*

97. *See Congress Asked to Hold Inquiry on Landis's Jobs: Resolution Calls for Decision on Federal Judge Also Holding $42,500 Baseball Position*, N.Y. TRIB., Feb. 3, 1921, at 2. *See also Wants a Landis Inquiry: Welty Urges Congress to See if He Can Be Judge and Baseball Arbiter*, N.Y. TIMES, Feb. 3, 1921, at 5.

98. *See Would Bar Landis as Baseball Head: Representative Welty Proposes Bill Limiting Federal Judges to Government Salaries—No Law Now Covers Case: Attorney General Declares Present Statutes Apply Only to Compensation as Lawyers*, N.Y. TIMES, Feb. 12, 1921, at 3.

99. *See Landis Impeached by Welty in House: Action is Based on Five Charges Alleging Neglect of Duty Because of Baseball Job; Trial of Judge Unlikely—Dial Renews Attack in Senate and Asserts He Will Press for Impeachment*, N.Y. TIMES, Feb. 15, 1921, at 1.

100. *See Committee Doubts Right of Landis to Baseball Job: Hearing of Impeachment Charge Against Federal Jurist is Begun*, ATLANTA CONST., Feb. 22, 1921, at 1. *See also Landis Won't be Impeached; Censure Likely—Bribed by Baseball Welty Cries*, CHI. DAILY TRIB., Feb. 22, 1921, at 1.

101. *See Hit Action of Judge Landis—House Judiciary Committee for Investigation: Taking Baseball Job Would be Improper; Volstead's [Minority] Report Disagrees with Majority*, L.A. TIMES, Mar. 3, 1921, at 13.

102. *See Full Probe Ordered of the Landis Affair: Acceptance of Baseball Arbiter Position Termed Serious Impropriety*, ATLANTA CONST., Mar. 3, 1921, at 11.

103. *See Volstead Opposes Landis Impeachment: Presents Minority Report Upholding Judge's Acceptance of Office of Baseball Arbiter*, N.Y. TIMES, Mar. 4, 1921, at 4.

104. *See* PIETRUSZA, *supra* note 1, at 198.

105. *Senator Dial Makes Reply to Attack of Judge Landis: Says Federal Judge's Utterances Show That He is Not Qualified to Sit on Any Bench—"The Most Bolshevik Doctrine I Ever Heard,"* CHARLOTTE OBSERVER (NC), Feb. 15, 1921, at 1.

106. *Judge Landis in Limelight Again with Release of Bank Embezzler: Federal Judge Says Bank Directors Responsible for Theft of $96,000 by Clerk Receiving $90 Per Month*, ARIZ. REPUBLIC (Phoenix), Feb. 13, 1921, at 1.

107. *See Landis Defies Dial to Stand Wage Probe; Judge Asks What Senator Pays in His Banks and Mills in South Carolina; He Speaks of 11-Year Girls—Laughs at Impeachment Talk and Describes It as "Pish-Posh,"* SUN (Balt.), Feb. 14, 1921, at 1.

108. *See* Arthur Sears Henning, *'Barrage on Landis a Dud,' is Consensus: Welty and Dial Fire Both Barrels*, CHI. DAILY TRIB., Feb. 15, 1921, at 1, 2.

109. *See Landis Resolution and Discussion of Landis Resolution, in* REPORT OF THE FORTY-FOURTH ANNUAL MEETING OF THE AMERICAN BAR ASSOCIATION HELD AT CINCINNATI, OHIO, AUGUST 31, SEPTEMBER 1 AND 2, 1921, at 61–67 (1921).

110. *See id.* at 61 (remarks of former ABA president Hampton L. Carson).

111. *Id.* at 61 (text of the resolution), 67 (results of the vote).

112. *See Landis Protest in Senate: Bar Association's Criticism of Baseball Arbiter Starts Short Debate*, N.Y. TIMES, Oct. 18, 1921, at 10.

113. *See Landis Resigns from the Bench: Will Devote Entire Time to Work as Baseball Head—Retires as Judge on March 1*, BOS. SUN. GLOBE, Feb. 19, 1922, at 21.

114. *Landis on Last Day Both Gay and Stern: Quits Federal Bench After Seventeen Years to Devote Himself to Baseball; Brusque Words Hide Tears; Is Hard on Volstead Violators, Easy on a Tax Delinquent—Many Farewells*, N.Y. TIMES, Mar. 1, 1922, at 3.

115. Alexander F. Jones, *Landis Leaves Judges' Bench for Baseball: Fact He's Quitting Court Doesn't Bring Last-Day Defendants Luck*, ATLANTA CONST., Mar. 1, 1922, at 1.

116. *See* RAYMOND J. MCKOSKI, JUDGES IN STREET CLOTHES: ACTING ETHICALLY

Off-the-Bench 10–13 (2017). The CJE's text can be found at American Bar Association, *Judicial Ethics & Regulation*, https://www.americanbar.org/content/dam/aba/administrative/professional_responsibility/pic_migrated/1924_canons.pdf (last visited July 1, 2024) (under "1924 Canons of Judicial Ethics").

117. *Proceedings of 47th Annual Meeting: 5th Session, in* Report of the Forty Seventh Annual Meeting of the American Bar Association Held at Philadelphia, Pennsylvania, July 8, 9, and 10, 1924, at 68 (1924).

118. *See supra* the sources cited in note 116.

119. *See supra* note 11. Landis, an atheist, was cremated, after which his ashes were interred at Chicago's Oak Woods Cemetery. *Id. See also* Pietrusza, *supra* note 1, at 399 (discussing Landis's atheism).

120. *See $100,000 Left to Widow by Judge Landis*, Chi. Daily Trib., Dec. 5, 1944, at 22. *See also* Friedman, *supra* note 56 (converting 1944 dollars to 2023 dollars).

121. *See supra* the sources cited in note 1 for examinations of Landis's tenure as commissioner. *See also* David George Surdam & Michael J. Haupert, The Age of Ruth and Landis: The Economics of Baseball During the Roaring Twenties (2018); Jan L. Jacobowitz, *Baseball, Kenesaw Mountain Landis, and the Judicial Strike Zone—Home Run or Foul on the Play?*, 13:1 J. Tex. Sup. Ct. Hist. Soc'y 9 (2023); Shayna M. Sigman, *The Jurisprudence of Judge Kenesaw Mountain Landis*, 15 Marq. Sports L. Rev. 277 (2005). As these sources collectively point out, Landis banned for life the Black Sox Eight, even though the octet had been acquitted in court and similar incidents almost certainly had occurred during the 1905, 1912, 1914, and 1918 World Series; made it a point to enforce baseball's anti-barnstorming rules, despite the public's interest in seeing the sport's leading players; attempted to break up baseball's farm system, an important pipeline for both players and teams; fiercely maintained baseball's color line (it was broken shortly after his death); discouraged the growth of night baseball; prohibited women from participating in organized baseball after Virne B. "Jackie" Mitchell, a 17-year-old southpaw, struck out George H. "Babe" Ruth and Henry L. "Lou" Gehrig in a 1931 exhibition game in Chattanooga, Tennessee; and, in the face of irrefutable evidence, covered up the fact that in 1919 stars Tyrus R. "Ty" Cobb and Tristam E. "Tris" Speaker had thrown a game to ensure that the Detroit Tigers, and not the New York Yankees, finished in third place (in 1919, the third place team received a small share—approximately $500 a player—of the post-season pot).

122. Ford C. Frick, Games, Asterisks, and People: Memories of a Lucky Fan 215 (1973).

123. 49 F.2d 298 (N.D. Ill. 1931).

124. Bennett had played for the Browns from 1923 to 1927 and had compiled a .276 batting average. Beginning in 1928, he was stashed in the minor leagues. After becoming a free agent, Bennett failed to make it back to the majors and retired in 1932. For Bennett's career statistics, see *Herschel Bennett*, Baseball-Reference.com, https://www.baseball-reference.com/players/b/bennehe01.shtml (last visited July 1, 2024).

125. *Milwaukee Am. Ass'n*, 49 F.2d at 302, 304. For an obituary of Lindley (1880–1958), see *Judge Walter C. Lindley, 77, Ruled in A & P Trust Case*, Evening Star (DC), Jan. 4, 1958, at A10. *See also Judge Walter Charles Lindley*, Find-a-Grave.com, https://www.findagrave.com/memorial/95411981/walter-charles-lindley (last visited July 1, 2024).

126. *See* Dan Schlossberg, *Kenesaw Mountain Landis Name Comes Off Baseball's MVP Trophies*, Forbes, Oct. 3, 2020, https://www.forbes.com/sites/danschlossberg/2020/10/03/kenesaw-mountain-landis-name-comes-off-baseballs-mvp-trophies/?sh=797d48f74536.

127. *See* John Drebinger, *Baseball Pays Tribute to Landis by Picking Him for Hall of Fame: Late Commissioner's Name to Be Inscribed at Cooperstown—Major Leagues to Open Winter Meetings Here Today*, N.Y. Times, Dec. 11, 1944, at 18.

128. *Kenesaw Mountain Landis*, National Baseball Hall of Fame and Museum, https://baseballhall.org/hall-of-famers/landis-kenesaw (last visited July 1, 2024).

CHAPTER 2

Hugh Ambrose "Hughie" Jennings (1945)

SAVANNA L. NOLAN

Hugh Ambrose "Hughie" Jennings (April 2, 1869–February 1, 1928), named midway through U.S. Supreme Court Justice Harry A. Blackmun's famous list of 88 notable baseball players,[1] was inducted into the Baseball Hall of Fame in 1945 for his superlative work as a shortstop.[2] Jennings played on the Baltimore Orioles during their three consecutive Temple Cup seasons (1894–96); subsequently won two National League pennants with the Brooklyn Superbas (1899–1900); later piloted the Detroit Tigers to three consecutive American League pennants (1907–09); and still later coached (and at times managed) the New York Giants as they won two World Series (1921–22) and two National League pennants (1923–24).[3]

Jennings, however, was more than a ballplayer, for he also attended Cornell University's law school. Although he left before graduating (1904), he became a member of the Maryland (1905) and Pennsylvania (1908) bars and built a thriving law practice in Scranton, Pennsylvania, with his younger brother William.

A Large Family

Jennings was born in the Browntown section of the coal mining town of Pittston, Pennsylvania (12 miles south of Scranton). Although his birthday now routinely is reported as April 2, 1869, Jack Smiles, his principal biographer, gives the date as April 2, 1871, apparently confusing Jennings with his brother William.[4]

Jennings's parents were Honora (often incorrectly reported as "Nora," likely due to confusion resulting from the fact that Jennings's second wife's name was Nora) (née Feehan) (c. 1828–83) and James J. Jennings,

Sr. (1823–98), both of whom were Irish immigrants.[5] Like so many others (including the parents of James H. O'Rourke, the subject of Chapter 3 of this book), Honora and James left Ireland during the Great Potato Famine,[6] a time of mass starvation and disease that lasted from 1845 to 1850.[7]

It is not known when Honora and James met or when they married; according to one source, they arrived in Pittston from Ireland in 1849.[8] It also is not known how many children the couple had—while various sources report they had 12,[9] Smiles simply describes Jennings as their "ninth child."[10] Based on the 1860 and 1880 federal censuses (the family does not appear in the 1870 federal census), however, it appears that Honora and James had 10 children and that Jennings was their eighth child: Thomas E. (1854–1923)[11]; John (1855–1925)[12]; James R. (1858–1943)[13]; Henry (1859–1915)[14]; Bridget A. (later Walsh) (1864–1940)[15]; Frank E. (1866–1949)[16]; Ellen (1868–?)[17]; Jennings (1869–1928)[18]; William A. (1871–1922)[19]; and Dr. Joseph A. (1873–1920).[20]

Jennings, whose nickname originally was spelled "Hughey," but today routinely appears as "Hughie,"[21] dropped out of school when he was 11 or 12 to become a "breaker boy." For 15 cents a day, he would separate pieces of rock, slate, and wood from lumps of coal for the Pennsylvania Coal Company, working in the same mine as his father and brothers.[22] As Smiles explains:

> Pittston sat at the base of the Pocono Mountains in the northeastern part of [Pennsylvania] … in the middle of a huge coalfield…. The coalfield in Northeastern Pennsylvania contained anthracite, or "hard" coal, in such quantities that three-quarters of the known deposits in the Earth were within 480 square miles. While soft coal could be more cheaply mined—and was practically unlimited in other parts of Pennsylvania and Kentucky and West Virginia—anthracite was much more in demand.[23]

When they were not working, Jennings and the other breaker boys would play baseball.[24] Although not the best player, Jennings's fearlessness made him stand out, and when he was 13 he was recruited to play catcher on a local men's team known as the Moosic Pounders.[25]

By the time he was 15, Jennings's family had moved to Stark's Patch, just north of Pittston but still part of "Greater Pittston."[26] Jennings also had received a promotion at work, for he now was a mule driver, a coveted position in the mines.[27] Jennings lost this job, however, after skipping work to play in a baseball game:

> One afternoon [Jennings] asked permission of the foreman to be excused to play in a critical game against the Bark Peelers of Minooka, a rival village. After consultation with [Jennings's] father, the foreman denied the request. Undeterred, Jennings left work. His father caught him on the way home and made him put on a dress, saying to him: "If you go, you'll go in that!"

Hughie went to the game anyway, borrowing an extra pair of clothes from his teammates. The following day he was fired by the mine foreman for insubordination and forced to return to his old job as a breaker boy picking slate.[28]

During the next five years, Jennings played for various town teams in the Greater Pittston area, including Avoca, Minooka, and Moosic. In 1889, when he was 20, he agreed to play with a semi-professional club in Lehighton, Pennsylvania, for $5 a game. Based on his play, the club offered to pay him $50 a month (some sources say $75 a month) if he returned for the 1890 season.[29] Although Jennings accepted this offer,[30] in June 1890 he jumped to the newly formed Allentown (Pennsylvania) Colts of the minor league Inter-State League (also called the Eastern Inter-State League—both names are misnomers, as all of the league's teams were located in Pennsylvania).[31] When the Colts folded in July 1890,[32] Jennings returned to Lehighton and finished out the year with it.[33]

In the Majors

In April 1891, Jennings signed with the Harrisburg Ponies, one of the teams expected to be represented in the new Pennsylvania State League ("PSL") (the successor to the Inter-State League).[34] When the PSL failed to get off the ground,[35] Jennings returned to Lehighton for a third season.[36]

In late May 1891, the Louisville Colonels of the American Association ("AA"), at the time one of baseball's two major leagues, called Jennings up.[37] Although the Colonels were woeful (the team finished the season in eighth place, with a record of 54–83, ahead of only the even more woeful Washington Statesmen, who finished last with a record of 44–91[38]), the callup meant that Jennings had made it to the major leagues.

The callup happened so quickly that when the elfin Jennings showed up, the Colonels had trouble dressing him:

Unfortunately, the club did not have a uniform that even remotely fit the slight Jennings. The one they gave him was so large it seemed he was encased in about three large pillowcases. Samuel N. Crane, the sportswriter for the *New York Journal*, wrote that Hughie's red head stuck up through his uniform "like a red peony in a field of chrysanthemums."[39]

Although Jennings always had been a catcher, the Colonels needed a shortstop. Following his first game, the *Freeland Tribune* newspaper gushed: "Jennings made his debut at Louisville on Monday [June 1]. The club was defeated, but it was not any fault of Hughey's. He played short and accepted eight chances without an error."[40]

Despite having been thrown into extremely deep waters, Jennings immediately dazzled at his new position. In August 1891, the *Freeland Tribune* again gushed:

> Jennings stands third in Association shortstops and is playing a game that brings the highest praise from the critics in every city where he appears. In Sunday's *Press* he is spoken of as follows: Louisville may have a death grip on … last place, but the past few weeks have demonstrated one thing—that it has the coming shortstop of the country in Hugh Jennings. He was practically an amateur when he joined the club, but by conscientious work he has advanced to the front ranks, and now is one of Louisville's favorites. He goes after any and everything, and covers as much territory as any shortstop in the country. He is also extremely handy with the bat, and there is not a more reliable hitter in the club. Jennings attended school last year on money borrowed from his brother, and since he joined the Louisville Club he has been sufficiently frugal to enable him to return it. He not only tries to attain the highest round in the ladder of base ball fame, but when not on the diamond he devotes himself to improving his mind.[41]

Following the end of the season, Jennings was asked to describe his improbable ascent into the major leagues:

> Hugh Jennings, Louisville's shortstop, who is destined to obtain an even greater reputation than [shortstop] Herman Long [of the Boston Beaneaters], is in many respects a very interesting character. Jennings, before his entrance into base ball two years ago, worked in a coal mine in a small town in Pennsylvania. His advent on the diamond was made at Lehighton, where he signed as a backstop. Jennings describes Lehighton as being a beautiful place of about 3,000 inhabitants, but he was somewhat lost while there, for of the 3,000 residents all were Dutch except two, an Irish saloonkeeper and his sister. "I would never have come to Louisville," said [Jennings,] "if Manager [John C. 'Jack'] Chapman had not sent me [a] $100 advance. To come from a place like [Lehighton] into the American Association was more than I could have hoped for, and I would never have reached Kentucky soil had I not been given the money in advance. I felt sure that I would prove a failure, and I only brought enough wearing apparel to last me two weeks."[42]

For the next 11 seasons (1892–1902), Jennings, standing 5'8" and weighing 165 pounds, would remain in the major leagues, first with the Colonels (1892–93), then with the Baltimore Orioles (1893–99), then with the Brooklyn Superbas (1899–1900), and finally with the Philadelphia Phillies (1901–02).[43] During these years, Jennings found his greatest success with the Orioles, hitting .355 in 1894, .386 in 1895, .401 in 1896 (finishing second to Jesse C. Burkett of the Cleveland Spiders, who hit .410), .355 in 1897, and .328 in 1898.[44]

As already noted, Jennings was recruited by the Moosic Pounders because of his fearless style of play. In the major leagues, the story was the same. Crowding the plate and refusing to concede an inch, Jennings was hit a remarkable 287 times, a major league record that still stands.[45] The most harrowing of these at-bats occurred on June 28, 1897, when Amos W. "The Hoosier Thunderbolt" Rusie of the New York Giants "uncorked a fastball that rammed into Hughie's skull just above his ear with a sickening crack."[46] Years later one sportswriter recalled that he "thought [Jennings] was dead to a certainty."[47] Although bleeding badly and having suffered a concussion (which caused him to stagger around the field), Jennings refused to stop playing, scored a run, and only left the game after his teammates insisted that he do so.[48]

Remarkably, Jennings returned just four days later in a game against the Washington Senators:

> Jennings—the brilliant and plucky Hugh Jennings—who was nearly killed in New York by being hit in the head by one of Rusie's catapult inshoots, insisted upon playing.... Jennings's nerve and loyalty to the club was fully appreciated by the crowd, and he was cheered heartily.[49]

A few days later, another newspaper correctly predicted: "Jennings ... will continue to take every chance. The aggressiveness of Jennings is the wonder of every player who knows the tractable disposition the lad possesses."[50]

Law School (But No Degree)

In the Winter of 1895, Jennings, along with his Orioles teammate John J. McGraw,[51] began taking classes at St. Bonaventure College ("SBC") (now St. Bonaventure University) in Allegany, New York (70 miles south of Buffalo).[52] In exchange for coaching SBC's baseball team, the pair were allowed to attend classes for free.[53]

In a February 1896 interview, Jennings explained that he planned to get his degree from SBC, even though it likely would take him another three winters of work, and then was set on going to law school, following in the footsteps of his former teammate Harry L. Taylor (1866–1955), who in 1893 had graduated from Cornell University's law school and now was a practicing lawyer in Buffalo[54]:

> This is Jennings's second year at St. Bonaventure, and he will probably spend two or three more winters there. After that it is his ambition to devote himself to the study of law.... The example of Harry Taylor, who is a great friend of Jennings, has had no small influence in determining the shortstop in his course.[55]

In October 1897, however, Jennings's plans changed after he married Elizabeth C. Dixon (1871–98), like Jennings a resident of Avoca, Pennsylvania.[56] Although Jennings honored his commitment to coach at SBC during the winter of 1898,[57] he stopped taking classes. While some sources now report that Jennings earned a degree from SBC, the SBC alumni directory makes it clear that he did not.[58]

Following a brief honeymoon (during which they accompanied the Orioles on a tour of the western United States), Elizabeth and Jennings settled in Baltimore.[59] On September 4, 1898, Elizabeth gave birth to a daughter named Grace E. (later McWilliams) (1898–1964).[60]

In November 1898, Jennings suffered two terrible blows. First, on November 20, his father James died from pleurisy.[61] Then, on November 26, Elizabeth died from complications suffered while giving birth to Grace.[62] In March 1899, life became even more unsettled when Jennings, along with the Orioles' other top players, was "transferred" to the Brooklyn Superbas in a shady business deal engineered by Orioles owner Harry Von der Horst, who had bought his way into the Superbas (having ownership interests in two or more clubs soon would become a prohibited practice).[63]

Eleven games after being transferred to the Superbas, Jennings blew out his arm, ending his days as a shortstop. Upon learning of Jennings's injury, manager Edward H. "Foxy Ned" Hanlon, who also had been transferred to the Superbas, "tried to trade Jennings to Pittsburgh but Hughie was an honest man and wrote the Pirates that he was damaged goods. Hanlon then tried to return Jennings to the Orioles, but after only two games Hughie was back with Brooklyn."[64]

Unwilling to retire, Jennings learned to play first base and soon became one of the best "cold corner" men in the National League.[65] Nevertheless, it was evident that Jennings's playing days were coming to an end: in 1899, his batting average slipped to .299, while in 1900 it fell to .272.[66] With the handwriting on the wall, Jennings decided it was time to start law school. Thus, in January 1901, he entered Cornell's law school at Ithaca, New York (150 miles to the east of Buffalo):

> Hughey Jennings, the ball player, has left his home and gone to Cornell, where he will enter the law department and incidentally coach the base ball candidates of the college. Jennings … declares he will never again play professional base ball, but will enter a law firm in New York as soon as his studies are completed at Cornell.[67]

By this time, Cornell's law school offered two separate programs of instruction, one lasting three years and the other lasting four years. As the school's brochure explained, the latter

> includes the same law subjects as the three-year course and in addition the equivalent of one year's work in the College of Arts and Sciences. It is designed to afford to law students an opportunity to pursue some of the courses in

History, Political Science, Political Economy and Finance, which have a direct bearing upon the history and the business aspects of law.[68]

Jennings chose the four-year program,[69] which meant that he would have to complete the following courses to graduate:

FIRST YEAR
Torts (including Master and Servant). Three hours.
English History. Three hours.
Elementary Economics. Three hours.
Electives (Arts and Sciences). Six or seven hours.

SECOND YEAR
Contracts and Agency. Four hours.
Real Property. Three hours.
Criminal Law. First Term. Four hours.
Civil Procedure. Second Term. Four hours.
Brief Making. One hour.
Electives (Arts and Sciences). Three to six hours.

THIRD YEAR
Equity Jurisdiction. Three hours.
Sales. First term. Three hours.
Suretyship. Second term. Three hours.
Insurance. First term. Two hours.
Domestic Relations and the Law of Persons. Second term. Two hours.
Civil Procedure. First term. Three hours.
Evidence. Second term. Three hours.
Probate Law. First term. Three hours.
Procedural Papers. Second term. Three hours.
College Court. One hour.
Electives. (Not required).

FOURTH YEAR
Partnership. First term. Three hours.
Corporations. Second term. Four hours.
Quasi-Contracts. First term. Two hours.
Carriers. Second term. Two hours.
Bills Notes and Checks. First term. Two hours.
Constitutional Law. Second term. Two hours.
Civil Procedure. First term. Four hours.
Property. Second term. Four hours.
Conveyancing. First term. Two hours.
Practice Court. One hour.
Electives. (Not required).[70]

Despite insisting that he was through with baseball, in June 1901 Jennings returned to the big leagues:

> To the surprise of many, the Phillies purchased future Hall of Famer Hugh Jennings from Brooklyn on June 20 for $3,000. Jennings had refused to report to the Superbas that spring while studying law at Cornell….
>
> While his early play did not draw praise (*Sporting Life* wrote, "Hugh Jennings' batting eye is not quite as bright as it should be for a '$6,000 beaut'" [referring to Jennings's salary with the Phillies]), his addition to the Phillies coincided with their rise in the National League standings. Philadelphia, 24–24 when Jennings joined the club, went 59–33 the remainder of the season to finish in second place, only 7½ games behind the pennant-winning Pirates; it was their closest finish to first place since 1887, and the Phillies would not exceed their .593 winning percentage until 1916. More relevantly, they outperformed the upstart [Philadelphia] Athletics [of the new American League] (who finished 74–62). [For the season, Jennings hit .262.][71]

In January 1902, Jennings returned to Cornell; in June 1902, when his exams were done, he re-joined the Phillies.[72] In what would prove to be his final full season as a major league player, Jennings hit .272 (the same as in 1900).[73]

In 1903, Jennings became the player-manager of the recently formed Baltimore Orioles of the Class A Eastern League.[74] Jennings would end up managing the Orioles for four seasons (coming in fourth, second, second, and third) before leaving in 1907 to become the manager of the American League's Detroit Tigers.[75]

The added demands of being a player-manager, coupled with an unfortunate accident in February 1904 in the Cornell natatorium,[76] caused Jennings to leave Cornell in the spring of 1904, "two semesters short of graduating [but with] enough classes to take the bar exam."[77]

During his time coaching the Cornell baseball team, one of Jennings's players (and classmates) was outfielder William George "Billy" Evans.[78] Born in 1884 in Chicago, Illinois, but raised in Youngstown, Ohio, Evans entered Cornell Law School in 1901 as a member of the Class of 1905.[79] In 1902, however, Evans's father John D. Evans died unexpectedly at the age of 50,[80] which forced Evans to drop out of Cornell in 1903.[81] Returning to Youngstown, Evans became a sportswriter for the local newspaper (the *Youngstown Daily Vindicator*).[82] In 1906, at the age of 22, Evans was hired as an American League umpire (earning him the nickname "The Boy Umpire").[83] After retiring as an umpire in 1927, Evans wrote a book called *How to Umpire* (1929); worked in the front offices of the Boston Red Sox, Cleveland Indians, and Detroit Tigers (becoming the first person in baseball history to hold the title "general manager"—previously, all such executives had used the title "business manager"); and served as the president of the minor league Southern Association.[84] In 1973, Evans was elected to the Baseball Hall of Fame.[85]

Jennings & Jennings

In January 1905, Jennings took and passed the Maryland bar exam.[86] By this time, he had agreed to join the Baltimore law firm of Willis, Homer, France & Smith ("WHFS").[87] The firm had been started in 1894 by George R. Willis (1851–1919), an 1873 graduate of the Dickinson Law School, and Francis T. Homer (1872–1930), an 1894 graduate of the University of Maryland's law school. In 1899, the firm's name expanded when Joseph C. France (1862–1938), an 1883 graduate of the Baltimore City Law School, and Samuel K. Smith (1869–1940), an 1893 graduate of the University of Maryland, were admitted as partners.[88]

Jennings was not with WHFS for very long and little is known about his work at the firm. It is known, however, that when the firm defended Robert P. McCloskey, a local Black man accused of "keeping a disorderly house" (i.e., an unlicensed bar), Jennings cross-examined one of the state's witnesses.[89]

In November 1907, following his first season as the manager of the Detroit Tigers, Jennings opened a law firm in Scranton, Pennsylvania, with his younger brother William, a 1904 graduate of the University of Pennsylvania's law school, called Jennings & Jennings.[90] Initially, Jennings worked as an out-of-state lawyer (relying on his Maryland license), but in December 1908 he took and passed the Pennsylvania bar exam.[91]

Although Jennings was able to practice law only in the winters, it seems clear that he considered law his true calling. On January 9, 1911, for example, when Jennings married his second wife—schoolteacher Nora M. O'Boyle (1883–1943)[92] in Scranton—Jennings put down "lawyer" as his occupation on the couple's wedding license.[93]

Jennings practiced with William until William's death in 1922.[94] During their time together, the pair handled a variety of cases. One of their first involved representing a farmer named Thomas Royce, whose rooster was killed by a foul ball. The ball had been hit during a baseball game by a player named James Donovan, Jr. In court, Rufus Clarke, Donovan's attorney, argued that the killing was unavoidable and warned "that the great American game of baseball must not be trammeled and hand-icapped by ... absurd lawsuits."[95] Jennings responded that by failing to properly control his bat, Donovan had "lessened and cheapened the noble and desirable accomplishment of batting, distinctly injur[ing] the great national game."[96] Swayed by Jennings's argument, the jury returned a verdict of $750 (the full amount sought by Jennings) after deliberating for just seven minutes.[97]

Jennings and William also handled at least two murder cases. In the first, the brothers represented John Marmo, who was accused of killing John Hunold when Hunold attempted to steal one of Marmo's chickens.[98] On February 3, 1910, the jury deadlocked 11–1 in favor of acquittal.[99] By the time the case was retried, Jennings had left town to rejoin the Tigers. As a result, William, aided by a young lawyer named John J. Memolo (Dickinson Law School, Class

Hugh A. "Hughie" Jennings (*c.* 1921) (National Baseball Hall of Fame and Museum).

of 1909), argued that Marmo could not be retried because jeopardy had attached. The government responded that because Marmo had only been tried for manslaughter, and now was on trial for murder, he remained prosecutable. William, however, pointed out that Marmo's original indictment had been for both manslaughter *and* murder and that the jury had been discharged without rendering a verdict. Although agreeing with William (and ordering Marmo freed), Judge Edward C. Newcomb severely chastised William and Memolo and pointedly suggested that they had breached their duties as officers of the court by using such a hyper-technical defense.[100]

In their second murder case, Jennings and William represented five men who were accused of beating 22-year-old John (some sources say Felix) Slesonski to death following a bar fight.[101] In explaining how he planned to defend the group, Jennings told reporters, "I think they have the wrong men in this affair. I must forget baseball until this thing is over with, and I'm glad I have the time to give to the case."[102] Ten days later, however, Jennings was involved in a near-fatal automobile accident,[103] thereby ending his involvement in the case.[104]

Conclusion

In October 1920, after 14 seasons at the helm, Jennings stepped down as the Tigers' manager.[105] Within weeks, however, Jennings agreed to become the coach and assistant manager of the New York Giants, whose manager was Jennings's old Orioles teammate John McGraw.[106]

In 1925, with McGraw out ill, Jennings became the Giants' acting manager. Although the club had won the last four National League pennants (1921–24), under Jennings the team finished second with a record of 86–66.[107] Jennings held himself responsible for the team's performance and, as a result, suffered a nervous breakdown. In February 1926, Dr. Martin T. O'Malley sent Jennings to the Winyah Sanitarium in Asheville, North Carolina, for a "complete rest."[108] Although Jennings was discharged after just three months,[109] he never fully recovered.

In December 1926, Jennings issued a public statement in which he placed much of the blame for his continuing ill health on the Giants' owners, Judge Francis X. McQuade and Charles A. Stoneham, who, he claimed, have "absolutely deserted me, cut me off the payroll and … to this [day] never directly asked me by wire or letter or word of mouth how I felt."[110]

On January 29, 1928, Jennings, having contracted meningitis, fell into a coma and died three days later at his home in Scranton.[111] Subsequently, it was reported that he had left the bulk (77%) of his $87,000 estate, the equivalent today of $1.58 million, to his wife Nora.[112]

Nearly 50 years later, in April 1996, the University of Maryland's law school in Baltimore held its first "Hughie Jennings Memorial Baseball Lecture"—the inaugural speaker was noted Stanford University law professor William B. Gould IV.[113] A short time later, in November 2001, Christopher A. Doherty, Jennings's great-grandson (and like Jennings a Democrat) was elected mayor of Scranton.[114]

NOTES

1. *See* Flood v. Kuhn, 407 U.S. 258, 262 (1972). For a further look at Blackmun's list, see, e.g., Savanna L. Nolan, *Inside Baseball: Justice Blackmun and the Summer of '72*, 2020 THE GREEN BAG ALMANAC & READER 351; Ross E. Davies, *A Tall Tale of The Brethren*, 33 J. SUP. CT. HIST. 186 (2008); Roger Abrams, *Blackmun's List*, 6 VA. SPORTS & ENTM'T L.J. 181 (2007).

2. *See* James P. Dawson, *Old Timers' Committee Selects Ten for Baseball Hall of Fame: Bresnahan, Brouthers, Clarke, Jim Collins, Delehanty, Duffy, Jennings, King Kelly, James O'Rourke and Robinson Named*, N.Y. TIMES, Apr. 26, 1945, at 18. Jennings's Hall of Fame plaque can be viewed at *Hughie Jennings*, NATIONAL BASEBALL HALL OF FAME AND MUSEUM, https://baseballhall.org/hall-of-famers/jennings-hughie (last visited July 1, 2024) (describing Jennings as "a star shortstop" and "a constant threat at the plate").

3. For Jennings's career statistics as a player, see *Hughie Jennings*, BASEBALL-REFERENCE. COM, https://www.baseball-reference.com/players/j/jennihu01.shtml (last visited July

1, 2024) [hereinafter *Jennings Player Stats*]. For Jennings's career statistics as a manager, see *Hughie Jennings*, Baseball-Reference.com, https://www.baseball-reference.com/managers/jennihu01.shtml (last visited July 1, 2024) [hereinafter *Jennings Managerial Stats*] (indicating that as a manager, Jennings went 1,184–995–23 [.543]). All the baseball statistics for Jennings cited in this essay come from these sources.

4. See Jack Smiles, "Ee-Yah": The Life and Times of Hughie Jennings, Baseball Hall of Famer 7 (2005). The title of Smiles's book refers to the unusual sound ("Ee-Yah") that Jennings would make while coaching—Jennings would do so while raising his hands above his head, balling his fists, and hoisting his right leg. For a further discussion, see C. Paul Rogers III, *Hughie Jennings*, SABR, https://sabr.org/bioproj/person/hughie-jennings/ (last visited July 1, 2024) ("[Jennings's] shrill yell became one of baseball's historic trademarks and, in modified form, even became a rallying cry of the U.S. Marines in World War I, who often went into battle shouting 'Ee-yah-yip!'.... There are two stories for the origin of 'Ee-yah.' One is that it came originally from Johnny Williams, a pitcher from Hawaii, who used it. Jennings was enamored with the yell and learned from Williams that it was Hawaiian for 'Look out.' The fact that Williams was not with the Tigers until 1914 casts some doubt on [this] version. The other, more likely story is simply that it was a perversion of 'That's the way,' which evolved to 'Way-yah' and then to its final [form of] 'Ee-yah.").

5. Almost no information has been found for Honora, who sometimes (as in the 1880 federal census) is listed as "Hannah." *See Hannah Jennings in the 1880 United States Federal Census*, Ancestry.com, https://www.ancestry.com/discoveryui-content/view/37499214:6742 (last visited July 1, 2024) (at Line 2). For an obituary of James, see *James Jennings Dead: Was the Father of Hughey, the Famous Baltimore Shortstop*, Scranton Trib., Nov. 22, 1898, at 3. *See also James Jennings*, Find-a-Grave.com, https://www.findagrave.com/memorial/151247147/james_jennings (last visited July 1, 2024) (reporting that James was a native of Westport, County Mayo, Ireland, and that his wife, who is not named, predeceased him by 15 years). As a teenager, James was one of the thousands of people who took the Reverend Theobald Mathew's pledge of total abstinence. Following his death, James's obituaries unfailingly reported that James never broke his pledge, proudly wore the medal he had been given after taking the pledge, and regularly participated in local temperance gatherings. For a biography of Mathew, see Paul A. Townend, Father Mathew, Temperance, and Irish Identity (2002).

6. *See* Smiles, *supra* note 4, at 10 ("[T]he Jenningses ... left Ireland ... to escape the Great Famine").

7. For a further discussion, see Susan Campbell Bartoletti, Black Potatoes: The Story of the Great Irish Famine, 1845–1850 (2001).

8. *See Death of a Well Known Resident—James Jennings, Sr.: Passes Away After a Few Days' Illness*, Scranton Republican, Nov. 22, 1898, at 8. It seems likely that the pair married before immigrating to the United States, for a search of Pennsylvania's marriage records reveals no trace of them.

9. *See, e.g.*, Rogers, *supra* note 4 ("Hugh Ambrose Jennings was born on April 2, 1869 in Pittston, Pennsylvania, the ninth of twelve children of a miner's family"). Rogers does not provide any proof for his statement. Another source that reports that Honora and James had 12 children is David Clark, *James J Jennings Sr.*, Ancestry.com, https://www.ancestry.com/family-tree/person/tree/195585902/person/282549968250/story (last visited July 1, 2024). Clark, however, gets matters wrong because he relies on an 1875 New York State census that provides information on a different couple—Nora (née Rooney) (1838–1905) and James Jennings (?–1906)—who lived in Brooklyn and who did not have a son named Hugh in 1875. *See James Jennings in the New York, U.S., State Census, 1875*, Ancestry.com, https://www.ancestry.com/discoveryui-content/view/1366159077:7250 (last visited July 1, 2024).

10. *See* Smiles, *supra* note 4, at 7.

11. For an obituary of Thomas, see *Thomas Jennings Dies at Home in Colorado: Native of Avoca and Brother of Hugh Jennings*, Scranton Republican, Oct. 20, 1923, at 17. *See also Thomas E Jennings*, Find-a-Grave.com, https://www.findagrave.com/memorial/94641382/thomas-e-jennings (last visited July 1, 2024).

12. For an obituary of John, see *Pioneer Mining Man Dies at Age of 61*, SANTA FE NEW MEXICAN, Jan. 12, 1925, at 4 ("John Jennings, one of the pioneer mining men of northern New Mexico, passed away at the Dawson hospital.... Mr. Jennings had been a resident of this city for many years and was a brother to Hughie Jennings, formerly manager of the Detroit Tigers..."). *See also John Jennings*, FIND-A-GRAVE.COM, https://www.findagrave. com/memorial/94641383/john-jennings (last visited July 1, 2024) (listing John's birth year as unknown). The 1855 date used in the text comes from the 1860 federal census. *See John Jennings in the 1860 United States Federal Census*, ANCESTRY.COM, https://www.ancestry. com/discoveryui-content/view/1969377:7667 (last visited July 1, 2024) (listing John, at Line 22, as being five in 1860). In 1912, it was erroneously reported that John had been killed in a mining accident. *See Hugh Jennings' Brother Dead*, TRIB.-REPUBLICAN (Scranton), July 5, 1912, at 2.

13. For an obituary of James, see *James R. Jennings, 80, Dies in Mercy Hospital: Brother of Late Hughie Jennings of Baseball Fame; Funeral Will Be Held Tuesday*, SCRANTON TIMES, Jan. 18, 1943, at 11. *See also James R. Jennings*, FIND-A-GRAVE.COM, https:// www.findagrave.com/memorial/151248247/james_r_jennings (last visited July 1, 2024). This website lists James's birth year as 1866 but provides no proof. The 1858 date used in the text comes from the 1880 federal census. *See James Jennings in the 1880 United States Federal Census*, ANCESTRY.COM, https://www.ancestry.com/discoveryui-content/ view/50232235:6742 (last visited July 1, 2024) (listing James, at Line 4, as being 22 in 1880).

14. For an obituary of Henry, see *Hughey Jennings' Brother is Dead at Rendham Home*, SCRANTON REPUBLICAN, Mar. 16, 1915, at 14. Henry does not have a *Find-a-Grave* webpage.

15. For an obituary of Bridget, see *Mrs. Edward Walsh, Sister of Hughey Jennings, is Dead*, PITTSTON GAZ. (PA), Dec. 2, 1940, at 3. *See also Bridget A Jennings Walsh*, FIND-A-GRAVE.COM, https://www.findagrave.com/memorial/238448513/bridget_a_walsh (last visited July 1, 2024) (this webpage includes a copy of Bridget's death certificate).

16. For an obituary of Frank, see *Frank Jennings Dies; Brother of Late Baseball Chief*, SCRANTON TRIB., May 5, 1949, at 22. Frank, whose real name probably was Francis, does not have a *Find-a-Grave* webpage.

17. Ellen appears only twice in public records. In the 1880 federal census, she is listed as a 12-year-old student. *See Ellen Jennings in the 1880 United States Federal Census*, ANCESTRY.COM, https://www.ancestry.com/discoveryui-content/view/50232238:6742 (last visited July 1, 2024) (at Line 8). She also appears in an 1886 newspaper notice reporting that a letter is waiting for her at the Pittston post office. *See Advertised Letters*, EVENING GAZ. (Pittston, PA), June 12, 1886, at 4. In one of his obituaries, James is reported as being survived by eight sons and one daughter. No mention is made of Ellen, which suggests that she died sometime between 1887 and 1897. *See Death of James Jennings*, DOLLAR WKLY. NEWS-DEALER (Wilkes-Barre, PA), Nov. 26, 1898, at 3 (listing James's children as Jennings; his seven brothers Frank, Henry, James, John, Joseph, Thomas, and William; and his sister "Mrs. Edward Walsh").

18. For an obituary of Jennings, see *Hugh Jennings Dies After Long Illness: Famous Baseball Veteran, Ailing for Three Years, Succumbs in Scranton—Was Picturesque Figure—Captained Old Orioles, Won Three Pennants for Detroit and Helped Giants Take Four*, N.Y. TIMES, Feb. 1, 1928, at 1 [hereinafter *Jennings Dies*]. *See also Hugh Jennings*, FIND-A-GRAVE.COM, https://www.findagrave.com/memorial/3696/hugh_jennings (last visited July 1, 2024) (indicating that Jennings is buried in Saint Catherine's Cemetery in Moscow, Pennsylvania).

19. For an obituary of William, see *W.A. Jennings Claimed by Death: Well Known Attorney Dies Suddenly at His Home in Dunmore—Ailing for Some Time; Brother of Hughie Jennings, Assistant Manager of New York Giants*, SCRANTON REPUBLICAN, Nov. 25, 1922, at 2. William does not have a *Find-a-Grave* webpage.

20. For an obituary of Joseph, see *Death Summons Dr. Jennings: Brother of Hugh Jennings Passes Away After Long Illness*, SCRANTON REPUBLICAN, June 7, 1920, at 2. Joseph does not have a *Find-a-Grave* webpage.

21. *See* SMILES, *supra* note 4, at 5 ("'Hughie' is the more common [form] ... and ... is the spelling used on his Hall of Fame plaque and in various baseball encyclopedias.... In

the early part of his career, especially before 1900, sportswriters often spelled the name 'Hughey.'").

22. *See id.* at 10. Rogers claims that Jennings was paid 90 cents a day, see Rogers, *supra* note 4, but this almost certainly is incorrect. According to another source, breaker boys were making just 25 cents a day in the 1920s. *See* WILLIAM C. KASHATUS, DIAMONDS IN THE COALFIELDS: 21 REMARKABLE BASEBALL PLAYERS, MANAGERS, AND UMPIRES FROM NORTHEAST PENNSYLVANIA 13 (2002).

23. SMILES, *supra* note 4, at 7. As Smiles further reports:

> Rated chemically for hardness and luster, anthracite is the highest grade of coal in the earth.... Anthracite burns cleaner, hotter and four times longer than bituminous [coal] and is virtually smoke free.... As the demand for [anthracite] grew, so did Pittston.... Fed by thousands of English, Welsh and Irish immigrants who came specifically to work in the mines, the area grew rapidly. By 1869, the anthracite fields around Pittston were producing 25,000,000 tons of hard coal a year, double that by 1900. During this time the population of Pittston increased from 2,500 to 15,000.

Id. at 8.

24. *Id.* at 11 ("[Jennings] played with the other breaker boys in pickup games during lunch break and accident or machinery breakdowns. Sometimes breaker boys purposely caused these breakdowns").

25. *Id.* at 13 ("The Pounders' next youngest player was 17 and most [of the team members] were adults. It wasn't Hughie's talent that made the Pounders seek him out, but his fearlessness"). Moosic is four miles north of Pittston. During this time, "Neither Pittston nor West Pittston [had] a base ball club." *Local Gleanings*, EVENING GAZ. (Pittston, PA), June 6, 1884, at 4.

26. As Smiles explains, "Greater Pittston, as the 50 square miles of 15 attached and fragmented little towns around it is called, was a boom area in the late 1800s and downtown Pittston was its hub." SMILES, *supra* note 4, at 8.

27. *See id.* at 12 ("Breaker boys coveted mule-driving jobs, even though it was fraught with its own dangers. A driver might fall under the mule's hoofs or the car [or suffer some other type of grievous injury]"). As this description suggests, mining companies used mule-powered carts to move coal from where it was mined to where it was refined. The mule driver was responsible for steering the mule. *See id.* at 10.

28. KASHATUS, *supra* note 22, at 12–13.

29. *See* SMILES, *supra* note 4, at 17–19; Rogers, *supra* note 4.

30. *See Base Ball*, CARBON ADVOC. (Lehighton, PA), Mar. 22, 1890, at 3 ("Lehighton will play ball during the coming season in splendid shape.... Ball players who have signed with Manager Clauss thus far are Hugh Jennings...").

31. The first inkling that Jennings might leave Lehighton came in a news report in May 1890. *See Base Ball Chit-Chat*, HARRISBURG TELEGRAPH (PA), May 28, 1890, at 1 ("Catcher Young has been released by Easton at his own request. Catcher Jennings, of the Lehighton club, will probably be signed in his stead"). Two weeks later, Jennings did leave Lehighton, but for Allentown rather than Easton. *See An Exhibition Game at Easton*, PHIL. INQUIRER, June 16, 1890, at 3 (reporting on an exhibition game between Allentown and Easton. In the accompanying box score, Jennings is listed as having played catcher for Allentown and having driven in a run on a sacrifice). Allentown joined the league on June 12, 1890, taking Lancaster's place. *See Pennsylvania State League*, BASEBALL-REFERENCE.COM, https://www.baseball-reference.com/bullpen/Pennsylvania_State_League (last visited July 1, 2024) (under "Cities Represented 1890–1890 Eastern Inter-State League"). This explains why Allentown needed to play an exhibition game in the middle of the season.

32. *See Players Left in a Lurch: Manager Mason, of the Allentown Club, Disappears and the Team Disbands*, PHIL. INQUIRER, July 6, 1890, at 3. The rest of the league folded three weeks later. *See The Inter-State's Fall: Harrisburg's Withdrawal Sends the League to the Wall; Causes Leading to the Break; President Voltz Censured—Small Towns and Smaller Backing Two of the Reasons for the Failure*, TIMES (Phil.), July 27, 1890, at 14. *See also* "YankeeBiscuitFan," *Minor League History: Eastern Interstate [sic] League*, DUTCH BASEBALL

HANGOUT, Mar. 27, 2016, https://dutchbaseballhangout.blog/2016/03/27/minor-league-history-eastern-interstate-league/ (pointing out that despite the recent institution of baseball's color line, the league included the York (Colored) Monarchs).

33. *See Base Ball Gossip*, LEBANON DAILY NEWS, Aug. 25, 1890, at 1 ("Hugh Jennings, of Lehighton, formerly of the Allentown base ball club, has declined the offer of $100 per month by the Lebanon base ball club [of the Atlantic Association], and will continue with the Lehighton team").

34. *See Base Ball Gossip*, CARBON ADVOC. (Lehighton, PA), Apr. 11, 1891, at 3.

35. For a look at the PSL's lost season, see PAUL BROWNE, THE COAL BARONS PLAYED CUBAN GIANTS: A HISTORY OF EARLY PROFESSIONAL BASEBALL IN PENNSYLVANIA, 1886–1896, at 121–29 (2013). As Browne explains:

> The failure of a Pennsylvania state league to launch in 1891, the only time between 1886 and 1897, was at least in part due to fallout from the Players' League war [in 1890].... Having been burned by failure when baseball's popularity was growing, many who had backed teams in Pennsylvania cities before were unwilling to take that risk in a year when public opinion was at least somewhat soured on the baseball business.

Id. at 123–24.
The Players League (also spelled Players' League), of course, was the brainchild of John Montgomery Ward, the subject of Chapter 5 of this book, and operated as one of the three major leagues during the 1890 season. For a further discussion, see ROBERT B. ROSS, THE GREAT BASEBALL REVOLT: THE RISE AND FALL OF THE 1890 PLAYERS LEAGUE (2016).

36. *See, e.g., Base Ball Gossip*, CARBON ADVOC. (Lehighton, PA), May 16, 1891, at 3 ("Lehighton shut out Allentown in a spiritless game Saturday—the score standing 12 to 0. The features of the game were a home run [by] Jennings and Loken's pitching").

37. The Colonels were a charter member of the AA (founded 1882). When the AA folded after the 1891 season, the Colonels became part of the National League (which expanded from eight teams to 12). The Colonels disbanded after the 1899 season as many of its best players, along with Colonels' owner Bernhard "Barney" Dreyfus, became part of the Pittsburgh Pirates. For a history of the Colonels, see ANNE JEWELL, BASEBALL IN LOUISVILLE 13–24 (2006). For a history of Dreyfus, see BRIAN MARTIN, BARNEY DREYFUSS: PITTSBURGH'S BASEBALL TITAN (2021). For a history of the AA, see DAVID NEMEC, THE BEER AND WHISKEY LEAGUE: THE ILLUSTRATED HISTORY OF THE AMERICAN ASSOCIATION—BASEBALL'S RENEGADE MAJOR LEAGUE (1994).

38. *See 1891 American Association Team Statistics*, BASEBALL-REFERENCE.COM, https://www.baseball-reference.com/leagues/AA/1891.shtml (last visited July 1, 2024).

39. Rogers, *supra* note 4.

40. *Base Ball*, FREELAND TRIB. (PA), June 4, 1891, at 1.

41. *Baseball*, FREELAND TRIB. (PA), Aug. 13, 1891, at 4.

42. *The Star of the Season*, FREELAND TRIB. (PA), Oct. 1, 1891, at 1.

43. *See Jennings Player Stats*, *supra* note 3.

44. *Id.* Ironically, during Jennings's best season (1896), a woman named Caroline B. Newman filed a $5,000 lawsuit against the Orioles, claiming that during a game with the Philadelphia Phillies on September 22, 1896, she was hit in the head by a Jennings fly ball. *See Fly May Come High: Baltimore Club Sued by Woman for Injuries Caused by Foul Fly*, BOS. DAILY GLOBE, Oct. 30, 1896, at 2. Unfortunately, due to a lack of further public reporting, the outcome of the lawsuit is unknown.

45. *See Career Leaders & Records for Hit by Pitch*, BASEBALL-REFERENCE.COM, https://www.baseball-reference.com/leaders/HBP_career.shtml (last visited July 1, 2024).

46. SMILES, *supra* note 4, at 79.

47. *Hughey Jennings' Head was Stone: Shaved Eternity by a Fraction the Day That Amos Rusie Hit Him with a Pitched Ball—Story of a Remarkable Game*, BUFF. ENQUIRER, Feb. 16, 1905, at 8.

48. *See Well, Well, What Next?: Jennings and Doyle Gone to Join Keeler, Robinson and Clarke's Sick List; Badly Bunged-Up Orioles; Hugh's Head Hit by One of Rusie's Swift Shoots*, SUN (Balt.), June 29, 1897, at 6.

49. *Orioles Got This, Too: A Sort of Farewell Engagement Won from the Washingtons by 6 to 4; It was an Exciting Game—Jennings and Doyle Back in the Infield Again,* Sun (Balt.), July 3, 1897, at 6.

50. *He'll Keep It Up,* Wilkes-Barre Rec. (PA), July 7, 1897, at 3.

51. Jennings (shortstop) and McGraw (third base) were part of the Orioles' "Big Four," the other members of the quartet being Joseph J. "Joe" Kelley (center field) and William H. "Wee Willie" Keeler (right field). *See generally* Stephen Fox, Big Leagues: Professional Baseball, Football, and Basketball in National Memory 206 (1994) ("In [their] 'Big Four' of McGraw, Jennings, Kelley, and Keeler, [the Orioles] in effect had four managers on the field, all of them popping with tricks and strategies. They called their own signals, ranging at will with their speed, always pushing and taking risks…. Although weak at pitching, fielding, and first base, the Orioles still pestered the enemy into exasperated defeats").

52. *See M'Graw and Jennings: Getting in a Winter's Work at College—Other Baseball News,* Sun (Balt.), Jan. 26, 1895, at 7.

53. Jennings soon worked out a somewhat similar arrangement with the University of Georgia ("UGA"). As a result, from 1895 to 1897, while participating in spring training with the Orioles in Macon, Georgia, Jennings regularly made the 90-mile trip north to Athens, Georgia, where UGA had its campus. *See* Smiles, *supra* note 4, at 65–66. During his three years as UGA's coach, Jennings compiled a record of 5–17. *See* University of Georgia Athletics, *All-Time Georgia Baseball Coaches,* https://georgiadogs.com/sports/2017/6/17/sports-m-basebl-spec-rel-baseball-former-coaches-html (last visited July 1, 2024) (listing Jennings as UGA's second head baseball coach). *See also* William F. Ross III, *Spring Training in Georgia: The Yannigans are Coming!,* SABR, https://sabr.org/journal/article/spring-training-in-georgia-the-yannigans-are-coming/ (last visited July 1, 2024) (explaining that the Orioles held spring training in Macon from 1894 to 1898).

54. For a biography of Taylor, see Charlie Bevis, *Harry Taylor,* SABR, https://sabr.org/bioproj/person/harry-taylor-3/ (last visited July 1, 2024). As Bevis explains, Taylor earned his bachelor's degree from Cornell in 1888; played minor league baseball in 1889; played for the Louisville Colonels from 1890 to 1892 (where he first became teammates with Jennings); entered Cornell's law school in 1891 and earned his law degree in 1893; played for the Baltimore Orioles in 1893 (again teaming with Jennings); and then, after passing the bar exam in January 1894, opened his own law firm in Buffalo (where he continued to play on various amateur baseball teams). In December 1906, Taylor was appointed to the New York State Supreme Court (a trial court) in Erie, where he remained until 1924, when he was appointed to the Appellate Division, a position he held until mandatory retirement at the age of 70 forced him off the bench in December 1936. For a further discussion, see *Harry L. Taylor,* Historical Society of the New York Courts, https://history.nycourts.gov/biography/harry-l-taylor/ (last visited July 1, 2024).

55. *Jennings in Buffalo: Two Columns Devoted to Him in the Buffalo Times,* Scranton Republican, Feb. 11, 1896, at 3.

56. *See Wedding at Avoca: Miss Elizabeth Dixon Becomes the Bride of Hugh Jennings, of Baltimore Club—Brilliant Social Event,* Scranton Trib., Oct. 15, 1897, at 6 (reporting on the wedding, which took place at St. Mary's Catholic Church, and describing Elizabeth as "one of Avoca's most graceful and accomplished daughters, and her family [as] one of the [town's] most prominent…. She was educated in St. Cecilia's convent in this city and has a large number of warm admiring friends in the various towns and cities of [this region]").

57. *See St. Bonaventures: Hughey Jennings, Who is Coaching the Boys, is Satisfied,* Buff. Courier, Feb. 14, 1898, at 7.

58. *See* Alumni Directory of Saint Bonaventure's College and Seminary 1859–1930, at 116 (Oct. 1, 1930) (listing Jennings as having failed to earn a degree).

59. *See Wedding at Avoca, supra* note 56.

60. *See Round About Town: Hughey is a Papa,* Wilkes-Barre Rec. (PA), Sept. 7, 1898, at 10. For an obituary of Grace, see *Grace McWilliams Dies; Was Ill for Three Weeks—Daughter of a Baseball Great,* Scranton Trib., Aug. 29, 1964, at 3. Grace does not have a *Find-a-Grave* webpage.

61. *See supra* note 5.

62. *See Mrs. Elizabeth C. Jennings*, Sun (Balt.), Nov. 28, 1898, at 7. *See also Elizabeth C. Jennings*, Find-a-Grave.com, https://www.findagrave.com/memorial/158431621/elizabeth-c-jennings (last visited July 1, 2024).

63. For a further discussion, see Burt Solomon, Where They Ain't: The Fabled Life and Untimely Death of the Original Baltimore Orioles, the Team That Gave Birth to Modern Baseball (1999). As Solomon explains, the transfer marked the beginning of the end of the Orioles. After finishing in fourth place with a record of 86–62, the team was "contracted" (folded) by the National League. Three other teams also were contracted: the Cleveland Spiders, Louisville Colonels, and Washington Senators. *See Eight Clubs Will Constitute National League This Season: Louisville, Cleveland, Washington and Baltimore are Left Out in the Deal*, Dayton Evening Herald, Mar. 9, 1900, at 6. In return for agreeing to be contracted, the Colonels were paid $10,000 and had their debts ($104,000) assumed; the Orioles were paid $30,000 and given the right to dispose of their players as they saw fit; the Senators were paid $39,000 for both their players and their stadium; and the Spiders were paid $25,000 for both their players and their stadium. *See The Big League*, Sporting Life, Mar. 17, 1900, at 2. In 1900, $1 was the equivalent of $18.20 today. *See* Morgan S. Friedman, *The Inflation Calculator*, https://westegg.com/inflation/ (last visited July 1, 2024) (converting 1900 dollars to 2023 dollars).

64. Rogers, *supra* note 4.

65. *Id.*

66. *See Jennings Player Stats, supra* note 3. During the 1900 season, Jennings was elected secretary of the Players' Protective Association, baseball's second union, but played only a minor role in its affairs. *See* Ross E. Davies, *Along Comes the Players Association: The Roots of Organized Labor in Major League Baseball*, 16 N.Y.U. J. Legis. & Pub. Pol'y 321, 325–27 (2013).

67. *Live Sporting Gossip*, Brooklyn Daily Eagle, Jan. 7, 1901, at 10.

68. Cornell University, Announcement of the College of Law, 1898–99, at 15 (Apr. 1898) [hereinafter College of Law Announcement].

69. *See Hughey Jennings Quits [Professional Baseball]; Will Be Cornell's Coach*, Buff. Sun. Times, Dec. 16, 1900, at 6. As this article explains, Jennings had agreed, in addition to his law studies, to continue as Cornell's baseball coach. In exchange, Cornell agreed to pay Jennings $1,500 a year and waive his tuition. *Id.* During this time, Cornell's law school tuition was $100 a year. *See* College of Law Announcement, *supra* note 68, at 18. Jennings had been coaching Cornell's baseball team since February 1899. *See New Coach for Cornell Baseball Men*, N.Y. Times, Dec. 23, 1898, at 3 ("Capt. Murtaugh of the Cornell Varsity baseball team has secured the services of 'Hughey' Jennings … to coach the Varsity players…. He will begin about Feb. 15[, 1899] and continue until the National League season begins").

70. College of Law Announcement, *supra* note 68, at 15.

71. Andrew Milner, *June 24, 1901: He Didn't Have the Energy to Strike a Lucifer*, SABR, https://sabr.org/gamesproj/game/june-24-1901-he-didnt-have-the-energy-to-strike-a-lucifer/ (last visited July 1, 2024) (footnotes omitted).

72. *See Hugh Jennings to Report Saturday*, Pitt. Press, June 12, 1902, at 12. In his first game back (June 16, 1902, versus the Chicago Orphans (later Cubs)), Jennings got a single and a double and scored a run but the Phillies lost 9–4). *See Chick Fraser was Easy and Wild: Hugh Jennings Rejoined the Phillies, But Could Not Avert Defeat*, Phil. Inquirer, June 17, 1902, at 10.

73. *See Jennings Player Stats, supra* note 3. After 1902, Jennings played in 13 more major league games spread out over 16 years (1903–18). *See id.* His last major league game occurred on September 2, 1918 (the last day of the war-shortened 1918 season), when, at the age of 49, he manned first base for the Detroit Tigers for one inning in the second game of a doubleheader against the Chicago White Sox. *Id. See also Sox Do a Fadeout by Dropping Pair to Detroit Tigers*, Chi. Daily Trib., Sept. 3, 1918, at 13 (reporting that the Tigers won the first game by a score of 11–5 and the second game by a score of 7–3).

74. Prior to the start of the 1903 season, Ned Hanlon of the Superbas purchased the

Montreal Royals and moved the club to Baltimore. *See Baltimore Joins Eastern League: Hanlon and Mose Frank Give Dooley $5,000 for Montreal Franchise and Players*, BUFF. EVE-NING NEWS, Feb. 6, 1904, at 8. Jennings started the 1903 season with the Superbas but after six games was traded down to the Orioles. *See Jennings to Manage Orioles*, WILKES-BARRE REC. (PA), July 4, 1903, at 8 (explaining that the Orioles sent outfielder John F. "Jack" Hayden to the Superbas in return for Jennings, catcher Hughey Hearne, outfielder Walter H. McCredie, and pitcher Jeared W. "Bill" Pounds, with Orioles player-manager Wilbert Robinson relinquishing his managerial duties to Jennings but staying on as catcher).

75. *See Jennings Managerial Stats, supra* note 3; Rogers, *supra* note 4.

76. On February 25, 1904, after holding baseball practice, Jennings took a shower and then decided to go for a swim. The lights in the natatorium were off, and without pausing to turn them on—which would have revealed that there was no water in the pool—Jennings dove off the diving board, fracturing his skull, knocking him unconscious, and spraining his wrists. *See Hughey Jennings is Injured: Plunges into an Empty Tank at Cornell College, Breaking Wrist and Cutting His Head*, CHI. DAILY TRIB., Feb. 26, 1904, at 10. Remarkably, Jennings was able to make a complete recovery. *See Local Gleanings: Town Talk and Events in and About the City*, PITTSTON GAZ. (PA), Mar. 11, 1904, at 3 ("Hugh Jennings has completely recovered from the injuries he received at Ithaca [two weeks ago] by accidentally jumping into an empty swimming pool, and will be on hand to play the opening game with Baltimore on Apr. 5").

77. Rogers, *supra* note 4. *See also Jennings Resigns as Cornell Coach*, N.Y. TIMES, May 4, 1904, at 6. Although Smiles claims that Jennings did graduate, *see* SMILES, *supra* note 4, at 102, the Cornell alumni directory makes it clear that this is incorrect. *See* 13:12 CORNELL UNIVERSITY, ALUMNI DIRECTORY 165 (May 15, 1922) (indicating that Jennings attended the school from 1901 to 1904 but did not graduate). In place of a degree, the directory puts an "sp" next to Jennings's name, which, as explained *id.* at vi, indicates that he pursued a "Special Course" of instruction. While at Cornell, Jennings did find time to become a member of Conkling Inn, the local chapter of the Phi Delta Phi national legal fraternity. *See* DIRECTORY OF THE LEGAL FRATERNITY OF PHI DELTA PHI 276 (George A. Katzenberger, ed.) (8th ed. 1909).

78. For a profile of Evans, see David W. Anderson, *Billy Evans*, SABR, https://sabr.org/bioproj/person/billy-evans/ (last visited July 1, 2024).

79. *Id.*

80. *See John D. Evans*, FIND-A-GRAVE.COM, https://www.findagrave.com/memorial/92738294/john_d_evans (last visited July 1, 2024). An obituary for John has not been found.

81. *See* 13:12 CORNELL ALUMNI DIRECTORY 100 (May 15, 1922) (reporting that Evans entered Cornell Law School in 1901 as a member of the Class of 1905 but left in 1903 without a degree).

82. *See* Anderson, *supra* note 78.

83. *Id.*

84. *Id.* Evans died in 1956 at the age of 71. *See Billy Evans Dies in Miami at 71; Major League Umpire 22 Years; Noted for Commentaries*, N.Y. TIMES, Jan. 24, 1956, at 31. *See also William George "Billy" Evans*, FIND-A-GRAVE.COM, https://www.findagrave.com/memorial/6960/william-george-evans (last visited July 1, 2024).

85. *See Name Kelly, Evans to Hall of Fame*, HOME NEWS (New Brunswick, NJ), Jan. 29, 1973, at A11. *See also* Arthur Daley, *Sometimes He Erred*, N.Y. TIMES, Mar. 1, 1973, at 33 (describing Evans as "the best umpire in the American League" and commending him for his willingness to admit that he sometimes made mistakes). For Evans's Hall of Fame plaque, see *Billy Evans*, NATIONAL BASEBALL HALL OF FAME AND MUSEUM, https://baseballhall.org/hall-of-famers/evans-billy (last visited July 1, 2024) (pointing out that Evans, who officiated in six World Series, is the youngest umpire in major league history).

86. *See Admissions to the Bar: Seventeen Young Lawyers Passed Upon by Court of Appeals*, SUN (Balt.), Jan. 19, 1905, at 10 ("Hughey Jennings, the well-known professional baseball player, who played on the Baltimore Eastern League team last season, was admitted to the bar yesterday").

87. *See Baseball Notes*, PITT. PRESS, Jan. 10, 1905, at 12.

88. *See* 16 THE NATIONAL CYCLOPEDIA OF AMERICAN BIOGRAPHY 123 (1918) (under entry "Willis, George Roberts"). As this source reports, the firm disbanded in 1912. *Id.* For an obituary of Willis, see *George R. Willis Dies: Succumbs to Long Illness in Country Home at Bengies—Widely Known as Lawyer, Attained Prominence as Head of Police Board and Served City in Many Capacities*, SUN (Balt.), Sept. 12, 1919, at 16. *See also George Roberts Willis*, FIND-A-GRAVE.COM, https://www.findagrave.com/memorial/99348850/george-roberts-willis (last visited July 1, 2024). For an obituary of Homer, see *Francis T. Homer, 58, Lawyer, Dies: Retired Six Years Ago After Practicing in Baltimore and in New York; Educated at Loyola—Leaves Widow and Daughter, Latter Now Traveling Abroad*, SUN (Balt.), Mar. 4, 1930, at 30. *See also Francis Theodore Homer*, FIND-A-GRAVE.COM, https://www.findagrave.com/memorial/62259259/francis-theodore-homer (last visited July 1, 2024). For an obituary of France, see *J.C. France, Dean of Bar, Dead at 75: Served More Than Thirty Years as Counsel for United Railways; Took Part in Probe of State Roads Commission in 1928 and 1929*, SUN (Balt.), July 27, 1938, at 20. France does not have a *Find-a-Grave* webpage. For an obituary of Smith, see *Samuel K. Smith*, TIMES-HERALD (DC), Jan. 10, 1940, at 7. *See also Samuel King Smith*, FIND-A-GRAVE.COM, https://www.findagrave.com/memorial/8482080/samuel-king-smith (last visited July 1, 2024).

89. *See Jennings' Client Fined*, SUN (Balt.), Feb. 4, 1905, at 7 (explaining that McCloskey was found guilty and was sentenced to 30 days in jail and fined $100). *See also Life Story of Great and Only Hughey Jennings: Avoca Boy's Career as Told by Frank F. Patterson, Famous Baltimore Sporting Writer—Breaker to the Bar*, WILKES-BARRE LEADER (PA), Feb. 13, 1905, at 10 ("That Hughey's client was convicted was no fault of his, however. He acquitted himself with credit at the trial, but the police had a clear case against Hughey's negro and he went to jail").

90. *See Jennings Now a Lawyer: Starts Active Practice at Scranton in Partnership with Brother*, WASH. POST, Nov. 14, 1907, at 8 (noting that Jennings had just arrived from Detroit and would practice with his brother until returning to the Tigers in March 1908). *See also* GENERAL ALUMNI CATALOGUE OF THE UNIVERSITY OF PENNSYLVANIA 1922, at 456 (1922) (indicating that William earned his LL.B. in 1904).

91. *See Baseball Briefs*, PITT. PRESS, Dec. 11, 1908, at 27 ("Hugh Jennings did not attend the American League meeting Wednesday, as he was taking the Pennsylvania bar examinations"). *See also News of the Profession*, 13 L. NOTES 15 (Apr. 1909) ("Hugh Jennings, manager of the Detroit baseball team and formerly one of the greatest shortstops that the game has ever known, has been admitted to the Pennsylvania bar"). In addition to having to pass Pennsylvania's state bar exam, Jennings also was required to pass a local bar exam. *See No Flunker*, WILKES-BARRE REC. (PA), Feb. 12, 1909, at 20 (reporting on Jennings passing the Lackawanna County bar exam).

92. For an obituary of Nora, see *Mrs. Nora Jennings is Dead; Ill Four Months—Widow of Hugh Jennings, Famous Baseball Player and Manager—Funeral Tomorrow*, SCRANTON TIMES, Oct. 25, 1943, at 20. *See also Nora Ann M. O'Boyle Jennings*, FIND-A-GRAVE.COM, https://www.findagrave.com/memorial/151221436/nora_ann_m_jennings (last visited July 1, 2024). Nora and Jennings had one child, a daughter named Amelia, who died when she was two months old. *See Death of Daughter of Mr. and Mrs. Jennings*, SCRANTON TRUTH, Feb. 6, 1912, at 9. *See also Amelia Jennings*, FIND-A-GRAVE.COM, https://www.findagrave.com/memorial/222660073/amelia_jennings (last visited July 1, 2024). For Amelia's death certificate, see *Amelia Gennings [sic] in Pennsylvania, U.S., Death Certificates, 1906–1970*, ANCESTRY.COM, https://www.ancestry.com/discoveryui-content/view/373501:5164 (last visited July 1, 2024) (stating that Amelia was born on December 14, 1911, and died on February 5, 1912, from convulsions and indigestion).

93. *See "Hughie" Passes Round the Smokes: Signs Long-Term Contract and Then Distributes Cigars in Court House—Occupation: "Lawyer,"* TRIB.-REPUBLICAN (Scranton), Jan. 10, 1911, at 2.

94. *See supra* note 19.

95. *Jennings at the Bar: Makes Impassioned Appeal in Live Chicken Case—A $600 Rooster Killed; Eminent Attorney Carries Law Books into Court in a Baseball Bag—Manager*

of Detroit Tigers is Quite Busy These Days, Clients Fairly Swarming into His Office at Scranton, WASH. POST, Jan. 3, 1910, at 8.

96. *Id.*

97. *Id.*

98. *See Out on Bail*, WILKES-BARRE SEMI-WKLY. REC. (PA), Nov. 26, 1909, at 8.

99. *See Jury Failed to Agree in Murder Case; Scored by Judge Newcomb: Stood Eleven to One for Acquittal in Marmo Case—In Discharging Jury Judge Referred to Practice of Taking Life in Cold Blood*, SCRANTON TIMES, Feb. 3, 1910, at 3.

100. *See Technicality Secures the Discharge of John Marmo: He was Indicted for the Killing of John Hunold at Old Forge Last November; Counsel Censured by Judge Newcomb—Taken an Unfair Advantage—Marmo Tried Once and Acquitted*, SCRANTON TRUTH, Apr. 8, 1910, at 1. For a profile of Newcomb (1856–1935), see *President Judge E.C. Newcomb Dies: Blood Clot Kills County Jurist at 77; Veteran Member of Common Pleas Bench Loses Long Fight Against Illness as Brain Ailment Develops; Funeral Tomorrow Afternoon*, SCRANTON REPUBLICAN, Feb. 11, 1935, at 1. *See also Judge Edwin Charles Newcomb*, FIND-A-GRAVE.COM, https://www.findagrave.com/memorial/198943049/edwin-charles-newcomb (last visited July 1, 2024). Years later, Memolo (1885–1954) *did* breach his professional ethics by helping to obstruct an investigation into allegations that U.S. District Judge Albert W. Johnson was accepting bribes. When the facts came out, Memolo gave up his law license and later served two years in prison. *See Death Claims John Memolo: Long Illness Fatal; Funeral on Tuesday*, SCRANTON TRIB., Mar. 1, 1954, at 9. *See also John Memolo*, FIND-A-GRAVE.COM, https://www.findagrave.com/memorial/40343728/john-memolo (last visited July 1, 2024). For more about Johnson, who resigned his seat in the face of certain impeachment, see Johnson v. United States, 79 F. Supp. 208 (Ct. Cl. 1948).

101. *See Assassins of Slesonski Have Retained Counsel: Hugh and W.A. Jennings Will Defend Five Men Under Arrest*, SCRANTON TIMES, Nov. 23, 1911, at 12.

102. *Jennings Retained in Homicide Case*, PITT. POST, Nov. 23, 1911, at 11.

103. *See Hugh Jennings Hurt; Auto Ran Off Bridge: Car Driven by Detroit Team's Manager Fell to River When Steering Gear Failed; Priest in Car Also Injured—Couple Just Married by the Rev. P.J. Lynott Escaped Injury—Car was Gift of Detroit Fans*, N.Y. TIMES, Dec. 3, 1911, at 10. *See also Hughey Jennings is Not the Same Person*, TAMPA MORN. TRIB., May 18, 1912, at 2 (describing the enormous physical toll the accident took on Jennings).

104. There is no further public reporting about the case. Smiles claims that William continued to handle the case and got two of the defendants (brothers Edward and Stanley Papsch) off by having them agree to testify against the other three defendants (Frank Kerdoski, Peter Strounka, and Martin Toskoski), who were convicted. *See* SMILES, *supra* note 4, at 170. Smiles's account seems improbable because if true, William would have violated his ethical duties to Kerdoski, Strounka, and Toskoski.

105. *See Hughey Jennings Quits as Detroit Manager: Ty Cobb, Jimmy Burke and Clarence Rowland are Mentioned as Prospective Candidates to Succeed Veteran Pilot of Benegal Squad*, ST. LOUIS STAR, Oct. 15, 1920, at 22. In his letter of resignation, Jennings told Tigers owner Francis J. "Frank" Navin that he thought "a change would be beneficial to you and the Detroit baseball club, and perhaps to myself." *In Letter to Navin, Jennings Announces Retirement as Boss*, ST. LOUIS STAR, Oct. 15, 1920, at 22. After winning the American League pennant in each of his first three years as manager of the Tigers (1907–09), Jennings had guided the team to two second place finishes, two third place finishes, three fourth place finishes, two sixth place finishes, and two seventh places, with the 1920 season being the worst of the lot (61–93, 37 games behind the first place Cleveland Indians). *See Jennings Managerial Stats, supra* note 3.

106. *See* W.J. Macbeth, *McGraw Ready to Give Reins to Jennings: Short Training Trip Leads to Belief Giants' Manager is Through as Active Pilot*, N.Y. TRIB., Dec. 28, 1920, at 10. As matters turned out, McGraw was *not* ready to hand the reins over to Jennings, and remained the manager of the Giants until June 1932, when ill health finally forced him to resign. *See* Alan Gould, *M'Graw Resigns, Terry to Manage Giants: Poor Health is Reason Given for His Action—Former Atlanta Boy Gets Chance as Veteran Gives Up Helm*, ATLANTA CONST., June 4, 1932, at 8.

107. *See Jennings Managerial Stats, supra* note 3.

108. *See Smiles, supra* note 4, at 189. During this period the Winyah Sanitarium exclusively served patients with tuberculosis. As a result, many newspapers reported that Jennings was suffering from the disease, a claim that Dr. O'Malley emphatically denied. *See Hugh Jennings Seeks Rest in Sanitarium,* DAILY NEWS (NY), Feb. 15, 1926, at 25. It is difficult to determine the truth, especially because some sources claim that Jennings contracted tuberculosis while at Winyah. *See, e.g.,* ROY KERR, SLIDING BILLY HAMILTON: THE LIFE AND TIMES OF BASEBALL'S FIRST GREAT LEADOFF HITTER 187 (2010).

109. *See Asheville Hospital Discharges Jennings,* N.Y. TIMES, May 27, 1926, at 18 (giving Jennings's discharge date as May 26). Smiles claims that Jennings was discharged on June 12. *See* SMILES, *supra* note 4 at 189.

110. *Jennings Explains Break with Giants: Says He Was Deserted by the Club Officials and Cut Off Payroll; McGraw Gets Praise—Stood by His Former Assistant, Who Declares He Sought Only Confidence of Employers,* N.Y. TIMES, Dec. 10, 1926, at 32. McQuade (1878–1955) was a New York City municipal court judge. In 1919, he became (with McGraw and Stoneham) a co-owner of the Giants and was made the team's treasurer. When Stoneham (as majority owner) abruptly fired McQuade as treasurer in 1928, McQuade sued Stoneham. Although McQuade was successful in the lower courts, the New York State Court of Appeals ruled that McQuade could not legally serve as both a judge and the Giants' treasurer. *See* McQuade v. Stoneham, 189 N.E. 234 (N.Y.), *reargument denied,* 191 N.E. 514 (N.Y. 1934). For a further discussion, see Bill Lamb, *Frank McQuade,* SABR, https://sabr.org/bioproj/person/Frank-McQuade/ (explaining that in addition to not getting back his job with the Giants, McQuade was forced to resign from the bench for violating a state law that prohibited judges from accepting outside employment).

111. *See Jennings Dies, supra* note 18.

112. *See Jennings' Estate Valued at $87,000,* BOS. GLOBE, Feb. 7, 1928, at 19 (reporting that Jennings left $10,000 to his sister Bridget; $10,000 to his daughter Grace; and the rest to his wife Nora). *See also* Friedman, *supra* note 63 (converting 1928 dollars to 2023 dollars).

113. Gould's talk was titled, "My Fifty Years in Baseball: Ways in Which the Game Has Changed and Stayed the Same." *See Faculty Notes,* 31:1 STANFORD LAWYER (alumni magazine of Stanford University law school), Fall 1996, at 27. Regrettably, the lecture appears to have fallen by the wayside in recent years.

114. *See* Kristin Wintermantel, *Grace Notes: A Conversation with the Mayor-Elect's Mother, Grace Doherty,* SUN. TIMES (Scranton), Jan. 6, 2002, at F1.

CHAPTER 3

James Henry "Jim" O'Rourke (1945)

GEOFFREY CHRISTOPHER RAPP

James Henry "Jim" O'Rourke (September 1, 1850–January 8, 1919) was one of the stars of baseball's pre-deadball era.[1] Prominent throughout the Northeast, O'Rourke achieved fame as a player, manager, team owner, league executive, and advocate for players' rights. He also earned a law degree at Yale University (1887) and practiced law both during and after his baseball career.

The Family Farm

O'Rourke, who eventually acquired the nickname "Orator Jim" due to his large vocabulary and penchant for long-winded speechmaking,[2] was born in Bridgeport, Connecticut. His birth date usually is reported as September 1, 1850, although there is some evidence to suggest that his birthday was August 24 and that he was born in either 1852 or 1854.[3]

O'Rourke's parents—Catherine (née O'Donnell) (1822–1907)[4] and Hugh O'Rourke[5] (1812–68)[6]—had married in 1836 (some sources say 1835)[7] in County Mayo, Ireland, and had immigrated to the United States in 1844–45 at the onset of the Great Potato Famine.[8] Within a few years, as the crisis raged on, the parents of Hugh A. Jennings, the subject of Chapter 2 of this book, also would leave Ireland and make their way to the new world.[9]

Upon arriving in the United States, O'Rourke's parents, like others fleeing the Famine, found conditions "harsh" and the "opportunities open to them limited."[10] Bridgeport's evolution from a whaling town to a manufacturing center, however, provided some hope for new arrivals. Factories in the city required workers to turn out a variety of products, including "sewing machines, brass lamps, and rifle cartridges."[11] Thaddeus Barnes moved to Bridgeport from New Haven, Connecticut, in 1849 and eventually launched the Burlock Shirt Factory, taking advantage of the soft, spring-fed waters on Golden Hill (a small rise overlooking the city's commercial district).[12] Leather manufacturing began in 1845, and in 1849 S.J. Patterson and Stephen Tomlinson launched the Bridgeport Patent Leather Company.[13] Tomlinson also helped spur the city's burgeoning carriage industry.[14] Likewise, the production of steam engines and boilers was "well represented" in Bridgeport during the 1840s.[15]

In 1851, six years after settling in America, O'Rourke's parents managed to put down $200 on a plot of land, signing the mortgage with an "X" because neither had learned to read or write.[16] They later would save up enough money to buy and then expand a small farm.[17] In addition to being a farmer, O'Rourke's father worked as a night watchman.[18] O'Rourke and his older brother John W. (1849–1911)[19]—also destined to play professional baseball—along with their younger sister Sarah J. "Sara" (later Grant) (1854–1931)[20] spent many hours doing chores on the family's farm.[21]

O'Rourke attended Bridgeport's local schools (the Waterville Grammar School and Strong's Military Academy) and began playing baseball as a youngster. In 1866, he was a member of the Bridgeport Ironsides; in 1867, he played for the Bridgeport Unions; and in 1868, he joined the Stratford Osceolas, a newly formed semi-professional team named after the famous Seminole Indian leader.[22]

On December 31, 1868, O'Rourke's father died unexpectedly from tetanus at the age of 56.[23] Hugh left behind an estate valued at $11,232.05.[24] After the payment of debts and expenses ($2,411.06) and Catherine's dower share ($2,583.33), Jim, John, and Sarah each inherited a one-third share of the family farm, with each share worth $2,079.22,[25] the equivalent today of $48,374.90.[26]

In the Major Leagues—and the Ivy League

Stratford borders Bridgeport to the east, and the Osceolas, with O'Rourke playing catcher, quickly became southwest Connecticut's premier baseball team.[27] In 1871, the Osceolas won the Connecticut state championship by beating the Middletown Mansfields, the defending champion, in a best-of-three series.[28]

One year earlier, the *Bridgeport Daily Standard* had singled O'Rourke out for "special notice," describing his "catching and throwing" as "splendid" and, among catchers, "as good as any in the State."[29] Time would prove that O'Rourke was even better than the paper had reported.

Playing catcher in the early 1870s was a dangerous undertaking. As O'Rourke later noted, "there was no paraphernalia with which one could protect himself. No mitts; no, not even gloves; and masks, why you would have been laughed off the diamond had you worn one behind the bat."[30]

In 1872, O'Rourke's professional career began when he agreed to play for the Mansfields, who had just joined the National Association of Professional Base Ball Players (the country's first professional baseball league).[31] In a provision rare, if not unique, in baseball contracts, O'Rourke reportedly insisted that the team hire a worker to replace him on his family's farm.[32] In mid–August 1872, the 5–19 (.208) Mansfields suddenly folded,[33] causing O'Rourke to return home to Bridgeport. In the team's 24 contests, O'Rourke had played 15 games at shortstop and nine games at catcher and hit .273.[34]

Shortly after the season started, O'Rourke had gotten married (May 15, 1872) in Bridgeport.[35] His bride was Anna "Annie" Kehoe (1854–1910),[36] a recent immigrant from Ireland.[37] During their long marriage (38 years), the couple had eight children (seven girls and one boy): Sarah J. "Sadie" (later Grant) (1873–1941)[38]; Anna "Annie" (1874–83)[39]; Agnes G. (later Kaesmann) (1879–1968)[40]; James S. "Queenie" (1880–1955)[41]; Ida M. (later Hilt, then Dean) (1883–1959)[42]; Lillian N. "Lillie" (later Brotherton, then Waugh) (1885–1977)[43]; Irene M. (later Wintter) (1886–1968)[44]; and Edith F. (later Hanke) (1889–1979).[45] It has been theorized that James was called "Queenie" due to his "growing up the only male child in a household full of women."[46]

In 1873, O'Rourke joined the National Association's Boston Red Stockings and began to show his true potential, hitting .350 in 1873 (57 games), .314 in 1874 (70 games), and .296 in 1875 (75 games).[47] During these seasons O'Rourke, while continuing to catch, also began to play first base, third base, and the outfield. With O'Rourke's help, the Red Stockings won the pennant each season.

According to many sources, the Red Stockings, whose owners were Protestant, asked the Catholic O'Rourke to drop the "O'" from his last name. O'Rourke supposedly replied that he "would rather die than give up my father's name. A million dollars would not tempt me."[48]

Following the National Association's demise in 1875, O'Rourke signed a $1,600 contract with the Boston Red Caps,[49] a franchise in the newly-formed National League.[50] (In later years, the Red Caps would change their name to the Braves [1912] and relocate first to Milwaukee [1953] and then to Atlanta [1966]).[51] On April 22, 1876 [Opening Day], O'Rourke recorded the first hit in National League history, a sharply driven single to left field off pitcher Alonzo P. "Lon" Knight, in a game between the Red Caps and the Philadelphia Athletics at Philadelphia's Jefferson Street Grounds [a 6–5 Red Caps victory].[52]

In 1877, O'Rourke protested owner Arthur H. Soden's plan to charge players $30 for their uniforms. When Soden agreed to exempt O'Rourke from the fee, O'Rourke's reputation as an advocate for players' rights was born.[53] During the season, O'Rourke hit a career high .362 while helping lead the Red Caps to the pennant.

In 1878, Soden announced plans to impose a $20 laundry charge on the Red Caps' players for cleaning their road uniforms. Once again, O'Rourke protested, and once again Soden exempted O'Rourke from the charge.[54] As before, the season ended with the Red Caps winning the pennant.

In 1879, O'Rourke moved to the Providence (Rhode Island) Grays and helped the club win its first pennant.[55] While with the Grays, O'Rourke was teammates with pitcher John Montgomery Ward, the subject of Chapter 5 of this book and the person who later would help inspire O'Rourke to attend law school.

In 1880, O'Rourke returned to the Red Caps, where he now was paired with his older brother John, who played center field.[56] In 1881, with John having left baseball (he would return in 1883 for one last season), O'Rourke joined the Buffalo Bisons and served as the team's third baseman, captain, and manager.[57] In 1884, O'Rourke led the league in hitting with a .347 batting average, although the Bisons finished third in the standings, 19½ games behind the Grays.

In 1885, O'Rourke left the Bisons and signed a league-leading $4,000 contract (the equivalent today of $138,000) with the New York Giants.[58] Part of O'Rourke's motivation for joining the Giants appears to have been a desire to play closer to home following the recent death of his second daughter Annie (September 15, 1883).[59]

As a player, O'Rourke, who stood 5'8" and weighed 185 pounds, was unusual because he neither drank alcohol nor smoked tobacco—"as a milk drinker," it was said, O'Rourke "was always great."[60] O'Rourke also was a talker, earning the nickname "Orator Jim" because of his "commanding speaking voice"[61] and practice of offering lengthy comments.

While disputing an umpire's foul ball call he believed should have been a home run, for example, O'Rourke told the befuddled official, "I am conversant with the conglomeration of facts in this case, and as my optical eyesight is of extreme excellence, I am positive of your misinformation."[62] Likewise, while serving as the Bisons' manager in 1881, O'Rourke turned down shortstop John "Johnny" Peters' request for a $10 salary advance by telling Peters:

> The exigencies of the occasion and the condition of our exchequer will not permit anything of that sort at this period of our existence. Subsequent developments in the field of finance may remove the present gloom and we may emerge

into a condition where we may see our way clear to reply in the affirmative to your exceedingly modest request.[63]

Even O'Rourke's youngest daughter Edith later recalled O'Rourke scolding her in "five-syllable words."[64]

In signing with the Giants in 1885, O'Rourke was reunited with his former Grays teammate John Montgomery Ward. During the 1885 season, Ward graduated from Columbia University's law school. Motivated by Ward's example, O'Rourke decided to enroll in the law school at Yale University in New Haven (a mere 20 miles from his home and at the time the only law school in Connecticut).[65] Lacking a college degree, O'Rourke "was required to pass a compulsory entrance exam that required him to exhibit 'satisfactory knowledge on the outlines of History of the United States and England, and on the text of the Constitution of the United States.'"[66]

Yale during this period offered both a two-year and a three-year course of instruction.[67] O'Rourke opted for the former, which focused on "the practical side of legal education" and included courses on "American Law, international law, public and private general jurisprudence, political science, the Institutes of Justinian, and the Pandects."[68]

With the Giants having agreed to pay his tuition,[69] O'Rourke took his studies seriously, at one point turning down a chance to be a polo referee because his law studies were "too demanding."[70] O'Rourke made "great headway" in his studies at Yale, with one newspaper reporting that he "studies ten hours a day."[71] Yet despite his demanding schedule, in 1886 O'Rourke found time to coach the Yale baseball team after being asked to do so by Professor Theodore S. Woolsey (the law school's international law professor).[72]

As has been reported elsewhere, O'Rourke's schedule while in law school *was* demanding: "[The] thirty-five-year-old [O'Rourke] would board a New Haven-bound train at daybreak, six days a week. After attending classes and studying, he would return home on the five o'clock coach for Bridgeport. Quick to fit in, he was soon considered one of the most promising students in the law school."[73] O'Rourke also had to put up with kidding from some of his teammates:

> [Near the end of his first year of law school, O'Rourke] reported back to the Giants on April Fool's Day, 1886. He was scheduled to leave the club in June to take his regular exams in New Haven. While in New York, [O'Rourke] took some ribbing from his teammates. [First baseman] Roger Connor joked that his friend amused him by throwing "quietams, assumptis and quo warrentos" at [him] instead of baseballs. Big Roger laughed, "He would rather have O'Rourke bang him over the head with a bat than hear him talk [law] French in that way." [O'Rourke] took the wisecracks in stride.[74]

Although it always has been part of the Ivy League, Yale Law School in the 1880s was a relatively modest institution with a small enrollment—O'Rourke's class consisted of just 30 students.[75] Despite this fact, O'Rourke crossed paths with two individuals who today are recognized as legal trailblazers. The first was Warner T. McGuinn (1859–1937), one of the law school's first African American students. McGuinn was an acquaintance of Samuel L. Clemens (better known as Mark Twain), who helped pay McGuinn's way through Yale. As a student, McGuinn won the law school's Townshend Prize for distinguished oration. Years later, McGuinn served as a mentor to future U.S. Supreme Court Justice Thoroughgood "Thurgood" Marshall when Marshall was a young lawyer in Baltimore.[76]

O'Rourke also crossed paths with Alice R. Jordan (later Blake) (1863–93), who was a year ahead of him. Jordan was the law school's first female student. Having been denied admission by both Columbia's law school and Harvard's law school due to her gender, Jordan applied to Yale using only her first initials. When she later showed up for class, the university reluctantly allowed her to enroll after it could not find a rule prohibiting her admission.[77]

O'Rourke's encounters with Jordan and McGuinn undoubtedly reinforced his egalitarian views, which likely were the product of his immigrant heritage.[78] Notably, O'Rourke was an early supporter of integration in baseball—in 1895, while operating the minor league Bridgeport Victors, O'Rourke signed outfielder Harry Herbert, the city's first Black resident to play professional baseball.[79] In 1910, O'Rourke, still ahead of his time, famously told a reporter that baseball is "a game for all creeds and nationalities, as well as for all political parties."[80]

In June 1887, O'Rourke graduated from Yale with a B.C.L. (Bachelor of Civil Law),[81] and on November 5, 1887, he was sworn into the Connecticut bar.[82] O'Rourke could have been sworn in earlier (most of his classmates were sworn in right after graduation[83]), but because of his baseball schedule O'Rourke was forced to wait until the season was over.[84]

After receiving his law license, O'Rourke rented an office on Bridgeport's Main Street.[85] In an interview with the *Sporting Life,* O'Rourke explained that from now on he planned to divide his time, playing baseball in the summer (at a salary of several thousand dollars a season) and poring over "briefs [and] musty law books" in the winter, for which he expected to earn a few hundred dollars a year.[86]

In 1888, O'Rourke hit a disappointing (by his standards) .274. Despite this performance, the Giants won their first National League pennant. In 1889, O'Rourke returned to form, hitting .321 and helping the Giants repeat as National League champions. Despite this fact, in 1890 O'Rourke agreed to jump to the New York Giants of the upstart Players League (also spelled Players' League), the brainchild of John Montgomery Ward. As envisioned by Ward, the Players League would provide players with a fair wage, improved working conditions, and a say in management decisions. Although an enormous success on the field, the league folded after the 1890 season when its financial backers pulled their support.[87]

In 1891, O'Rourke returned to the National League's New York Giants. In addition to his salary, O'Rourke was given a small interest in the franchise.[88] Following the end of the 1892 season, the Giants, having decided to clean house, released O'Rourke despite his hitting .304.

In 1893, O'Rourke played his final season in the majors. In 129 games as the Washington Senators' player-manager, the 42-year-old O'Rourke hit .287 while mostly playing in the outfield (87 games) but also manning first base (33 games) and occasionally catching (nine games).[89]

After the Majors

O'Rourke's exit from the major leagues did not signal the end of his baseball career. In 1894, he was hired as a major league umpire but quit after just two months because the job was "too trying."[90] O'Rourke found greater success (and satisfaction) as a baseball executive, running both teams and leagues from his law office, including the Connecticut State League (originally known as the Naugatuck Valley League) and the previously-mentioned Bridgeport Victors (renamed the Orators in O'Rourke's honor in 1898).[91]

On August 13, 1897, while serving as the Victors' catcher, O'Rourke was involved in a play that badly tarnished his reputation as a clean player. In the fifth inning of the first game of a doubleheader, with the fourth place Victors leading the first place Meriden Bulldogs 10–9, George H. Courtney, the Bulldogs' shortstop, hit a long fly ball over the head of the previously mentioned Harry Herbert, the Victors' left fielder. Trying to turn a double into a home run, Courtney charged around the bases. When he reached home plate, he barreled into O'Rourke, who dropped the ball. Having failed to touch home plate, Courtney began to crawl back to it. Before he could reach it, O'Rourke, who had scrambled to his feet, punched Courtney, causing both benches to clear. The resulting melee took 12 plain-clothes policemen to break up.

After the game O'Rourke apologized to Courtney and Courtney agreed to let the matter drop.[92] The next day, however, the *Meriden Daily Republican* deplored O'Rourke's "upper cut" and called it "the most disgraceful act that ever took place on a diamond in this state[.]"[93]

In 1902, O'Rourke helped found the National Association of

Professional Base Ball Leagues ("NAPBBL") to improve the organizational structure of the minor leagues and see that their rights were respected by the now two major leagues (American and National).[94]

During the 1903 season, O'Rourke appeared in the Orators' line-up with his son Queenie.[95] In 1908, Queenie made it to the majors, playing 34 games for the New York Highlanders (now Yankees).[96]

In 1904, at the age of 54, O'Rourke appeared in his final major league game. With the Giants on the verge of clinching their first National League pennant since 1889, John J. McGraw, the Giants' superstitious future Hall of Fame manager, asked O'Rourke to catch future Hall of Fame pitcher Joseph J. "Joe" McGinnity. O'Rourke agreed and played all nine innings, collecting a hit, scoring a run, and helping the Giants beat the Cincinnati Reds 7–5.[97] With this game in the record books, O'Rourke's major league stat line was complete: in 1,999 games, he had collected 2,639 hits, driven in 1,208 runs, compiled a .310 batting average, and played on nine pennant winning teams (1873, 1874, 1875, 1877, 1878, 1879, 1888, 1889, and 1904).[98]

In addition to baseball and his law practice, O'Rourke was active in a variety of civic undertakings and social organizations. In 1894, for example, he ran (as a Democrat) for a seat in the Connecticut legislature "but fell victim to the Republican landslide that swept the nation."[99] From 1901 to 1903, he served on Bridgeport's fire commission.[100] Later (1909–19), he was on the city's paving and sewer commission.[101] O'Rourke also was an active member of the Connecticut Bar Association, Elks, Knights of Columbus, and Royal Arcanum.[102]

James H. O'Rourke, Attorney at Law

In 1910, O'Rourke's former teammate Timothy H. "Tim" Murnane (the two had played together on both the Mansfields and the Red Caps) visited O'Rourke in Bridgeport and then wrote a widely circulated story about his visit.[103] After an evening at the Bridgeport Club, the two men walked to O'Rourke's law office in the Meigs building. (The Meigs building was an impressive five story building that had been erected in 1897 by the Meigs department store.[104]) There, the words "James H. O'Rourke, Attorney at Law" were stenciled on the outer glass door leading to Room 203,[105] which O'Rourke had been renting since 1902.[106] Inside, O'Rourke's furniture included a "comfortable swinging chair."[107] The office also was filled with pictures of O'Rourke's heroes, including

> Presidents Lincoln, McKinley and Garfield, famed orator Senator Daniel Webster, and abolitionist Senator Charles Sumner. Other luminaries were poet Henry Wadsworth Longfellow and yachtsman Commodore Francis Burritt....

The portrait of Virginia Governor Fitzhugh Lee, a post–Civil War Democrat, was also displayed, along with a photograph of Robert "Bob" Ingersoll, a free-thinker who believed in the sanctity of the family and women's suffrage.... Also honored with a picture was Chief Justice of the United States Melville Weston Fuller.... [O'Rourke's] office also contained a few pictures of baseball executives and players.[108]

After looking around, Murnane asked O'Rourke what he liked to read. O'Rourke replied: "Oh, my law books, and Shakespeare on the side."[109]

During Murnane's visit, O'Rourke railed against the growing trend among law schools to require applicants to have a bachelor's degree. If universally implemented, O'Rourke worried that the policy would produce much "hardship," with fewer lawyers from lower income backgrounds and the profession robbed of "eminent legal luminaries [who happened to have] little learning in the classics."[110] The final result, O'Rourke predicted, would be "much weaker lawyers[.]"[111]

At the time of Murnane's visit, O'Rourke, who by now had acquired the additional nickname of "Uncle Jeems,"[112] was still living at 274 Pembroke Street, the massive (4,000 square feet) Victorian style house he had built in 1891.[113] Murnane pronounced it a "fine home," just 15 minutes by streetcar from O'Rourke's law office.[114] While giving Murnane a tour of the house, O'Rourke pointed out the spot where he planned to build a garage for his new automobile, which he intended to use "for touring purposes."[115] Regrettably, the house was razed in 2009 after a long effort to turn it into a baseball museum failed.[116]

In 1903, a local newspaper had called O'Rourke a "successful" lawyer.[117] Years later, following his death, O'Rourke was described as having had an "office practice,"[118] with his handling of the matters entrusted to his care being both "honorable and valuable."[119] In *Martindale's American Law Directory*, O'Rourke was rated "good" on legal ability, "very high" on moral character (the directory's top rating), and "good" on paying his bills (also the directory's top rating).[120]

O'Rourke's practice primarily focused on trusts and estates.[121] In 1906, for example, O'Rourke was appointed administrator of the $4,000 estate of William S. Schreiber, Bridgeport's popular town clerk, following Schreiber's death at the age of 42 from asphyxiation.[122] Because Schreiber's body was discovered in a hotel room, many people were convinced that he had killed himself because he had been implicated in a ballot box stuffing scandal.[123]

In 1916, O'Rourke found himself in the middle of a high-profile dispute pitting the widow of William Dunn against the couple's four children. O'Rourke had drawn up Dunn's will, which left his entire estate, estimated to be worth as much as $40,000, to his wife Margaret. Because

"Mr. Dunn was too ill to write his name at the time the document was drawn … he held the pen while [O'Rourke] signed for him."[124] Believing that Dunn had lacked testamentary capacity, his children sued to prevent the will from being admitted to probate. Finding that Dunn had understood what he was doing when he cut his children out of his will, the probate court ordered the will admitted.[125] In reporting on the case, one local newspaper remarked:

> [Dunn's] will was drawn by Attorney James H. O'Rourke and is one of the most terse documents ever submitted for probate here. The will is so clear in its diction that lawyers who have seen it [scoff at] the idea that, by any legal process, it may be set aside as defective.[126]

Although the exact date is unclear, at some point O'Rourke formed an affiliation with Charles W. Mann, another local trusts and estates lawyer. As one of city's best-known probate lawyers, Mann handled many of its largest estates, including, in 1896, the $150,000 estate of retired dry goods merchant William H. Fitzgerald.[127]

In 1899, Mann was appointed the guardian of William Bochek (some sources say "Boebek"), a minor who had been left an estate valued at $94. In 1902, after he turned 21, Bochek discovered that Mann had stolen his money. As a result, Bochek hired attorney Thomas C. Coughlin, who asked O'Rourke how he (Coughlin) should proceed. Having ended his affiliation with Mann some time earlier (again, the exact date is unknown), O'Rourke advised Coughlin to file criminal charges against Mann.[128] When Coughlin did so, Mann agreed to pay Bochek $88[129] and then moved to Boston.[130]

James H. "Jim" O'Rourke (1891) (National Baseball Hall of Fame and Museum).

O'Rourke's practice also included some trial work. In 1890, in *Rowen v. New York, New Haven & Hartford Railway Company*,[131] for example, O'Rourke and Robert E. De Forest, a former Fairfield County common pleas court judge (1874–77), three-time mayor of Bridgeport (1878, 1889, 1890), and two-term U.S. congressman (1891–95),[132] represented Edward Rowen, whose wife Catherine had been killed when she was run over by an express train. Finding that the accident was Catherine's fault, the superior court awarded Catherine's estate $50 in nominal damages.[133] On appeal, the Connecticut Supreme Court affirmed.[134]

In 1896, O'Rourke represented Bridgeport High School student Thomas Foster in proceedings before the Connecticut Interscholastic Athletic Association ("CIAA"). According to one "Cottrell," the trainer at the Hopkins Grammar School, Foster had accepted money the year before to pitch for Edgewood High School in Westerly, a violation of the CIAA's rules.[135] At the end of the hearing, the CIAA ruled that there was no merit to the charges.[136]

In 1904, in *Parotte v. Holbrook, Cabot and Rollins*,[137] John Parotte had been a member of a Bridgeport labor gang digging a new city pier. During the excavation, a 300-pound stone fell on Parotte, resulting in Parotte suffering a broken right leg. O'Rourke filed a $5,000 negligence lawsuit in state court against Parotte's employer (a Massachusetts company), which removed the case to the local U.S. district court based on diversity of citizenship. Deciding that the company had not been negligent, District Judge James P. Platt awarded Parotte $10 in nominal damages.[138]

In 1915, O'Rourke represented Nelson D. Judd, the father of a four-year-old boy named Clarence E. Judd. When Nelson's wife Helen W. Judd was killed in an automobile accident, Helen's mother (Nelson's mother-in-law) Margaret Gilson sought custody of Clarence on the ground that Nelson was an unfit parent. Nelson retained O'Rourke to oppose Margaret's petition. After several acrimonious court hearings before Probate Judge Paul L. Miller,[139] the parties agreed to place Clarence in the care of a woman named Luella R. Watrous.[140]

In 1916, O'Rourke represented himself in an action against Bridgeport City Sheriff James F. Beck. For a time, Beck had rented space in O'Rourke's law office. After Beck moved out, O'Rourke sued him for $157.20 in unpaid rent. Beck responded by countersuing O'Rourke for $250 in unpaid service fees. After hearing from both sides, Fairfield County Common Pleas Judge Howard B. Scott dismissed Beck's countersuit and awarded O'Rourke $152.25.[141]

During his legal career, O'Rourke also handled numerous pro bono cases. "Asked by his daughters why he did not charge the poor, [O'Rourke] answered, 'I get my money from the rich.'"[142]

Conclusion

In 1910, O'Rourke's wife Annie died from the lingering complications of a fall.[143] In 1911, O'Rourke's brother John died in Boston from a heart attack he suffered while working as a railway baggage handler (a job he had held since before his baseball days).[144]

On September 14, 1912, O'Rourke, now 62, played in his final baseball game, catching nine innings for the New Haven Wings against the Waterbury Spuds in a Connecticut State League game.[145] In 1916, O'Rourke gave up baseball for good after losing a bitter fight over the future of minor league baseball in New England.[146] Subsequently, O'Rourke devoted himself to his law practice, his sizeable real estate holdings, and his grandchildren.[147]

During a blizzard on New Year's Day, 1919, O'Rourke left his home to meet with a client.[148] The decision to do so proved fatal, as he contracted pneumonia and died one week later at the age of 68.[149] Following a funeral mass at Bridgeport's St. Mary's Church, O'Rourke was laid to rest in the O'Rourke family plot at Saint Michael's Cemetery in nearby Stratford.[150] Although it is not known how much O'Rourke's estate was worth at the time of his death, in 1913 it had been publicly reported that O'Rourke was worth $75,000,[151] the equivalent today of $1.35 million.[152] O'Rourke's will, dated July 31, 1917, specified that his assets were to be divided equally among his surviving seven children.[153]

In 1945, O'Rourke was elected to the Baseball Hall of Fame.[154] Emphasizing his longevity as a ball player, his Hall of Fame plaque advises: "'Orator Jim' played ball until he was past fifty, including twenty-one major league seasons."[155] Not a word is said about either his law degree or his many years at the bar.

Notes

1. For a discussion of baseball's different eras, see, e.g., Michael T. Woltring et al., *Examining Perceptions of Baseball's Eras: A Statistical Comparison*, Sport J., Oct. 25, 2018, https://thesportjournal.org/article/examining-perceptions-of-baseballs-eras/.

2. *See* Chris Bodig, *Hall of Famer Jim O'Rourke: Yale Law Grad in a Blue Collar Game*, CooperstownCred.com, Sept. 1, 2018, https://www.cooperstowncred.com/hall-famer-jim-orourke-yale-law-grad-blue-collar-game/ ("O'Rourke's nickname was 'Orator Jim' because of his loquaciousness. Orator Jim would entertain (or annoy) his teammates by reciting Hamlet's soliloquy ['To be, or not to be'] before every game").

3. *See* Bill Lamb, *Jim O'Rourke*, SABR, https://sabr.org/bioproj/person/jim-orourke-2/ (last visited July 1, 2024).

4. For an obituary of Catherine, see *Mrs. O'Rourke Dead*, Meriden Daily J. (CT), July 29, 1907, at 3. *See also Catherine O'Rourke*, Find-a-Grave.com, https://www.findagrave.com/memorial/149061255/catherine-o'rourke (last visited July 1, 2024).

5. At some point—it is not clear when—the family's last name changed from "O'Rourk" to "O'Rourke." In the 1850 federal census, the family's last name is spelled "O'Rourk." *See*

Hugh O [sic] Rourk in the 1850 United States Federal Census, ANCESTRY.COM, https://www.ancestry.com/discoveryui-content/view/18076214:8054 (last visited July 1, 2024) (at line 1). In the 1860 federal census, however, the family's last name is spelled "O'Rourke." *See Hugh Orourke [sic] in the 1860 United States Federal Census*, ANCESTRY.COM, https://www.ancestry.com/discoveryui-content/view/14745529:7667 (last visited July 1, 2024) (at line 12).

6. *See Hugh O'Rourke*, FIND-A-GRAVE.COM, https://www.findagrave.com/memorial/17852992/hugh-o'rourke (last visited July 1, 2024). An obituary for Hugh has not been found, although various sources say a two-sentence death notice appeared in the January 2, 1869, issue of the *Bridgeport Daily Standard*.

7. *See Orator O'Rourke*, MIKEROER.COM, updated June 1, 2011, http://mikeroer.com/sport/oratororourke.html [hereinafter *Orator O'Rourke*] (under "Parents of James H. O'Rourke" in Excel box) (discussing the discrepancy).

8. *Id.* (speculating that Catherine and Hugh "may have been sent [to the United States] by their landlord as part of [a] humane system of population thinning during the early months of the famine").

9. *See generally* JAMES S. DONNELLY, JR., THE GREAT IRISH POTATO FAMINE (2001). *See also* Lorna Siggins, *Famine Dead to be Remembered in Mayo*, IRISH TIMES, May 10, 2010, https://www.irishtimes.com/news/famine-dead-to-be-remembered-in-mayo-1.663153.

10. Tyler Anbinder et al., *"The Best Country in the World": The Surprising Social Mobility of New York's Irish-Famine Immigrants*, 53 J. INTERDISCIPLINARY HIST. 407, 409 (2022).

11. MIKE ROER, ORATOR O'ROURKE: THE LIFE OF A BASEBALL RADICAL 8 (2005) [hereinafter BASEBALL RADICAL]. Although rough in places, Roer's book has been considered the definitive account of O'Rourke's life since its publication. For a review, see David Ball, *Book Review*, 15:2 NINE: J. BASEBALL HIST. & CULTURE 141 (2007). Recently, however, a new biography has appeared. *See* BERNARD J. CROWLEY, THE REMARKABLE LIFE OF JAMES HENRY O'ROURKE: A CONNECTICUT FARM BOY'S JOURNEY TO BASEBALL'S HALL OF FAME (2022).

12. *See* 1 GEORGE C. WALDO, JR., HISTORY OF BRIDGEPORT AND VICINITY 155 (1917).

13. *Id.* at 156.

14. *Id.* at 158.

15. *Id.* at 157.

16. *See* BASEBALL RADICAL, *supra* note 11, at 8.

17. *Id.*

18. *See* Lamb, *supra* note 3.

19. *See John W. O'Rourke*, FIND-A-GRAVE.COM, https://www.findagrave.com/memorial/46840195/john-w-o'rourke (last visited July 1, 2024). For John's obituary, see *infra* note 144.

20. *See Sarah J. O'Rourke*, FIND-A-GRAVE.COM, https://www.findagrave.com/memorial/155341852/sarah-j.-grant (last visited July 1, 2024). *See also Sarah Jane O'Rourke 1854–1931*, ANCESTRY.COM, https://www.ancestry.com/family-tree/person/tree/159725966/person/282094461903//story (last visited July 1, 2024). An obituary for Sarah has not been found.

21. *See* CROWLEY, *supra* note 11, at 12. In addition to Jim, John, and Sarah, O'Rourke's parents had a son named Patrick F. (1837–52). *See Patrick F. O'Rourk*, FIND-A-GRAVE.COM, https://www.findagrave.com/memorial/85230169/patrick-f-o'rourk (last visited July 1, 2024). *See also Melancholy*, HARTFORD DAILY COURANT, Oct. 6, 1852, at 2 (reporting that Patrick died after falling out of a maple tree). It is believed that the couple also had other offspring who did not survive childhood and whose names now are unknown. *See* Lamb, *supra* note 3, at n.2.

22. *See* CROWLEY, *supra* note 11, at 12–14. *See also* MICHAEL J. BIELAWA, BRIDGEPORT BASEBALL 9 (2003).

23. *See* Lamb, *supra* note 3, at n.4.

24. *See Hugh O'Reuke [sic] in the Connecticut, U.S., Wills and Probate Records, 1609–1999*, ANCESTRY.COM, https://www.ancestry.com/discoveryui-content/view/1713894:9049 (last visited July 1, 2024).

25. *Id.*

26. *See* S. Morgan Friedman, *The Inflation Calculator*, https://westegg.com/inflation/ (last visited July 1, 2024) (converting 1869 dollars to 2023 dollars). In discussing Hugh's death, Crowley remarks: "In a short 25 years since arriving in Bridgeport from Ireland, [Hugh] had succeeded in securing his family's future. He left his family rental property, land to be developed in the future, and a working farm, all valued at $170,000 in twenty-first-century dollars." CROWLEY, *supra* note 11, at 14. Crowley is a bit off in his figuring—rather than $170,000, Hugh's estate in current dollars was worth $261,000. *See* Friedman, *supra*.

27. *See* Mike Roer, *Annual Baseball Highlights: 1870–1879*, http://www.mikeroer.com/ bridgeporthistory1870.html (last visited July 1, 2024).

28. *Id.*

29. *Id.*

30. BIELAWA, *supra* note 22, at 9. *See also* CROWLEY, *supra* note 11, at 19 (quoting O'Rourke as saying that the pain of catching was "intense" and inflicted "unbelievable torture"). *See generally* Chuck Rosciam, *The Evolution of Catcher's Equipment*, SABR, https:// sabr.org/journal/article/the-evolution-of-catchers-equipment/ (last visited July 1, 2024) (explaining that catchers began wearing masks in 1876; padded gloves in 1877; chest protectors in 1883; and shin guards in 1890).

31. Lamb, *supra* note 3. For a history of the National Association, see WILLIAM J. RYCZEK, BLACKGUARDS AND RED STOCKINGS: A HISTORY OF BASEBALL'S NATIONAL ASSOCIATION, 1871–1875 (1992).

32. Lamb, *supra* note 3. Crowley tells this story a little differently: "[O'Rourke] settled on a salary that included adequate funds for his mother to hire a man to help with the farm work." CROWLEY, *supra* note 11, at 23.

33. *See Disbanded*, DAILY CONST. (Middletown, CT), Aug. 14, 1872, at 2. *See also* DAVID ARCIDIACONO, MAJOR LEAGUE BASEBALL IN GILDED AGE CONNECTICUT: THE RISE AND FALL OF THE MIDDLETOWN, NEW HAVEN AND HARTFORD CLUBS 91–94 (2009). As these and other sources report, the team collapsed due to a lack of funds.

34. For O'Rourke's statistics as a player, see *Jim O'Rourke*, BASEBALL-REFERENCE.COM, https://www.baseball-reference.com/players/o/o'rouji01.shtml (last visited July 1, 2024) [hereinafter *O'Rourke Player Statistics*]. For O'Rourke's statistics as a manager, see *Jim O'Rourke*, BASEBALL-REFERENCE.COM, https://www.baseball-reference.com/managers/ o'rouji01.shtml (last visited July 1, 2024) (indicating that as a manager, O'Rourke went 246–258–6 (.488)). All the baseball statistics for O'Rourke cited in this essay come from these sources.

35. *See Orator O'Rourke*, *supra* note 7 (under "James H. O'Rourke").

36. *Id. See also Annie O'Rourke*, FIND-A-GRAVE.COM, https://www.findagrave.com/ memorial/143137280/annie-o'rourke (last visited July 1, 2024). For Annie's obituary, see *infra* note 143.

37. As Crowley explains, "The exact date of … Annie Kehoe's arrival in America is unknown. The U.S. Census of 1900 states that Annie immigrated in 1870, but the 1910 Census gives her immigration date as 1860." CROWLEY, *supra* note 11, at 24.

38. *See Sarah Jane "Sadie" O'Rourke Grant*, FIND-A-GRAVE.COM, https://www. findagrave.com/memorial/172701562/sarah-jane-grant (last visited July 1, 2024). An obituary for Sadie has not been found.

39. *See Annie O'Rourke*, FIND-A-GRAVE.COM, https://www.findagrave.com/memorial/ 143137369/annie-orourke (last visited July 1, 2024). An obituary for Annie has not been found, although CROWLEY, *supra* note 11, at 158, reports that the *Bridgeport Daily Standard* did run a story about her death.

40. For an obituary of Agnes, see *Mrs. Kaesmann, 88, Ex-Teacher, Dies*, BRIDGEPORT POST, Jan. 29, 1968, at 24. *See also Agnes G O'Rourke Kaesmann*, FIND-A-GRAVE.COM, https://www.findagrave.com/memorial/262162043/agnes-g-kaesmann (last visited July 1, 2024).

41. For an obituary of Queenie, see *Deaths—O'Rourke*, SUN (Balt.), Dec. 23, 1955, at 20. *See also James Stephen "Queenie" O'Rourke*, FIND-A-GRAVE.COM, https://www.findagrave. com/memorial/13508299/james_stephen_o'rourke (last visited July 1, 2024). As

Crowley points out, "The O'Rourke family name in [O'Rourke's] family tree died with Queenie's son, James John O'Rourke, in 1968." CROWLEY, *supra* note 11, at 426.

42. For an obituary of Ida, see *Obituary—Mrs. Rollin C. Dean*, BRIDGEPORT POST, Apr. 20, 1959, at 31. *See also Ida May O'Rourke Dean*, FIND-A-GRAVE.COM, https://www.findagrave.com/memorial/245728522/ida-may-dean (last visited July 1, 2024).

43. For an obituary of Lillian, see *Deaths—Waugh*, FORT LAUDERDALE NEWS, Apr. 18, 1977, at 4B. Lillian does not have a *Find-a-Grave* webpage.

44. For an obituary of Irene, see *Mrs. Irene Wintter, Teacher, Succumbs*, BRIDGEPORT POST, Sept. 9, 1968, at 30. *See also Irene Mabel O'Rourke Wintter*, FIND-A-GRAVE.COM, https://www.findagrave.com/memorial/47247105/irene_mabel_wintter (last visited July 1, 2024).

45. For an obituary of Edith, see *Obituaries—Hanke*, ST. PETERSBURG TIMES (FL), Feb. 6, 1979, at 7B. *See also Edith Frances O'Rourke Hanke*, FIND-A-GRAVE.COM, https://www.findagrave.com/memorial/196481443/edith-frances-hanke (last visited July 1, 2024).

46. *See* Lamb, *supra* note 3.

47. *See O'Rourke Player Statistics, supra* note 34.

48. This story almost certainly is fictional:

> For almost a century, no account of ... O'Rourke['s] signing with Boston was complete without reference to [Harry] Wright's alleged request that Jim drop the O' from his surname, lest offense be given to the "Puritan" backers of the Red Stockings club.... O'Rourke's [principal] biographer, however, suspects the anecdote is apocryphal, tracing its print origins to a 1906 column by Boston sportswriter (and former O'Rourke teammate) Tim Murnane.... The [present] writer is also skeptical, as the business entrepreneur/sportsmen who backed the Boston club (Ivers Adams, John Conkey, N.T. Apollonio, et al.) were hardly Puritan or Boston Brahmin types. And whatever anti-Irish prejudice they may have harbored privately would have been more than offset by the financial attraction of drawing the city's burgeoning Irish population to the ballpark. Perhaps to that end, the 1873 Boston Red Stockings would occasionally feature an all-Irish-Catholic outfield, with O'Rourke in center flanked by Andy Leonard and Jack Manning.

Lamb, *supra* note 3, at n.8.

Crowley, however, believes the story likely is true, citing O'Rourke family historian Paul B. Conan. *See* CROWLEY, *supra* note 11, at 44–45.

49. *See* BIELAWA, *supra* note 22, at 10.

50. The National League was founded in 1876. For a history of the National League, see GLENN DICKEY, THE HISTORY OF NATIONAL LEAGUE BASEBALL, SINCE 1876 (1982).

51. For more about the team's history, see BRADSHER HAYES, 150 YEARS OF THE BRAVES: FROM BOSTON TO MILWAUKEE TO ATLANTA (2022).

52. *See* BIELAWA, *supra* note 22, at 10. Following the end of the 1876 season, the National League expelled the Athletics for failing to play all their scheduled games. *See National Base Ball League: The Athletics and the [New York] Mutuals Expelled*, PHIL. INQUIRER, Dec. 8, 1876, at 1 (explaining that the Mutuals were expelled for the same reason]. Although many subsequent Philadelphia baseball teams have been called the Athletics, none are related to the 1876 Athletics. For a further discussion, see RICHARD WORTH, TEAMS NAMES: A WORLDWIDE DICTIONARY, 1869–2011, at 232 (2011) (pointing out that the name "Athletics" has been used by Philadelphia baseball teams since 1859).

53. *See* BASEBALL RADICAL, *supra* note 11, at 68.

54. *Id.* at 71.

55. *See* BIELAWA, *supra* note 22, at 11.

56. For John's career and yearly statistics, see *John O'Rourke*, BASEBALL-REFERENCE.COM, https://www.baseball-reference.com/players/o/o'roujo01.shtml (last visited July 1, 2024). All the baseball statistics for John cited in this essay come from this source.

57. *See* Lamb, *supra* note 3.

58. *Id. See also* Friedman, *supra* note 26 (converting 1885 dollars to 2023 dollars). For a history of the Giants, see NOEL HYND, THE GIANTS OF THE POLO GROUNDS: THE GLORIOUS TIMES OF BASEBALL'S NEW YORK GIANTS (rev. ed. 2018).

59. *See* CROWLEY, *supra* note 11, at 158 (reporting that Annie died of dysentery, "a fatal illness before the advent of antibiotics").

60. T.H. Murnane, *James H. O'Rourke Quits Baseball After 38 Years*, BRIDGEPORT EVENING FARMER, Mar. 7, 1910, at 8.

61. BASEBALL RADICAL, *supra* note 11, at 1.

62. BIELAWA, *supra* note 22, at 14.

63. Lamb, *supra* note 3.

64. BIELAWA, *supra* note 22, at 14.

65. According to Crowley, O'Rourke's decision to attend Yale also was "influenced by his former schoolmaster, Emory Strong, who sent many of his students on to Yale." CROWLEY, *supra* note 11, at 178.

66. *Id.* at 177.

67. *See* REPORT OF THE COMMISSIONER OF EDUCATION FOR THE YEAR 1880, at 43 (1882).

68. CROWLEY, *supra* note 11, at 177.

69. BIELAWA, *supra* note 22, at 14. During this period the law school's tuition was $100 for the first year of study and $200 for the second year of study. *See* CATALOGUE OF YALE UNIVERSITY 1887–88, at 153 (1887).

70. *See Polo Notes*, MERIDEN DAILY REPUBLICAN (CT), Jan. 16, 1886, at 4 (incorrectly identifying O'Rourke as his brother John).

71. *See Base Ball Notes*, MERIDEN DAILY REPUBLICAN (CT), Feb. 16, 1886, at 4.

72. *See News of the State*, MERIDEN DAILY REPUBLICAN (CT), Dec. 9, 1885, at 1. For an obituary of Woolsey (1852–1929), see *Prof. T.S. Woolsey Dead in 77th Year: On Yale Faculty for 32 Years—Was an Authority on International Law; Son of University Head, Related to Two Other Famous Presidents of Yale—Professor Emeritus Since 1911*, N.Y. TIMES, Apr. 25, 1929, at 29. *See also* Charles Cheney Hyde, *In Memoriam: Theodore Salisbury Woolsey: October 22, 1852–April 24, 1929*, 23 AM. J. INT'L L. 616 (1929). Woolsey does not have a *Find-a-Grave* webpage.

73. CROWLEY, *supra* note 11, at 179.

74. *Id.* at 181.

75. *See* BASEBALL RADICAL, *supra* note 11, at 124. *See also* CROWLEY, *supra* note 11, at 178 (reporting that the law school's total enrollment was 82 students and that the faculty consisted of nine professors and eight lecturers).

76. For a further look at McGuinn's life, see Judith Ann Schiff, *Old Yale—Pioneers*, YALE ALUMNI MAG., Jan./Feb. 2006, http://archives.yalealumnimagazine.com/issues/2006_01/old_yale.html. *See also Warner T. McGuinn*, FIND-A-GRAVE.COM, https://www.findagrave.com/memorial/230425214/warner-t-mcguinn (last visited July 1, 2024).

77. After graduating in 1886, Jordan moved to California and continued her legal studies. In 1888, she married fellow lawyer George D. Blake. The pair later moved to Seattle. Following Jordan's graduation, Yale adopted a policy forbidding women from enrolling in the law school (the policy remained in force until 1920). For a further look at Jordan's life, see Judith Schiff, *Yale's First Female Graduate*, YALE ALUMNI MAG., Sept./Oct. 2013, https://yalealumnimagazine.org/articles/3742-yales-first-female-graduate (explaining that due to her untimely death, Jordan never practiced as a lawyer). *See also Alice Rufie Jordan Blake*, FIND-A-GRAVE.COM, https://www.findagrave.com/memorial/101966512/alice-rufie-blake (last visited July 1, 2024).

78. *See* BIELAWA, *supra* note 22, at 41.

79. *See* Andrew Fowler, *A History of Baseball in Connecticut*, YANKEE INST., July 8, 2023, https://yankeeinstitute.org/2023/07/08/a-history-of-baseball-in-connecticut/.

80. Murnane, *supra* note 60.

81. *See* CROWLEY, *supra* note 11, at 177. *See also Hits Outside the Diamond*, NEW HAVEN DAILY MORN. J. & COURIER (CT), May 13, 1887, at 3 (previewing O'Rourke's graduation).

82. *See O'Rourke Becomes a Lawyer*, N.Y. TIMES, Nov. 6, 1887, at 10 [hereinafter *Becomes a Lawyer*]. *See also* Welton Ulbrich, *Orator Jim O'Rourke, Connecticut's Brilliant Baseball Pioneer*, THE BAT AND BALL, Mar. 1, 2022, https://ghtbl.org/orourke. Connecticut at this time did not have a state bar exam. *See* DWIGHT LOOMIS & JOSEPH GILBERT CALHOUN, THE

JUDICIAL AND CIVIL HISTORY OF CONNECTICUT 186 (1895) (explaining that the state's first bar exam was given in 1891).

83. *See Blackstone's Disciples: Twenty-Two Admitted to the Bar from the Law School Yesterday*, NEW HAVEN DAILY MORN. J. & COURIER (CT), June 30, 1887, at 3.

84. *See Becomes a Lawyer*, *supra* note 82.

85. *See* BASEBALL RADICAL, *supra* note 11, at 132.

86. *See O'Rourke's Plans: Not Yet Ready to Give Up Ball Entirely for the Law*, SPORTING LIFE, Dec. 21, 1887, at 1.

87. For a further look at the Players League, see ROBERT B. ROSS, THE GREAT BASEBALL REVOLT: THE RISE AND FALL OF THE 1890 PLAYERS LEAGUE (2016).

88. *See* Lamb, *supra* note 3.

89. These Washington Senators (1891–99) should not be confused with the Washington Senators of the American League (1901–71). *See further* FREDERIC J. FROMMER, THE WASHINGTON NATIONALS 1859 TO TODAY: THE STORY OF BASEBALL IN THE NATION'S CAPITAL (2006).

90. *See* Lamb, *supra* note 3.

91. *Id.*

92. *See O'Rourke's Dirty Blow: Causes a Great Deal of Feeling in this City—Chapman Kicks at Tyler, Says He Should Have Fined the Bridgeport Slugger; President Whitlock to Investigate the Matter*, MERIDEN DAILY REPUBLICAN (CT), Aug. 14, 1897, at 1.

93. *Id.*

94. *See* Lamb, *supra* note 3. For a further discussion of the association's founding, see JOHN B. FOSTER, A HISTORY OF THE NATIONAL ASSOCIATION OF PROFESSIONAL BASEBALL [SIC] LEAGUES [SIC]—SILVER JUBILEE: 1902–1926 (1926). For a look at the American League, which had become the country's second major league in 1901, see WARREN N. WILBERT, THE ARRIVAL OF THE AMERICAN LEAGUE: BAN JOHNSON AND THE 1901 CHALLENGE TO [THE] NATIONAL LEAGUE MONOPOLY (2007).

95. *See, e.g., The Diamond: Dan O'Neills Walloped the Jim O'Rourkes; The Trick was Turned in Holyoke—Hartford is a Great Finisher, But Just Misses a Win—Springfield Does Things to Norwich—New London Outplayed New Haven*, WATERBURY EVENING DEMOCRAT (CT), July 18, 1903, at 9 ("'Sunny Jim' and 'Sonny Jim' played the heavy parts in yesterday's [9–3 thrashing by Holyoke]").

96. *See* Lamb, *supra* note 3. *See also Jimmy O'Rourke*, BASEBALL-REFERENCE.COM, https://www.baseball-reference.com/players/o/o'rouqu01.shtml (last visited July 1, 2024). According to Crowley, the impatient Highlanders cut Queenie before he had time to develop. *See* CROWLEY, *supra* note 11, at 373. Following his playing days, Queenie took a job with the Bethlehem Steel Corporation ("BSC") and eventually ended up working as a weighmaster at the Patapsco and Back Rivers Railroad Company, a BSC subsidiary in Sparrows Point, Maryland. *See Ada E O'Rourke in the 1950 United States Federal Census*, ANCESTRY.COM, https://www.ancestry.com/discoveryui-content/view/60208876:62308 (last visited July 1, 2024) (at line 4).

97. *See Old Jim O'Rourke with the Giants: Caught Iron Man M'Ginnity's Delivery as Faultlessly as a Youngster*, THE DAY (New London, CT), Sept. 23, 1904, at 2.

98. *See O'Rourke Player Statistics*, *supra* note 34. O'Rourke also played on two World Series-winning teams. In 1888, the Giants beat the St. Louis Browns, the American Association's champion, in a hotly contested 10-game series. In 1889, the Giants beat the American Association's Brooklyn Bridegrooms (later Dodgers) in a lopsided nine-game series. For a further discussion, see JERRY LANSCHE, GLORY FADES AWAY: THE NINETEENTH-CENTURY WORLD SERIES REDISCOVERED (1991). As Lansche explains, the modern World Series began in 1903, following the formation of the American League in 1901. Accordingly, not everyone recognizes the 19th century contests as being true World Series.

99. Lamb, *supra* note 3.

100. *See* CROWLEY, *supra* note 11, at 343–47 (detailing O'Rourke's stormy tenure on the commission).

101. *See J.H. O'Rourke to Succeed Himself: Mayor Buckingham Names Him for Paving*

Commission—Appointment is for 6 Years and Choice is Most Excellent, BRIDGEPORT EVENING FARMER, June 30, 1910, at 1 (explaining that O'Rourke, having served a one-year term from 1909 to 1910, now was being appointed for a full six-year term); *Mayor Wilson Appoints Recreation Commission*, BRIDGEPORT EVENING FARMER, July 3, 1916, at 12 (reporting that O'Rourke had been appointed to the paving and sewing commission for a second six-year term).

102. *See* Lamb, *supra* note 3.

103. *See* Murnane, *supra* note 60.

104. *See* ANDREW PEHANICK, BRIDGEPORT: 1900–1960, at 34 (2009).

105. *See* Murnane, *supra* note 60; *James H. O'Rourke, in* BIOGRAPHIES OF GRADUATES OF THE YALE LAW SCHOOL 1824–1899, at 548 (Roger W. Tuttle ed., 1911).

106. Prior to moving into the Miegs Building, O'Rourke had operated his law office out of several different locations, including the Fairfield County Courthouse. *See Orator O'Rourke*, *supra* note 7 (under "James H. O'Rourke").

107. *See* Murnane, *supra* note 60.

108. CROWLEY, *supra* note 11, at 367–68.

109. Murnane, *supra* note 60.

110. *Id.*

111. *Id.*

112. *See* BIELAWA, *supra* note 22, at 54.

113. *See* BASEBALL RADICAL, *supra* note 11, at 187. This house was just a few blocks from where the O'Rourke family farm had been (664 Pembroke Street). *See Orator O'Rourke*, *supra* note 7 (under "James H. O'Rourke"). *See also* CROWLEY, *supra* note 11, at 15 (explaining that in 1899, 102 Pembroke Street had been renumbered 274 Pembroke Street).

114. Murnane, *supra* note 60.

115. *Id.* In 1913, while returning with family members from a baseball game at Savin Rock in West Haven, Connecticut, O'Rourke was involved in a serious accident when the car's steering gear gave way, causing the vehicle to crash into a stone wall. Luckily, the only damage was a broken axle. *See J.H. O'Rourke's Car Bumps into Woodmont Ditch*, BRIDGEPORT EVENING FARMER, July 7, 1913, at 4.

116. *See* Bob Tedeschi, *Touching All the Bases for a Legend*, N.Y. TIMES, Feb. 20, 2009, https://www.nytimes.com/2009/02/22/nyregion/connecticut/22colct.html (describing the house's razing); C.J. Hughes, *Famous and Forgotten: A Baseball Legend from Bridgeport*, N.Y. TIMES, Aug. 8, 2004, at CT7 (describing the effort to save the house). Subsequently, a full-size bronze statue of O'Rourke was erected in 2010 at Bridgeport's Ballpark at Harbor Yard (the home of the independent Bridgeport Bluefish). *See James Henry O'Rourke Monument*, CONNECTICUT IRISH HISTORY, https://www.ctirishhistory.org/website/publish/trail/inventoryDetail.php?104 (last visited July 1, 2024). The statue was put into storage after the team folded and the stadium closed in 2017. *See On His Way Back Home*, STEELPOINTE HARBOR, Jan. 14, 2019, https://www.bldsteelpointe.com/2019/01/14/on-his-way-back-home/ (describing plans to relocate the statue to Steelpointe Harbor, a new mixed-used development project that has been slowed by various problems; the project is just a few blocks from where O'Rourke's home stood). For more about these matters, see CROWLEY, *supra* note 11, at vii–viii.

117. *See Baseball Lawyers Quite Successful*, MERIDEN DAILY J. (CT), Feb. 17, 1903, at 4.

118. *Resolutions on J.H. O'Rourke*, BRIDGEPORT EVENING FARMER, Jan. 31, 1919, at 11.

119. *Id.*

120. CROWLEY, *supra* note 11, at 392–93.

121. According to Crowley, O'Rourke also handled a fair number of family and labor law matters and, when Bridgeport experienced a land boom in 1916 (a by-product of the city's new arms factories built for World War I), O'Rourke found himself busy with "legal work settling property disputes and real estate sales." *Id.* at 393–94, 413. Crowley also considers O'Rourke one of the country's first sports lawyers (due to his legal work for the NAPBBL). *See id.* at 392.

122. *See Made No Contest*, MERIDEN MORN. REC. (CT), Jan. 31, 1906, at 1.

123. *See Inquiry Worried Clerk Schreiber: Bridgeport Official Driven to Suicide by Alleged*

Stuffing of Ballot Box, THE DAY (New London, CT), Jan. 20, 1906, at 1 ("It is generally accepted here by his friends that Mr. Schreiber was driven to [suicide] through incessant worrying over the investigation into the ballot box stuffing case of Donnelly vs. Gotthard, which was heard before Judge George W. Wheeler and also before Judge Elmer and an investigating committee. Despite the fact that Judge Wheeler in his second decision on the case completely exonerated Mr. Schreiber from all blame in connection with the alleged ballot box stuffing, the town clerk has worried a great deal over the fact that his name was connected with the affair").

124. *Dunn Estate in Superior Court: Judge Miller Admits Last Testament—Relatives to Appeal Decision*, BRIDGEPORT EVENING FARMER, Feb. 5, 1916, at 1.

125. *See id.*

126. *Grandchildren to Battle for Dunn's Estate: Milkman Left Fortune from Sale of Sites to U.M.C. Plant; Son's Widow Takes Preliminary Steps, Contends that Late Husband Laid Foundation of Dunn Fortune*, BRIDGEPORT EVENING FARMER, Jan. 27, 1916, at 1. In January 1917, the plaintiffs dropped their lawsuit after it was discovered that the actual value of Dunn's estate was just $3,000. *See Dunn Appeal Withdrawn*, THE FARMER (Bridgeport), Jan. 29, 1917, at 2.

127. *See Big Will Case*, MERIDEN DAILY REPUBLICAN (CT), Apr. 27, 1896, at 1.

128. *See Former Meriden Lawyer: Charles W. Mann Held to Answer for Embezzlement*, MERIDEN DAILY J. (CT), July 9, 1902, at 5.

129. *See Mann's Case Settled*, MERIDEN DAILY J., July 14, 1902, at 4.

130. *See William Heath Dead: Former Meriden Man*, MERIDEN DAILY J. (CT), Sept. 12, 1906, at 2 ("Mr. Heath was a well known printer in this city ... [and] was a brother-in-law of Attorney Charles W. Mann, formerly of Meriden and Bridgeport, and now of Boston"). Mann (1855–1910) was born in London and arrived in the United States in 1877. For an obituary of Mann, see *Charles W. Mann Dead; Attorney Formerly Well Known in Connecticut Passes Away in Somerville Hospital*, BOS. GLOBE, Oct. 18, 1910, at 11. Mann does not have a *Find-a-Grave* webpage.

131. 21 A. 1073 (Conn. 1890).

132. *See DE FOREST, Robert Elliott 1845–1924*, BIOGRAPHICAL DIRECTORY OF THE UNITED STATES CONGRESS, https://bioguide.congress.gov/search/bio/D000190 (last visited July 1, 2024). *See also Robert Elliott De Forest*, FIND-A-GRAVE.COM, https://www.find agrave.com/memorial/22047726/robert-elliott-de_forest (last visited July 1, 2024).

133. *See City News*, WATERBURY EVENING DEMOCRAT (CT), Feb. 15, 1890, at 4.

134. *See Rowen*, 21 A. at 1075.

135. *See School Boy on Trial: Bridgeport High School Player Accused*, MORN. REC. (Meriden, CT), Apr. 25, 1896, at 1.

136. *Id.*

137. 127 F. 1013 (D. Conn. 1904).

138. *Id.* at 1015. For a further look at the case, see *Orator Jim's Case: He Won It but Damages Were Put at $10*, MERIDEN DAILY J. (CT), Feb. 18, 1904, at 5 (reporting that O'Rourke believed he would have done better if the case had remained in state court). For a biography of Platt (1851–1913), see *Platt, James Perry*, FEDERAL JUDICIAL CENTER, https://www.fjc. gov/node/1386381 (last visited July 1, 2024) (explaining that Platt was an 1875 graduate of Yale's law school and served on the federal bench from 1902 to 1913). *See also Judge James Perry Platt*, FIND-A-GRAVE.COM, https://www.findagrave.com/memorial/30119589/james-perry-platt (last visited July 1, 2024).

139. *See, e.g., Auto Victim's Mother Fight for Grandchild: Child of Woman Killed in Sommers' Machine is Subject of Legal Contest*, BRIDGEPORT EVENING FARMER, Mar. 24, 1915, at 5 (reporting on O'Rourke's heated cross-examination of police officer Edward Cronan, one of Gilson's character witnesses).

140. *See Father Wins in Action to Keep Clarence Judd: Judge Paul Miller Decides Against Foster Mother of Automobile Victim*, BRIDGEPORT EVENING FARMER, Apr. 23, 1915, at 1. For an obituary of Miller (1885–1962), see *Former Judge Dies: Rites Wednesday for Paul Miller—Former City Court Judge and Civic Leader Dies in 78th Year*, BRIDGEPORT POST, Dec. 3, 1962, at 1. *See also Paul Lathrop Miller*, FIND-A-GRAVE.COM, https://www.findagrave.com/memorial/82262747/paul-lathrop-miller (last visited July 1, 2024).

141. *See Attorney O'Rourke Winner Over Beck in Legal Action*, BRIDGEPORT EVENING FARMER, Sept. 13, 1916, at 2. For an obituary of Scott (1851–1918), see *Judge Scott Passes Away at Danbury: Native of Bridgeport, Long Ill, Dies at Age of 67 Years*, REPUBLICAN FARMER (Bridgeport, CT), Feb. 8, 1918, at 1. *See also Judge Howard Burr Scott*, FIND-A-GRAVE.COM, https://www.findagrave.com/memorial/179024274/howard-burr-scott (last visited July 1, 2024).

142. CROWLEY, *supra* note 11, at 393.

143. *See Died—O'Rourke*, FARMER (Bridgeport, CT), June 15, 1910, at 2. *See also* Lamb, *supra* note 3.

144. *See Jno. H. O'Rourke, Former Baseball Star, Passes Away: Brother of James H. O'Rourke and Formerly of This City; Mourned by Many Friends Here—Had Been 35 Years in Railroad Service*, FARMER (Bridgeport, CT), June 24, 1911, at 2. *See also* Lamb, *supra* note 3.

145. *See* Lamb, *supra* note 3. Crowley, however, claims that O'Rourke's last game occurred on August 17, 1918, when "a team captained by [O'Rourke] traveled to Easton's Sport Hill to play their annual game against the local nine." CROWLEY, *supra* note 11, at 417. It appears that Lamb is talking about O'Rourke's last game in organized baseball, while Crowley is talking about O'Rourke's last baseball game of any sort.

146. The battle had been particularly hard on O'Rourke because it involved his old friend and teammate Tim Murnane:

> In February 1916 [O'Rourke] lost a protracted battle with New England League President Tim Murnane over the direction of minor-league baseball in the region. Among the casualties of the New England Baseball War was an O'Rourke/Murnane friendship that dated to when the two had been young teammates on the Stratford Osceolas.

Lamb, *supra* note 3.

For a further look at the fight, see CHARLIE BEVIS, THE NEW ENGLAND LEAGUE: A BASEBALL HISTORY, 1885–1949, at 159–65 (2008); BASEBALL RADICAL, *supra* note 11, at 253–70; CROWLEY, *supra* note 11, at 406–16.

147. *See* Lamb, *supra* note 3.

148. According to one of O'Rourke's biographers,

> [O'Rourke's] daughters asked him to stay home, but he refused. He planned to meet a woman being evicted from her home, and considering his habit of providing services for the needy, he was likely handling the matter pro bono. Anxious to be on time for his appointment, when no trolley arrived, he walked the half mile to his office through the storm.

CROWLEY, *supra* note 11, at 419.

149. *See Old Giant Player Dies: Jim O'Rourke Played with New York from 1885 to 1889*, N.Y. TIMES, Jan. 9, 1919, at 8. *See also A Notable in Baseball was James O'Rourke: 'Orator' Who Died a Few Days Ago was One of Game's Greatest Hitters; Played Ball at Age 56—O'Rourke was One of Original Members of Famous 'Big Four' at Buffalo*, ST. LOUIS STAR, Jan. 14, 1919, at 13 (noting that O'Rourke was "the originator of the 'rabbit ball' trick, which consisted of slipping into play, at a critical point of the game with the opposing side at bat, a nice, soft, soggy ball, which the heaviest batsman couldn't drive past the pitcher's box").

150. *See James Henry "Orator Jim" O'Rourke*, FIND-A-GRAVE.COM, https://www.findagrave.com/memorial/21216/james-henry-o'rourke (last visited July 1, 2024).

151. *See Orator O'Rourke*, *supra* note 7 (under "James H. O'Rourke") (citing the September 28, 1913, issue of the *Bridgeport Herald*).

152. *See* Friedman, *supra* note 26 (converting 1913 dollars to 2023 dollars).

153. *See* CROWLEY, *supra* note 11, at 421.

154. *See* James P. Dawson, *Old Timers' Committee Selects Ten for Baseball Hall of Fame: Bresnahan, Brouthers, Clarke, Jim Collins, Delehanty, Duffy, Jennings, King Kelly, James O'Rourke and Robinson Named*, N.Y. TIMES, Apr. 26, 1945, at 18. Ironically, one of the committee members casting a vote for O'Rourke was Connie Mack (born Cornelius McGillicuddy), the longtime manager of the American League's Philadelphia Athletics. In 1893, as both men were nearing the end of their major league playing days, Mack had tricked O'Rourke into striking out:

[O'Rourke] was quite a man…. [He was] educated, dignified and a lawyer with a great vocabulary…."

"[In 1893] I was catching for Pittsburgh … and O'Rourke was at bat for Washington. My pitcher was Billy Terry, who was a pretty tricky sort."

"O'Rourke had one foot on the boundary of the batter's box." "Mr. O'Rourke, I asked him, would you be so good as to remove your foot from the line?"

"Why certainly," he replied. "I'm sorry."

O'Rourke glanced down at his feet and just then Terry sneaked a third strike past him.

"A contemptible trick," [O'Rourke howled]. "Contemptible."

Connie chuckled with pleasure.

"Afterwards," Mack explained, "we got to be good friends."

Mack Recalls Tricky Strike, Paterson Morn. Call (NJ), June 20, 1945, at 9.

155. *See Jim O'Rourke*, National Baseball Hall of Fame and Museum, https://baseballhall.org/hall-of-famers/orourke-jim (last visited July 1, 2024). One observer, unimpressed with O'Rourke's career statistics, has claimed that O'Rourke was "elected more for his fame than for his greatness." Jay Jaffe, The Cooperstown Casebook: Who's in the Baseball Hall of Fame, Who Should Be In, and Who Should Pack Their Plaques 268 (2017).

CHAPTER 4

Miller James "Hug" Huggins (1964)

STEPHANIE HUNTER MCMAHON

At an exaggerated 5'6" and 140 pounds (the truth was somewhere closer to 5'2" and 120 pounds),[1] Miller James "Hug" Huggins (March 27, 1878–September 25, 1929) looked more like the lawyer he had trained to be than the baseball player he had become. A local boy, Huggins had entered the University of Cincinnati ("UC") in 1897 and graduated from its law school in 1902.[2] Although he never practiced law, Huggins nevertheless became, in the words of one anonymous pundit, "the greatest lawyer who ever sat on a bench."[3]

It was Huggins's father who pushed Huggins to get a law degree—Huggins wanted to play baseball. After fulfilling his father's wish, Huggins became a better-than-average player with the Cincinnati Reds (1904–09) and the St. Louis Cardinals (1910–16). Halfway through his tenure with the Cardinals, Huggins also began to manage the team (1913–17). Huggins found his greatest success, however, piloting the New York Yankees (1918–29) during the team's boisterous first dynasty.[4]

Throughout his time at UC, Huggins continuously felt the pull of baseball, and in the summers between classes he played both semi-professional and minor league ball. But it was only after he had his law degree that Huggins was able to devote himself fully to baseball. As he later remarked, "I fell in love…. The object of my love, though, was no lady; it was instead baseball."[5]

Family Matters

Huggins's parents were Sarah A. (née Reid) (1848–96)[6] and James T. Huggins (1843–1913).[7] Sarah was a native Cincinnatian,[8] while James was an immigrant from London who had arrived in the United States in

1866 (many sources incorrectly report that James was from Scotland).[9] The pair had married in the early 1870s (the exact year is unknown) and had four children: Arthur W. (1874–1963), a New Jersey salesman[10]; Clarence W. (1875–1955), the owner of a Massachusetts automobile parts company[11]; Huggins[12]; and Myrtle M. "Myrtie" (1882–1938), who ended up being Huggins's housekeeper.[13]

While most sources say that Huggins was born on March 27, 1878, some give his birth year as 1879 or 1880.[14] In its report of Huggins's death, for example, the *New York Times* wrote that Huggins was born "on April 19, 1879, according to the family records, though the baseball records give the date as March 27, 1880."[15]

Huggins's father James was a grocer,[16] and the Hugginses were residents of "The Bottoms," a working-class neighborhood in downtown Cincinnati.[17] Wanting a better life for his children, James insisted that each of them obtain an education.[18] While James pushed Huggins to become a lawyer and run for public office, Sarah hoped her youngest son would become a minister.[19] Huggins himself dreamed of becoming either a drum major[20] or a seaman.[21]

Years later, Huggins claimed that his father chose law as Huggins's future profession because of Huggins's fondness for arguing:

> When I was a mere lad it had been decided that I was to be a lawyer. This was due to a tendency on my part to enter into long arguments over any question that arose, whether in the back yard playing baseball or in the parlor.
>
> "Mr. Huggins," the neighbors used to say to my father, "that boy is bound to be a lawyer. Anyone who can persistently argue every side of a question like him has got to go into law."[22]

Although he "had been an amateur cricket player of note in his home country,"[23] James, a devout Methodist, did not think much of "athletes and the life they were likely to lead."[24] Thus, he frowned upon Huggins's participation in sandlot baseball—which included playing for such well-known local teams as Wesley W. Elberfeld's Bond Hills and Frank J. Behle's Shamrocks[25]—and repeatedly told Huggins that he was wasting his time on a "frivolity."[26]

In 1898, when he was 20, Huggins spent the summer playing for the Wapakonetas, a semi-professional team in Wapakoneta, Ohio.[27] In 1899, Huggins joined his first minor league team, the Class B Mansfield (Ohio) Haymakers.[28] While with these clubs, Huggins used the name "Jack Procter" (misspelled "Proctor" in many news accounts) to hide his ballplaying from his father.[29] According to most sources, Huggins picked the name "Procter" because of his familiarity with the soap company Procter & Gamble, a Cincinnati institution since 1837.[30]

Whether to pursue baseball or a law degree led to numerous quarrels between Huggins and his father. As Huggins later recalled: "We argued the matter at length. I was stubborn and argumentative, and in a way I did win. I got a compromise by which I could play ball at times and study law at others."[31]

Legal Studies and a Word of Advice

Following his graduation from Walnut Hills High School in 1897 (James had been able to move the family out of The Bottoms and into successively better neighborhoods as his grocery business prospered),[32] Huggins became a pre-law student at UC.[33] After two years of preparatory work, during which he nearly failed out of UC,[34] Huggins entered UC's law school in 1899.[35] Because he had a high school diploma, Huggins did not have to take the law school's entrance examination.[36]

UC had been founded in 1870, although it did not begin holding classes until 1873.[37] In 1896, the UC Law Department was started.[38] In 1897, Cincinnati College's law school (founded 1833), the oldest law school in the state, agreed to a merger with UC's Law Department, with "the degree of Bachelor of Laws ... [to be conferred] by the concurrent action of the Board of Directors of the University of Cincinnati and the Directors of the Cincinnati College."[39] As a result, by the time Huggins entered UC's law school, it had approximately a dozen faculty members, one of whom was William Howard Taft, the future U.S. president (1909–13) and Chief Justice of the United States (1921–30).

Taft had earned his undergraduate degree at Yale University (1878) and his law degree from Cincinnati College's law school (1880). In 1896, he became the latter's dean while retaining his seat on the U.S. Court of Appeals for the Sixth Circuit (a position he had been appointed to in 1891). As part of the 1897 merger, Taft became the dean of UC's Law Department as well as its property professor.[40] In 1900, Taft left the school (and the Sixth Circuit) after President William McKinley placed him in charge of the Philippines, which had become a U.S. territory following the end of the 1898 Spanish-American War.[41]

Prior to the merger, Cincinnati College's law school had used the textbook method of instruction (which relied on memorization and recitation of legal treatises), while UC's Law Department had adopted the Harvard case method of instruction (which involved reading and dissecting appellate cases).[42] As part of the merger, it was agreed that the latter method of instruction would be used:

The course and methods of study in the new school are the same as those marked out by the faculty of the Law Department of the University before the union. The endowment [of the Law School of the Cincinnati College] enables the new school to enlarge the course of study, and to come nearer to its Harvard model than would have been possible had the two schools continued separate.[43]

During Huggins's time, UC law students had to take 10 credits during their first year (consisting of courses in civil procedure, contracts, criminal law, the law of persons [*i.e.*, domestic relations], [property, and torts]); 13 credits during their second year [agency, equity, evidence, jurisprudence, procedure in equity, property, quasi-contracts, sales of personal property, and suretyship]; and 14 credits during their third year [bailments and common carriers, bills and notes, code pleading, constitutional law, corporations, equity, partnership, and property]).[44] No elective courses were offered, and students had to complete all of the listed courses to graduate.[45]

Huggins found it relatively easy to juggle his law studies and baseball. The Law Department conducted courses six days a week (Monday–Saturday), with all courses being held either in the morning (9:00 a.m.–12:00 noon) or late afternoon (4:00–6:00 p.m.).[46] The school's Fall semester began on the first Monday in October, while its Spring semester began on the first Monday in February.[47] Exams, administered annually, took place during the first week of June.[48] As a result, Huggins would leave the law school after spring classes were over, start playing baseball, return for exams, and then resume playing baseball.

During the Spring 1900 semester, Huggins was the captain and shortstop of UC's college baseball team.[49] On April 14, 1900, the National League's Cincinnati Reds beat Huggins and his teammates in a sparsely attended exhibition game at League Park (the Reds' home field) by a score of 13–2.[50] The rest of UC's season, played against other college teams, was more successful.[51]

In the summer between his first and second year of law school (1900), Huggins played for the semi-professional New York Mountain Tourists (also known as the Mountaineers), a team financed by Julius A. Fleischmann, a wealthy Cincinnati businessman.[52] In the summer between his junior and senior year of law school (1901), Huggins played for the minor league Saint Paul Saints of the Class A Western League, even though he had been drafted by the Philadelphia Athletics of the new American League.[53]

In addition to fulfilling his true ambition, playing baseball allowed Huggins to pay for law school:

To keep faith with what I had told my father, I matriculated in the law school of the University of Cincinnati and dived into Blackstone with almost as much spirit as I had in baseball.... Still, I stuck to my studies. I stuck to them for three years.

Mind you, I was paying my own way through the law school. At no time did I call on my father.... [I]t occurred to me that I could play professional baseball during the warm months and earn enough to keep up my studies in the fall.[54]

During Huggins's time, tuition at UC's law school was $100 a year, payable in advance,[55] the equivalent today of $3,575.[56] Textbooks cost an additional $40 to $50 per year, while room and board ran anywhere from $3.50 to $8.00 a week for the typical law student.[57] Being local, Huggins avoided these last two costs by living at home.[58]

On December 14, 1901, Huggins became a member of the law school's Hamilton Inn, the local chapter of the national legal fraternity Phi Delta Phi. Two weeks later, the chapter's president reported:

Hamilton was a little late with its initiation this year. The results, however, justified the delay. A most excellent set of candidates were produced by the process of selection and survival. We initiated on the night of December 14 ... Frank W. Moulton, A.B., Ohio University; Miller James Huggins; John F. Neilan, Jr., A.M., St. Xavier's; Glendinning Burnet Groesbeck; Wilfred Marshall Tyler; [and] Paul Lincoln Mitchell, A.B. Yale, 1901.[59]

In January 1902, just before his final semester of law school, Huggins briefly clerked for St. Paul (Minnesota) Municipal Court Judge Grier M. Orr (1856–1939),[60] an 1883 graduate of the Cincinnati College School of Law and an expert in family law.[61] As matters turned out, it was the only law job Huggins ever held.

In June 1902, Huggins graduated from UC's Law Department with an LL.B.[62] Shortly before graduation, Huggins was selected to give a talk to his classmates. The next day, Dean Gustavus H. Wald (1853–1902)[63] asked Huggins: "[D]o you intend to be a lawyer or a ball player? It's time for you to decide. Law, you know, is a jealous mistress."[64] Huggins responded that he was not certain and might try to do both. Upon hearing this, Wald replied: "I would advise you to center on baseball. I heard you talk last night and I have heard you talk on the ball field. I think your baseball argument the more interesting."[65] Years earlier, Taft, who had been Huggins's property professor, supposedly had given him the same advice: "You can become a pleader or a player—not both. Try baseball, you seem to like it better."[66]

Passing the Bar and Forsaking the Law

In the summer of 1902, Huggins returned to Saint Paul and again played for the Saints, hitting .328.[67] In the fall, he began preparing for the

Miller J. Huggins (bottom row, second from the right) and his law school graduating class (1902) (University of Cincinnati College of Law).

Ohio bar exam. In December 1902, Huggins traveled to Columbus to take the exam.[68]

The exam consisted of 98 short-answer questions on a variety of topics.[69] The following 12 questions provide a sense of the exam's scope and difficulty:

Question 1: Give an example of an equitable and legal title existing at the same time and in the same piece of real estate.

Question 17: Is it perjury in Ohio to swear falsely to an application for a marriage license, the applicant not being one of the parties to the intended marriage?

Question 30: Is an agent personally liable on a note signed by himself as "Agent of the K.C. Co.," the payee knowing that he is acting as agent and the name of his principal? State your reasons.

Question 31: A client on the eve of trial for the sole purpose of obtaining a continuance of his case, and against the advice and protest of his attorney, who refused to prepare the affidavit, himself prepared and falsely swore to an affidavit, proper in form, disqualifying the sitting judge on the ground of bias and prejudice, presented the same to the sitting judge, who thereupon continued the case for trial to another judge. What course should the attorney pursue on the presentation of such affidavit? Give reason for answer.

Question 33: A died possessed of a large amount of real estate and personal property devising all to his only son. If you were attorney for A's widow, how would you advise her?

Question 44: If the owner of an article, which has been stolen, finds it in a pawn shop, where it has been pledged by the thief for a sum of money, can he recover it without paying the sum for which it was pledged? State your reasons.

Question 48: What are the elements of a sale of chattels?

Question 52: A farmer went to a miller and said: "I have a thousand bushels of wheat in sacks in my barn, for which I want one dollar per bushel." The miller said: "I will give you $500 for 500 bushels." "It's a bargain," said the farmer. An hour afterwards, before the farmer got home and before the miller saw the wheat, it was destroyed by fire. How is the loss borne? Why?

Question 54: What is a nuncupative will, and what are the requisites for a valid execution and probate of the same? And what is the force and effect of a duly executed nuncupative will in Ohio?

Question 67: To what extent is a moral obligation a good and legal consideration to support a contract?

Question 81: Give five instances where, one of the parties being an executor, the other party may testify.

Question 97: The court is to pass upon a statute partly unconstitutional. Is the court to declare the whole statute unconstitutional or not?[70]

Within days, Huggins found out that he had passed the exam.[71] Having fulfilled his father's wishes, Huggins was done with the law. From now on, his sole focus would be baseball. Huggins's father, however, would not let go of his dream for his son:

For some time after he went into baseball Hug's father was hopeful that he might yet give up the game in favor of law. He urged him frequently not to give up legal practice entirely but to maintain his office during the off season. This Hug refused to do. "You can't do two jobs at once," he declared. "Either I'm a lawyer or a ball player. I can't be both."[72]

Huggins never wavered in his conviction to stick to baseball. In a long piece published after his death, a reporter noted:

The other day in the county clerk's office, in Columbus, Ohio, an aging and gray-haired clerk, going through his files, came across a card yellow with dust and gray with age. That card bore the name "Miller James Huggins" and showed that Hug has been admitted to the bar and was entitled to practice law in the common courts of the State of Ohio.

The old clerk surveyed the card for a moment, lifted it from its fellows, took up his pen and wrote across it the single word "deceased."

Miller Huggins's legal career was officially closed. Had that clerk but known, he was thirty years late in his notations. Miller Huggins' life span had ended on the day the clerk made his notation—[but] his legal career had ended ... years before....[73]

Baseball, Finally

Having committed himself to baseball, Huggins gave everything he had to the game. In 13 seasons as a major league player, he collected 1,474 hits and compiled a .265 batting average.[74] In 17 seasons as a major league manager, he was 1,413–1,134, a winning percentage of .555.[75] As a manager, Huggins found his greatest success with the Yankees, whom he led to six pennants (1921, 1922, 1923, 1926, 1927, and 1928) and three World Series championships (1923, 1927, and 1928). In these campaigns, Huggins had the good fortune to have teams that boasted a bevy of future Hall of Famers, including Earle B. Combs, Henry L. "Lou" Gehrig, Jr., Waite C. Hoyt, Anthony M. "Tony" Lazzeri, Herbert J. "Herb" Pennock, and, of course, the incomparable George H. "Babe" Ruth.[76] But he also was aided by his superior intellect, which allowed him to outthink his opponents, and his calm but determined demeanor, which helped him handle difficult situations with aplomb.[77]

Huggins never married—instead, following his father's death in 1913, he lived quietly with his unmarried sister Myrtie, who kept house for Huggins and served as his chief confidant.[78] Outside baseball, Huggins's principal interests were billiards, fishing, golf, pinochle, and roller skating. Huggins was particularly taken with roller skating, regularly visiting rinks on his days off and eventually becoming the part-owner of one.[79] In 1925, when the Yankees shifted their spring training headquarters from New Orleans to St. Petersburg, Florida, Huggins briefly dabbled in the local real estate market but got out in 1926 after finding the time commitment to be too burdensome.[80] As for politics, Huggins almost never spoke of the subject. In 1928, however, he publicly supported Republican Herbert C. Hoover for president.[81]

In 1917, Huggins, who desperately wanted to own a major league team, nearly succeeded in buying the St. Louis Cardinals with the help of Julius

Fleischmann, the Cincinnati business magnate he had known for years.[82] But when owner Helene Hathaway Robison Britton, who had inherited the team from her uncle Martin S. "Stanley" Robison in 1911, ended up selling the club to her attorney James C. Jones for $350,000,[83] Huggins realized he had no future with the club and departed when his contract expired at the end of the 1917 season. A short time later, he agreed to become the Yankees' new manager.[84] In explaining the change, Huggins told reporters: "I gave Branch Rickey [the president of the Cardinals, and the subject of Chapter 6 of this book] a proposition and he failed to meet my terms. I was given to understand that I was free to dispose of my services wherever I pleased."[85]

On January 1, 1925, Huggins became a part-owner of the minor league Saint Paul Saints, for whom he had played for three seasons (1901–03).[86] Huggins's partners were Yankees head scout Robert J. "Bob" Connery and St. Louis banker Leo L. Daly, with each man owning one third of the team. Due to the obvious conflict of interest (the Yankees ended up benefiting time and again from the arrangement), Huggins kept his position a secret (some sources say he did so by putting his stock in his sister Myrtle's name).[87]

Conclusion

In 1924, while talking to sportswriter Bill Corum in New Orleans during spring training, Huggins, in a rare moment of self-reflection, observed: "My chief regret is that I haven't a boy of my own to take an interest in. I could give him so many things I didn't have. A first-class college education would be one of them. Money doesn't mean much, unless you have somebody to spend it on."[88]

In August 1929, Huggins began to feel ill and started losing weight. He also developed a ghastly red blotch under his left eye. Although the Yankees were out of the pennant race (having fallen badly behind the Philadelphia Athletics[89]), Huggins refused to leave the team to seek medical care.[90] Finally, however, on September 20, 1929, Huggins went to Saint Vincent's Hospital in Manhattan.[91] Five days later, he died there from a combination of influenza and pyemia (a form of sepsis).[92] Subsequently, he was laid to rest in Cincinnati's Spring Grove cemetery next to his parents.[93]

On the day of Huggins's funeral (September 27, 1929), the American League cancelled all its games to honor Huggins.[94] Three years later, on May 30, 1932, the Yankees erected a monument to Huggins in center field at Yankees Stadium[95]—the start of what would become the franchise's fabled "Monument Park."[96]

In 1938, Huggins's beloved sister Myrtle killed herself by taking an overdose of sleeping pills.[97] In his will, Huggins had left the bulk (80%) of his $250,000 estate (worth $4.53 million today) to her.[98]

In 1964, Huggins was elected to the Baseball Hall of Fame.[99] In all, it had taken him nine tries to gain entry.[100] The next day, *New York Times* reporter Arthur J. Daley penned a column with the headline: "What Took So Long?"[101]

Notes

1. *See Miller Huggins Taking on Weight*, N.Y. AM., Oct. 22, 1926, at 19.

2. *See* Louis D. Bilionis, *[Dean's] Opening Statement*, 20:3 COUNSELOR (alumni magazine of the University of Cincinnati College of Law) 1, 1 (Spring 2007) ("[O]ne of our College's famous graduates, Miller Huggins[,] took his degree with the Class of 1902, passed the Ohio bar, and [then] went on to a [storied] career [in baseball]"). In his autobiography "On Top of the Baseball World," which he co-wrote with noted sports reporter Bozeman Bulger, and which appeared in serialized form in newspapers across the country in 1924, Huggins erroneously claimed that he received his law degree in 1903. *See, e.g.,* Miller Huggins, *Huggins Tells of His Choice Between the Law and Following Baseball: Dean of Law School Advises Him to Center on the National Pastime and Not to Play to Both Diamond and Legal Work*, S.F. CHRON., Jan. 30, 1924, at 2H [hereinafter *Choice*].

3. *How the Yanks' "Four Straight" Gave Baseball a Good Name*, 95 LITERARY DIG. 64, 65 (Oct. 22, 1927).

4. For biographies about Huggins, see, e.g., STEVE STEINBERG & LYLE SPATZ, THE COLONEL AND HUG: THE PARTNERSHIP THAT TRANSFORMED THE NEW YORK YANKEES (2015); GARY A. SARNOFF, THE FIRST YANKEES DYNASTY: BABE RUTH, MILLER HUGGINS AND THE BRONX BOMBERS OF THE 1920S (2014); Kirk H. Beetz, *Huggins, Miller James, in* 1 SCRIBNER ENCYCLOPEDIA OF AMERICAN LIVES, THEMATIC SERIES: SPORTS FIGURES 434–36 (Arnold Markoe ed., 2002); Sam Gazdziak, *Grave Story: Miller Huggins (1878–1929)*, RIP BASEBALL, July 10, 2021, https://ripbaseball.com/2021/07/10/grave-story-miller-huggins-1878-1929/; Steve Steinberg, *Miller Huggins*, SABR, https://sabr.org/bioproj/person/miller-huggins/ (last visited July 1, 2024). For Huggins's career statistics as a player, see *Miller Huggins*, BASEBALL-REFERENCE.COM, https://www.baseball-reference.com/players/h/huggimi01.shtml (last visited July 1, 2024) [hereinafter *Huggins Player Statistics*]. For Huggins's career statistics as a manager, see *Miller Huggins*, BASEBALL-REFERENCE.COM, https://www.baseball-reference.com/managers/huggimi01.shtml (last visited July 1, 2024) [hereinafter *Huggins Managing Statistics*]. All of the baseball statistics for Huggins cited in this essay come from these sources.

5. Miller Huggins & Ruth Crawford, *How I Got That Way*, BROOKLYN DAILY EAGLE, Oct. 3, 1926, at 2C.

6. *See Sarah A. Reed [sic] Huggins*, FIND-A-GRAVE.COM, https://www.findagrave.com/memorial/83374099/sarah_a_huggins (last visited July 1, 2024). An obituary for Sarah has not been found.

7. *See James Thomas Huggins*, FIND-A-GRAVE.COM, https://www.findagrave.com/memorial/83295569/james_thomas_huggins (last visited July 1, 2024). Although this source reports that James was born in 1846, it also includes a photograph of his headstone with the dates "1843–1913." *Id.* James's obituary reports that he died at the age of 70, which also would make his birth year 1843. *See Jas T. Huggins Dies*, CIN. POST, Apr. 21, 1913, at 1.

8. Some sources claim that Sarah was born in Ireland, but this clearly is incorrect. *See, e.g., Sarah Reid in the 1860 United States Federal Census*, ANCESTRY.COM, https://www.ancestry.com/discoveryui-content/view/43676800:7667 (last visited July 1, 2024) (indicating, at Line 7, that Sarah was born in Ohio). The mistake is explained easily: as Line 5 of the 1860 census reports, Sarah's father Robert Reid, a shoemaker, was a native of Ireland. *Id.*

9. *See James Thomas Huggins Find-a-Grave Webpage, supra* note 7.

10. For an obituary of Arthur, see *Funeral Notices—Huggins*, St. Petersburg Times, June 27, 1963, at 23B. *See also Arthur W. Huggins*, Find-a-Grave.com, https://www.findagrave.com/memorial/83374632/arthur_wilson_huggins (last visited July 1, 2024).

11. For an obituary of Clarence, see *Brother of Former Yankee Pilot Dies*, Tampa Morn. Trib., July 14, 1955, at 28. *See also Clarence Walter Huggins*, Find-a-Grave.com, https://www.findagrave.com/memorial/83294409/clarence_walter_huggins (last visited July 1, 2024).

12. *See Miller James Huggins*, Find-a-Grave.com, https://www.findagrave.com/memorial/2038/miller_james_huggins (last visited July 1, 2024). For Huggins's obituary, see *infra* note 15.

13. *See Myrtle Marie Huggins*, Find-a-Grave.com, https://www.findagrave.com/memorial/11551182/myrtle_marie_huggins (last visited July 1, 2024). For Myrtie's obituary, see *infra* note 97.

14. On his World War I draft registration card, Huggins reported his birthday as March 27, 1878. *See* Sarnoff, *supra* note 4, at 35.

15. *See Miller Huggins Dies; Many Pay Tribute: Manager of Yankees' Baseball Team for 12 Seasons is a Victim of Blood Poisoning—League's Games Today Off—Group He Led to Three World Championships Will Attend the Funeral Here Tomorrow*, N.Y. Times, Sept. 26, 1929, at 1 [hereinafter *Huggins Dies*].

16. *See* Henry F. Pringle, *A Small Package*, 3:34 New Yorker 25, 25 (Oct. 8, 1927).

17. *See* Joe Heffron & Jack Heffron, The Local Boys: Hometown Players for the Cincinnati Reds 98 (2014). For more about The Bottoms, see Jeff Suess, *Remembering Cincy's Notorious The Bottoms*, Cin. Enquirer, Mar. 3, 2024, at A4 (explaining that during Huggins's childhood, The Bottoms was "the poorer section of town, … where immigrants and the free Black population could find meager living accommodations"). Living in The Bottoms meant that Huggins learned to fight at an early age. *See* Sarnoff, *supra* note 4, at 35 ("In spite of his size, [Huggins] always held his own against the bigger kids").

18. *See* Myrtle Huggins & John B. Kennedy, *Mighty Midget: The Career of Miller Huggins*, 85:21 Collier's: The Nat'l Wkly. 18, 18 (May 24, 1930).

19. *See* Sarnoff, *supra* note 4, at 35.

20. *See Miller Huggins Had Desire to Shine as Real Drum Major*, Long Beach Press (CA), Mar. 9, 1924, § 3, at 9.

21. *See* Sarnoff, *supra* note 4, at 35.

22. *Choice, supra* note 2.

23. Pringle, *supra* note 16, at 25.

24. *Id.*

25. *See* Tom Swope, *Yankee Victory is Triumph of Cincinnati Man Who Overcomes Handicap of Size: Long Fight Starts with Hug Studying Law in Order to Play Ball*, Cin. Post, Oct. 5, 1921, at 1.

26. Steinberg & Spatz, *supra* note 4, at 29.

27. *See* Swope, *supra* note 25.

28. *Id.*

29. *See* Steinberg, *supra* note 4.

30. *See, e.g.*, Fred Glueckstein, The '27 Yankees 65 (2005). The company's first name often is misspelled "Proctor." *See A Long History of Misspelling Our Company's Name*, P & G Blog, Apr. 5, 2023, https://us.pg.com/blogs/pg-misspelling-procter-and-gamble/ (giving numerous examples of the mistake, which sometimes has been made by the company itself).

31. Miller Huggins, *Writer of Sports on a Cincinnati Paper Given Credit as Discoverer: Moses Isaacs Enthusiastic Over Huggins, Then Known as Proctor, and Boosted Him into Salary of Some $80 Per Month*, S.F. Chron., Feb. 1, 1925, at 2H.

32. *See* Walnut Hills High School Alumni Hall of Fame Program 26 (Apr. 21, 2007), http://www.walnuthillseagles.com/pdfs/alumni/hof/2007.pdf (indicating that Huggins graduated as a member of the Class of 1897).

33. *See* Catalogue of the University of Cincinnati—Founded by Charles McMicken—1897–1898, at 95 (1898) [hereinafter 1898 UC Catalogue] (listing Huggins

as a freshman and giving his address as "2937 Gilbert Ave., W. Hills"). In 2022, UC cut all ties with McMicken (1782–1858) because he had been a slaveholder. *See* Madeline Mitchell, *McMicken Name Struck from UC Campus in Unanimous Board Vote*, CIN. ENQUIRER, June 29, 2022, at A3. Huggins also is listed as a college freshman in UNIVERSITY OF CINCINNATI, CINCINNATIAN 1898 (yearbook of the University of Cincinnati), at 31 (1898).

34. In June 1898 and again in February 1899, Huggins was ordered to appear before UC's Examinations Committee and explain why he should not be expelled for poor grades. Both times, he managed to convince the Committee to let him stay. For a copy of Huggins's "Remark Card" listing his appearances before the Committee, see KEVIN GRACE, THE CINCINNATI REDS: 1900–1950, at 18 (2005). As the card indicates, Huggins was particularly bad at French and Latin. *Id.*

35. *See* UNIVERSITY OF CINCINNATI, CINCINNATIAN 1900 (yearbook of the University of Cincinnati), at 75 (1900) [hereinafter 1900 UC YEARBOOK] (listing Huggins as a first-year law student).

36. *See* 1898 UC CATALOGUE, *supra* note 33, at 161.

37. *Id.* at 11–12.

38. *Id.* at 161.

39. *Id.* at 162. Byron B. "Ban" Johnson (1864–1931), the founder of the American League (1901), briefly was a law student at Cincinnati College but dropped out halfway through his sophomore year (1886) to become a sportswriter. *See* Joe Santry & Cindy Thomson, *Ban Johnson*, SABR, https://sabr.org/bioproj/person/ban-johnson/ (last visited July 1, 2024).

40. *See* 1898 UC CATALOGUE, *supra* note 33, at 160, 164.

41. *See Civil Government for the Filipinos: Judge Taft the Head of a New Commission to Establish It—He Will Sail About March 15; Likely That Judge Taft Will Be the First Civil Governor of the Philippine Archipelago*, N.Y. TIMES, Feb. 7, 1900, at 1. Following his return from the Philippines in 1904, Taft served as the U.S. Secretary of War and then was elected president in 1908. After losing his re-election bid in 1912, Taft joined Yale's law faculty. In 1921, Taft was named Chief Justice of the United States, a position he had been seeking for more than 20 years. Taft remained Chief Justice until February 3, 1930, when ill health forced him to resign. Five weeks later, Taft died from a combination of heart disease, high blood pressure, and inflammation of the liver. For a further look at Taft's life, see Jonathan Lurie's two-volume biography titled, respectively, WILLIAM HOWARD TAFT: THE TRAVAILS OF A PROGRESSIVE CONSERVATIVE (2011) (recounting Taft's life from his birth to 1921), and THE CHIEF JUSTICESHIP OF WILLIAM HOWARD TAFT, 1921–1930 (2019) (recounting Taft's life from 1921 to his death). Taft remains the only person in history to serve as both president of the United States and Chief Justice of the United States.

42. For a further description of the two methods, see Susan Katcher, *Legal Training in the United States: A Brief History*, 24 WIS. INT'L L.J. 335, 349–61 (2006).

43. THE UNIVERSITY OF CINCINNATI—FOUNDED BY CHARLES MCMICKEN—CATALOGUE 1901–1902, at 218 (Feb. 1902) [hereinafter 1902 UC CATALOGUE]. This document lists Huggins as a third-year law student. *See id.* at 275.

44. *Id.* at 222.

45. *Id.* at 223.

46. *Id.* at 221.

47. *Id.* at 222.

48. *Id.*

49. *See Varsity Baseball*, CIN. POST, Mar. 16, 1900, at 2.

50. *See Reds: Won in a Gallop from Diamond Representatives of University; Several Players Released by the Pittsburgh Club; Billy Hoy, the Clever Outfielder, Goes with Comiskey; Tommy Corcoran is Able to be Out—Accorsini Goes to Elmira—Indianapolis Plays Today*, ENQUIRER (Cin.), Apr. 15, 1900, at 10. Due to the possibility of inclement weather, fans had been warned to call ahead to see if the game would be played, which likely kept the attendance down. *See Baseball Gossip*, ENQUIRER (Cin.), Apr. 14, 1900, at 3.

51. *See* 1900 UC YEARBOOK, *supra* note 35, at 135 (reporting that UC went 2–2, beating Miami University, losing to DePauw University, and splitting a pair of games with Indiana University).

52. As previously explained, see *supra* text accompanying note 28, Huggins had played with the Mansfield Haymakers of the Interstate League during the Summer of 1899. When the Haymakers refused to give up their rights to Huggins for the 1900 season, Huggins was unable to play professional baseball and therefore agreed to play for the Tourists. *See [No Headline in Original],* ENQUIRER (Cin.), Dec. 20, 1900, at 4 (explaining that the Haymakers invoked the reserve clause in Huggins's contract, even though they had no plans to play him).

53. *See Huggins Player Statistics, supra* note 4 (under "Minor, Independent & Cuban Lg Stats"). *See also Postponed Once More: Western League Magnates Will Not Meet Again Until Next Week; Denver Said to be Out of It, Representatives from Indianapolis and Louisville to Attend the Conference and Ask for Admission,* ST. PAUL GLOBE (MN), Mar. 6, 1901, at 5. As this source explains, Huggins turned down the Athletics' offer "[o]n account of the fight between the American and National leagues[,] [prefer[ing] to come to St. Paul and play under the national agreement." *Id.* For more about the fight between the American and National Leagues, see WARREN N. WILBERT, THE ARRIVAL OF THE AMERICAN LEAGUE: BAN JOHNSON AND THE 1901 CHALLENGE TO [THE] NATIONAL LEAGUE MONOPOLY (2007).

54. Miller Huggins, *Miller Huggins Earned His Way Through Law School by Playing Ball: Manager of New York Yankees Declares He Never Regretted Forsaking Blackstone for Baseball Diamond,* TACOMA DAILY LEDGER (WA), Feb. 4, 1924, at 10.

55. *See* 1902 UC CATALOGUE, *supra* note 43, at 224.

56. *See* S. Morgan Friedman, *The Inflation Calculator,* https://westegg.com/inflation/ (last visited July 1, 2024) (converting 1902 dollars to 2023 dollars).

57. *See* 1902 UC CATALOGUE, *supra* note 43, at 227.

58. *See Miller J Huggins in the 1900 United States Federal Census,* ANCESTRY.COM, https://www.ancestry.com/discoveryui-content/view/40189409:7602 (last visited July 1, 2024) (showing, at Lines 13–17, that Huggins and his three siblings were living with their widowed father James in 1900).

59. Charlton Thompson, *Hamilton—Cincinnati University Law School,* 4:1 THE BRIEF (quarterly magazine of the national legal fraternity Phi Delta Phi) 75 (1902).

60. *See* STEINBERG & SPATZ, *supra* note 4, at 30.

61. For a profile of Orr, see SAINT PAUL LEGAL LEDGER, MEMORIAL SERVICES FOR DECEASED MEMBERS [OF THE] RAMSEY COUNTY BAR, HELD AT THE COURTHOUSE, APRIL 8, 1939, at 2–4 (1939), http://www.minnesotalegalhistoryproject.org/assets/Ramsey%20 Mem%20-%201939.pdf. See also *Judge Grier Malancthore or Malancthon Orr,* FIND-A-GRAVE.COM, https://www.findagrave.com/memorial/162612266/grier-malancthore_or_ malancthon-orr (last visited July 1, 2024).

62. *See* UNIVERSITY OF CINCINNATI, DIRECTORY OF LIVING GRADUATES 109 (May 1920) (listing Huggins as a member of the Law School's 1902 graduating class).

63. Wald had become dean in 1900 following Taft's resignation and relocation to Manila. *See Wald: Chosen Dean of Law Department of Cincinnati University to Succeed Judge Taft,* ENQUIRER (Cin.), Mar. 27, 1900, at 5. For a profile of Wald, see 2 CHARLES THEODORE GREVE, CENTENNIAL HISTORY OF CINCINNATI AND REPRESENTATIVE CITIZENS 690–91 (1904). Ward died suddenly on June 28, 1902. *See Gustavus H. Wald,* AM. ISRAELITE (Cin.), July 3, 1902, at 6.

64. *Choice, supra* note 2.

65. *Id.*

66. In his autobiography, Huggins mentions having Taft as a professor but says nothing about Taft's supposed advice. *See id.* The first person to report Taft's alleged remark was NEA sportswriter Harry M. Grayson (1894–1968), who did so in a nationally syndicated article that appeared in June 1943 (many years after both Huggins and Taft had died). *See, e.g.,* Harry Grayson, *Huggins Excelled as Lead-Off Man: 'Little Everywhere' Was as Durable as He Was Frail; Concentrated on Getting on Base—Cultivates Knack of Walking,* PITT. PRESS, June 5, 1943, at 8. It seems likely that Grayson made up the tale (or, alternatively, conflated Taft and Wald). For a profile of Grayson, see *Harry Grayson, Editor, 74, Dead: N.E.A. Sports Chief for 30 Years was Boxing Expert,* N.Y. TIMES, Oct. 1, 1968, at 47.

67. *See Huggins Player Statistics, supra* note 4 (under "Minor, Independent & Cuban Lg Stats").

68. *See Baseball Gossip*, ENQUIRER (Cin.), Dec. 3, 1902, at 3 ("Miller Huggins has gone to Columbus to stand his law examination").

69. *See Ohio Bar Examination: Questions and Answers, December, 1902*, 11:2 L. STUD.'s HELPER 50–54 (Feb. 1903) (Part I) (reprinting Questions 1–47 and providing suggested answers), and 11:3 L. STUD.'s HELPER 85–92 (Mar. 1903) (Part II) (reprinting Questions 48–98 and providing suggested answers).

70. *See id.*

71. *See New Lawyers*, OHIO L. BULL., Dec. 15, 1902, at 868 ("At the examination of students for admission to the bar, held at Columbus, December 2 and 3, out of 130 applicants, 93 were successful. This is considered a fair percent of the number that usually pass.... The following are the names of the successful applicants ... Miller James Huggins, Cincinnati..."). Huggins was admitted to the Ohio bar on December 6, 1902. *See* The Supreme Court of Ohio Attorney Directory, *Attorney Directory Search*, https://www.supremecourt. ohio.gov/AttorneySearch/#/61429/attyinfo (last visited July 1, 2024) (under "Miller J. Huggins").

72. Ford C. Frick, *Huggins Chose Ball Instead of Law*, WASH. TIMES, Oct. 2, 1929, at 22.

73. *Id.*

74. *See Huggins Player Statistics, supra* note 4.

75. *See Huggins Managing Statistics, supra* note 4.

76. See the biographical sources cited *supra* note 4. As they report, Huggins found it difficult to manage Ruth, the game's biggest star and, at 6'2" and 215 pounds, a veritable giant when standing next to Huggins. In 1925, Huggins famously suspended Ruth, and fined him $5,000, for misconduct, a punishment Ruth protested profusely. *See* Dave Anderson, *When the Babe Almost Hit Huggins*, N.Y. TIMES, Mar. 31, 1977, at D15. The pair later reconciled, and in 1927 had their finest season together, with Ruth hitting 60 home runs (a new record), the Yankees (110–54–1) sweeping the Pittsburgh Pirates in the World Series in four games, and the team's fearsome lineup being nicknamed "Murderer's Row." For a further discussion, see HARVEY FROMMER, FIVE O'CLOCK LIGHTNING: BABE RUTH, LOU GEHRIG AND THE GREATEST BASEBALL TEAM IN HISTORY, THE 1927 NEW YORK YANKEES (2007).

77. *See* William F. Kirk, *A Midget Manager*, S.F. EXAMINER, July 20, 1919, at 12 ("Huggins is the smallest big league manager ever in captivity, physically. Mentally he is equipped above the average handler of ball players. He stands in no awe of big men, always keeping in mind the fact that Old Jule Caesar was just about his build when Jule was winning pennants for Rome back in the old days"). For a further discussion, see Samuel Shapiro, "A Necessary Evil: A Leadership Analysis of Major League Baseball's Best Managers," at 36–42 (unpublished honors thesis, University of Richmond, Apr. 28, 2023), https://scholarship. richmond.edu/honors-theses/1716/ (describing Huggins's talents as a manager).

78. *See* Steinberg, *supra* note 4. During his second year at UC, however, Huggins had raised eyebrows after taking an obvious interest in a fellow student named Cora Kahn, a "basket-ball player, talker, hustler, linguist, and society leader." *See* UNIVERSITY OF CINCINNATI, CINCINNATIAN 1899, at 205–06 (1899). Kahn later became a leader in Cincinnati's Jewish community. *See Mrs. Rosenthaler Dies; Active in Jewish Affairs*, CIN. ENQUIRER, Aug. 24, 1950, at 12. Huggins's poems to a different classmate, identified only as "Katharine," also drew notice. CINCINNATIAN 1899, *supra*, at 179. Later, while playing for the Saint Paul Saints in 1902 (just after his graduation from law school), Huggins

> became a fan favorite[, p]articularly among the female fans, according to the *Saint Paul Globe*. "[H]e is frequently seen escorting some vision of loveliness to Wildwood [Amusement Park] when he should be learning more about the statute in such case made and provided [*i.e.*, criminal indictments]," the *Globe* said of the erstwhile law student. "He admits his weakness in this respect, but insists that it will wear off as he grows older."

Gazdziak, *supra* note 4.

79. *See* John Kieran, *Sports of the Times*, N.Y. TIMES, Sep. 27, 1929, at 36. As Kieran reports:

> [Huggins] was fond of roller skating ... and, as a young ball player, worked in a

Cincinnati rink in the off-season. He thought there was a great future for him in the business. At one time he was part owner and director of a rink. It wasn't a tremendous success, but he thought he knew what was wrong and how to remedy the defect in his next venture along that line. As he went from town to town with ball clubs with which he was playing, he inspected every roller-skating rink he could discover, estimated its income, [and] made visionary improvements and imaginary offers for the place.

Id.

80. *See* SARNOFF, *supra* note 4, at 225–26.

81. *See* Robert Chiles, *Brown Derby Bambino: Babe Ruth's Celebrity Endorsement and the 1928 Presidential Campaign, in* SPORTS AND THE AMERICAN PRESIDENCY: FROM THEODORE ROOSEVELT TO DONALD TRUMP 211, 216 (Adam Burns & Rivers Gambrell eds., 2022).

82. Fleischmann was the owner of both the Shamrocks, one of the sandlot teams Huggins had played for as a boy, and the Mountain Tourists, the semi-professional team Huggins had spent time with in 1900 when the Haymakers had kept him out of organized baseball. *See supra* notes 25 and 52 and accompanying text. For a profile of Fleischmann, see *Julius Fleischmann Dies Playing Polo in Tourney at Miami: Head of Yeast Firm, Stricken in Saddle, Dismounts and Falls Dead of Heart Disease; Teammates Rush to Him But Reach His Side Too Late to Aid—Body to Be Sent North in Private Car; Twice Mayor of Cincinnati, Financier, Philanthropist, Sportsman, Had Lived in New York in Recent Years*, N.Y. TIMES, Feb. 6, 1925, at 1.

83. Because Jones could not come up with the full amount, Britton agreed to take $175,000 in cash and a note for the remainder. *See First Payment on Cardinals Ready; Free Score Cards for Fans Today*, ST. LOUIS POST-DISPATCH, Mar. 31, 1917, at 8. In May 1920, after much struggling, the Cardinals finally paid off the note. *See Cards Arrange to Pay $75,000 Note; Club Out of Debt—Issue of $100,000 Stock to Note-Holders Removes Last of Ball Club's Obligations*, ST. LOUIS POST-DISPATCH, May 11, 1920, at 18. For a profile of Britton, see JOAN M. THOMAS, BASEBALL'S FIRST LADY: HELENE HATHAWAY ROBISON BRITTON AND THE ST. LOUIS CARDINALS (2010). For a profile of Jones (1866–1946), who specialized in insurance law, see *James C. Jones Dies; Ex-Head of State Bar: Onetime President of Cardinals—Worked to Help the Blind*, ST. LOUIS POST-DISPATCH, July 15, 1946, at 3B. As this source reports:

Before World War I Mr. Jones brought into the Cardinals ball club, sponsoring a syndicate which attempted to keep the club's ownership in St. Louis. Previously he had been attorney for the club. He sold his interest to Sam Breadon at about the time America entered World War I. In his presidency of the club he organized the Knothole Gang, providing admission for children unable to afford to buy tickets.

Id. See also James Coulter Jones, Sr., FIND-A-GRAVE.COM, https://www.findagrave.com/memorial/170674318/james-coulter-jones (last visited July 1, 2024).

84. *See Miller Huggins is Named Manager of New York Club: Succeeds Wild Bill Donovan as Pilot of Yankees—Man of Wide Experience in Baseball Affairs*, BUFF. ENQUIRER, Oct. 26, 1917, at 12.

85. *Id.*

86. As explained *supra* note 53 and accompanying text, Huggins first played for the Saints during the summer between his second and third year of law school (1901). After graduating from law school, Huggins returned to the Saints and played for them for two more seasons (1902–03). *See Huggins Player Statistics, supra* note 4 (under "Minor, Independent & Cuban Lg Stats"). In September 1903, having hit .309 for the Saints, *id.*, Huggins agreed to play for the Reds beginning in 1904. *See Miller Huggins to Play with the Reds: St. Paul Infielder Picks the Cincinnati Team for His Big League Berth*, ST. PAUL GLOBE (MN), Sept. 13, 1903, at 6 (reporting that Huggins's contract with the Saints did not include a reserve clause because "Huggins in signing with St. Paul at the close of [the 1902] season insisted upon being allowed to join the team of his choice at the end of the [1903] season").

87. For a further discussion, see Steve Steinberg, *The St. Paul-New York Underground Railroad*, SABR, https://sabr.org/journal/article/the-st-paul-new-york-underground-railroad/ (last visited July 1, 2024). *See also* Steve Steinberg, *Bob Connery*, SABR, https://sabr.org/bioproj/person/bob-connery/ (last visited July 1, 2024).

88. Bill Corum, *Give This Little Guy a Hand*, N.Y. EVENING J., Mar. 9, 1927, at 22. As Corum explains, although the conversation took place in 1924, he did not report it until 1927.

89. The Athletics, powered by future Hall of Famer James E. "Jimmy" Foxx and managed by future Hall of Famer Connie Mack (born Cornelius McGillicuddy), ended up winning three consecutive pennants (1929–31) and two consecutive World Series championships (1929–30). For a further look at the team, the last competitive squad the Athletics would field until 1972 (by which time they had moved to Oakland after a brief sojourn in Kansas City), see BRETT TOPEL, SIMPLY THE BEST: THE STORY OF THE 1929–31 PHILADELPHIA ATHLETICS (2011).

90. *See* Steinberg, *supra* note 4 ("Huggins showed up at Yankee Stadium with a red blotch under his left eye, which unnerved coaches and players. 'Go see a doctor because I have a red spot on my face? Me? Who took the spikes of Frank Chance and Fred Clarke?' he retorted…. [Yet] [e]verybody could see Huggins was exhausted [and] a young Yankee shortstop named Leo Durocher, a Huggins favorite, pleaded with his manager to take the rest of the season off[.]").

91. *See Huggins in Hospital with 104 Temperature*, BROOKLYN DAILY EAGLE, Sept. 21, 1929, at 8.

92. *See Huggins Dies*, *supra* note 15.

93. *See Miller James Huggins Find-a-Grave Webpage*, *supra* note 12.

94. Following this announcement, the league realized that the only game on the schedule was a contest between the Yankees and the Washington Senators. *See* William J. Chipman, *Sport World Mourns Passing of Manager Miller Huggins: Mite Pilot Gave His Life for Game He So Dearly Loved; Funeral Service Friday—Failure to Heed Doctor's Orders Proves Fatal; Ruth Severely Shocked at Death of Man Who Once Fined Him $5,000 for Insubordination*, BUFF. TIMES, Sept. 26, 1929, at 17.

95. *See Dedication of Memorial Tablet to Miller Huggins at the Stadium*, N.Y. TIMES, May 31, 1932, at 24. For a photograph of the monument, see Wally Gobetz, *Yankee Stadium: Monument Park—Miller Huggins Monument*, FLICKR.COM, July 18, 2006, https://www.flickr.com/photos/wallyg/192159189. In pertinent part, the inscription on the monument's plaque reads: "A tribute to a splendid character who made priceless contribution [sic] to baseball."

96. For a history of Monument Park, see Daniel R. Epstein, *Of Monuments and Men: The Story of Monument Park at Yankee Stadium*, SABR, https://sabr.org/journal/article/of-monuments-and-men-the-story-of-monument-park-at-yankee-stadium/ (last visited July 1, 2024).

97. *See Miller Huggins' Sister Dead in St. Petersburg*, TAMPA MORN. TRIB., Nov. 3, 1938, at 8.

98. *See Bulk of Huggins' $250,000 Estate Goes to Sister*, DAILY NEWS (NY), Oct. 15, 1929, at 53 (reporting that Huggins left $200,000 to Myrtie; $10,000 to each of his two brothers; and the remaining $30,000 for expenses and various small legatees). *See also* Friedman, *supra* note 56 (converting 1929 dollars to 2023 dollars).

99. *See Grimes, Huggins, Faber and Manush Gain Baseball Hall of Fame: Keefe and Ward are Also Named; 2 Pre-1900 Stars Among 6 Selected by Old-Timers Hall of Fame Board*, N.Y. TIMES, Feb. 3, 1964, at 33. For a photograph of Huggins's Hall of Fame plaque, which recites his career statistics but provides no information about his life (fitting for a man who valued his privacy), see *Miller Huggins*, NATIONAL BASEBALL HALL OF FAME AND MUSEUM, https://baseballhall.org/hall-of-famers/huggins-miller (last visited July 1, 2024).

100. According to his *Wikipedia* page, Huggins's previous eight tries came in 1937, 1938, 1939, 1942, 1945, 1946, 1948, and 1950. *See Miller Huggins*, WIKIPEDIA: THE FREE ENCYCLOPEDIA, https://en.wikipedia.org/wiki/Miller_Huggins (last visited July 1, 2024).

101. *See* Arthur Daley, *What Took So Long?*, N.Y. TIMES, Feb. 4, 1964, at 26.

CHAPTER 5

John Montgomery "Monte" Ward (1964)

WALTER T. CHAMPION, JR.

John Montgomery Ward (March 3, 1860–March 4, 1925) ranks as one of the greatest baseball players in history. He also ranks as one of the game's most erudite players: in addition to having earned a law degree from Columbia University (1885), Ward spoke five languages (English, French, German, Italian, and Latin). Indeed, one would be hard pressed to name a player equal to Ward in both skill *and* intelligence. Equally difficult would be naming a player with a greater impact on the game—in this regard, only the legendary George H. "Babe" Ruth (like Ward a "two-way" player) and the iconic Jack R. "Jackie" Robinson come to mind.[1]

In 1964, Ward was enshrined in the Baseball Hall of Fame, a long overdue tip of the hat to his many contributions to the sport.[2] Ward's failure to be elected earlier (when the Hall opened in 1936, he received just three votes) can be attributed to three factors: (1) his anti-management activities as a player (even though he later served in various front office positions); (2) his progressive politics (Ward openly challenged baseball's color line after it was established in 1887 and forcefully advocated for Black, Latin, and Native American players); and (3) his numerous post-baseball triumphs as an amateur golfer, which had caused some people to forget how good he had been on the diamond.[3]

Of course, like other members of baseball's "pioneer era" (1871–92), Ward also has suffered from the fact that there is no footage of him playing. Instead, there are merely posed photographs showing Ward, 5'9" and 165 pounds, sporting a handlebar mustache and wearing the outlandish uniforms characteristic of early baseball (*i.e.*, flat top cap with narrow bill; high-collared shirt with crossed laces at the neck; impossibly wide belt; and fitted pants ending just below the knees).[4]

Ward's life has been the subject of two full-length biographies[5] and numerous shorter works.[6] With Ward having accomplished so much as an athlete, these undertakings tend to give short shrift to Ward's other career. Following his admission to the bar in 1895 (a decade *after* he graduated from law school), Ward became one of the most successful lawyers in New York City. To the extent that his biographers mention Ward's legal career, they tend to focus on his baseball cases (ironically, in these lawsuits Ward often flipped from being pro-player to pro-management). But these engagements, although helpful in keeping Ward's name in front of the public, are outliers and one-offs—Ward's bread-and-butter as a lawyer was his representation of well-heeled corporations.

Early Years

Ward was born in the small but prosperous iron mining town of Bellefonte in central Pennsylvania.[7] His parents were Ruth A. (née Hall) (1826–74), an elementary school teacher,[8] and James E. Ward (1806–71), a dealer in farm equipment.[9] The couple, strict Presbyterians, had married on May 12, 1849, in Bellefonte and had three children: Ida M. (1850-died soon after birth); Charles L. (1855–1906); and Ward.[10] Ward additionally had three half-siblings from his father's two earlier marriages.[11] The family tree also included a distant relative named Aaron Montgomery Ward (1844–1913), who in 1872 founded the famous Chicago mail order business Montgomery Ward & Company.[12]

Growing up, Ward detested the name "Montgomery" and therefore was called "Monte" by family members and close friends. When he was an adult, newspapers typically referred to him as either "John M. Ward" or, more colloquially, "Johnny Ward." In modern works, Ward usually appears as "Monte Ward."[13]

Any description of Ward's life must be careful to avoid confusing him with two other lawyers named "John M. Ward" whose careers overlapped Ward's. The first is John Metcalfe Ward (1867–99), an 1894 graduate of Columbia University's law school who earned much acclaim as a Brooklyn assistant district attorney.[14] The second is John Marcy Burnoise Ward (1880–1970), who attended New York University's law school and later became a Passaic County (New Jersey) district court judge.[15] This John often did not use his second middle name, causing him to appear in print as "John M. Ward."[16]

Following the death of his mother in 1874 (which left him an orphan), *our* John M. Ward was sent by his Uncle Philoh (his father's brother) to the prep school at nearby Pennsylvania State College ("PSC") (now Pennsylvania State University). In 1876, Ward was expelled for having taken part in a midnight prank that involved stealing a local farmer's chickens.[17] During his short time at PSC, Ward became (according to many sources) the first pitcher in history to throw a curveball.[18]

After his expulsion from PSC, Ward became a traveling flower salesman.[19] Ward had no aptitude for his new profession, however, and in 1877 began playing semi-professional baseball. In 1878, he signed as a pitcher with the recently formed Providence (Rhode Island) Grays[20] of the fledgling National League of Professional Baseball Clubs, which in 1876 had become the country's second professional baseball league[21] following the collapse of the National Association of Professional Base Ball Players (1871–75).[22] Ward later mused that if he had not rediscovered baseball, he would have been at a loss for how to make a living.[23]

During his first season with the Grays, Ward performed brilliantly, going 22–13 with a 1.51 earned run average.[24] Ward was even better in 1879, when he went 47–19 with a 2.15 earned run average and led the Grays to their first National League pennant. In 1880, Ward threw baseball's second perfect game, a 5–0 triumph over the Buffalo Bisons, and late in the season also served as the team's manager. Two years later, Ward pitched the longest complete game shutout in baseball history, beating the Detroit Wolverines 1–0 in 18 innings.

A Shift to the Infield, Law School, and First Marriage

Following the 1882 season, the Grays traded Ward to the New York Gothams (soon to be renamed the Giants).[25] Judged by his own high standards, Ward fared poorly during the 1883 season, going 16–13 on the mound and hitting a mere .255 at the plate. Now recognizing that he would not be able to play baseball forever, Ward enrolled in Columbia University's law school in the Fall of 1883.[26] As matters turned out, Ward's former (and future) teammate James H. "Jim" O'Rourke, the subject of Chapter 3 of this book, was so impressed by Ward's decision that he later entered, and in 1887 graduated from, Yale University's law school.

While running the bases in an 1884 game, Ward injured his right arm, thereby ending his pitching career. Over the course of seven seasons, he had compiled a glittering 164–103 record (a .614 winning percentage) with a 2.10 earned run average. Refusing to call it quits, Ward learned to play the infield and became a superb shortstop and second baseman. During the 1884 season Ward also became the Giants' captain—a position he would hold until 1887—and briefly served as the team's manager.

In 1885, Ward received his LL.B., with honors, from Columbia University's law school.[27] It was during this time that Ward organized the

Brotherhood of Professional Base Ball Players, baseball's first union, and began a determined (but ultimately unsuccessful) campaign to rid the sport of the reserve clause, by which players were contractually bound to their teams indefinitely.

In 1886, Ward earned a second degree from Columbia (a bachelor's in philosophy), thereby making up for the degree he had failed to obtain from PSC.[28] On October 12, 1887, Ward married the actress Helen Dauvray (1859–1923), a star of the Broadway stage, at her Manhattan apartment.[29] Dauvray had become smitten with Ward after meeting him at a social function, and throughout the 1887 season she frequently could be seen at the Polo Grounds (the Giants' home ballpark) rooting for Ward. Dauvray's infatuation with Ward was so great that she created the Helen Dauvray Cup, a large silver trophy that from 1887 to 1893 was awarded initially to the winner of the World Series and later to the winner of the National League pennant. (The cup mysteriously disappeared following the 1893 season, just after the finalization of Dauvray's divorce from Ward for adultery, a charge Ward did not contest.[30])

In 1888, Ward, who by now was writing articles for many of the country's leading magazines and newspapers, published *Base-Ball: How to Become a Player, with the Origin, History and Explanation of the Game.*[31] The book, which proved to be an instant classic, is the earliest known attempt to detail baseball's history. During the same year, Ward helped the Giants win their first World Series, besting the American Association's St. Louis Browns in a 10-game match.

The 1890 Players League

In 1889, Ward and the Giants won their second consecutive World Series, this time besting the American Association's Brooklyn Bridegrooms in a nine-game match. Following the season, Ward founded the Players League (also spelled Players' League) to improve salaries and working conditions and provide players with a say in management decisions.

Eager to prevent the Players League from getting off the ground, the Giants took Ward to court, where they claimed that the reserve clause in his 1889 contract prevented him from playing for any team but the Giants. To defend himself, Ward hired Henry E. Howland and George W. Murray of the New York City law firm of Anderson, Howland & Murray, one of the forerunners of the law firm now known as Milbank LLP (previously Milbank Tweed).[32]

On January 28, 1890, in *Metropolitan Exhibition Co. v. Ward,*[33] Justice Morgan J. O'Brien of the New York Supreme Court (the city's principal trial court) denied the Giants' request for a preliminary injunction and referred the matter to trial.[34] On March 31, 1890, just a few weeks before the start of the season, Justice Abraham R. Lawrence, who was scheduled to preside over the trial, issued the following one sentence order:

> As I am informed by counsel for the plaintiff that they do not intend to submit a brief in this case, and as I am of the opinion that the contract referred to in the complaint is one which a court of equity will not enforce, judgment will be granted dismissing the complaint with costs.[35]

With the Giants' legal challenge behind him, Ward moved forward with his plans to break the reserve clause. On the field, the Players League proved enormously successful, with the Boston Reds finishing in first place and Ward's team (the Brooklyn Wonders) finishing in second place in the eight-team league. Off the field, however, the Players League was beset by a host of problems. When the league's investors withdrew their financial support, the Players League was finished.[36]

Return to the National League

Following the collapse of the Players League, Ward returned to the National League and spent two seasons (1891–92) as the player-manager of the Brooklyn Grooms, who had jumped from the American Association to the National League after the 1889 season and who had just shortened their name from the Bridegrooms.[37] In 1893, Ward reunited with the Giants and spent the next two years (1893–94) as their player-manager.

In 1894, Ward had his best year as a manager, leading the Giants to a second-place finish (88–44, .667), three games behind the powerful Baltimore Orioles, whose roster boasted six future Hall of Famers (including future lawyer Hugh A. Jennings, the subject of the second essay of this book). Following the end of the regular season, the Giants and the Orioles played a best-of-seven match to determine the winner of the inaugural Temple Cup. (Due to the lack of another major league, a true World Series could not be staged. As a result, from 1894 to 1897 the National League's top two teams vied for the Temple Cup, which was donated by, and named for, William C. Temple, a part-owner of the Pittsburgh Pirates.[38]) In four straight games, the Giants beat the heavily favored Orioles 4–1, 9–6, 4–1, and 16–3. A short time later, Ward, who by now was 34, announced his retirement from baseball.[39]

Shortly before the start of the 1895 season, a rumor began circulating that Ward intended to keep playing. Seeking to quell the rumor, Ward told reporters:

I have certainly retired for good from active participation in baseball affairs. I have disposed of my stock in the [Giants, which Ward had received upon returning to the team] and I will not again be seen in any team. The change from baseball to law is a particularly inviting one to me. I can sleep now at nights, and all worriment is gone. As a star player the life of the average green-diamond knight is a pleasant one, but when he assumes the captaincy and management of a team his troubles begin. I have had my share of the sport, for I have been in baseball for many years. I shall attend the games as a spectator, not as a player.[40]

While Ward was sincere that he was finished as a player,[41] he was eager to be named managing director of the Giants in the wake of Edward B. Talcott's decision to resign from the position and, along with the rest of the board of directors, sell the team. As the public soon learned from sportswriter Oliver P. Caylor, Ward's interest in the position stemmed from his need for money:

There is a growing opinion, however, that ex–Capt. John M. Ward will show an inconstancy to his new love—the law—and bob up [as] a candidate for Talcott's shoes when the club holds its annual meeting on February 14[, 1895], in spite of his repeated assertions to the contrary.

Some time ago I announced that owing to "Johnnie's" fondness for the good and beautiful things of life, his assets consisted of six suits of clothes, seven lop-eared dogs, a conscience, some hope and little else in sight. Several days ago John stopped me on Broadway and reported that the inventory which I had made must be revised. One suit of clothes, he said, had already been worn out in the assiduous labor of reading Blackstone, two of his lop-eared dogs had died of "pip" or some insidious disease, his conscience was suffering from an ingrowing conviction and the price of the good and the beautiful [had] not been lowered by the tariff [i.e., the Wilson-Gorman Tariff Act of 1894, which was supposed to lower consumer prices]. He hinted that unless he could get a job with a fat salary attachment, [or] someone ... die[d] and [left] him a leg-acy[,] or dogs [went] up in price, he would have to sacrifice some real estate of which he had great expectations, provided he could hold it for a few years longer.[42]

In the end, Talcott and his fellow investors skipped over Ward and sold the Giants to Andrew Freedman, a wealthy local businessman.[43] With his short temper and imperious manner, Freedman quickly became "the most-hated man in turn-of-the-century baseball."[44]

Starting Life at the Bar

In June 1895, Ward took and passed the New York bar exam and then opened his own law office in Brooklyn. While preparing for the exam,

Ward clerked for Austin B. Fletcher (1852–1923), the future namesake of Tufts University's graduate school of law and diplomacy.[45] (Ward landed this position through his wealthy friend Albert L. "Al" Johnson, soon to become Ward's most important client.[46]) Born in Mendon, Massachusetts, Fletcher, an 1879 graduate of Boston University's law school, had moved to New York City in 1882 and had rapidly built a burgeoning legal practice representing banks and trusts.[47]

In addition to clerking for Fletcher, Ward found work as a court referee. In May 1895, for example, he submitted a report to the New York Supreme Court recommending that George W. Proctor Knott, the past president of the Manhattan Athletic Club, pay his ex-wife Eleanor $25 a week in alimony. Ward also recommended that Knott pay Eleanor's counsel $500 in attorneys' fees.[48]

When the bar exam finally arrived, Ward passed easily. The test, administered orally, took place on Saturday, June 15, 1895, "in the General Term room of the [New York] Supreme Court" before "Austen G. Fox, of [New York City]; F.M. Donaher, of Syracuse, and William F. Goodelle, of Albany."[49] In all, 215 persons (including five women) presented themselves, "the largest number of applicants examined in [New York] county at one time."[50]

One month later, it was reported that Ward, along with just about every other applicant, had passed the exam.[51] Four days later, on July 19, 1895, Ward officially became a lawyer.[52] On October 21, 1895, Ward added to his resume by being admitted to New York's federal courts.[53]

Ward did not have to wait long for his first case. In August 1895, Samuel N. Crane, a former ballplayer now working as a reporter for the *New York Morning Advertiser,* hired Ward after Crane was barred from the Polo Grounds.[54] Crane had written several negative articles about Andrew Freedman, the Giants' new owner, leading Freedman to ban Crane from the ballpark. When other reporters came to Crane's defense, the matter quickly blew over.

In November 1895, Ward asked the National League to remove his name from the reserve list:

> The board of directors of the National League began business at 11 o'clock and handled a good deal of matter during their session. Ex-Captain John M. Ward requested them to have his name erased from the reserve list of the New-York Baseball Club, claiming that under the rules a contract should have been proffered to him at the close of the season of '94 and as this was not done, he asserted that this omission released him. Furthermore, he claimed that the keeping of his name on the list injured him in his profession as a lawyer, as it would lead persons to suppose that he had not retired permanently from the ball field. Ward's protest was laid over in order that the board could take further testimony in regard to the matter.[55]

Ward's request to have his name removed from the reserve list, although entirely reasonable, was strenuously opposed by Freedman and the Giants (in part out of personal enmity and in part out of fear that Ward might be thinking of trying to make a comeback as a player). Thus, it was not until February 1896 that Ward's request was granted. Following his victory, Ward icily told reporters that he wanted no "courtesies from Mr. Freedman."[56]

In April 1896, reports circulated that the National League's Louisville Colonels had offered Ward a salary of $5,000 to serve as the team's general manager and manager.[57] Ward, however, turned the offer down. A rumor then began to spread that Andrew Freedman, having grown tired of baseball, was getting ready to sell the Giants and that a syndicate headed by Ward was poised to buy the team.[58] Whether there was any truth to this rumor is hard to say; in any event, Freedman held onto the Giants until 1903, when he sold the club to John T. Brush, the owner of the Cincinnati Reds.[59]

In July 1896, the Atlantic League of Professional Baseball Clubs, a minor league headquartered in New York City, expelled the New York Metropolitans and replaced them with the Philadelphia Athletics. The Metropolitans were a "farm team" of the New York Giants and Freedman, who had worn out his welcome with the league's other owners, threatened to sue the Atlantic League for the profit (later estimated at $3,950) that the Metropolitans stood to lose by being unable to play the final 64 games of the season.[60] When Freedman made good on his threat, Samuel B. Crane (no relation to sportswriter Samuel N. Crane), the Atlantic League's president, hired Ward to defend the league. After years of delaying tactics, Freedman finally dropped the lawsuit. Not satisfied with having won, Ward obtained an order requiring Freedman to pay the defense's costs.[61]

Although the two *Crane* cases certainly brought welcome attention to Ward's fledgling legal practice, they did not pay the bills. What was paying them was Ward's growing roster of corporate clients, of which the most important was Al Johnson's Nassau Electric Railroad Company ("NERC").[62] In an April 1900 article, for example, the *Brooklyn Citizen* newspaper urged more ballplayers to go to law school in the off-season to secure their post-baseball lives. For incentive, the paper pointed to Ward's representation of the NERC:

> There is no reason why a ball player [cannot study law in the off-season.] [G]ranted that he has to report in March [for spring training], a course of instruction could be mapped out for him so that he could keep up with his class. This is what John M. Ward did, and today he is counsel for a local railroad corporation, with an income of several thousand dollars[,] more yearly than he received as a ball player, and Ward always got the best salary going at that.[63]

In November 1900, the public learned still more about Ward's finances. During a talk in Chicago, baseball executive (and future American League president) Byron B. "Ban" Johnson explained how Ward had turned down a lot of money at the end of his baseball career because he was eager to start his legal career:

> [L]ess than a week after the announcement of Ward's retirement [from baseball in 1894,] he received a bona-fide offer of $6,000 to manage, captain and play second base for a certain [National] League team, and he turned this offer down…. I happened to be present at that memorable conference between the player and the magnate, and if I live to be 100 I will never forget the expression of blank astonishment and dismay on the face of the club owner when Ward made this little speech to him:
>
> "I realize that you have made me a big offer, and $6,000 for six months' work on the diamond is big money for any man, but I cannot accept it. I do not know how good a lawyer I will make, but the chances are that it will be many a year before I can pull a regular income of $6,000 a year out of my practice, if I have any, but at the same time I mean to try. I have a few dollars saved up and I won't go hungry, even if I fail to get a case for a year or two[.]"[64]

Baldwin & Ward

By the time the two articles discussing Ward's finances appeared, Ward, who previously had been a sole practitioner, had formed a partnership ("Baldwin & Ward") with the eminent New York City trial lawyer Stephen C. Baldwin (1864–1923). The son of Christian missionaries, Baldwin had read law, first in the offices of former Probate Judge Clinton G. Reynolds and then in the offices of David Dudley Field (the author of New York's Code of Civil Procedure). Following his admission to the bar in 1885, Baldwin was hired in 1887 by future U.S. Supreme Court Justice Benjamin N. Cardozo's law firm (Cardozo & Newcombe). In 1893, Baldwin left Cardozo & Newcombe and started his own firm, where he cemented his reputation as one of the city's top courtroom advocates.[65]

During Baldwin & Ward's existence, Ward continued to grow his non-baseball practice[66] but also handled several high-profile baseball cases, including second baseman Nathaniel F. "Fred" Pfeffer's lawsuit against the Giants[67] and two actions on behalf of the National League's Brooklyn Superbas (the Superbas being the defendant in both cases).[68] Ward's retention by the Superbas was the product of his growing friendship with team owner Charles H. Ebbets, Sr. The two had become professionally acquainted several years earlier when Ward represented the NERC and Ebbets was a Brooklyn councilman and a member of the local improvements board.[69]

Golf, Second Marriage, and a Bruising Lawsuit

Although Baldwin and Ward got along well, in January 1903 the pair decided to end their partnership. In a long article, the *Brooklyn Daily Eagle* reported on the split:

> The firm of Baldwin & Ward, attorneys, with offices at 86 Livingston Street, Brooklyn [Ward's location], and 277 Broadway, Manhattan [Baldwin's location], and composed of Stephen C. Baldwin and John M. Ward, has been dissolved by mutual consent.
>
> The firm has been in existence for more than three years, and during that time was concerned in many important cases. As to the cause of the dissolution[,] one of the firm when seen said: "There has been no disagreement at all. We are the best of friends, but circumstances have arisen which have created individual plans for the future which would not be furthered by a partnership arrangement."[70]

Based on subsequent events, it seems likely that the "individual plans" that caused the split were Ward's. First, Ward had become infatuated with the game of golf and was devoting every free minute he had to it. He had taken to the game quickly, mastered its finer points with ease, and in March 1903 finished second at the "North and South," the country's top amateur tournament (held annually since 1901 at the Pinehurst [North Carolina] Golf Club).[71] Ward was such a natural that observers agreed that if he had started playing as a youngster, he could have become a champion professional golfer.

Second, Ward had fallen in love. Katherine M. "Kate" Waas (1877–1966) was a Manhattan social worker that Ward had met (if stories are to be believed) on a golf course.[72] On September 17, 1903, the couple married in a small private ceremony at the home of the Rev. Dr. Newell D. Hillis, the pastor of Brooklyn's historic Plymouth Church of the Pilgrims.[73] Immediately upon returning from their honeymoon, Ward started a campaign to have his home golf club (Staten Island's Fox Hills) admit women so that he and Kate could play together.[74]

Not everything in Ward's life was perfect, however, for 1903 also was the year of the George S. Davis affair. Davis was a star shortstop who, following the establishment of the American League in 1901, had jumped from the Giants to the Chicago White Sox. When Davis subsequently jumped back to the Giants, the White Sox obtained first a state injunction (issued by Judge Edward F. Dunne of the Cook County [Illinois] Circuit Court) and then a federal injunction (issued by Judge Edward B. Thomas of the U.S. District Court for the Eastern District of New York) prohibiting Davis from playing for the Giants.

In signing his contracts, Davis had been counseled by Ward, who now opined that both were valid and that Davis therefore was free to pick his preferred team. This contention caused Ward tremendous grief, both in and out of court:

> To no great surprise, [Ward's] doublespeak did not play well in court. Worse yet was [the] reaction in the court of public opinion, with baseball voices leading the chorus of disapproval. "Great is the power of the retaining fee over the legal mind," observed *The Sporting News*. "It can make black appear white and vice versa in a twinkling." Chicago Cubs president James Hart characterized Ward's reasoning as "trumped up" and liable to "ruin his standing with any reputable bar association," while American League President Ban Johnson denounced Ward as a "trickster" and "as crooked as any player who ever jumped his agreement." In the end, the court ordered Davis's return to Chicago, where he ... completed his Hall of Fame playing career ... without incident.[75]

Following the demise of Baldwin & Ward, Ward formed a new partnership with Frederick S. Martyn (1874–1957), one of the firm's junior lawyers.[76] By 1906, however, Ward and Martyn had gone their separate ways.[77] Undoubtedly, Ward once again was the cause of the separation, for shortly after the dissolution he and Kate closed on the purchase of a 200-acre farm in North Babylon, Long Island, where they resided for the rest of their marriage and where Ward slipped easily into the role of gentleman farmer.[78]

A few months later, on November 5, 1906, Ward's brother Charles died in Brooklyn from complications caused by his chronic alcoholism.[79] His death certificate lists his occupation as "law clerk,"[80] but whether he was working for Ward at the time of his death is unknown.

In 1907, the Long Island Republican party flirted with the idea of making Ward its candidate for Babylon justice of the peace.[81] In the end, however, it was decided that Ward was too new to the town to be a viable choice.[82]

By this time, Ward had been a lawyer for just over a decade and had relied heavily on corporate clients to build his practice. Nevertheless, when the right opportunity presented itself, Ward did not hesitate to turn the tables. As a result, Ward ended up suing some of New York's best-known businesses, including the Degnon–McLean Contracting Company (one of the principal builders of the city's new subway system)[83]; the Hinkle Iron Company (Manhattan's biggest steel supplier)[84]; and the Hyde & Behman Amusement Company (Brooklyn's largest theater owner).[85]

On August 26, 1909, Ward found himself on the other side of the courtroom when he was called for jury duty. Although lawyers in New York were not required to serve on juries, Ward declined the statutory exemption and took his seat in the box and listened to the evidence in the case of the People vs. Frank Kahn, a local contractor, charged with assault in the third degree by Henry P. Schroeder.

Schroeder's eye was blacked on the afternoon of August 19 at Broring's Hotel, in West Babylon. A fine of $15 was imposed and paid.[86]

By now, Ward was a candidate to succeed Harry C. Pulliam, the president of the National League, who had committed suicide one month earlier (July 29, 1909). Although Ward initially was considered a shoo-in, by the time of the vote the league's owners were split 4–4, with half supporting Ward and the other half favoring Robert W. Brown, the editor of the *Louisville Times*.[87] The stalemate finally was broken on December 18, 1909, when Thomas J. Lynch, a former major league umpire, was picked as a compromise candidate.[88]

Believing that his defeat was attributable, at least in part, to American League president Ban Johnson reminding everyone of Ward's role in the George Davis affair, Ward sued Johnson for defamation in the U.S. District Court for the Southern District of New York. By random draw, the case was assigned to Judge (Billings) Learned Hand, who just recently (April 26, 1909) had been appointed to the bench and who knew nothing at all about baseball.[89]

As noted by one of Ward's biographers, the lawsuit ended in a technical victory for Ward, although both men came out of the brawl with their reputations in tatters:

> Smarting from the public aspersion cast upon his character, Ward filed a $50,000 defamation suit against Ban Johnson. The action was tried in federal court, where Ward came off as the stereotypical shifty lawyer on the witness stand. Fortunately for him, Johnson was worse, a pompous blowhard who probably perjured himself during his testimony. In the end, the jury returned a modest $1,000 judgment in Ward's favor, but the suit had done little credit to the reputation of either party.[90]

Rather than pushing Ward away from baseball, the lawsuit made him eager to rejoin the game:

> The unpleasantness [of the case] notwithstanding, the episode seemed to rekindle Ward's interest in baseball, at least temporarily. In December 1911, he became part-owner and president of the National League Boston Braves. But less than a year later, Ward stepped down, citing the press of his legal practice. By doing so, he missed out on the glory of the Miracle Braves' improbable 1914 world championship. By then Ward was tending to his final baseball-connected job: business manager of the Brooklyn [Tip-Tops] in the upstart Federal League [a third major league that operated during the 1914 and 1915 seasons]. His retirement from that post in April 1915 brought a near-40-year association with the game to an end.[91]

John Montgomery "Monte" Ward in his law office (1914) (Library of Congress/ Bain News Service).

Final Years and Death

After resigning from the Tip-Tops, Ward spent the last decade of his life primarily engaged in fishing, golfing, hunting, and traveling. He also continued to practice law, but at a somewhat slower pace.[92]

Ward's last reported case was *In re Wiemann's Estate*,[93] a 1922 decision in which he represented various parties who objected to the closing of an estate. In February 1925, while on a hunting trip, Ward was stricken with pneumonia and died four days later in Augusta, Georgia (one day after his 65th birthday).[94] After being taken back to New York, Ward was laid to rest at Greenfield Cemetery in Uniondale, Long Island.[95]

Ward's only immediate survivor and heir was Kate (Ward did not have any children). Subsequently, it was reported that Ward had left behind an estate worth $58,000,[96] the equivalent today of $1.03 million.[97] In 1960, Ward's longtime home in North Babylon, having passed through several subsequent owners, became part of a public park (Phelps Lane Park).[98]

Conclusion

Those who spend any time studying Ward's life never fail to mention that Ward was an arrogant jerk. In its review of Ward's principal biography, for example, the *New York Times* ended its assessment by warning readers to keep Ward at arm's length:

> Ward was standoffish—"there exists no known likeness of him smiling." His teammates disliked him, especially when he was in charge. He was smarter than they were and made sure they knew it. Ward is to be admired from afar, but he isn't someone you would want to spend too much time with, either in a dressing room or in a book in your lap.[99]

Every successful lawyer, of course, has some character flaw.

Notes

1. In 2014, John A. Thorn, Major League Baseball's official historian, ranked Ward the 16th most important person in baseball history. *See* Alan Schwarz & John Thorn, *Baseball's 100 Most Important People, Part 4*, Our Game, Nov. 13, 2014, https://ourgame. mlblogs.com/baseballs-100-most-important-people-part-4-e99029f88a5b. Thorn ranked Ruth first and Robinson second. *See* Alan Schwarz & John Thorn, *Baseball's 100 Most Important People*, Our Game, Nov. 10, 2014, https://ourgame.mlblogs. com/baseballs-100-most-important-people-dfd3189f96de.

2. *See John Ward*, National Baseball Hall of Fame and Museum, https:// baseballhall.org/hall-of-famers/ward-john (last visited July 1, 2024). After recounting his lifetime statistics—Ward is the only player in the Hall of Fame with 2,000 hits as a batter and 100 wins as a pitcher—Ward's plaque ends: "Played important part in establishing modern organized baseball."

3. *See, e.g.*, George Trevor, *Gamest of Golfers Passed on When John M. Ward Dropped His Final Putt*, Brooklyn Daily Eagle, Mar. 6, 1925, at A3 (reporting that Ward preferred golf to baseball); William Everett Hicks, *John M. Ward Will Be Missed in Met Golfing*, Brooklyn Daily Times, Mar. 6, 1925, at 15 (describing golf as "brighten[ing]" and "happify[ing]" Ward's "later years").

4. The most often seen photograph of Ward is the one that now appears at the start of his *Wikipedia* page—it shows Ward in a baseball uniform leaning against a bat. *See John Montgomery Ward*, Wikipedia: The Free Encyclopedia, https://en.wikipedia.org/wiki/John_ Montgomery_Ward (last visited July 1, 2024). Regrettably, the picture's date is unknown. Another familiar photograph of Ward, which appears further down on his *Wikipedia* page, is an 1888 reenactment of Ward stealing a base. (In 1887, Ward led all National Leaguers with 111 stolen bases.) Not realizing that the photograph is a reenactment, Wikipedia lists its date as 1887.

5. *See* Bryan Di Salvatore, A Clever Base-Ballist: The Life and Times of John Montgomery Ward (1999) (considered the definitive account of Ward's life); David Stevens, Baseball's Radical for All Seasons: A Biography of John Montgomery Ward (1998). Ward also is the main character in an entertaining novel. *See* James Hawking, Strikeout: Baseball, Broadway and the Brotherhood in the 19th Century (2012).

6. *See, e.g.*, Christopher W. Schmidt, *John Montgomery Ward: The Lawyer Who Took on Baseball*, in Then and Now: Stories of Law and Progress 44–50 (Lori Andrews & Sarah Harding eds., 2013); David Jones, *Ward, John Montgomery*, in 2 Scribner Encyclopedia of American Lives, Thematic Series: Sports Figures 479–80 (Arnold Markoe ed., 2002); Benjamin Hoffman, *A 19th-Century Pioneer of Perfection, and a Whole Lot More*, N.Y. Times, July 1, 2023, at B8; Dustin Elder, *Changing the Game: John Montgomery Ward*, Town & Gown Mag., June 1, 2022, https://www.statecollege.com/town-and-gown/ changing-the-game-bellefontes-john-montgomery-ward-made-history-on-the-diamond-in-the-courtroom%ef%bf%bc/; Bill Lamb, *John Montgomery Ward*, SABR, https://sabr. org/bioproj/person/john-montgomery-ward/ (last visited July 1, 2024). As Lamb notes:

"No essay-length biography could possibly do full justice to John Montgomery Ward. His life, both on and off the diamond, was entirely too eventful." *Id.*

7. *See John Montgomery Ward,* FIND-A-GRAVE.COM, https://www.findagrave.com/memorial/6169/john_montgomery_ward (last visited July 1, 2024). Although all sources report that Ward was born on March 3, 1860, Ward inexplicably gave his birth date as March 3, 1867, when he applied for a U.S. passport. *See John M Ward in the U.S., Passport Applications, 1795–1925,* ANCESTRY.COM, https://www.ancestry.com/discoveryui-content/view/887197:1174 (last visited July 1, 2024). In this application Ward also misstated his father's death year, writing "1874" (the year his mother died) instead of "1871." *Id.*

8. For an obituary of Ruth, see *State Items,* LEWISBURG CHRON. (PA), Dec. 18, 1874, at 2. *See also Ruth A. Hall Ward,* FIND-A-GRAVE.COM, https://www.findagrave.com/memorial/112323546/ruth_a_ward (last visited July 1, 2024). Ruth died of pneumonia. *See* STEVENS, *supra* note 5, at 234.

9. For an obituary of James, see *Things About Town & Country,* DEMOCRATIC WATCHMAN (Bellefonte, PA), May 12, 1871, at 8. *See also James Edward Ward,* FIND-A-GRAVE.COM, https://www.findagrave.com/memorial/112323462/james_edward_ward (last visited July 1, 2024). James died of tuberculosis. *See* DI SALVATORE, *supra* note 5, at 36. *See also Threshing Machines &c.,* CENTRE DEMOCRAT (Bellefonte, PA), Oct. 18, 1860, at 4 (one of James's business ads—in pertinent part it reads: "[I am] determined to ... furnish the farmers of Centre and the surrounding counties, with Threshing Machines, Shakers &c., superior to those made by any other mechanic in the country.... Repairing done on the shortest notice").

10. *See* STEVENS, *supra* note 5, at 1 (religion); Robert Beach, *James Edward Ward,* ANCESTRY.COM, https://www.ancestry.com/family-tree/person/tree/45157508/person/25126710061/facts (last visited July 1, 2024) (wedding date); *James Ward in the 1860 United States Federal Census,* ANCESTRY.COM, https://www.ancestry.com/discoveryui-content/view/26714364:7667 (last visited July 1, 2024) [hereinafter 1860 Census] (listing Charles and Ward's births at Lines 24–25); *James Ward in the 1850 United States Federal Census,* ANCESTRY.COM, https://www.ancestry.com/discoveryui-content/view/4694801:8054 (last visited July 1, 2024) (Ida's birth at Line 4).

11. Ward's father's earlier wives were a woman named Caroline (last name unknown) (1815–39) and Ellen Moore (1811–48). *See Caroline Ward,* FIND-A-GRAVE.COM, https://www.findagrave.com/memorial/205881602/caroline_ward (last visited July 1, 2024); *Ellen Moore,* ANCESTRY.COM, https://www.ancestry.com/family-tree/person/tree/48376510/person/12885082917//facts (last visited July 1, 2024). With Caroline, Ward's father had a son named William (1837–41). *See William Ward,* FIND-A-GRAVE.COM, https://www.findagrave.com/memorial/205881660/william_ward (last visited July 1, 2024). With Ellen, Ward's father had a daughter, Mary C. (later Goodrich) (1840–1907), and a son, James M. Sr. (1846–71). *See Mary Caroline Ward Goodrich,* FIND-A-GRAVE.COM, https://www.findagrave.com/memorial/186031675/mary_caroline_goodrich (last visited July 1, 2024); *James Moore Ward, Sr.,* FIND-A-GRAVE.COM, https://www.findagrave.com/memorial/112323508/james_moore_ward (last visited July 1, 2024). For Mary's obituary, see *Deaths and Funerals,* TOPEKA DAILY HERALD, Apr. 15, 1907, at 7 (reporting that Mary died of heart failure). James, on the other hand, died in a railroad collision. *See The P. & E. Railroad Accident,* TITUSVILLE MORN. HERALD (PA), Aug. 29, 1871, at 2 ("James M. Ward, of Renovo, conductor of freight train, killed. Body forwarded to Belfonte [sic] to friends"). Obituaries have not been found for Caroline, Ellen, or William. Likewise, a *Find-a-Grave* webpage has not been found for Ellen.

12. *See* Lamb, *supra* note 6, at n.1. The company, whose slogan for more than a century was "Satisfaction Guaranteed," filed for bankruptcy in 2000 and closed in 2001. In 2004, its name was revived by an unrelated online merchant. *See* ROBIN CHERRY, CATALOG: THE ILLUSTRATED HISTORY OF MAIL ORDER SHOPPING 18–19 (2004).

13. *See* Lamb, *supra* note 6, at n.2.

14. *See Death of John M. Ward—A Well Known Lawyer and a Member of Many Social, Political and Secret Organizations,* BROOKLYN DAILY EAGLE, Feb. 28, 1899, at 16. *See also*

John M. Ward, Find-a-Grave.com, https://www.findagrave.com/memorial/196444219/john-w-ward (last visited July 1, 2024).

15. *See John M.B. Ward Dies at 89; Retired District Court Judge*, Paterson News (NJ), Feb. 16, 1970, at 24. *See also Judge John Marcy Burnoise Ward*, Find-a-Grave.com, https://www.findagrave.com/memorial/254405400/john-marcy_burnoise-ward (last visited July 1, 2024).

16. *See, e.g.*, U.S. Trust Co. of Paterson v. Giveans, 117 A. 46 (N.J. 1922) (listing, *id.* at 46, "John M. Ward" as appellant's counsel).

17. *See* Di Salvatore, *supra* note 5, at 56–58.

18. *See, e.g.*, Lamb, *supra* note 6 ("At age 14, he was dispatched to Penn State, which, like many other colleges, also maintained a prep school for younger students. Here, as Johnny Ward, he first attracted public notice. In the spring of 1875, Ward, a member of Penn State's first baseball team, astounded several thousand onlookers on the Old Main Lawn by demonstrating that a thrown ball could actually be made to curve").

19. *Id.*

20. For a history of the Grays, see Thomas Carson, *Baseball's First World Champions: The Providence Grays*, in Basepaths: The Best of the Minneapolis Review of Baseball: 1981–1987, at 161–66 (Ken LaZebnik & Steve Lehman eds., 1991). As Carson explains, *id.* at 161, the Grays existed from 1878 to 1885.

21. For a history of the National League, see Donald Honig, The National League: An Illustrated History (rev. ed. 1987).

22. For a history of the National Association, see William J. Ryczek, Blackguards and Red Stockings: A History of Baseball's National Association (1992).

23. *See The National Game … Johnny Ward's Brooklyn Debut*, Brooklyn Times, Jan. 2, 1895, at 6.

24. Ward's career statistics as a player can be found at *John Ward*, Baseball-Reference.com, https://www.baseball-reference.com/players/w/wardjo01.shtml (last visited July 1, 2024) [hereinafter *Ward Career Playing Statistics*]. For Ward's managerial statistics, see *John Ward*, Baseball-Reference.com, https://www.baseball-reference.com/managers/wardjo01.shtml (last visited July 1, 2024) (reporting that as a manager, Ward went 412–320, a .563 winning percentage). All the baseball statistics for Ward cited in this essay come from these sources.

25. For a history of the Giants, see Noel Hynd, The Giants of the Polo Grounds: The Glorious Times of Baseball's New York Giants (rev. ed. 2018). *See also infra* note 37.

26. As Di Salvatore points out, Ward missed his first day of law school (Oct. 1, 1883) because he was required to take part in an exhibition game between the Giants and a Brooklyn minor league team. *See* Di Salvatore, *supra* note 5, at 181.

27. In his book, Di Salvatore recounts Ward's time in law school:

> [A]s one of [the law school's] 365 enrollees, [Ward] studied municipal law, constitutional history, political science, and international and constitutional law, and took part in moot courts. He read Blackstone's Commentaries, Perry on trusts, Washburn on real property, Fisher on mortgages, Stephen on pleading, Ortolan's Roman law, Wietersheim's *Geschichte der Volkerwanderung*, Maten's *Recueil des Traites de La Paix*, Calvo's *Droit International*, and many others, including, possibly, Ordronaux's Judicial Aspects of Insanity….
>
> Ward's 1885 law degree was cum laude, by virtue of both his simultaneous study of political science and the fact that he had received an award: second prize (and $50) for "distinction" in constitutional history and constitutional law.

Id. at 183.

Ward also was a member of Story Inn, the local chapter of the Phi Delta Phi national legal fraternity. *See* Directory of the Legal Fraternity of Phi Delta Phi 314 (George A. Katzenberger, ed.) (8th ed. 1909).

28. Ward's dogged pursuit of this degree (which required much more work than his law degree) is recounted in *Sound Body an Aid to the Mind: John M. Ward an Example, Good Work Done by Him in College and on the Diamond*, Buff. Evening News, Jan. 16, 1903, at 7.

29. *See Helen Dauvray's Wedding: A Home Run with Short Stop Ward, of the New York Team; After Meeting Him Socially, the Actress Fell in Love with Baseball—She Attended the Games and Presented a Championship Cup—The Engagement Kept a Secret—The Bridegroom a Lawyer*, EVENING WORLD (NY), Oct. 12, 1887, at 1. For an obituary of Dauvray, see *Famous Actress Dies in D.C. Hotel: Mrs. Helen G. Winterhalter was Known on Stage as Helen Dauvray*, EVENING STAR (DC), Dec. 5, 1923, at 7. *See also Helen Gibson Winterhalter*, FIND-A-GRAVE.COM, https://www.findagrave.com/memorial/49367090/helen-winterhalter (last visited July 1, 2024).

30. For more about Dauvray, her marriage to Ward, and the disappearance of the Dauvray Cup, see John Thorn, *Baseball's Lost Chalice*, SABR, Nov. 3, 2011, https://sabr.org/latest/our-game-baseballs-lost-chalice/. *See also* HELEN DAUVRAY: THE ACTRESS WHO LOVED BASEBALL (Greg Gubi ed., 2024). Two years after the couple's divorce, Ward was sued by the Hotel Vendome when Dauvray failed to pay a $260.61 bill. In court, Ward successfully disclaimed liability on the ground that the charges had been incurred after the couple had separated. *See Johnny Ward Wins His Suit*, BUFF. EVENING NEWS, May 16, 1895, at 5 (reporting that the suit "was dismissed by Judge [Simon M.] Ehrlich in the city court").

31. Originally released by Philadelphia's Athletic Publishing Company, the book now is in the public domain and numerous reprints (of varying quality) are available. A digital version of the original can be found on the website of the Library of Congress at https://www.loc.gov/item/05023915/ (last visited July 1, 2024).

32. *See* John Q. Barrett, *Milbank Loses Hope ... and Hadley and Tweed and McCloy*, N.Y. L.J., Mar. 5, 2019, at 6 (recounting the firm's history). For an obituary of Howland (1835–1913), see *Henry E. Howland Dead: Was Former Justice of Marine Court and Prominent at Bar—Ancestor on Mayflower—Served City as Alderman, as Head of Tax Department and in Militia*, N.Y. TRIB., Nov. 9, 1913, at 11. *See also Henry Elias Howland*, FIND-A-GRAVE. COM, https://www.findagrave.com/memorial/94830753/henry-elias-howland (last visited July 1, 2024). For an obituary of Murray (1856–1943), see *George W. Murray, Lawyer Since 1876: Leader of New York Bar for Many Years and Counsel to Rockefellers is Dead—Columbia Paid Honor—Chair Founded in Recognition of Aid to Foundations in Their Legal Researches*, N.Y. TIMES, Apr. 26, 1943, at 19. *See also George Welwood Murray*, FIND-A-GRAVE.COM, https://www.findagrave.com/memorial/228417295/george-welwood-murray (last visited July 1, 2024).

33. 24 Abb. N. Cas. 393 (Sup. Ct. 1890). A less complete version of the case is available at 9 N.Y.S. 779.

34. *See Metropolitan Exhibition*, 24 Abb. N. Cas. at 418–19. For an obituary of O'Brien (1852–1937), see *Morgan J. O'Brien Dead at Age of 85: Former Member of Supreme Court Succumbs at His Park Av. Home of Pneumonia—A Lawyer for 62 Years—Was an Equitable Trustee with Cleveland and Westinghouse—Prominent Catholic Layman*, N.Y. TIMES, June 17, 1937, at 23. *See also Judge Morgan Joseph O'Brien*, FIND-A-GRAVE.COM, https://www.findagrave.com/memorial/184230275/morgan-joseph-o'brien (last visited July 1, 2024).

35. *Metropolitan Exhibition*, 24 Abb. N. Cas. at 419 n.a1. For an obituary of Lawrence (1832–1917), see *A. Riker Lawrence, Ex-Justice, is Dead: Jurist of New York Supreme Court for 28 Years Expires in His Eighty-Fifth Year—Once Nominee for Mayor—Author of Legal Works was Twice the President of the St. Nicholas Society*, N.Y. TIMES, Feb. 15, 1917, at 11. *See also Judge Abraham Riker Lawrence*, FIND-A-GRAVE.COM, https://www.findagrave.com/memorial/69566688/abraham-riker-lawrence (last visited July 1, 2024).

36. For a further history of the Players League, see ROBERT B. ROSS, THE GREAT BASEBALL REVOLT: THE RISE AND FALL OF THE 1890 PLAYERS LEAGUE (2016). The third major baseball league during the 1890 season was the American Association. It folded following the 1891 season. For a history of the American Association, see DAVID NEMEC, THE BEER AND WHISKEY LEAGUE: THE ILLUSTRATED HISTORY OF THE AMERICAN ASSOCIATION—BASEBALL'S RENEGADE MAJOR LEAGUE (2004). With the demise of the American Association, the National League once again had a monopoly, which ended in 1901 with the emergence of the American League. *See* WARREN N. WILBERT, THE ARRIVAL OF THE AMERICAN LEAGUE: BAN JOHNSON AND THE 1901 CHALLENGE TO [THE] NATIONAL LEAGUE MONOPOLY (2007).

37. For the team's history, see, e.g., DONALD HONIG, THE BROOKLYN DODGERS: AN ILLUSTRATED TRIBUTE (1981). During its time in Brooklyn (1883–1957), the club went by many different names: Atlantics, Bridegrooms, Dodgers, Grays, Grooms, Robins, Superbas, and Trolley Dodgers. Following the 1957 season, both the Dodgers (Los Angeles) and the Giants (San Francisco) moved to California. *See* ROBERT E. MURPHY, AFTER MANY A SUMMER: THE PASSING OF THE GIANTS AND DODGERS AND A GOLDEN AGE IN NEW YORK BASEBALL (2009).

38. For more about the Temple Cup, see, e.g., JERRY LANSCHE, GLORY FADES AWAY: THE NINETEENTH-CENTURY WORLD SERIES REDISCOVERED (1991).

39. *See John M. Ward Will Retire: He Says That This Will be His Last Season in Baseball*, SUN (NY), Oct. 2, 1894, at 5.

40. *In the Field of Sports—John M. Ward Says His Retirement is Final*, N.Y. DAILY TRIB., Feb. 3, 1895, at 4. Despite Ward's emphatic denial, some observers refused to believe him. *See, e.g., On the Ball Field: Pick Up from the Amateur and Professional Diamonds*, BROOKLYN CITIZEN, Mar. 30, 1895, at 3 ("[Sportswriter] O.P. Caylor still insists that John M. Ward will don a uniform and return to New York's second base before the season is half over"). When Ward did not return, Caylor, ignoring his earlier prediction, congratulated Ward for refusing to come back:

> While many of the New-York papers are clamoring loudly for the return of Johnny Ward to the [on-field] management of the Giants, O.P. Caylor comments as follows in the New-York Herald: "I give Johnny Ward credit for being as shrewd as men grow, and for that reason he should make a good lawyer if he has the courage to stick to it. He was shrewd enough to get out of baseball last year at the right time."

Diamond Gossip: News of the Professional Players and Matters of Interest to the Amateurs, BUFF. COURIER EXPRESS, July 3, 1895, at 10.

41. From time to time, however, Ward did play in various amateur games. In July 1896, for example, Ward participated in two games (held on consecutive Saturdays) that pitted the Manhattan Elks Lodge against the Brooklyn Elks Lodge. In the second game, while manning second base for the Manhattanites, Ward engineered a triple play and hit a home run. *See Local Elks Lose Again: Deciding Game with the New Yorkers at Eastern Park—A Wonderful Contest Which Came to an End When Umpire Simpson Fled; Johnny Ward Triple Play*, BROOKLYN DAILY EAGLE, July 24, 1896, at 4.

42. *Baseball is Risky: [The Owners of the] New-York [Giants Have] Sunk More Than a Quarter of a Million [Dollars] in Three Years*, BUFF. EXPRESS, Jan. 1, 1895, at 9 (paragraphing slightly altered for improved readability).

43. For a further discussion, see Bill Lamb, *Edward B. Talcott*, SABR, https://sabr.org/bioproj/person/edward-b-talcott/ (last visited July 1, 2024). Although they later would become adversaries, Ward initially approved of the sale to Freedman and willingly sold his Giants stock (30 shares) to Freedman, which helped Freedman gain majority control of the team. *Id.*

44. *Id.*

45. *See* DI SALVATORE, *supra* note 5, at 356. Stevens claims that Ward did not stay with Fletcher's firm because he found Fletcher too conservative. *See* STEVENS, *supra* note 5, at 181.

46. *See Countryman Who Turned Out to be a Phenom*, BUFF. EVENING TIMES, Nov. 15, 1900, at 10. Johnson and Ward's relationship is described further *infra* notes 62 and 66 and accompanying text.

47. For biographical materials about Fletcher, see *Austin Fletcher*, HOPEDALE LEGACY, https://www.hope1842.com/mendonfletcher-html/ (last visited July 1, 2024). *See also Object to Probate of $3,000,000 Will; Cousins of Austin B. Fletcher Protest Bequest of Bulk of Estate to Tufts College, Charge Undue Influence; Other Schools, Including Boston University, Receive Bequests of Small Amounts*, N.Y. TIMES, Sept. 12, 1923, at 31. Fletcher does not have a *Find-a-Grave* webpage.

48. *See G.W.P. Knott Must Pay Alimony*, N.Y. TIMES, May 18, 1895, at 8.

49. *Johnny Ward, Lawyer: One of 215 Candidates, Male and Female, for Admission to the Bar*, EVENING WORLD (NY), June 15, 1895, at 5.

50. *Id.*

51. *See Lawyer John M. Ward Now: The Ex-Ball Player Has Passed the Examination*, BROOKLYN DAILY EAGLE, July 15, 1895, at 1 (explaining that "Out of this large class there were but few rejected...").

52. *See Lawyers Sworn In*, BROOKLYN DAILY EAGLE, July 19, 1895, at 12.

53. *See News of the Courts in Brief*, N.Y. TIMES, Oct. 22, 1895, at 14 ("John M. Ward of 11 Pine Street, the ball player, was sworn in before United States Commissioner [John A.] Shields yesterday as an attorney at law, and admitted to practice in the Federal courts").

54. *See Sporting*, BUFF. SUN. MORN. NEWS, Aug. 25, 1895, at 9.

55. *League Magnates—No Sign of Friction Seen at Yesterday's Meeting*, BUFF. EXPRESS, Nov. 14, 1895, at 11.

56. *J.M. Ward Gets His Release: The National Board Decides Against President Freedman—His Reservation Illegal*, BROOKLYN DAILY EAGLE, Feb. 24, 1896, at 4.

57. *See Louisville After Johnny Ward*, BROOKLYN DAILY EAGLE, May 1, 1896, at 11.

58. *See Base Ball Notes*, BROOKLYN DAILY EAGLE, May 16, 1896, at 4.

59. *See* John Saccoman, *John T. Brush*, SABR, https://sabr.org/bioproj/person/john-t-brush/ (last visited July 1, 2024). Brush, who also owned the Baltimore Orioles, was forced to sell both teams following his purchase of the Giants. *Id.*

60. *See Freedman's "Mets" Ousted: The Atlantic League Magnates Weary of an Autocrat—Representatives of the New-York Club's President Make a Strenuous Protest, But It Avails Them Naught*, N.Y. DAILY TRIB., July 11, 1896, at 12. At the time of their expulsion, the Metropolitans were 30–32. The Athletics went 27–37 in finishing the Metropolitans' schedule. *See Atlantic League*, BASEBALL-REFERENCE.COM, https://www.baseball-reference.com/bullpen/Atlantic_League#Minor_League_1896-1900 (last visited July 1, 2024).

61. *See* National Exhibition Co. v. Crane, 66 N.Y.S. 361 (App. Div. 1900), *aff'd*, 60 N.E. 768 (N.Y. 1901).

62. Johnson and Ward had met during the Players League, when Johnson, a baseball enthusiast and the scion of a wealthy family that owned trolley car companies in Brooklyn, Cleveland, and Indianapolis, had financially backed the Cleveland Infants. *See General*, MORN. REC. MERIDEN (CT), Nov. 13, 1897, at 5 ("John M. Ward has struck it rich through baseball. He does all the law work for Al Johnson, the rich street railway owner and rail manufacturer. Johnson, it will be remembered, backed the Cleveland brotherhood team in royal style"). Unsurprisingly, much of Ward's work for Johnson involved defending the NERC against negligence lawsuits. *See, e.g.*, New York Condensed-Milk Co. v. Nassau Elec. R. Co., 60 N.Y.S. 234 (App. Div. 1899); Cunningham v. Nassau Elec. R. Co., 58 N.Y.S. 22 (App. Div. 1899); McNamara v. Nassau Elec. R. Co., 57 N.Y.S. 504 (App. Div. 1899); Harvey v. Nassau Elec. R. Co., 55 N.Y.S. 20 (App. 1898). For a further look at the NERC (which later became the Brooklyn and Queens Transit Corporation), see JAMES CLIFFORD GRELLER, BROOKLYN TROLLEY CARS FROM THE BRT TO THE B&QT (3d ed. 2013). The last trolley car in Brooklyn stopped operating in 1956. *See Trolleys Just a Memory Now in Boro*, BROOKLYN DAILY, Nov. 7, 1956, at 15.

63. *Brooklyns to Play the Phillies*, BROOKLYN CITIZEN, Apr. 24, 1900, at 6. The paper's claim that Ward already was making more money as a lawyer than as a ballplayer is incorrect. Ward's highest salary as a ballplayer was $7,000 (earned in 1891 while playing for the Grooms). *See Ward Career Playing Statistics*, *supra* note 24 (under "Salaries"). Ward eventually did top this figure as a lawyer, see *infra* note 64, but it would take him several more years to do so.

64. *Countryman*, *supra* note 46. As explained *supra* note 63, Ward's salary as a lawyer eventually did exceed the club's offer—in 1907, for example, it was reported that Ward was earning $10,000 a year from his law practice. *See John M. Ward a Farmer: Noted Lawyer-Golfer-Ball Player Raising Garden Truck and Chickens on Long Island*, BROOKLYN DAILY EAGLE, Jan. 7, 1907, at 10.

65. For a further profile of Baldwin, whose daughter Faith became a famous romance novelist, see *Stephen C. Baldwin*, YONKERS HERALD (NY), July 30, 1923, at 6. *See also Stephen Charles Baldwin*, FIND-A-GRAVE.COM, https://www.findagrave.com/memorial/108539445/stephen-charles-baldwin (last visited July 1, 2024).

66. *See, e.g.*, Perry v. Metropolitan St. Ry. Co., 74 N.Y.S. 1 (App. Div. 1902); Hubener v. Heide, 70 N.Y.S. 1115 (App. Div. 1901); Schriever v. Brooklyn Heights R. Co., 63 N.Y.S. 217 (App. Div. 1900); Kennedy v. Allentown Foundry & Mach. Works, 63 N.Y.S. 195 (App. Div. 1900). Ward's practice suffered a blow, however, in 1901 when Al Johnson, Ward's biggest client, unexpectedly died at the age of 40. *See Albert L. Johnson, the Trolley Magnate, Dead: One of Brooklyn's Most Enterprising Citizens Succumbs to Heart Disease—Built the Nassau Railroad; Revolutionized the Street Railroad Service Here*, Brooklyn Times, July 3, 1901, at 3.

67. *See* Russell v. National Exhibition Co., 69 N.Y.S. 732 (App. Div. 1901), *appeal after remand*, 93 N.Y.S. 1145 (App. Div. 1905), *aff'd*, 81 N.E. 1175 (N.Y. 1907) (ordering the Giants to pay Frank Russell, Pfeffer's assignee, the balance due on Pfeffer's contract). Along with the *Russell* case, Ward also represented pitcher Amos W. Rusie in a similar successful lawsuit against the Giants that settled out of court and produced no reported decisions.

68. *See* Griffin v. Brooklyn Ball Club, 73 N.Y.S. 864 (App. Div. 1902), *aff'd*, 66 N.E. 1109 (N.Y. 1903); Boston Baseball Ass'n v. Brooklyn Baseball Club, 75 N.Y.S. 1076 (Sup. Ct. 1902). The *Griffin* case is particularly notable because in it, Ward argued for, rather than against, the reserve clause. Despite Ward's efforts, Griffin won a $2,349 judgment, after which he retired from baseball. For a further discussion, see Scott Fiesthumel, *Mike Griffin*, SABR, https://sabr.org/bioproj/person/mike-griffin-2/ (last visited July 1, 2024).

69. *See Local Improvements Board: That of the Sixth District Transacts Much Business*, Brooklyn Daily Eagle, Oct. 18, 1898, at 13 (describing Ward's appearance before the board to respond to a citizens' petition complaining about the NERC's equipment depots).

70. *Baldwin & Ward No More: Members of Law Firm Agree to Dissolve, But Will Finish Up Pending Business*, Brooklyn Daily Eagle, Jan. 25, 1903, at 3.

71. *See Pinehurst Golf Finals—Beckwith Defeats Staten Island Champion in Men's Event—Women's Championship Won by Mrs. M.D. Patterson—Keen Competitions Mark Ending of the Tournament*, N.Y. Times, Apr. 1, 1903, at 6. The reference in this headline to "Staten Island Champion" is a reference to Ward.

72. For Kate's obituary, see *infra* note 95.

73. *See "Johnny" Ward Married: Former Baseball Player Quietly Weds Miss Katherine Waas*, Brooklyn Citizen, Sept. 19, 1903, at 2 (reporting that the only guests were Kate's cousin (a "Mrs. Leslie," often incorrectly identified as Kate's sister); Brooklyn Superbas manager Edward H. "Ned" Hanlon; and Frederick S. Martyn, Ward's new law partner). Because Ward's divorce decree from Helen included a clause prohibiting him from remarrying during Helen's lifetime (a standard punishment imposed on the party whose actions had caused the divorce), Ward had to go to court to have the ban lifted. *See John M. Ward Marries Again*, Balt. Sun, Sept. 21, 1903, at 3 ("A few hours before the ceremony Supreme Court Justice [D. Cady] Herrick, in Brooklyn, on the presentation of affidavits by Mr. Ward's lawyer, granted an order dissolving the injunction against his remarrying, which had been in force since his first wife, Helen Dauvray, the actress, obtained a divorce decree 10 years ago").

74. *See Golf Club in Arms: Fox Hills, a Bachelor Organization, Opposes the Invasion of Women Golfers*, Buff. Comm., Nov. 2, 1903, at 5.

75. Lamb, *supra* note 6 (footnotes omitted). Neither Judge Dunne nor Judge Thomas published an opinion.

76. For Martyn's obituary, see *Frederick S. Martyn*, Daily News (NY), May 25, 1957, at K3. Martyn does not have a *Find-a-Grave* webpage. Martyn was a graduate of Dartmouth College (B.A., 1894) and Yale University (LL.B., 1896) and had worked for the well-known Manhattan law firm of Evarts, Choate & Beaman before joining Baldwin & Ward.

77. *See* The Trow (formerly Wilson's) Copartnership and Corporation Directory of the Boroughs of Manhattan and the Bronx—City of New York 761 (Mar. 1906) (listing Ward & Martyn as "dissolved").

78. *See Ward a Farmer, supra* note 64. *See also John M. Ward to Join Long Island Golfers: New Jersey and Staten Island Champion Will Soon Be Enrolled in Garden City Club*, Brooklyn Daily Eagle, Apr. 18, 1906, at 14 ("John M. Ward, golfer, baseball player and all-around sportsman, is soon to transfer his golfing allegiance to Long Island. He recently

brought a historic residence with a large tract of land, a trout lake, etc., at Babylon and so will give up his summer residence in New Jersey. His name is now on the waiting list at the Garden City Golf Club. This does not necessarily mean that he will drop his connection with the Fox Hills and Montclair clubs, at least not for the present...."); *John M. Ward's Country Home Near Babylon*, BROOKLYN DAILY EAGLE, Dec. 8, 1907, at 8 (explaining that the estate's name was "The Reel" because its previous owner was the Rod & Reel fishing club).

79. *See Charles Ward in the New York, New York, U.S., Index to Death Certificates, 1862–1948*, ANCESTRY.COM, https://www.ancestry.com/discoveryui-content/view/1462416: 61778 [hereinafter Charles Ward Death Certificate]. *See also Charles L Ward*, FIND-A-GRAVE.COM, https://www.findagrave.com/memorial/111536664/charles_l_ward (last visited July 1, 2024). An obituary has not been found for Charles.

80. *See* Charles Ward Death Certificate, *supra* note 79.

81. *See J.M. Ward in Politics: One Time "Pro" Ball Player May Dispense Justice in Babylon Town; Belmont Leaders Beaten*, BROOKLYN DAILY EAGLE, Mar. 14, 1907, at 18.

82. *See Babylon Politics Quite Strenuous: A Review of the Situation Just Prior to the Final Nominations; Republicans are Chirking Up a Bit, But Politics are Generally Acknowledged to be Uncertain—John Montgomery Ward, Former Ball Player, Suggested for Justice*, BROOKLYN TIMES, Mar. 15, 1907, at 8 ("There was talk of running John Montgomery Ward, the old-time professional ball tosser, for Justice of the Peace in the Second District.... Mr. Ward, who is a practicing lawyer in New York, is a very estimable gentleman, but his residence in Bablyon has been so brief that it is hardly fair to name him for so important a position").

83. *See* McDonald v. Degnon-McLean Cont. Co., 109 N.Y.S. 519 (App. Div. 1908), *decision after remand*, 125 N.Y.S. 295 (App. Div. 1910), *aff'd*, 98 N.E. 1107 (N.Y. 1912) (Ward represented a pedestrian who was injured when he fell into a poorly marked open subway trench).

84. *See* Stewart v. Hinkle Iron Co., 125 N.Y.S. 1073 (App. Div. 1910) (Ward represented an iron worker who was struck by a girder due to the alleged negligence of his co-workers).

85. *See* Walsh v. Hyde & Behman Amusement Co., 98 N.Y.S. 960 (App. Div. 1906) (Ward represented a theater patron who was injured when he was ejected from a production of "The Empire Show," allegedly because he was drunk and behaving obnoxiously).

86. *John M. Ward Served on the Jury*, BROOKLYN TIMES, Aug. 27, 1909, at 5.

87. Ward's main backer was Charles Ebbets, the Superbas' owner, while Brown's candidacy was pushed by Martin S. "Stanley" Robison, the owner of the St. Louis Cardinals. *See Ebbets Takes Stand; Will Support Ward—President of Brooklyn Club Issues Statement About the National League*, BROOKLYN DAILY EAGLE, Dec. 7, 1909, at 15.

88. For a further look at the election, see Marshall Adesman, *1909 Winter Meetings: If It Takes All Winter*, SABR, https://sabr.org/journal/article/91198/ (last visited July 1, 2024).

89. When the White Sox were mentioned during opening argument, for example, a befuddled Hand asked: "What are the White Sox?" William F. Lamb, *The Ward v. Johnson Libel Case: The Last Battle of the Great Baseball War*, 2 BASE BALL: A JOURNAL OF THE EARLY GAME 47, 47 (Fall 2008). Hand (1872–1961), of course, later would become one of the most famous judges in American history. For a further discussion, see GERALD GUNTHER, LEARNED HAND: THE MAN AND THE JUDGE (2d ed. 2010).

90. Lamb, *supra* note 6. Although Johnson appealed the jury's decision to the U.S. Court of Appeals for the Second Circuit, on the day the appeal was supposed to be heard Johnson sent Ward a check for $1,000, thereby mooting the appeal. *See Johnson Pays $1,000 to Ward*, CHI. DAILY TRIB., Nov. 23, 1912, at 10.

91. Lamb, *supra* note 6. For a history of the Braves (founded 1871), see BRADSHER HAYES, 150 YEARS OF THE BRAVES: FROM BOSTON TO MILWAUKEE TO ATLANTA (2022). For a history of the Federal League, see ROBERT PEYTON WIGGINS, THE FEDERAL LEAGUE OF BASE BALL CLUBS: THE HISTORY OF AN OUTLAW MAJOR LEAGUE, 1914–1915 (2009). As Wiggins mentions, *id.* at 339–40, a piece of the Federal League persists to this day in the form of Wrigley Field. Home since 1916 to the National League's Chicago Cubs, it was built in 1914 for the Federal League's Chicago Whales and originally was known as Weeghman Park (in honor of Whales' owner Charles H. Weeghman).

92. *See, e.g.,* Central Trust Co. of N.Y. v. Dewey, 120 N.E. 859 (N.Y. 1918) (will construction case); Wenzel v. Patrick Ryan Const. Corp., 119 N.E. 1085 (N.Y. 1918) (wrongful death case); *In re* Atterbury, 118 N.E. 858 (N.Y. 1918) (attorney's lien case); and Larkin v. New York Tel. Co., 114 N.E. 1043 (N.Y. 1917) (wrongful death case).

93. 195 N.Y.S. 957 (Surr. Ct. 1922).

94. *See John M. Ward Dies Suddenly in South: Famous Baseball Player and Noted Golfer Succumbs Suddenly in Georgia Hospital: Was with Giants in '80s: Led Them to Two World's Titles—Organized Players' League to Fight National—Friends Shocked,* N.Y. Times, Mar. 5, 1925, at 17. For a copy of Ward's death certificate, see *Katherine [sic] Ward in the Georgia, U.S., Death Records, 1914–1940,* Ancestry.com, https://www.ancestry.com/discoveryui-content/view/45218307:2562.

95. *See Services Are Held for John M. Ward: Funeral for Noted Baseball Star and Golfer Takes Place at West Islip Episcopal Church,* N.Y. Times, Mar. 8, 1925, at 3 (Sports). *See also supra* note 7 (*Ward's Find-a-Grave Webpage*). Kate is buried next to Ward. *See Katherine Waas Ward,* Find-a-Grave.com, https://www.findagrave.com/memorial/144025036/katherine_ward (last visited July 1, 2024). *See also Mrs. K.M. Ward Dies; Widow of Hall of Famer,* Daily Argus (Mount Vernon, NY), Apr. 13, 1966, at 2.

96. *See Estate of John M. Ward Appraised at $58,122,* Brooklyn Daily Eagle, Nov. 3, 1925, at 2.

97. *See* S. Morgan Friedman, *The Inflation Calculator,* https://westegg.com/inflation/ (last visited July 1, 2024) (converting 1925 dollars to 2023 dollars).

98. *See* Town of Babylon, *North Babylon Community Profile,* https://www.townofbabylon.com/624/North-Babylon-Community-Profile (last visited July 1, 2024).

99. Burt Solomon, *Same Old Ball Game: How One 19th-Century Player Organized Against Management Tactics,* N.Y. Times, Sept. 19, 1999, at BR24 (reviewing Di Salvatore, *supra* note 5). *See also* Lamb, *supra* note 6 ("Cool and with an innate aura of superiority about him, Ward was respected, but never much liked by teammates. Several were reportedly not even on speaking terms with him").

CHAPTER 6

Wesley Branch Rickey (1967)

RICHARD D. FRIEDMAN

When Wesley Branch Rickey (December 20, 1881–December 9, 1965)[1] of Portsmouth, Ohio (in the southeastern corner of the state, along the Ohio River), applied to the University of Michigan ("UM") Law School in Ann Arbor in 1909, the application process was both informal and simple. It is amusing, therefore, to think about the personal statement he might have submitted if he had to deal with today's much more imposing on-line application form.[2] Perhaps he would have written something like this:

> I have a combination of credentials that I suspect will make me unique not only in this year's entering class, but among all the students you ever have admitted or ever will admit. Though I have no high school diploma,[3] I have not one but two college degrees, a B. Litt. (1904) and a B.A. (1906), both from Ohio Wesleyan University ("OWU").[4] What is more, I have done a good deal of teaching, at both the preparatory[5] and college levels,[6] and among the wide variety of college courses I have taught has been a series in law, for when my law teacher at OWU died, I took over his courses.[7] I have read law on my own[8] and have done extra class work in law at the Ohio State University ("OSU")— but to be the kind of lawyer I aspire to be I need a law degree.[9]
>
> I was an athlete in college.[10] While still working towards my degrees, I began my coaching career, in baseball, basketball, and football,[11] and I have served as the athletic director at both OWU[12] and at Allegheny College ("AC").[13]
>
> I also have been a temperance and political campaigner.[14] As administrator of our YMCA, I have hosted such speakers as Jane Addams, Jacob Riis, and Booker T. Washington.[15] And for parts of four summers, I have had a job that would be the envy of just about any boy in America—I have been a big-league baseball player.[16]

Rickey would have had to think hard in deciding which optional supplemental essays to write. For fear of over-eagerness—and Rickey certainly was eager—UM limits students to two such essays.[17] Rickey might have

106

chosen to respond to a request to "[d]escribe a challenge, failure or set-back" in his life and state how he overcame it.[18] Even then, he would have had to make a choice. He probably would *not* have chosen to elaborate on his interest in the law school by saying that he was motivated in large part by a desire to make himself appear more suitable to his father-in-law.[19] (On June 1, 1906, Rickey had married Jane ["Jennie"] Moulton [1882–1971],[20] who had been his hometown sweetheart, in Lucasville, Ohio.[21]) Rather, he might have explained that by determined effort he had overcome a child-hood stutter that had caused him to be mocked by his peers[22]; or that he had failed by a small margin to gain admission to the service academies, apparently because he knew so little history[23]; or that when he first came to college his Latin was not up to the expected level, but by hard work he had excelled at it.[24]

Perhaps even better, Rickey might have described how, to his bitter disappointment, he had lost his eligibility for college sports due to a short stint with a semi-professional baseball team,[25] and how the shutting of this door had opened the door to his becoming first a college coach[26] and then a college athletic director at an extraordinarily young age. Or he might have mentioned that his refusal, on religious grounds, to play on Sundays had hampered his baseball career, but he had adhered to his principles—and even insisted that a clause be included in his contracts excusing him from Sunday play.[27]

But a more gripping story would have been how he was at the time confronting and beating a life-threatening illness—tuberculosis—with treatments at the Trudeau Sanatorium at Saranac Lake, New York.[28]

If Rickey had not yet caught the attention of the dean of admissions, he could have done so with an optional essay describing his "experiences and perspectives" that would contribute to the law school's goal "to expand and diversify the identities of people in the legal profession"[29]:

> When I coached the OWU baseball team, we had a black member on the team named Charles Thomas. At one point, the University of Kentucky refused to play us if Thomas played; I insisted vigorously that we would play with him or not at all, and the Kentuckians relented.[30]
>
> On another occasion, when we checked into a hotel in South Bend, Indiana, the hotel clerk would not let Thomas check in because he was black. I arranged for Thomas to share my room. When I came up to the room, he was rubbing at his skin, saying he wished it were white.[31] Confronted with such a blatant display of prejudice and the harmful consequences of it, I was reminded of the reaction of my great hero Abraham Lincoln, who, when as a very young man, witnessed a slave auction in New Orleans and afterwards said: "If ever I get a chance to hit that thing [meaning slavery], I'll hit it hard!"[32] I felt the same way, and I still do. I still hear Thomas crying, and I expect I always will.[33]

Life as a Law Student

Throughout his already extraordinarily accomplished career, Rickey's goal had been to put himself in a position, educationally and financially, to attend law school.[34] Discharged from the Trudeau Sanitarium with a warning that his health was still vulnerable,[35] Rickey arrived alone in Ann Arbor in the fall of 1909 while Jennie stayed with family in Ohio.[36]

William W. Cook, of the Class of 1882, had not yet made the huge gift that financed the magnificent set of buildings that UM's law school still occupies.[37] Founded in 1859, the law school was housed in a single building along State Street, northwest of the main university quadrangle; in what must be a rare anomaly in university development, the space occupied by a large building a century ago is now a grassy, tree-shaded plot.[38]

UM's law school—at the time still designated a department—was much more closely integrated with the rest of the university than U.S. law schools are today. Most law students did not have an undergraduate degree, and they were treated on a par with undergraduates in other fields. They appeared in the university yearbook alongside students of literature and engineering, and some of them participated in varsity sports. The law school, however, was in the midst of a significant transition. It was instituting more demanding admissions standards and, beginning with the class graduating in 1910, it was granting a new degree—the J.D. (juris doctor)—to go along with the traditional LL.B. (bachelor of laws). The J.D. was reserved for students who had already received a bachelor's degree in another field from a reputable college or university (OWU was safely on the list), or who were simultaneously working towards one from UM, and who performed to a high standard in three-quarters of their classes.[39]

Harry B. Hutchins (1847–1930), the longtime dean of the law school (1895–1910), would soon take over as UM's president upon the retirement of the venerable James B. Angell.[40] The small law faculty was composed entirely of white men. But not so the student body. The law school always had been integrated racially and had graduated its first African American student, Gabriel F. Hargo, in 1870.[41] Likewise, women had been welcomed for decades, and by 1910 nearly 40 had graduated.[42] Among Rickey's more than 200 classmates were at least two women and at least four African Americans—not, to be sure, a "critical mass," but a genuine presence, nonetheless.

Because Rickey already had studied some law, he hoped to be granted advanced standing. This matter was left to be determined later.[43] Evidently, the school administration concluded that Rickey had most, but not all, of the credits necessary for him to begin as a second-year student, so he took the full 30-credit second-year curriculum supplemented by nine first-year credits of contracts and torts. With matters resolved, Rickey was admitted to the class of 1911, thereby allowing him to graduate in just two years.

Rickey proved to be a very capable student. In his first semester, although still affected by his tuberculosis—he wrote to Jennie that he was exhausted after attending a UM football game[44]—he received a "+" mark, indicating performance qualifying towards the J.D., for 13 of his 15 second-year credits.[45] (Rickey's "make-up" first-year courses appear not to have been graded.) And yet, Rickey was not happy with himself or with his situation. As a result, he experienced a sense of drift that plagued his stern conscience. In a remarkable letter to his parents—Emily (née Brown) (1858–1935)[46] and Jacob F. Rickey (1854–1939)[47]—dated January 13, 1910, he wrote:

> Yes I'm tired and sick of college. I've been around one too long & I want to get out and do some one thing and bend every effort—I may fizzle about for a while but if I get a good grip on some one thing—& have a purpose—well I guess I'll do my best not to make God as ashamed of me as he has been these last few years.

Almost as an afterthought, the end of the letter revealed news that suggested that Rickey perhaps had found the path that would lead to his life's mission:

> I have secured the position of Baseball coach here—thanks to many good friends. It was really their victory for the odds were against me & I counted for very little. My greatest joy is not the paltry job or its incidents but the fact of being known by men of such standing and character that their commendation places me above the pull and push of the other fellow. It shall ever be my steadfast purpose to keep, increase and yet merit the esteem those men have expressed for me. No more time or space—Love to all Branch[48]

Cloying as that passage may have been, in at least two respects Rickey's reporting was accurate. The pay *was* rather paltry—$700 for the season, but with UM having an option (perhaps reflecting lack of faith in a law student's ability to coach the team) to deduct up to $100 to pay one or more assistant coaches.[49] And it does appear that many friends had written in support of Rickey—though he did not mention to his parents that he had carefully orchestrated the campaign, which seems to have been so persistent that UM athletic director Philip G. Bartelme concluded that the only way to stop the flood of letters was to hire the young man behind them.[50]

There was one other aspect of the incident that Rickey did not report: The consent of the law school was essential to the deal. The story often has been told that Hutchins and Rickey had a long meeting, at the end of which Hutchins agreed, contingent on a promise by Rickey that he would be in class and prepared every day.[51] Even while throwing himself with characteristic vigor into his new job, and carrying an overload of courses, Rickey performed creditably, with 11 "+" credits and four "-" credits.[52]

Although it sometimes has been said that Rickey made the law review,[53] this is inaccurate. In this period, the faculty chose the review's members, and Rickey was not among those selected, at least not formally.[54] While his grades were good enough to have made him a marginal candidate, it is likely that the time burdens of his coaching job rendered the question of his candidacy moot.

The UM baseball team had an excellent record under Rickey's predecessor, Lewis W. "Sport" McAllister, but it had lost several key players, not only to graduation but also to charges of professionalism, the same issue that had ended Rickey's own college playing career. Rickey's coaching style was didactic—he limited scrimmage time, held evening lectures on the finer points of the game, and seems always to have been talking and giving instruction, baseball-related or otherwise[55]—but also was inventive and even daring; he actively promoted "adventure."[56]

Bolstered by Rickey's energy, enthusiasm, and deep knowledge, the team finished the season with a 17–8 record—not outstanding but very satisfactory given its low expectations.[57] Clearly Rickey's superiors were pleased; in June 1910, just a week after his contract expired, Rickey signed a new contract to coach the 1911 season, this time for $1,000 and with no contingent deduction for an assistant coach.[58]

Rickey and Jennie spent the summer of 1910 in the Rockies, where he felt deeply refreshed by the mountain air.[59] Returning to UM for the Fall 1910 semester, and without the distraction of his coaching job, Rickey earned 15 "+" credits and only one "-" credit. In the spring, while coaching once again, his numbers were 13 and three. One of the minus credits was for Practice Court. By this point, perhaps some wiggle room in Rickey's deal with Hutchins had developed, or perhaps the law school's new dean (Henry M. Bates) was less demanding, because the times for baseball practice and Practice Court were in direct conflict.[60] In any event, Rickey easily satisfied the requirements for the J.D.[61]

Meanwhile, just before UM's first game in 1911, Rickey signed contracts to manage the team in 1912 and 1913, with a provision of $300 for expenses, presumably to account for the fact that he would no longer be residing in Ann Arbor, and his salary rising to a relatively munificent $1,200 in 1913.[62] In the end, the 1911 team, beset with injuries, turned in a disappointing 16–10–1 record.[63] But Rickey's leadership still drew plaudits. In the yearbook, the student manager—who did not hesitate to offer critical comments—noted:

[Rickey] was the hardest worker on the squad, kept everyone working to correct this or that mistake, and taught the game from the beginning to the end. He had the "pep" and the head for the team, and without him there would have been no season to write up.[64]

Rickey, Crow & Ebbert

With his long-sought law degree in hand, Rickey intended baseball to be a sideline. In early August 1911, at a national convention of his college fraternity (Delta Tau Delta) in Chicago, he met with two fraternity brothers from OWU, Howard M. Crow (1882–1963)[65] and Frank B. Ebbert (1879–1938).[66] Like Rickey, both men were recent law school graduates. Crow and Rickey had been roommates during Rickey's senior year at OWU, and they had daydreamed about being law partners together. Now, with Ebbert, they decided to make the dream a reality, and they quickly settled on Boise, Idaho, as an ideal place, by virtue of climate, geography, and growth potential, to hang their shingles.[67]

The fledgling partnership—dubbed Rickey, Crow & Ebbert[68]—took offices on the fourth floor of the elegant new Idaho Building[69] at $17.50 per month.[70] Rickey was admitted to the Idaho bar on September 19, 1911.[71] True to form, soon afterwards he successfully tutored at least one other bar exam candidate.[72]

Rickey later recalled that during his time in Boise he handled only one case. His client was a man accused of, among other crimes, what now would be called human trafficking.[73] As Rickey recalled the matter, he was in court when the case was assigned to him. He visited the client in jail and was greeted by the snarled question, "Who the hell are you?" "Sir, my name is Branch Rickey," he responded. "The court has appointed me your attorney and I would like to talk to you." The client looked Rickey over, spat at his feet, and instructed, "Get the hell out of here."[74] Whether Rickey immediately complied or not, his subsequent assessment was succinct: "I never knew a man could be so guilty of so many crimes."[75]

In his later years, Rickey probably encouraged the view that the firm had essentially no business, but that seems to be incorrect. Howard Crow later recalled, "[W]e did not get rich but we had three meals a day."[76] The people of Boise were hospitable to the young trio and some gave them business. Thus, the firm had a variety of civil representations "of minor importance," including collections, divorces, and personal injury cases, and Rickey successfully defended a man charged with horse stealing, then considered a major crime.[77] Civically active, Rickey began to make a name for himself.[78]

In addition, Rickey spent "considerable time" as a paid temperance organizer in Idaho County, in the north-central part of the state, which, having gone "dry" two years before, was facing a hotly contested "local option" election.[79] This led to a remarkable, and to this day little-known, incident. At the trial of a hotel employee who was charged with selling liquor, his two customers testified that Rickey had put them up to it, hiring them and providing them with cash for the purchase, in an apparent effort to trap the "wets." Upon hearing the witnesses' testimony, James Woodward, the justice of the peace presiding over the case, ordered Rickey arrested.[80] The county went wet in the November election[81]; as for the charges against Rickey, there is no further reporting about them, which suggests they either were dropped or not pursued.

With some relief, Rickey returned to Ann Arbor for the 1912 baseball season.[82] The team nearly duplicated the prior year's performance with a 15–10–2 record.[83] But the development of greatest interest that year lay with a student who could not yet play in regular games for the varsity.

When practice began, George H. Sisler, a freshman engineering student from Manchester, Ohio, turned out. Rickey told him that the practice was for upperclassmen only, but some of the returning players urged him to give Sisler a look. Many years later, the noted sportswriter James P. "Jim" Murray said that Rickey could spot talent "from the window of a moving train,"[84] and that certainly was true in this case—although in Rickey's own account of the affair, it took no special skill for Rickey to realize, after a minute of watching Sisler pitch to the upperclassmen, that Sisler was a rare talent. Freshmen were not eligible to play on the varsity, but Rickey allowed Sisler to work out with them.[85]

Sisler spent the year pitching for the freshman team, but he also turned in a dazzling performance in an exhibition game against the alumni.[86] Norman H. Hill, who had been captain of the 1911 varsity team and was by then a reporter for the *Detroit News*, struck out three times. After the third time, he went over to the varsity dugout to congratulate Rickey on having such an outstanding pitcher. In Hill's presence, a scout offered Rickey $1,500 if he could sign Sisler for the New York Highlanders, Rickey's last major league team. Rickey declined to let Sisler know of the team's interest. No doubt it would have been improper for Rickey, while under contract with UM, to take a fee for sending an immensely talented player to the majors. Whether Rickey should have transmitted the team's offer to Sisler's parents, however, is a debatable question. Hill's interpretation was that Rickey simply wanted to keep Sisler "for Michigan."[87]

A new threat to Sisler remaining at UM arose in the summer of 1912. While still in high school, Sisler had signed a contract with the Akron (Ohio) Champs of the Ohio-Pennsylvania League, although he never played for them or received any money from them. In 1912, Bernhard "Barney" Dreyfuss, the owner of the Pittsburgh Pirates, purchased Sisler's contract from the Champs and then insisted that Sisler was bound to the Pirates and ineligible to continue playing college ball.[88] Drawing on his legal training, Rickey helped organize a campaign to persuade the National Commission, baseball's governing body, that the contract was void because Sisler had been a minor in 1910 and his parents had not approved the contract. In the end, the National Commission withheld judgment and Sisler retained his eligibility.[89]

Leaving the Law Behind

Although he had spent his entire adult life planning to be a lawyer, Rickey now was about to make a life-altering decision. Robert Hedges, the owner of the St. Louis Browns, the big league team with which Rickey had his best year as a player,[90] thought highly of Rickey and had had Rickey do some scouting for the Browns while Rickey was in law school.[91] In the spring of 1912, Hedges tried to hire Rickey to manage one of the Browns' minor league teams, but Rickey was committed to resuming his law practice in Boise; he agreed, however, to continue scouting for the Browns in the Rocky Mountains and on the West Coast.[92]

A few months later, Hedges sent Rickey a train ticket and asked Rickey to meet him in Salt Lake City, Utah. There, Hedges made Rickey a

Wesley Branch Rickey (*c.* 1913) (National Baseball Hall of Fame and Museum).

more appealing offer. He asked Rickey to be his assistant and the business manager of the Browns, with responsibilities for selecting and trading players, at a handsome annual salary of $7,500.[93] Rickey replied that he was under contract to coach the UM team for one more season. Hedges agreed that Rickey could fulfill his Michigan contract and then join the Browns full-time.[94]

Rather than accept immediately, Rickey returned to Boise. At just about the same time, Crow received an offer to return to the casualty firm for which he had worked in Cleveland, but in a better position. Rickey and Crow both accepted their offers, dissolving their nascent firm. Ebbert remained behind for a while and took over the defense of a pending criminal case that the firm was handling.[95] A short time later, however, he too left Boise, returning to Chicago as counsel to the Illinois Anti-Saloon League.

And so Rickey began intermittent work, and travel, for the Browns,[96] but not before suffering another life-threatening illness, a bout of blood poisoning that he contracted by cutting his finger while opening a box of books.[97]

During the 1913 season, UM's star pitcher, George Sisler, was limited by a sore arm. It turned out, however, that he also could hit, and the team posted the best record of Rickey's tenure: 22–5.[98] Following the season, the *Michigan Daily*, UM's main student newspaper, paid Rickey a warm tribute:

> [H]e leaves with a sterling record behind him, a loyal student body to thank him, and a host of friends to remember him…. Above all he taught clean ball, gentlemanly tactics, and clean living…. A gentleman, a true sportsman, and a man, he will long be remembered by those who love and help Michigan athletics.[99]

Rickey now took up his duties full-time with the Browns,[100] and never again practiced law,[101] even though Howard Crow, his former law partner, later opined: "[I]t is my firm conviction that if Rickey had spent his life in the practice of law, he would have long ago been recognized as one of the outstanding trial lawyers of the country."[102]

For the next four decades, Rickey was a fixture in the major leagues, occupying key positions with the Browns (1913–16), St. Louis Cardinals (1917–18, 1919–42), Brooklyn Dodgers (1942–50), and Pittsburgh Pirates (1951–59).[103] Years later, however, Rickey, in the orotund style that helped earn him the nickname "Mahatma," mused about being "a man trained for the law [who has] devote[d] his entire life and all his energies to something so cosmically unimportant as a game."[104]

During his tenure as a baseball executive, eight of Rickey's teams won National League pennants (1926, 1928, 1930, 1931, 1934, 1942, 1947, and 1949) and four went on to win the World Series (1926, 1931, 1934, and 1942). Of even greater significance, Rickey transformed the game in three momentous ways. First, while with the Cardinals, he invented the farm system, an idea that would revolutionize how major league teams cultivated future players.[105] Second, in 1945 he hired Jackie Robinson, who in 1947 broke baseball's color line.[106] And third, in 1959–60, he spearheaded the effort to start a third major league (known at the Continental League), which led to baseball's expansion era.[107] Yet at his core, Rickey remained stubbornly old-fashioned:

> Branch Rickey was a Midwestern Methodist Victorian and proud of it. He counseled all his players to marry. He wanted nothing to do with alcohol, or Democrats. Even with all his innovations in baseball, he was a man whose concept of marketing was to put a talented, interesting team on the field and let the fans flock to it.[108]

Conclusion

On November 13, 1965, while giving a speech in Columbia, Missouri, where he was being inducted into the Missouri Sports Hall of Fame, Rickey collapsed. Never regaining consciousness, he died four weeks later of heart failure, just days before his 84th birthday,[109] and was buried in the Rushtown Township (Ohio) Cemetery, a few miles from his birthplace.[110] A little more than a year later, in January 1967, Rickey was elected to the Baseball Hall of Fame.[111] His brief legal career also has been memorialized: since 2009, UM's law school has had a professorship named for Rickey.[112]

NOTES

1. Rickey's birth certificate erroneously records his birthday as November 20, 1881. *See* MURRAY POLNER, BRANCH RICKEY: A BIOGRAPHY 7 (1982). Rickey's first name is a tribute to the Reverend John Wesley (the founder of Methodism).

2. For an annotated copy of the law school's current application form, see https://michigan.law.umich.edu/system/files/2023-06/2023_2024_annotated_application_ally.pdf (last visited July 1, 2024) [hereinafter 2023–24 UM Application Form].

3. There was no high school near Rickey's home of Lucasville; many Ohio towns at this time did not have one. *See* Howard M. Crow, "Reply to Questions Asked by Arthur Mann," *in* Arthur Mann Papers, Box 3, Library of Congress Manuscript Division [hereinafter Crow Memorandum].

4. Notwithstanding the other demands on his time, Rickey earned his B. Litt. in three and a half years. *See* LEE LOWENFISH, BRANCH RICKEY: BASEBALL'S FEROCIOUS GENTLEMAN 25 (2007). Rickey finished his B.A. in 1906, see *id.* at 38; POLNER, *supra* note 1, at 45; *Registration Slip, in* Wesley Branch Rickey File, Bentley Historical Library at the University of Michigan [hereinafter WBR File]. It appears, however, that he did not receive this degree until 1908. *See* Letter from William E. Smyser, Registrar, OWU, dated Oct. 5, 1909, *in* WBR File, *supra*.

5. Beginning at the age of 17, Rickey taught for two years at a school in Turkey Creek near his home in Scioto County, Ohio. *See* LOWENFISH, *supra* note 4, at 13–15. He qualified, even without a high school diploma, by passing the state's certification exams. *See* POLNER, *supra* note 1, at 16–17. Maintenance of discipline sometimes required physical confrontations with students. *See id.* at 17–18; ARTHUR MANN, BRANCH RICKEY: AMERICAN IN ACTION 17–18 (1957).

6. Rickey, having just earned his B. Litt. at OWU, taught a variety of courses at Allegheny College while also coaching baseball and football. *See* LOWENFISH, *supra* note 4, at 28 (English, history, and Shakespeare); POLNER, *supra* note 1, at 39 (English, German, Greek drama, and Shakespeare).

7. *See* Affidavit of attorney (later judge) Benson W. Hough, dated Nov. 20, 1909 (on file with the author). This affidavit, apparently submitted by Rickey in his ultimately successful attempt to secure advanced standing, explains that beginning in 1904, Rickey "completed the entire law course provided for and prescribed in the law department of the Ohio Wesleyan University" under the instruction of Professor John H. Grove, and that during the 1907–08 school year, after Grove died, Rickey was "duly appointed instructor of said law department" and "acted as instructor and supervisor of the entire course of study." A letter from William E. Smyser, OWU's registrar, states that Rickey taught five recitations per week throughout a full academic term, using Blackstone among other texts. *See* Letter from William E. Smyser, Registrar, OWU, dated Nov. 20, 1909, *in* WBR File, *supra* note 4.

8. *See* POLNER, *supra* note 1, at 41.

9. Rickey attended night classes at OSU's law school while coaching and teaching at OWU, traveling between the two schools (a trip of 24 miles) by electric railway. *See* LOWENFISH, *supra* note 4, at 41; Crow Memorandum, *supra* note 3.

10. Rickey not only caught for the OWU baseball team, he was a running back on its football team and was voted starting halfback on the All-Ohio college team of 1901. *See* LOWENFISH, *supra* note 4, at 20.

11. Rickey coached baseball at OWU in 1903 and 1904; football at Allegheny College in 1904; baseball and football at Allegheny College in 1905; and football, baseball, and basketball at OWU in 1906–08. *See id.* at 22, 28–30, 39, 40–41; POLNER, *supra* note 1, at 31–35. Even while in law school at UM, Rickey coached basketball at OWU in 1909–10. *See* LOWENFISH, *supra* note 4, at 49.

12. *See* LOWENFISH, *supra* note 4, at 34, 41; POLNER, *supra* note 1, at 49; MANN, *supra* note 5, at 29, 45.

13. *See* Crow Memorandum, *supra* note 3; HARVEY FROMMER, RICKEY AND ROBINSON: THE MEN WHO BROKE BASEBALL'S COLOR BARRIER 42 (1982).

14. *See* LOWENFISH, *supra* note 4, at 42–43; FROMMER, *supra* note 13, at 43–44; POLNER, *supra* note 1, at 47–49.

15. *See* POLNER, *supra* note 1, at 46–47.

16. For Rickey's playing statistics, see *Branch Rickey*, BASEBALL-REFERENCE.COM, https://www.baseball-reference.com/players/r/rickebr01.shtml (last visited July 1, 2024) (listing Rickey as standing 5'9" and weighing 175 pounds). Rickey played semi-professional and then minor league ball in 1903 and 1904. Late in the 1904 season, his contract was bought by the Cincinnati Reds. He appeared with the Reds in exhibition games, but not in any regular-season games, and was released before the season ended because, for religious reasons, he declined to play on Sundays. *See* LOWENFISH, *supra* note 4, at 25–28; POLNER, *supra* note 1, at 37–39; MANN, *supra* note 5, at 37–38. Rickey played in only one major league game, for the St. Louis Browns in 1905, and then returned to the minors. In 1906, he was a semi-regular catcher for the Browns and performed well, batting .284 and playing solid defense. In December 1906, the Browns sold his contract to the New York Highlanders (later Yankees); at that time, Sunday baseball was illegal in New York, making the Highlanders a good fit for Rickey. Plagued by a sore arm, Rickey appeared only sporadically for the Highlanders. *See* LOWENFISH, *supra* note 4, at 39–40. As it happened, however, Rickey was planning for 1907 to be his last playing season, see *id.* at 35, 39; POLNER, *supra* note 1, at 42. Rickey had two final plate appearances in 1914, when he was the manager of the Browns. In his application essay, Rickey probably would not have felt the need

to mention the one enduring record he set as a player: most stolen bases allowed by a single catcher in a single game (13) (his arm was numb). *See* POLNER, *supra* note 1, at 45–46.

17. *See* 2023–24 UM Application Form, *supra* note 2, at 15.

18. *Id.* (Essay Two).

19. *See* LOWENFISH, *supra* note 4, at 22; POLNER, *supra* note 1, at 36, 38.

20. For an obituary of Jennie, see *Mrs. Rickey Dead at 89*, ST. LOUIS POST-DISPATCH, Oct. 17, 1971, at 10E. *See also Mrs Jane "Jennie" Moulton Rickey*, FIND-A-GRAVE.COM, https://www.findagrave.com/memorial/7341298/jane_rickey (last visited July 1, 2024).

21. *See Rickey to Marry*, DAILY SCIOTO GAZ. (Chillicothe, OH), May 25, 1906, at 6 (reporting that the pair had been classmates at OWU).

22. *See* POLNER, *supra* note 1, at 12–13.

23. *See* LOWENFISH, *supra* note 4, at 18; POLNER, *supra* note 1, at 16, 20; MANN, *supra* note 5, at 20.

24. Before entering OWU, Rickey, aware of his deficiency, walked miles to obtain tutoring in Latin. *See* LOWENFISH, *supra* note 4, at 13. He still was weak in the subject when he entered OWU, but with the help of early-morning tutoring sessions (after he had finished one of his jobs, stoking coal furnaces in college buildings), Latin became one of his strongest subjects. *Id.* at 19; FROMMER, *supra* note 13, at 39–40; POLNER, *supra* note 1, at 25–26; MANN, *supra* note 5, at 23–24.

25. Always short of cash as a student, Rickey played for pay for the Portsmouth Navvies, a team based near his home, in the summer of 1902. *See* LOWENFISH, *supra* note 4, at 21; POLNER, *supra* note 1, at 28–29. He also played football for a semi-professional team variously known as the Shelby Blues and the Shelby Steamfitters. *See* LOWENFISH, *supra* note 4, at 24–25; POLNER, *supra* note 1, at 29–30.

26. Ineligible to play beginning in the 1903 season, Rickey, who was 21, was made OWU's baseball coach. *See* LOWENFISH, *supra* note 4, at 22; POLNER, *supra* note 1, at 31. *See also supra* note 11.

27. *See* FROMMER, *supra* note 13, at 41–42; MANN, *supra* note 5, at 32. *See also supra* note 16. At one point, Rickey signed to play with the Chicago White Sox, but its owner, Charles A. Comiskey, decided he needed an everyday catcher and traded Rickey to the Browns. *See* LOWENFISH, *supra* note 4, at 30. Reflecting on the matter half a century later, Rickey acknowledged "the appearances of hypocrisy" in his position:

> Here we have the Sunday school mollycoddle, apparently professing a sort of public virtue in refraining from playing or watching a game of baseball on Sunday.
>
> And yet at the same time he is not above accepting money from a till replenished by Sunday baseball.

Gerald Holland, *Mr. Rickey and the Game*, SPORTS ILLUS., Mar. 7, 1955, at 38, 38.

28. *See* LOWENFISH, *supra* note 4, at 44–48.

29. 2023–24 UM Application Form, *supra* note 2 (Essay Seven).

30. *See* LOWENFISH, *supra* note 4, at 23; POLNER, *supra* note 1, at 32.

31. See LOWENFISH, *supra* note 4, at 23; POLNER, *supra* note 1, at 34.

32. William H. Herndon, Lincoln's law partner and biographer, reports that Lincoln's cousin, John Hanks, who claimed to have been at the auction, told Herndon this story. Herndon says he also heard Lincoln refer to it himself. *See* 1 WILLIAM H. HERNDON & JESSE WILLIAM WEIK, HERNDON'S LINCOLN: THE TRUE STORY OF A GREAT LIFE 75–76 (1889). Maybe it did not happen. *See* RALPH KEYES, THE QUOTE VERIFIER: WHO SAID WHAT, WHERE, AND WHEN 127 (2006); RECOLLECTED WORDS OF ABRAHAM LINCOLN 198 (Don E. Fehrenbacher & Virginia Fehrenbacher eds., 2006). In any event, Rickey would have been within his rights to believe and use the story.

33. Walter L. "Red" Barber, the famed baseball broadcaster, said that in 1945 Rickey told him that he still heard Thomas crying—and that now he was prepared to do something about it (which turned out to be the signing of Jack R. "Jackie" Robinson). *See International Baseball Players in MLB: Museum Exhibit Activity*, PBS, https://dptv.pbslearningmedia. org/resource/international-baseball-players-in-mlb-gallery/ken-burns-baseball/ (last visited July 1, 2024).

34. *See* POLNER, *supra* note 1, at 36, 38, 39, 43; MANN, *supra* note 5, at 41–42.

35. *See* LOWENFISH, *supra* note 4, at 47; POLNER, *supra* note 1, at 52.

36. *See* POLNER, *supra* note 1, at 53. The Rickeys were childless while Rickey was a law student; a baby girl born prematurely in January 1909 (sometimes reported as 1908, see, e.g., MANN, *supra* note 5, at 53) had died within hours. The couple later had six children: Mary E. (later Eckler) (1913–2005); Branch, Jr. (1914–61); Jane A. (later Jones) (1916–2004); Mabel A. "Alice" (later Jakle) (1918–96); Sue (later Adams) (1923–83); and Elizabeth A. "Betty" (later Wolfe) (1924–2009). *See Wesley Branch Rickey (1881–1965)*, WIKITREE, https://www.wikitree.com/wiki/Rickey-34#_note-birth (last visited July 1, 2024); JOHN BURROUGHS [SCHOOL] REPORTER, May 2010, at 14, https://www.yumpu.com/en/document/read/46736323/may-2010-john-burroughs-school (reporting on Elizabeth's death). Like his father, Branch, Jr., was admitted to UM's law school, but he was asked to withdraw before he was able to earn his degree. *See Faculty Records, Oct. 1930 to June 1940*, University of Michigan Law School Collection, Box 60, Bentley Historical Library at the University of Michigan, at 412 (July 6, 1937). Branch, Jr., later became a baseball executive and in 1960 was part of the front office when the Pittsburgh Pirates won the World Series by beating the New York Yankees in seven games. *See Rickey, Jr. Buc Farm Director, Dies: Son of Former General Manager Succumbs at 47*, PITT. POST-GAZ., Apr. 11, 1961, at 21 (reporting that Branch, Jr., died from the combined effect of diabetes, a heart condition, and hepatitis).

37. *See* MARGARET A. LEARY, GIVING IT ALL AWAY: THE STORY OF WILLIAM W. COOK & HIS MICHIGAN LAW QUADRANGLE (2011).

38. *See* University of Michigan Law School, *The First Law Building, 1863–1933*, https://repository.law.umich.edu /cgi/viewcontent.cgi?article=1023&context=about_buildings (last visited July 1, 2024).

39. The resolution prescribing requirements for the J.D. was adopted at the faculty meeting of January 12, 1909. *See Faculty Records, 1901–1910*, University of Michigan Law School Collection, Box 60, Bentley Historical Library at the University of Michigan, at 373 [hereinafter *Faculty Records, 1901–1910*]. LOWENFISH, *supra* note 4, at 25, indicates that a B.A. (which was more prestigious than an LL.B., *see* POLNER, *supra* note 1, at 39) was necessary for Rickey to attend law school, but this was not so. A college degree was necessary for the J.D., but not for the LL.B., and many of Rickey's classmates had only a high school education.

40. Angell served as UM's president from 1871 to 1909, with occasional leaves of absence for diplomatic assignments. For a biography of Angell, see SHIRLEY W. SMITH, JAMES BURRILL ANGELL: AN AMERICAN INFLUENCE (1954). For a biography of Hutchins, see SHIRLEY W. SMITH, HARRY BURNS HUTCHINS AND THE UNIVERSITY OF MICHIGAN (1951).

41. *See* Margaret A. Leary & Barbara J. Snow, *Gabriel Franklin Hargo: Michigan Law 1870* (July 9, 2009), https://repository.law.umich.edu/cgi/viewcontent.cgi?article=1142&context=miscellaneous.

42. *See* University of Michigan Law School, *Law School (University of Michigan) Records, 1852–2010*, https://findingaids.lib.umich.edu/catalog/umich-bhl-87235 (last visited July 1, 2024).

43. An admission slip, identifying Rickey as "Wesley B. Rickey," did not indicate to which class Rickey was being admitted but instead said "sp." (for "special") and noted "Adv. Standing to be determined later." A registration file indicates that Rickey paid the necessary $92 to attend for the year—a $25 matriculation fee, an annual fee of $65, and a library fee of $2. He also paid the latter two fees, a total of $67, for his second year. *See Registration Slip, in* WBR File, *supra* note 4. The present-day value of $92 is $3,170.03. *See* S. Morgan Friedman, *The Inflation Calculator*, https://westegg.com/inflation/ (last visited July 1, 2024). UM law school's current annual tuition and fees are $69,584 (in-state) and $72,584 (out-of-state). *See* University of Michigan Law School, *Student Budget Example*, https://michigan.law.umich.edu/resource-center/student-budget-example (last visited July 1, 2024).

44. *See* LOWENFISH, *supra* note 4, at 48.

45. *See* Wesley Branch Rickey 1909–11 UM Transcript (on file with the author) [hereinafter Rickey Transcript].

46. For an obituary of Emily, see *Mrs. Frank Rickey Dies from Paralytic Stroke*, ZANES-VILLE SIGNAL (OH), May 24, 1935, at 1. *See also Emily Brown Rickey*, FIND-A-GRAVE.COM, https://www.findagrave.com/memorial/33921748/emily_rickey (last visited July 1, 2024).

47. For an obituary of Frank, see *Branch Rickey's Father Passes Away at 85*, BROOKLYN EAGLE, Dec. 13, 1939, at 18. *See also J. Frank Rickey*, FIND-A-GRAVE.COM, https://www.finda grave.com/memorial/33921671/j_frank_rickey (last visited July 1, 2024).

48. *Letter to Parents*, dated Jan. 13, 1910, *in* Branch Rickey Papers, Box 2, Library of Congress Manuscript Division (emphasis in original). Emily and Frank (a farmer) had married on March 12, 1874, in Pike County, Ohio, and had, in addition to Rickey, two other sons: Orla E. (1875–1944), a shoe salesman, and Frank W. (1888–1953), a baseball scout. For an obituary of Orla, see *Orla E. Rickey, 68, Dies; Brother of Dodgers' Head*, EVENING STAR (DC), Apr. 28, 1944, at B18. *See also Orla Edwin Rickey*, FIND-A-GRAVE.COM, https://www.findagrave.com/memorial/33921980/orla_edwin_rickey (last visited July 1, 2024). For an obituary of Frank, see *Rickey's Brother Dies*, CIN. ENQUIRER, Oct. 27, 1953, at 30. *See also Frank Wanzer Rickey*, FIND-A-GRAVE.COM, https://www.findagrave.com/memorial/45401134/frank_wanzer_rickey (last visited July 1, 2024). Emily and Frank also had a fourth child who died either in childbirth or soon thereafter and whose name is not now known. *See* WIKITREE, *supra* note 36.

49. The contract, dated January 4, 1910, with a notation that it was ratified by the Board in Control of Intercollegiate Athletics ("BCIA") on January 14, 1910, can be found in Box 2 of the papers of the BCIA, Bentley Historical Library at the University of Michigan [hereinafter BCIA Papers]. Rickey's predecessor as coach (Lewis W. McAllister) had been paid $1,000, plus $100 for living expenses, for the 1909 season, with no provisional deduction for an assistant coach. *See id.* (contract dated Oct. 2, 1908).

50. *See* LOWENFISH, *supra* note 4, at 49–50; POLNER, *supra* note 1, at 55–56; MANN, *supra* note 5, at 56–57.

51. *See* LOWENFISH, *supra* note 4, at 50; POLNER, *supra* note 1, at 56. Assuming the story is true, it is noteworthy that Hutchins, who was both the university's acting president and the law school's dean, handled the matter himself. At this time, the practice was for the full faculty to be involved in student matters. Perhaps Hutchins had faith in Rickey; perhaps, however, he thought an informal agreement, giving Rickey the chance to prove that he could successfully take on the job, would be better than a formal faculty resolution.

52. *See* Rickey Transcript, *supra* note 45.

53. *See, e.g.*, LOWENFISH, *supra* note 4, at 48; POLNER, *supra* note 1, at 57.

54. The selection for the 1910–11 school year was made at a faculty meeting held on April 5, 1910. The names of those selected are listed in the minutes of that meeting. *See Faculty Records, 1901–1910*, *supra* note 39, at 437.

55. *See, e.g.*, POLNER, *supra* note 1, at 56.

56. *Id.* at 59. For a fuller discussion of Rickey's time as UM's baseball coach, see John D. Stevens, *As the Branch is Bent: Rickey as College Coach at the University of Michigan*, 2 NINE: J. BASEBALL HIST. & CULTURE 277 (1994).

57. *See* University of Michigan, MICHIGANENSIAN 1911 (yearbook of the University of Michigan), at 221–22 (1911) (noting that "[t]he season's success may be largely attributed to Coach Rickey, whose knowledge of inside baseball was what really counted," and that he had "start[ed] with a green team" but "closed the season with one that knew and played good baseball").

58. The contract, dated June 4, 1910, but not ratified until October 4, 1910, is in the BCIA Papers, *supra* note 49. In his spare time—and it is amazing that he had any—Rickey helped the legendary UM football coach Fielding H. Yost plan plays. *See* LOWENFISH, *supra* note 4, at 53.

59. LOWENFISH, *supra* note 4, at 52; MANN, *supra* note 5, at 53.

60. The schedule for third-year students is printed on an insert to page 459b of *Faculty Records, 1910–1920*, University of Michigan Law School Collection, Box 60, Bentley Historical Library at the University of Michigan [hereinafter *Faculty Records, 1910–1920*]. Practice Court was scheduled every weekday from 2:00–5:00 pm. *Id.* For a profile of Bates (1869–1949), see *Dr. H.M. Bates, 80, a Law Authority: Dean at U. of Michigan School in 1910–39 is Dead—Leader in National Societies*, N.Y. TIMES, Apr. 16, 1949, at 15.

61. There were 196 LL.B.'s in Rickey's class but only 28 J.D.'s. *See Faculty Records, 1910–1920, supra* note 60, at 476–77 (faculty meeting of June 24, 1911). Rickey's entry on the list of those awarded the J.D. was the only time his name appeared in the faculty minutes while he was in law school, no mean feat given the number of students who ran into academic or other difficulty.

62. Both contracts were signed on April 7, 1911; the one for 1912 kept Rickey's base salary where it had been at $1,000 but added the allowance for expenses; the payment schedule did not distinguish between salary and expenses or ask for an accounting of expenses. *See* BCIA Papers, *supra* note 49.

63. University of Michigan, Michiganensian 1912, at 231 (1912).

64. *Id.* at 233.

65. For an obituary of Crow, see *H.M. Crow, 54 Years at Law, is Dead,* Plain Dealer (Cleve.), Nov. 11, 1963, at 39 (reporting that Crow was a 1909 graduate of Case Western Reserve University's law school). *See also Howard Malley Crow,* Find-a-Grave.com, https://www.findagrave.com/memorial/101808856/howard-malley-crow (last visited July 1, 2024).

66. For an obituary of Ebbert, see *Col. Ebbert Dies in Walter Reed: Co-author of Volstead Act was National Counselor of Temperance Board,* Evening Star (DC), May 23, 1938, at 12 (reporting that Ebbert was a 1911 graduate of the Chicago-Kent law school). *See also Frank Baker Ebbert,* Find-a-Grave.com, https://www.findagrave.com/memorial/49177108/frank-baker-ebbert (last visited July 1, 2024).

67. *See* Crow Memorandum, *supra* note 3. Ebbert had transferred to DePauw University when his brother-in-law became president there. *Id.* Nevertheless, he remained loyal to OWU. *See* 15:5 Ohio Wesleyan U. Bull. 26 (Sept. 1, 1916) (listing Ebbert as the president of OWU's Chicago alumni club).

68. *See* Jim Poore, *From a Boise Lawyer to a Baseball Legend,* Idaho Statesman (Boise), Apr. 19, 1987, at 1B ("I called historian Arthur Hart [regarding the firm's name]. His research uncovered that [the] law firm of Rickey, Crow and Ebbert was listed in the 1912–13 Boise City Directory.... Rickey's law firm's office was located at 409 Idaho Building. The telephone number was 110. Rickey's residence—and that of his partners—was listed as 1602 W. Washington [suggesting that the men shared an apartment]").

69. *See* Crow Memorandum, *supra* note 3. The Idaho Building, consisting of six stories, had been designed by noted Chicago architect Henry J. Schlacks in the Second Renaissance Revival style. The building opened in 1911 and has been on the National Register of Historic Places since 1978. *See* Halle Fiderlick, *Idaho Building,* Idaho Architecture Project, https://www.idahoarchitectureproject.org/properties/idaho-building/ (last visited July 1, 2024).

70. *See* Mann, *supra* note 5, at 59.

71. *See* 20 Report of Cases Argued and Determined in the Supreme Court of the State of Idaho iv (1912). At this time, admission to the Idaho bar for those who were not able to waive in (as Crow may have been able to do) was formally by examination in open court before the justices of the state supreme court. *See* Idaho Rev. Code §§ 3991 and 3994, as amended by Idaho Sess. L., Sen. Bill No. 138 (Mar. 12, 1909). Rickey, however, took a two-day written test and, by his later account, passed easily. *See* Eugene H. Russell, *Rickey was Lawyer: Veteran Baseball Manager Passed Bar Exam in Idaho 42 Years Ago,* Seattle Times, Apr. 27, 1954, at 24.

72. The tutee was Oscar W. Worthwine (1885–1960), himself an athlete, having played football at the University of Chicago and having earned a law degree there in 1911. Worthwine was admitted on December 16, 1911 (the same day as Crow) and became a leading member of the Idaho bar. *See* Ernest A. Hoidal, *Oscar Worthwine & the "Greatest Event in Boise Football,"* 4:4 Idaho Legal Hist. Soc'y Newsl. 1 (Fall 2012). *See also Oscar W Worthwine Sr.,* Find-a-Grave.com, https://www.findagrave.com/memorial/61953399/oscar-w-worthwine (last visited July 1, 2024).

73. In contrast, Polner, *supra* note 1, at 58, asserts that "Rickey's only case was a minor civil dispute."

74. Holland, *supra* note 27, at 59.

75. LOWENFISH, *supra* note 4, at 54.

76. Crow Memorandum, *supra* note 3.

77. *Id.*

78. *See, e.g., Boys Ratify Big Cash Campaign Victory,* IDAHO STATESMAN (Boise), Feb. 4, 1912, at 9 ("W.B. Rickey, the attorney, was the toastmaster of the [YMCA] banquet").

79. *Id. See also Dry Campaign Manager Noted Baseball Player,* GRANGEVILLE GLOBE (ID), Oct. 26, 1911, at 1.

80. *See Dry Leader is Caught in Trap Set for Wets: Sensational Development in Fight for Control of Idaho County at Special Election,* IDAHO STATESMAN (Boise), Nov. 16, 1911, at 3.

81. *See Idaho and Kootenai are Wet: Both Counties Repudiate Local Option by Small Majorities; Contest in Idaho—Fight Bitterest Ever Known with Towns Against Drys,* IDAHO STATESMAN (Boise), Nov. 23, 1911, at 1.

82. It is sometimes reported that earlier that winter Rickey had telegraphed UM athletic director Bartelme: "AM STARVING. WILL BE BACK WITHOUT DELAY." *See, e.g.,* MANN, *supra* note 5, at 60.

83. *See* University of Michigan, MICHIGANENSIAN 1913, at 231 (1913). LOWENFISH, *supra* note 4, at 56, gives the record as 14–10–3. UM now lists the team's record as 14–10–2. *See* University of Michigan, *Michigan Baseball Year-By-Year Results,* https://mgoblue.com/sports/2017/6/16/michigan-baseball-year-by-year-results (last visited July 1, 2024) [hereinafter *Michigan Baseball Record*].

84. *See* Jim Murray, *He Brought Pirates and Fans Back,* L.A. TIMES, July 15, 1988, pt. III, at 1.

85. *See* LOWENFISH, *supra* note 4, at 54–55.

86. *See* MANN, *supra* note 5, at 62.

87. *See* Letter (undated; probably Sept. 1912 or Oct. 1912) from Norman H. Hill to the editor of *The Wolverine* (one of UM's auxiliary student newspapers), *in* BCIA Papers, *supra* note 49 ("[I]n my presence Rickey … refused a large sum to sign Sisler for New York. Sisler never heard of that offer. The coach wanted to keep him for Michigan").

88. *See Sisler Refuses to Report This Year,* PITT. PRESS, Aug. 27, 1912, at 16.

89. *See* LOWENFISH, *supra* note 4, at 57–58. Following Sisler's graduation in 1915, the National Commission ruled that the contract was void and that Sisler was a free agent. Sisler signed with the St. Louis Browns, by then Rickey's team, in part because he wanted to play for Rickey. *See* POLNER, *supra* note 1, at 71–72. For a look at the rest of Sisler's Hall-of-Fame career (almost all of it spent playing first base), see RICK HUHN, THE SIZZLER: GEORGE SISLER, BASEBALL'S FORGOTTEN GREAT (2004).

90. *See supra* note 16 (explaining that Rickey played with the Browns in 1905 and 1906).

91. *See* LOWENFISH, *supra* note 4, at 53.

92. *Id.* at 57. Rickey was too late by a few years to scout the pitcher who was the greatest prospect to ever come out of Idaho, future Hall-of-Fame pitcher Walter P. Johnson.

93. *See* POLNER, *supra* note 1, at 61–62.

94. *See* LOWENFISH, *supra* note 4, at 59.

95. *See* Crow Memorandum, *supra* note 3. The case involved a young girl who claimed that a man named Charles L. Blose had seduced her. *See Blose is Bound Over to District Court,* EVENING CAPITAL NEWS (Boise), Nov. 6, 1912, at 3 ("C.L. Blose, the automobile driver arrested last week on a statutory charge, was today bound over to stand trial…. Taking the stand, the young girl in the case, whose name is withheld for her own good, gave convincing and damaging testimony against Blose, although an attempt was made by his attorney to introduce testimony that the girl had a bad character…. Ebbert, Crow & Rickey are attorneys for the defendant."); *Brevities,* EVENING CAPITAL NEWS (Boise), Jan. 13, 1913, at 2 ("Charles L. Blose, sentenced to from six months to five years in the penitentiary for seduction, began his term today"). According to Crow, there was no defense on the facts and six months was the minimum sentence.

96. *See* POLNER, *supra* note 1, at 62–63.

97. *See* Crow Memorandum, *supra* note 3.

98. *See* University of Michigan, MICHIGANENSIAN 1914, at 237 (1914). LOWENFISH, *supra* note 4, at 60, again reports slightly different numbers: 22–4–1. UM now lists the team's record as 21–4–1. *See Michigan Baseball Record, supra* note 83.

99. *Coach Rickey,* MICH. DAILY, June 1, 1913, at 2.

100. Rickey did sneak back to UM for the annual alumni game. *See Rickey is Back for Tilt with Stars of Old,* MICH. DAILY, June 7, 1913, p. 1.

101. David Lipman asserts that following the Browns' 1913 season Rickey considered returning to law but was dissuaded when the team doubled his salary. *See* DAVID LIPMAN, MR. BASEBALL: THE STORY OF BRANCH RICKEY 57 (1966). I have found nothing to confirm Lipman's claim.

102. Crow Memorandum, *supra* note 3.

103. From 1913 to 1915, Rickey managed the Browns, compiling a 139–179 (.437) record. From 1919 to 1925, Rickey managed the Cardinals, where he finished with a 458–485 (.486) record. Thereafter, Rickey worked exclusively in his teams' front offices. For Rickey's managerial statistics, see *Branch Rickey,* BASEBALL-REFERENCE.COM, https://www.baseball-reference.com/managers/rickebr01.shtml (last visited July 1, 2024). Rickey briefly left baseball in 1918 to serve as a major in the Army's newly formed Chemical Corps. *See Branch Rickey is Major in Army's Chemical Section: President of Cardinals Gets Commission Under a Former Boston Baseball Man,* ST. LOUIS POST-DISPATCH, Aug. 24, 1918, at 2. *See also* JIM LEEKE, THE GAS AND FLAME MEN: BASEBALL AND THE CHEMICAL WARFARE SERVICE DURING WORLD WAR I (2024) (describing the Chemical Corps and Rickey's role in it).

104. Holland, *supra* note 27, at 59.

105. *See* Kevin Kerrane, *How Branch Rickey Invented Modern Baseball,* DEADSPIN.COM, Nov. 15, 2013, https://deadspin.com/how-branch-rickey-invented-modern-baseball-1458137692.

106. *See* ROGER KAHN, RICKEY & ROBINSON: THE TRUE, UNTOLD STORY OF THE INTEGRATION OF BASEBALL (2014); JOHN C. CHALBERG, RICKEY AND ROBINSON: THE PREACHER, THE PLAYER, AND AMERICA'S GAME (2000); FROMMER, *supra* note 13. As one of Rickey's biographers later put it, this act "raise[d] [Rickey] from talented baseball executive to sainted agent of progress" and "was a product of his religious beliefs; of his desire to win and draw fans; and of his ability to see baseball in the context of American society." Andy McCue, *Branch Rickey,* SABR, https://sabr.org/bioproj/person/branch-rickey/ (last visited July 1, 2024).

107. *See* G. SCOTT THOMAS, A BRAND NEW BALLGAME: BRANCH RICKEY, BILL VEECK, WALTER O'MALLEY AND THE TRANSFORMATION OF BASEBALL, 1945–1962 (2021); RUSSELL D. BUHITE, THE CONTINENTAL LEAGUE: A PERSONAL HISTORY (2014); MICHAEL SHAPIRO, BOTTOM OF THE NINTH: BRANCH RICKEY, CASEY STENGEL, AND THE DARING SCHEME TO SAVE BASEBALL FROM ITSELF (2009).

108. Andy McCue, *Los Angeles/Brooklyn Dodgers Team Ownership History,* SABR, https://sabr.org/bioproj/topic/los-angeles-brooklyn-dodgers-team-ownership-history/ (last visited July 1, 2024).

109. For an obituary of Rickey, see *Branch Rickey, 83, Dies in Missouri: A Leading Baseball Figure—Helped Break Color Bar,* N.Y. TIMES, Dec. 10, 1965, at 1. *See also Branch Rickey,* FIND-A-GRAVE.COM, https://www.findagrave.com/memorial/6644/branch_rickey (last visited July 1, 2024). For Rickey's death certificate (indicating that he died from heart disease), see *Frank [sic] Rickey in the Missouri, U.S., Death Certificates, 1910–1969,* ANCESTRY.COM, https://www.ancestry.com/discoveryui-content/view/64377116:60382 (last visited July 1, 2024). In 1970, it was reported that Rickey left behind an estate worth $379,475, the equivalent today of $3,029,819.52. *See Names and Faces—Baseball,* S.F. EXAM'R, Aug. 20, 1970, at 58 (reporting that Rickey "left half [his] estate for the benefit of his wife, and the remainder for his five daughters and [the] children of [his] deceased son [Branch, Jr.]). *See also* Friedman, *supra* note 43 (converting 1970 dollars to 2023 dollars).

110. *See Branch Rickey Buried Near Birthplace,* ST. LOUIS POST-DISPATCH, Dec. 15, 1965, at 5D. Just before his death, Rickey published an intensely personal and absorbing final love letter to the game. *See* BRANCH RICKEY WITH ROBERT RIGER, THE AMERICAN DIAMOND: A DOCUMENTARY OF THE GAME OF BASEBALL (1965). For a review, see Robert Cromie, *Mr. Baseball Speaks Out,* CHI. TRIB., Nov. 28, 1965, at 17 (Books Today) (describing the book as "the next best thing to attending a good game").

111. *See Rickey and Lloyd Waner Elected Unanimously to Baseball's Hall of Fame:*

Executive Set Up First Farm Clubs, He Also Broke Color Line; Waner Holds Singles Mark and Hit .316 for 19 Years, N.Y. TIMES, Jan. 30, 1967, at 38. For Rickey's Hall of Fame plaque, see *Branch Rickey,* NATIONAL BASEBALL HALL OF FAME AND MUSEUM, https://baseballhall. org/hall-of-famers/rickey-branch (last visited July 1, 2024).

112. *See Baseball Execs Honor Branch Rickey with New Law School Professorship,* 51:1 LAW QUADRANGLE: NOTES FROM MICHIGAN LAW (alumni magazine of the University of Michigan Law School) 45 (Winter 2009) (reporting on the professorship's creation and the selection of Dean Evan H. Caminker as its inaugural holder). *See also* Steve Kornacki, *Rickey of Michigan (Part II),* MGOBLUE.COM (news site of the University of Michigan Athletics Department), Feb. 25, 2016, https://mgoblue.com/news/2016/2/25/kornacki_rickey_of_michigan_part_ii_.

CHAPTER 7

Leland Stanford "Larry" MacPhail, Sr. (1978)

EDMUND P. EDMONDS

Leland Stanford "Larry" MacPhail, Sr. (February 3, 1890–October 1, 1975), described on his plaque at the Baseball Hall of Fame as a "dynamic, innovative executive,"[1] began his professional life in 1910 following his graduation from George Washington University's law school.[2] In contrast to his baseball career, MacPhail's legal career was both short and unremarkable.[3]

Birth and Childhood

MacPhail was born in a second-floor apartment in the Cass City State Bank Building in Cass City, Michigan (100 miles north of Detroit).[4] His parents were Catherine A. (née MacMurtrie) (1865–1931)[5] and Curtis W. "C.W." McPhail (1856–1939).[6] The pair had married in Cass City on December 26, 1887, shortly after the death of C.W.'s first wife.[7] Catherine was a native of Harrisburg, Ontario,[8] while C.W. was from Caro, Michigan.[9]

MacPhail's given name was the result of his parents' friendship with Jane E. and (Amasa) Leland Stanford, whose son, Leland Stanford, Jr., had died in 1884 while on a tour of Europe.[10] As a young man, MacPhail changed the spelling of his last name from "McPhail" to "MacPhail" to emphasize his father's Scottish roots.[11] As for his nickname, it is routinely claimed that "back in the Thirties[, when he was refereeing a Big Ten college football game,] along came a sportswriter who mistakenly called him Larry in a story and the name just stuck."[12] This explanation, however, is incorrect, for there are several 1929 newspaper articles about MacPhail's participation in the Columbus (Ohio) District Golf Association that identify him as "Larry."[13]

At the start of his career, MacPhail's father C.W. had been the owner of a general store. Because he would regularly extend credit and loan money to his customers, he got the idea to open a bank, and in 1882 started the Cass City State Bank.[14] When it proved to be a success, C.W. began to establish banks throughout western Michigan. As a result, MacPhail moved frequently as a child.[15]

Pre-Law Education

In September 1903, when MacPhail was 13, his parents sent him to the Staunton Military Academy ("SMA") in Staunton, Virginia. In a letter dated March 24, 1904, MacPhail's mother told Captain William H. Kable, the school's founder, how grateful she was for all that SMA was doing for MacPhail:

> I am convinced that he has received great benefit from the military drill, for we found him on our visit to your school in January with a much better chest development than when he entered your Academy last September....
>
> Your teachers appeared to be capable and worthy young men, and the thought that our son was under the supervision and instruction of exemplary and competent instructors has made his separation from us more endurable, as well as desirable for his ultimate advancement.[16]

Whether Catherine's comments about MacPhail's "chest development" were directed at his physique or a newfound sense of confidence is unknown.

MacPhail's stay at SMA turned out to be brief—by 1905, he was back home and attending Ludington High School ("LHS").[17] Although "[h]is teachers … claim[ed] they seldom saw him carry or open a book, … he was one of [LHS's] brightest students, earning nothing but A's and B's."[18] MacPhail also was the star first baseman of LHS's championship baseball team[19] and regularly played the organ at local Episcopal churches.[20]

During his senior year, MacPhail was offered a place in the U.S. Naval Academy's incoming class. Years later, MacPhail explained why he turned down the chance to be a midshipman: "I never could have passed the exams, because my background in mathematics was too skimpy."[21] Instead, in 1906 MacPhail enrolled in Beloit College ("BC"), a small liberal arts institution in Beloit, Wisconsin.[22]

MacPhail settled in quickly at BC. He pledged Beta Theta Pi fraternity[23] and in the winter played third base for its indoor baseball team.[24] In the spring, he joined the school's varsity baseball team, primarily playing first base but also spending time in the outfield.[25] In 1967, in recognition of his stellar play, MacPhail was inducted into the BC Athletic Hall of Honor.[26]

During his time at BC, MacPhail was a member of the debating club[27] and dated a fellow freshman named Ida D. Green, who was from Janesville, Wisconsin.[28] In her diary, Ida referred to MacPhail first as "Mr. McFail" (surely just a typo and not a comment on MacPhail's suitability as a boy-friend), then "Mr. McPhail," then "L. McPhail," and finally "Rusty" (due to MacPhail's red hair).[29] The couple was an item for five months, going to plays in Rockford, Illinois (where they saw productions of *Brown of Harvard* and *Strongheart*) and participating in a variety of BC social activities. After one such outing, Ida wrote in her diary that she had "never had a better time."[30] The romance ended, however, after MacPhail's temper caused a fight that lasted two days.[31]

Legal Education

Following his freshman year at BC, MacPhail decided that he wanted to be a lawyer. Because BC did not have a law school, MacPhail transferred to the University of Michigan ("UM"), which did have a law school (during this period a college degree was not a requirement for admission to law school).[32] According to many sources, MacPhail dropped out after his first semester due to vision problems,[33] but this seems unlikely given subsequent events.

MacPhail left UM at the end of the Spring 1908 semester. Had he stayed, he almost surely would have crossed paths with a later arriving student named Wesley Branch Rickey (Class of 1911), the subject of Chapter 6 of this book. MacPhail and Rickey later would meet (and eventually clash) after both became baseball executives.

In the Fall of 1908, MacPhail enrolled in the law school at George Washington University ("GWU") in Washington, D.C. Previously a night-only law school, GWU recently had started a day division. As *The Cherry Tree*, GWU's yearbook, explained:

> This wise arrangement makes the school available both to those who are unoc-cupied during the day and who can give their whole time to study, as well as to those employed in the Government Departments and who, in consequence, are able to devote only the late afternoons to the work.[34]

GWU allowed MacPhail to join its second-year class, meaning that he did not lose any time by transferring to GWU. (This fact makes it unlikely that MacPhail dropped out of UM's law school after his first semester.) Why MacPhail picked GWU is something of a mystery. It appears, however, that by this point he had decided to seek a position in the U.S. consular service and, as others have written, it is probable that he viewed GWU as providing him with a leg up.[35]

MacPhail likely also was drawn to GWU's law school because of its excellent faculty, one of whose members was U.S. Supreme Court Justice John Marshall Harlan (1833–1911).[36] In 1896, Harlan had been the only justice to register a dissent in *Plessy v. Ferguson,* the Court's notorious decision legitimizing the South's Jim Crow laws.[37]

While a student at GWU, MacPhail joined the John Marshall Inn (the law school's chapter of the national legal fraternity Phi Delta Phi); became a member of Theta Nu Epsilon (an offshoot of Yale University's Skull and Bones society); and served as an associate editor on *The Hatchet,* GWU's student newspaper.[38]

On June 7, 1910, MacPhail graduated from GWU with an LL.B.[39] That night, MacPhail and his fellow graduates held a farewell party at which the guest of honor was Dean William R. Vance (1870–1940). A short time earlier, Vance had announced that he was leaving GWU for a faculty position at Yale University's law school.[40]

By this time, a story had appeared in the *Washington Post* incorrectly identifying MacPhail as being a student at nearby Georgetown University.[41] As a result of this and subsequent erroneous reporting, MacPhail now often is described as having graduated from Georgetown's law school.

Admission to the Bar, Marriages, and Children

On October 15, 1910, MacPhail was admitted to the Illinois bar.[42] Five days later, he married Inez F. Thompson (1890–1965),[43] a striking brunette from Oak Park, Illinois.[44] Shortly before the wedding, Inez was forced to cancel the many "showers, card parties, and teas" that had been arranged in her honor due to the "unusual strain" they had placed on her.[45]

The couple had met three years earlier at a resort on Hamlin Lake, just a few miles north of Ludington, where their families both had summer cottages.[46] Inez's father Frank was the vice president of the American Car and Foundry Company, the country's leading manufacturer of railroad cars. At the 1903–04 World's Fair in St. Louis, Missouri, he had been recognized for his contributions in developing the country's first refrigerated railroad car.[47]

During their 35-year marriage (the pair divorced in 1945[48]), Inez and MacPhail had three children: Marian A. (later McDermott) (1912–93)[49]; Leland S. "Lee" Jr. (1917–2012)[50]; and William C. "Bill" (1920–96).[51] Like their father, both Lee and Bill ended up having great success in the sports world.

Lee became a widely respected baseball executive, serving as the general manager and president of the Baltimore Orioles (1959–65); the chief aide to Major League Baseball ("MLB") Commissioner William D. Eckert

(1965–66); the general manager of the New York Yankees (1967–73); and the president of the American League (1974–83). In 1998, he was elected to the Baseball Hall of Fame, making MacPhail and Lee the Hall's only father-and-son duo.[52]

Bill, on the other hand, went into broadcasting and became the president of CBS Sports and later the president of CNN Sports. While at CBS, he pioneered the use of "instant replay," which was employed for the first time during the storied 1963 Army-Navy football game.[53] In 1989, Bill became the first recipient of the Football Hall of Fame's Pete Rozelle Radio-Television Award.[54]

Within a week of his divorce from Inez becoming final, MacPhail married Jean B. Wanamaker (later Bauer) (1910–97), his secretary for the past seven years, in a small ceremony at the Belvedere Hotel in Baltimore, Maryland.[55] Together, they had one child, a daughter named Jean K. "Jennie" (later Duncan) (born 1946).[56]

Fowler, McDonnell, Rosenberg & MacPhail

Although it is agreed that MacPhail practiced law for only a short period of time, the exact details of his legal career are hazy and have been grossly embellished by later writers. In 1959, for example, *Sports Illustrated* overstated matters by gushing, "MacPhail argued his first case as a lawyer at 20. He found the courtroom a most congenial arena for his talents, and with his flaming red hair, his quick mind, his lung power and gift for nonstop oratory, he had all the equipment usually associated with great trial lawyers."[57]

After passing the Illinois bar and marrying Inez, many sources claim that MacPhail went to work for a law firm in Chicago but quit after six months because it refused to make him a partner.[58] Some of these sources hint that the unidentified law firm was Davis & Rankin ("D & R"),[59] and that while at D & R MacPhail lost 200 cases defending the Union Pacific Railroad Company.[60] These lawsuits supposedly were brought by shippers whose cargo was damaged, delayed, or destroyed due to the 1906 San Francisco earthquake. Just how this tale got started is impossible to say. There is no evidence, however, linking MacPhail and D & R.

Rather than the D & R story, it seems more likely that after passing the bar exam, MacPhail, in no immediate need of money, took his time looking for a job and only pursued firms that were willing to bring him in as a junior partner. While MacPhail's resume obviously was thin, his father's successful banking business, coupled with his father-in-law's railroad connections, would have allowed MacPhail to portray himself as a future rainmaker.

In early 1911, MacPhail found what he was looking for when the Chicago law firm of Fowler, McDonnell & Rosenberg offered to make him a partner. Following his acceptance, the firm reorganized itself as Fowler, McDonnell, Rosenberg & MacPhail ("FMRM").[61]

FMRM's lead partner was Frank L. Fowler (1870–1914).[62] After graduating from the University of Michigan's law school in 1892 and briefly working with John M. Harlan, the son of U.S. Supreme Court Justice John Marshall Harlan, Fowler opened a law office in his hometown of Manistee, Michigan. In 1906, he opened a second law office in Chicago and began splitting his time between the two locations. On June 29, 1911, MacPhail became a member of the Michigan bar, listing his local address as Manistee, Michigan.[63] (Some sources claim that MacPhail also was a member of the Washington, D.C., bar,[64] but no evidence supporting this assertion has been found.)

In July 1911, FMRM handled one of its very first cases when it petitioned the federal district court in Grand Rapids, Michigan, to place the Manistee Watch Company in bankruptcy.[65] After giving the company a year to try to work out its problems, the court granted trustee John A. Meier permission to liquidate the business.[66]

In December 1911, the first published case to list FMRM as counsel appeared. In *Maremont v. Muller,*[67] FMRM represented a party suing for specific performance on a real estate contract. To prevent the sellers from doing anything that might undermine its client's rights, FMRM obtained an interlocutory injunction. On appeal, the appellate court voted to keep the injunction in place.[68]

By now, MacPhail had been assigned to help reorganize the Rich Tool Company ("RTC"), a manufacturer of automobile parts and one of FMRM's most important clients.[69] MacPhail did an excellent job, and by September 1912 RTC had attracted new investors who had poured $90,000 (the equivalent today of $2.88 million[70]) into the company.[71]

With RTC back on its feet, MacPhail decided to leave FMRM—marking the end of his legal career—and go to work for RTC.[72] Thus, in the 1913 edition of *Martindale's American Law Directory*, MacPhail's office address is listed as the Railway Exchange Building,[73] which is where RTC had its offices.[74] Although he did not know it at the time, MacPhail had found what would become his lifelong calling card: the ability to turn around failing businesses.

Baseball Career

In 1915, MacPhail left RTC and moved to Nashville, Tennessee, where he became the new president of the troubled Huddleston-Cooper department store.[75] According to Lee MacPhail, his father had "bec[o]me close" with the store's owners (Ross H. Huddleston and Robert E. "Emmett" Cooper, Sr.) while working at FMRM. Thus, "when, in 1915, their store needed a reorganization, they hired him to come to Nashville and run the store."[76]

The remainder of MacPhail's life, extensively chronicled elsewhere,[77] can be quickly summarized here. In 1917, following the United States' entry into World War I, MacPhail left Huddleston-Cooper (which by now again was profitable) and joined the Army as a captain.[78] Sent to France, MacPhail was gassed and shot during the bloody Meuse-Argonne offensive but survived, although his eyesight was permanently impaired.[79] (Perhaps this is the basis for the claim that MacPhail left UM's law school due to vision trouble, although if so the timing is off by 10 years.)

In January 1919, MacPhail participated in an improbable plan to kidnap Kaiser Wilhelm II, who had been forced into exile at the Amerongen Castle in the Netherlands.[80] The plan was the brainchild of Colonel Luke Lea (1879–1945), an attorney, newspaper publisher, and politician whom MacPhail had known back in Nashville.[81] Although the plan failed, MacPhail managed to steal what later became a prized keepsake: a monogramed brass ashtray from the castle's library (often incorrectly identified as belonging to the Kaiser).[82]

In March 1919, MacPhail returned to the United States and, along with 1,200 other soldiers, was greeted by a delirious crowd in Knoxville, Tennessee.[83] After making his way back to Nashville, MacPhail soon decided to move to Columbus, Ohio.[84]

In the 1920 federal census, dated January 10, 1920, MacPhail is listed as the sales manager of the Prest-O-Lite Battery Company.[85] Whether he had this job before leaving Nashville, or found it after he moved to Columbus, is unknown. Soon, however, MacPhail was involved in many different businesses, including a car dealership selling Willys-Overland automobiles; several glass factories (which he ended up liquidating); a medical arts building (which he managed); and various real estate ventures.[86] While some sources claim that MacPhail also practiced law in Columbus,[87] there is no evidence to support this assertion. Moreover, MacPhail never joined the Ohio bar.

In 1930, MacPhail became part of a group seeking to save the Columbus Senators, a franchise in the Class AA American Association that was in danger of going under and leaving the city without a professional baseball team for the first time since 1883.[88] After paying $100,000 for the club, MacPhail immediately got to work reorganizing the Senators:

> MacPhail [first] brokered the sale of the club to Branch Rickey, and [the Senators, now renamed the Red Birds,] became part of the St. Louis Cardinals farm system, with MacPhail as president of the club.

[Then,] [t]hrough his entrepreneurial farsightedness and boldness, Mac-Phail brought the ailing Columbus team back to financial stability. He had a new stadium built and introduced three-dollar Ladies Day season tickets. He organized a knothole gang [to encourage youngsters to come to the ballpark] and also had lights installed [thereby making it possible for working men and women to attend games]. In 1932 the Columbus team outdrew the parent Cardinals 310,000 to 279,000. But MacPhail's insistence on putting the welfare of the Columbus team ahead of the parent team caused the first of his many rifts with Rickey, as they argued over the makeup of the Columbus and St. Louis rosters. [In May 1933, Rickey, having had enough, fired MacPhail, even though the Red Birds were in first place and on their way to winning the American Association's pennant.]

The personalities and lifestyles of MacPhail and Rickey made it highly unlikely they would ever get along. Rickey was an abstemious, churchgoing person; MacPhail was a drinker, a flashy dresser, and a loudmouth.[89]

Despite their differences, Rickey recognized that MacPhail had worked wonders with the Red Birds. Thus, in October 1933, when Powel Crosley, Jr., the new owner of the moribund Cincinnati Reds, asked Rickey to become the team's general manager, Rickey replied: "I've just the man for you. He's Larry MacPhail and he has great imagination. He'll come up with ideas to revive interest in your city. He's a wild man at times, but he'll do the job."[90]

Shortly after taking over the Reds, MacPhail made it the first MLB team to play night baseball: at 8:30 p.m. on May 24, 1935, Crosley Field suddenly was awash in artificial light after President Franklin D. Roosevelt pushed a ceremonial button at the White House.[91] Baseball would never be the same,[92] although at the time MacPhail was widely ridiculed for having the Reds play at night.[93] MacPhail, however, was untroubled by the criticism, although he later came to believe that too many baseball games were being played at night.[94]

In September 1936, MacPhail announced that he had decided to leave the Reds effective November 1, 1936.[95] By this time, MacPhail had built the foundation for the team's future success, which in 1939 bore fruit when the Reds went 97–57 and won the National League pennant. In 1940, the team did even better, going 100–53 and beating the Detroit Tigers in a thrilling seven-game World Series.[96]

After leaving the Reds, MacPhail briefly worked with his father C.W. and his half-brother Herman in the trio's newly formed investment company in Grand Rapids.[97] In January 1938, however, MacPhail agreed to become the general manager and vice president of the hapless Brooklyn Dodgers, who had not won anything in nearly two decades and were mired in debt.[98] Once again, MacPhail worked his magic, which resulted in the Dodgers becoming one of baseball's most valuable franchises and the winners of the National League's 1941 pennant.[99]

In September 1942, with the United States having entered World War II, MacPhail resigned from the Dodgers and rejoined the Army (this time as a lieutenant colonel).[100] In January 1945, MacPhail, although still in the service, became the general manager, president, and co-owner of the Yankees.[101] Immediately after the Yankees won the 1947 World Series (defeating the Dodgers in seven games), MacPhail sold his interest in the team to his fellow owners (Daniel R. Topping and Delbert E. "Del" Webb). While he made a profit estimated at $1 million,[102] the equivalent today of $13.88 million,[103] the sale marked the end of MacPhail's baseball career.

During his short stint with the Yankees, MacPhail authored what has become known as the "MacPhail Report." This document, which has no actual title, was presented to MLB's 16 team owners at a meeting held in Chicago on August 27, 1946. Although it identifies and discusses six "Problems" that baseball would have to confront in the aftermath of World War II, it is today almost exclusively remembered for its section dealing with the fifth problem, which it dubbed the "Race Question" (pages 18–20).

By this time, Rickey's plan to integrate the Dodgers (which he implemented in 1947) had become an open secret. MacPhail and his fellow committee members warned that if Rickey was successful in breaking baseball's color line (a fixture since 1887), the result would be twofold: (1) an increase in African American attendance at major league games, which would drive away White fans; and (2) the demise of the Negro Leagues, which would cost White owners revenue because many Black teams rented White-owned stadiums. The committee therefore recommended that Rickey be stopped. At the owners' meeting in Chicago, the report was approved 15–1, the Dodgers being the lone holdout.

Following the meeting, the owners were told to destroy their copies of the report. Years later, however, it was discovered that MLB Commissioner Albert B. "Happy" Chandler, Sr., the subject of Chapter 8 of this book, had kept his copy.[104]

In 1987, MacPhail's role in the affair was downplayed by Don Warfield, his principal biographer.[105] In a scathing review of Warfield's book, Professor Richard C. Crepeau of the University of Central Florida wrote:

> In treating these events Warfield does his best to denigrate Branch Rickey's motives and actions while absolving MacPhail from all charges of racism. In dealing with [the] MacPhail authored report, and its section on the race issue, Warfield writes: "The actual existence of this portion of the document seems never to have been entirely substantiated." (p. 207) A reading of Voigt's *American Baseball*, vol. III, or Tygiel's *Baseball's Great Experiment* negates this claim, and identifies MacPhail as one of the leaders of the forces opposing the desegregation of the National Pastime.[106]

Following his departure from the Yankees in 1947, MacPhail retired to his 960-acre cattle and horse breeding farm ("Glenangus") in Harford County, Maryland, later telling reporters: "I love this life, and I'll probably live 10 years longer than if I'd stayed in baseball. There's something about the turf—tomorrow is more appealing and interesting than today."[107] Even in this idyllic setting, however, MacPhail crossed swords with others:

Leland S. "Larry" MacPhail, Sr. (*c.* 1940) (**National Baseball Hall of Fame and Museum**).

In 1952, MacPhail headed a syndicate that purchased and refurbished the Bowie (Maryland) Race Track. He became president of the track, but served in that capacity for only a brief time.

Larry was involved in an altercation outside the track on April 12, 1953. He was upset and angry about the manner in which Maryland State Policemen were directing traffic leaving the facility. He became embroiled in an argument with one of the officers. The argument turned into an attack by MacPhail, [who was] arrested on a charge of being drunk and disorderly and assaulting a police officer.

Three days later, the Maryland Racing Commission barred [MacPhail] from his own track, pending a hearing. On April 17, the board of directors of the Bowie Race Track removed Larry from its presidency. The directors were responding to an incident involving MacPhail and three horse owners in the Bowie clubhouse earlier in the afternoon of the run-in with the State Police.

MacPhail won a judgment in court two years later, although he never regained his position at the race track. He was awarded $99,710.10 from the Bowie management in a breach-of-contract suit.[108]

Conclusion

MacPhail remained at Glenangus until June 1974.[109] In June 1975, Texas hamburger magnate James T. Dresher became the property's new owner after agreeing to pay $1.21 million for it.[110] By this time, MacPhail, in declining health, had moved into the Jackson Manor nursing home in Miami, Florida; in September 1975, just days before his death, he was transferred to the nearby Miami Veterans Administration Medical Center, where he died of pneumonia on October 1, 1975, at the age of 85.[111]

In 1966, when he had been out of baseball for nearly two decades, Minor League Baseball named a new award for MacPhail (the MacPhail Promotional Trophy), which for many years was given annually to the minor league team having the country's best marketing-and-promotions program.[112]

In July 1968, MacPhail, a lifelong Republican, returned to the public stage one last time when he announced that he was forming a group called "Athletes for Nixon."[113] On October 29, 1968, the group held a $500-a-plate fundraiser in Chicago; in large display ads inviting the public to send in contributions, MacPhail listed both his name and the names of the more than 500 athletes he had managed to sign up.[114]

In 1978, three years after his death, MacPhail was elected to the Baseball Hall of Fame.[115] His Hall of Fame plaque credits him as follows: "Pioneered night baseball at Cincinnati in 1935. Also installed lights at Ebbets Field and Yankee Stadium. Originated plane travel by playing personnel and idea of stadium club. Helped set up employee and player pension plans."[116] Left out of this summary is the fact that MacPhail also played significant roles in the invention of the batting helmet (after Dodgers outfielder Joseph M. "Ducky" Medwick was hit in the head during a game against the Cardinals at Ebbets Field on June 18, 1940)[117] and the creation of Old-Timer's Day (first held on September 22, 1940, at Ebbets Field).[118]

In 2012, when a reporter asked him to describe his grandfather, Andrew B. "Andy" MacPhail (himself an MLB executive), replied: "My grandfather was bombastic, flamboyant, a genius when sober, brilliant when he had one drink and a raving lunatic when he had too many."[119] Years earlier, Dodgers manager Leo Durocher had put matters more bluntly: "There is a thin line between genius and insanity. In Larry's case, it's sometimes so thin you can see him drifting back and forth."[120]

NOTES

1. MacPhail's plaque can be viewed at *Larry MacPhail*, NATIONAL BASEBALL HALL OF FAME AND MUSEUM, https://baseballhall.org/hall-of-famers/macphail-larry (last visited July 1, 2024) [hereinafter *MacPhail HOF Plaque*].

2. *See Many Get Degrees: Scholastic Honors for 166 Candidates; G.W.U. Commencement, Procession of Students in Academic Gowns and Caps; Gold Cane for [University President] Dr. Needham—Diplomas Awarded at Exercises in Belasco Theater This Morning*, EVENING STAR (DC), June 8, 1910, at 1. MacPhail's name appears with the other LL.B. recipients. *See id.* at 3.

3. Much of the information in this essay comes from the following sources: G. Richard McKelvey, The MacPhails: Baseball's First Family of the Front Office (2000) [hereinafter Front Office]; Lee MacPhail, My Nine Innings: An Autobiography of 50 Years in Baseball (1989) [hereinafter Nine Innings]; Don Warfield, The Roaring Redhead: Larry MacPhail—Baseball's Great Innovator (1987); *MacPhail, Larry, in* Current Biography 375–78 (Anna Rothe ed., 1945); Arthur Mann, *The Larry MacPhail Story*, 21:4 Sport 76 (Apr. 1956) (Part One) and 21:5 Sport 42 (May 1956) (Part Two).

4. See *Cass City Rotarians Honor Larry McPhail*, Sebewaing Blade (MI), Oct. 10, 1941, at 1. A slightly different description of MacPhail's birth appears in a 1947 magazine article. According to it, "MacPhail was born on February 3, 1890, in a small frame house in Cass City." Jack Sher, *Larry McPhail: The Man and the Mouth*, 3:1 Sport 61, 64 (July 1947). While filling out his World War I registration card, MacPhail listed his birth year as 1888. See *Leland Stanford Macphail [sic] in the U.S., World War I Draft Registration Cards, 1917–1918,* Ancestry.com, https://www.ancestry.com/discoveryui-content/view/22356281:6482 (last visited July 1, 2024). On his headstone, however, his birth year is listed as 1890. See *Leland MacPhail,* Find-a-Grave.com, https://www.findagrave.com/memorial/5860525/leland_macphail (last visited July 1, 2024).

5. For an obituary of Catherine, see *Mrs. C.W. M'Phail is Taken by Death; Ill Several Years,* Ludington Daily News (MI), Oct. 2, 1931, at 1. See also *Catherine Ann McMurtrie [sic] McPhail,* Find-a-Grave.com, https://www.findagrave.com/memorial/90158935/catherine_ann_mcphail (last visited July 1, 2024).

6. For an obituary of C.W., see *C.W. M'Phail, Banker, Dies: Prominent Grand Rapids Business Man Passes at Age of 83,* Herald-Press (St. Joseph, MI), May 11, 1939, at 6. See also *Curtis William McPhail,* Find-a-Grave.com, https://www.findagrave.com/memorial/90158672/curtis_william_mcphail (last visited July 1, 2024).

7. See *Curtis W. McPhail in the Michigan, U.S., County Marriage Records, 1822–1940,* Ancestry.com, https://www.ancestry.com/discoveryui-content/view/152167:61374 (last visited July 1, 2024). In 1879, C.W. had married Matilda A. Purvis (1860–86), with whom he had three children: Herman W. (1880–1944); Nina (1882–82); and Merritt G. "Glenn" (1886–86). See *Herman Ward MacPhail,* Find-a-Grave.com, https://www.findagrave.com/memorial/99996256/herman-ward-macphail (last visited July 1, 2024); *Nina McPhail,* Find-a-Grave.com, https://www.findagrave.com/memorial/90159124/nina_mcphail (last visited July 1, 2024); *Glenn McPhail,* Find-a-Grave.com, https://www.findagrave.com/memorial/90159026/glenn_mcphail (last visited July 1, 2024). Matilda died while giving birth to Glenn. See *Mathilda [sic] A McPhail in the Michigan, U.S., Death Records, 1867–1952,* Ancestry.com, https://www.ancestry.com/discoveryui-content/view/2829552:60872 (last visited July 1, 2024) (at Record 103). See also *Matilda A. "Tillie" Purvis McPhail,* Find-a-Grave.com, https://www.findagrave.com/memorial/90159076/matilda-a.-mcphail (last visited July 1, 2024).

8. See *Catherine Ann McMurtrie McPhail Find-a-Grave Webpage, supra* note 5.

9. See *Curtis William McPhail Find-a-Grave Webpage, supra* note 6.

10. In 1885, the Stanfords endowed Stanford University in their son's honor. For a further look at the Stanfords, see Roland De Wolk, American Disruptor: The Scandalous Life of Leland Stanford (2019).

11. See *What's in a Name?*, 33:4 The Way It Was (newsletter of the Cass City Area Historical & Genealogy Society) 1, 1 (Oct. 2022), https://www.rawsonlibrary.org/events/newsletters/historical-society-newsletter-november-2022-1.pdf. The earliest evidence I have found of MacPhail spelling his last name "MacPhail" is an April 1909 newspaper story. See L.S. MacPhail, *Colts Trim Locals: Commissioners No Match for Chicago Team—Anson's Playing a Feature,* Wash. Herald, Apr. 6, 1909, at 8 (reporting on a baseball game between the semi-professional Chicago Colts and the amateur Washington Commissioners).

12. John Dorsey, *The Lives of Larry MacPhail: He Has Been Baseball Magnate, Horse Breeder, Race Track Owner, Lawyer, Musician, Soldier,* Sun Mag. (Balt.), Nov. 27, 1966, at 18, 18.

13. For the earliest such article, see *Golf District to Propose a Merger,* Scioto Gaz.

(Chillicothe, OH), Apr. 18, 1929, at 11 ("Larry S. MacPhail, president of the Columbus District Golf Association, has extended a special invitation to officers of the Chillicothe Country Club to attend a meeting of Dayton and Columbus District Golf Associations here Monday to consider the proposed merger into one body to be known as the Central Ohio Golf Association").

14. See *Curtis William McPhail Find-a-Grave Webpage, supra* note 6.

15. *Id. See also* Rothe, *supra* note 3, at 375 ("During Larry's youth his father branched out into banking in Ludington, Michigan, and 'as he traveled from one town to another, establishing banks, the family went along.'").

16. STAUNTON MILITARY ACADEMY, 1904–05 CATALOG 100–01 (1904) (reproducing Catherine's letter).

17. In a 1941 article, sportswriter Leon S. "Lee" Kruska reported that MacPhail attended Scottville High School ("SHS") for two years before transferring to LHS for his junior and senior years. *See* Lee Kruska, *Memories of MacPhail: Present Brooklyn Manager Once Played on Championship Ludington Team*, LUDINGTON DAILY NEWS (MI), Oct. 6, 1941, at 6. The most likely scenario is that MacPhail started at SHS, then went to SMA, and then enrolled in LHS upon his return from Virginia.

18. *Id.*

19. *Id.* Among LHS's opponents was Paw Paw High School, whose star catcher was William L. "Bill" Killefer, a future battery mate of Hall of Famer Grover Cleveland Alexander. *See* Charlie Weatherby, *Bill Killefer*, SABR, https://sabr.org/bioproj/person/Bill-Killefer/ (last visited July 1, 2024).

20. *See* FRONT OFFICE, *supra* note 3, at 95. As an adult, MacPhail's love of music was well known. In 1941, composer (Robert) Russell Bennett, a former semi-pro baseball player, wrote *Symphony in D for the Dodgers.* The third movement, titled "Larry MacPhail Looks for a Pitcher," humorously imagines MacPhail trying to trade Brooklyn's Prospect Park to the Cleveland Indians for future Hall-of-Famer Robert W.A. "Bob" Feller. *See* Jimmy Wood, *Music Hath Charms*, BROOKLYN EAGLE, June 24, 1941, at 13.

21. Sher, *supra* note 4, at 64.

22. *See* Class of 1910, 53:1 THE ROUND TABLE (weekly newspaper of Beloit College) 7, 8 (Sept. 28, 1906) (listing McPhail as a member of the Class of 1910). For a history of BC (founded 1846), see EDWARD DWIGHT EATON, HISTORICAL SKETCHES OF BELOIT COLLEGE, WITH CHAPTERS BY MEMBERS OF THE FACULTY (1928).

23. *See* Beta Theta Pi, 53:11 THE ROUND TABLE 109 (Dec. 18, 1906).

24. *See* League Games, 53:18 THE ROUND TABLE 180 (Feb. 22, 1907); *Indoor Baseball*, 53:20 THE ROUND TABLE 204 (Mar. 8, 1907).

25. *See, e.g., College Takes First Two Games*, 53:25 THE ROUND TABLE 252 (Apr. 19, 1907) (MacPhail playing first base against the Freeport Pretzels of the Class D Wisconsin State League); *First Intercollegiate Game*, 53:26 THE ROUND TABLE 258, 259, 260 (Apr. 26, 1907) (MacPhail playing right field against Northwestern University and left field against the Pretzels). For a photograph of MacPhail with his teammates, see 53:32 THE ROUND TABLE 318 (June 7, 1907). In an accompanying article, MacPhail was described as having "surpassed everyone at first base." *The Base Ball Season: Captain Henry A. Arnold Reviews the Work of the Season*, 53:32 THE ROUND TABLE 319, 319 (June 7, 1907).

26. *See Two Named to BC Athletic Hall of Honor*, 117:7 THE ROUND TABLE 13 (Oct. 26, 1967).

27. *See* Robert Lewis Taylor, *Borough Defender–Part II*, NEW YORKER, July 19, 1941, at 20 (claiming that MacPhail was "one of the loudest debaters in the history of Beloit College").

28. Ida left BC before earning her degree. *See* 23:4 BELOIT COLLEGE BULL.: ALUMNI REG. 1925, at 49 (June 1925) (under listing for "Ida Green-Jeffris (Mrs. Malcom Jeffris)").

29. WARFIELD, *supra* note 3, at 4.

30. *Id.*

31. *Id.*

32. *See War Service Class Notes*, 49:1 MICHIGAN ALUMNUS 104–05 (Oct. 3, 1942) (listing MacPhail as a member of UM law school's class of 1907–08).

33. *See, e.g.,* G. Richard McKelvey, *MacPhail, Leland Stanford, Sr. ("Larry"), in* 2

SCRIBNER ENCYCLOPEDIA OF AMERICAN LIVES, THEMATIC SERIES: SPORTS FIGURES 98–99 (Arnold Markoe ed., 2002).

34. GEORGE WASHINGTON UNIVERSITY, THE CHERRY TREE 90 (1910).

35. *See, e.g.*, FRANK GRAHAM, THE BROOKLYN DODGERS: AN INFORMAL HISTORY 152 (2002 ed.) (1945) ("[With] his eyes ... on the diplomatic service, [MacPhail] soon ... left Ann Arbor for Washington, where he attended George Washington University, possibly because he believed that if he was on the spot, an appointment as a consul might come faster"). Numerous sources report that MacPhail ended up being "offered a consular appointment to a French seaport, which he declined." *See, e.g.*, Rothe, *supra* note 3, at 375. Although no source identifies the seaport, it seems likely that it was Fort-de-France on the Caribbean island of Martinique. On March 2, 1910, consul George B. Anderson, who had held the post since 1908, suffered a fatal heart attack while on a visit back home in the United States. *See George B. Anderson: Consul at Martinique Dies Suddenly on Train*, DAILY TIMES (Chattanooga), Mar. 3, 1910, at 3. On June 22, 1910, President William Howard Taft nominated Thomas R. Wallace to succeed Anderson. *See Taft Names Consuls*, COMM. APPEAL (Memphis), June 23, 1910, at 16. For a further discussion, see Sébastien Perrot-Minnot, *Once Upon a Time: The U.S. Consulate in Martinique*, 100:9 FOR. SERV. J. 53 (Nov. 2023) (explaining that the consulate closed in 1993).

36. *See* THE CHERRY TREE, *supra* note 34, at 90.

37. *See* Plessy v. Ferguson, 163 U.S. 537 (1896). For a biography of Harlan, nicknamed "The Great Dissenter" for his many dissents while on the Court, see LOREN P. BETH, JOHN MARSHALL HARLAN: THE LAST WHIG JUSTICE (1992).

38. *See* THE CHERRY TREE, *supra* note 34, at 213 (Phi Delta Phi), 231 (Theta Nu Epsilon), and 297 (*The Hatchet*). *See also Peeps into Frat House Disclose Students at Ease: Washington Contains Many Handsome Quarters; Keep College Days Green*, WASH. HERALD (DC), Mar. 13, 1910, at 8 (listing MacPhail as a student member of GWU's Phi Delta Phi chapter).

39. *See Many Get Degrees, supra* note 2.

40. *See Law School Graduates at Farewell Smoker: Dean Vance of George Washington University and Others Guests of the Class*, EVENING STAR (DC), June 8, 1910, at 3. During the party, the graduates adopted a resolution urging the university to name Professor Ernest G. Lorenzen (1876–1951) as Vance's replacement, with MacPhail being appointed to the committee charged with drafting the resolution. *Id.* Three days later, Lorenzen was given the job. *See Lorenzen to be Dean: Takes Vance's Post at G.W.U. Law School; Announces that this Department will be Maintained at Its Present Standard*, EVENING STAR (DC), June 11, 1910, at 7. For a profile of Vance, see *William R. Vance*, BOS. DAILY GLOBE, Oct. 24, 1940, at 19. *See also William Reynolds Vance*, FIND-A-GRAVE.COM, https://www.findagrave.com/memorial/147401408/william-reynolds-vance (last visited July 1, 2024). For a profile of Lorenzen, see *Prof. Lorenzen Rites Tomorrow*, OAKLAND TRIB., Feb. 13, 1951, at 27. Lorenzen does not have a *Find-a-Grave* webpage.

41. *See Met by Chance on Boat: University Student Gives Details of Trip to See Fleet Return*, WASH. POST, Mar. 7, 1909, at 14 ("Leland McPhail, a student at Georgetown University, explained yesterday how he and a companion, Harry Kitselman, happened to witness the review of the fleet in Hampton Roads, in company with the young ladies from a Washington seminary").

42. *See Many Chicagoans in 82 Admitted to Bar: Sixty-Four from City and Cook County Pass Examinations in Springfield, Supreme Court Issues Certificates to Applicants; Five from Capital City Among Fortunate Ones, Thirteen Others Entered from Edwards, Vermillion, Tazewell, Logan, Kane, Shelby, Montgomery, Madison and Effingham Counties*, INTER OCEAN (Chi.), Oct. 16, 1910, at 8 (listing MacPhail as being among the newly licensed). The Attorney Registration & Disciplinary Commission of the Supreme Court of Illinois gives MacPhail's admission date as October 18, 1910, likely the date MacPhail's admission was officially recorded. *See* https://www.iardc.org/ (last visited July 1, 2024) (under "Lawyer Search" for "L.S. MacPhail").

43. For Inez's obituary, see *Mrs. Inez T. MacPhail*, SUN (Balt.), June 20, 1965, at 25. Inez does not have a *Find-a-Grave* webpage.

44. *See [No Headline in Original]*, DET. FREE PRESS, Oct. 30, 1910, at 3 ("Mr. L.S. McPhail

and his bride, who was Miss Inez Thompson of Chicago, are spending some time … in [Detroit]…. [They were] married … October 20, in the home of her parents…. It was a small wedding for the families and … intimate friends only. Their future home will be in Chicago where Mr. McPhail is a young lawyer"). The pair's engagement had been announced just a few weeks earlier. *See In the World of Society: News of Official and Other Sets; Already a Bud is on Her Way to Bloom—Wedding Notes*, Evening Star (DC), Oct. 3, 1910, at 7. For a photograph of Inez, see *In the Society World*, Chi. Daily Trib., Oct. 19, 1910, at 6.

45. *See Too Many Teas Stop Fetes: Intended Bride, Overwhelmed by Trips to Dressmaker and Showers, Cancels Prenuptial Entertainment*, Chi. Daily Trib., Oct. 16, 1910, at 4.

46. *See* Nine Innings, *supra* note 3, at 15.

47. *Id.*

48. *See Larry MacPhail's Wife Wins Decree*, Daily News (NY), May 8, 1945, at 28 ("Inez T. MacPhail was granted a divorce today in Harford County [Mayland] Circuit Court from President Leland S. (Larry) MacPhail of the New York Yankees baseball club [after a separation of] more than five years…. [A] financial settlement ha[s] been made out of court").

49. For an obituary of Marian, see *Marian MacPhail McDermott, Retired Life Magazine Researcher*, Poughkeepsie J. (NY), Aug. 29, 1993, at 2B. *See also Marian MacPhail McDermott*, Find-a-Grave.com, https://www.findagrave.com/memorial/157702556/marian_mcdermott (last visited July 1, 2024).

50. *See Lee MacPhail*, Find-a-Grave.com, https://www.findagrave.com/memorial/100425484/lee_macphail (last visited July 1, 2024).

51. *See William Curtis "Bill" MacPhail*, Find-a-Grave.com, https://www.findagrave.com/memorial/262574561/william_curtis_macphail (last visited July 1, 2024).

52. For a further look at Lee's life, see Richard Goldstein, *Lee MacPhail, 95, Baseball Executive at Center of a Pine-Tar Uproar, Dies*, N.Y. Times, Nov. 10, 2012, at D8.

53. *See Greatest Moments in College Football—No. 2 Navy 21, Army 15—Municipal Stadium, Philadelphia, Dec. 7, 1963*, College Football Hall of Fame, Dec. 12, 2002, https://www.cfbhall.com/news-and-happenings/blog/greatest-moments-in-college-football-no-2-navy-21-army-15-municipal-stadium-philadelphia-dec-7-1963/ (explaining that because of the assassination of President John F. Kennedy just days before the game, CBS did not announce that it was going to be using the technology, which resulted in the network being inundated with phone calls from confused viewers after it replayed Army quarterback Carl R. "Rollie" Stichweh's five-yard touchdown run in the third quarter).

54. For a further look at Bill's life, see Richard Sandomir, *Bill MacPhail, 76, Pioneer in Development of TV Sports*, N.Y. Times, Sept. 5, 1996, at D21.

55. *See Larry M'Phail Weds Secretary Here*, Evening Sun (Balt.), May 16, 1945, at 1. For Jean's obituary, see *Bauer, Jean W.*, Sun (Balt.), July 15, 1997, at 11B. Jean does not have a *Find-a-Grave* webpage.

56. *See Jean MacPhail, J.W. Duncan Jr., Plan Marriage*, N.Y. Times, Sept. 24, 1972, at 84 ("Mr. and Mrs. Leland Stanford (Larry) MacPhail have announced the engagement of their daughter, Miss Jean Katherine MacPhail, to James W. Duncan Jr…. [The bride's] father is [the] former president of the Brooklyn Dodgers and New York Yankees Baseball Clubs").

57. Gerald Holland, *Horses, Carrots and Pimlico*, Sports Illus., Aug. 24, 1959, at 62.

58. *See, e.g.*, Taylor, *supra* note 27, at 20 ("The law firm MacPhail attached himself to neglected to make him a partner within six months, so he [left].."); Rothe, *supra* note 3, at 375 ("After six months, during which the Chicago firm failed to make him a partner, the impatient young lawyer left…").

59. Davis & Rankin's partners were Brode B. Davis (1868–1943) and John M. Rankin (1873–1947). In 1904, Rankin became a clerk in Davis's firm and in 1909 was elevated to partner. *See* The Book of Chicago 1911, at 64 (1911). For an obituary of Davis, see *Brode B. Davis*, N.Y. Times, May 20, 1943, at 21. Davis does not have a *Find-a-Grave* webpage. For an obituary of Rankin, see *Atty. Gen. Rankin, 74, Dies Here: Long Illness Fatal to High State Official*, Des Moines Trib., June 20, 1947, at 1 (explaining that Rankin moved to Iowa in 1917 and became the state's attorney general in 1940). *See also John Mercer Rankin*, Find-a-Grave.com, https://www.findagrave.com/memorial/157881542/john-mercer-rankin (last visited July 1, 2024).

60. *See, e.g.,* Steven P. Gietschier, Baseball: The Turbulent Midcentury Years 156 (2023); Front Office, *supra* note 3, at 2; Warfield, *supra* note 3, at 6.

61. A new partnership, consisting of Frank L. Fowler, Francis A. McDonnell, Joseph Rosenberg, and MacPhail, with locations at Chicago, Illinois (1444 First National Bank Building) and Manistee, Michigan (Fowler Building), appears at pages 17 and 42 of the November 1911 "Confidential Change Sheet" published by *Martindale's American Law Directory* (one of the forerunners of the current *Martindale-Hubbell Law Directory*). During this time, change sheets were used by *Martindale's* to keep its directory current between editions. *See id.* at 1 ("Attach this to your Law Directory—Always Consult It First, Before Referring to Directory—Destroy all former Change Sheets").

62. For an obituary of Fowler, see *Town Happenings*, Waukegan Daily Sun (IL), May 4, 1914, at 8 (indicating that Fowler died after a two-week fight with typhoid fever). *See also Frank Lincoln Fowler*, Find-a-Grave.com, https://www.findagrave.com/memorial/96591652/frank-lincoln-fowler (last visited July 1, 2024).

63. *See* 21 Proceedings of the Twenty-First Annual Meeting of the Michigan State Bar Association—Battle Creek, Michigan—Thursday and Friday, July 6 and 7, 1911, at 114 (1911) (listing MacPhail as a new member of the Michigan bar).

64. *See, e.g.,* Rothe, *supra* note 3, at 375.

65. *See* Andrew Dervan, *The Sad Tale of the Manistee Watch Co.*, 65:6 Watch & Clock Bull. 366, 378 (Nov./Dec. 2023) ("The petition was filed by four creditors, who allege[d] the company ha[d] liabilities amounting to $125,000.... The *Manistee Daily News* identified the four creditors [as being represented by] Fowler, McDonnell, Rosenberg, and McPhail...").

66. *See* In re Manistee Watch Co., 197 F. 455 (W.D. Mich. 1912).

67. 166 Ill. App. 503, 1911 WL 3053 (1911).

68. *Id.* at 506.

69. *See* Taylor, *supra* note 27, at 20.

70. *See* S. Morgan Friedman, *The Inflation Calculator*, https://westegg.com/inflation/ (last visited July 1, 2024) (converting 1912 dollars to 2023 dollars).

71. *See New Incorporations—Changes*, Chi. Daily Trib., Sept. 4, 1912, at 17.

72. Despite this fact, in June 1913 a court decision appeared listing FMRM as counsel. *See* Rosenberg v. Miller, 181 Ill. App. 443, 1913 WL 2568 (Ill. App. Ct. 1913). In all likelihood, the case began while MacPhail was still at FMRM and the court was never told about his departure.

73. *See* Martindale's American Law Directory (Annual)—January, 1913, at 996 (45th ed. 1912).

74. *See* Will R. MacDonald, *Automotive World*, Det. Free Press, Mar. 19, 1925, at 12 ("The Rich Tool Company has consolidated its office and executive, sales, engineering, treasury and accounting departments at the plant offices, 1501 Ferry Avenues East. The offices were formerly located in the Railway Exchange Building, Chicago").

75. *See* Front Office, *supra* note 3, at 2; Warfield, *supra* note 3, at 7.

76. Nine Innings, *supra* note 3, at 16.

77. *See, e.g.,* the sources cited *supra* note 3.

78. *See Display Ad*, Nashville Tennessean & Nashville Am., Nov. 15, 1917, at 16 ("Beginning this morning a stupendous dissolution & re-organization sale [will be held because] Mr. L.S. MacPhail, who is a member of this firm, has recently assumed the responsibility of commanding one of the many batteries now on the eve of departure for European battlefields. His withdrawal is due to the uncertainty of his return, and he requests that we take over his interest immediately. To satisfactorily expedite matters, we must materially reduce the tremendous stock we have on hand, hence this Dissolution Sale. In order to turn merchandise into money, and do it quickly, we have re-marked and placed at your disposal merchandise at 20 to 35 per cent off our regular selling prices").

79. *See* Rothe, *supra* note 3, at 376. For a detailed look at the offensive, which lasted 47 days and resulted in 26,000 American deaths, see Edward G. Lengel, To Conquer Hell: The Meuse-Argonne, 1918: The Epic Battle That Ended the First World War (2008).

80. To enter the Netherlands (a neutral country), MacPhail was required to obtain an emergency passport. A copy of his application, dated January 4, 1919, can be viewed at *Leland S Macphail [sic] in the U.S., Passport Applications, 1795–1925*, ANCESTRY.COM, https://www.ancestry.com/discoveryui-content/view/2106020:1174 (last visited July 1, 2024).

81. Lea, a 1903 graduate of Columbia University's law school, was the first editor of the *Nashville Tennessean* and served one term as Tennessee's U.S. senator (1911–17). In 1931, he was convicted of bank fraud and served two years in prison, although he later received a full pardon. For a further look at Lea's life, see *Col. Luke Lea, War Hero, Ex-Senator, Publisher Dies in Hospital Here: Gastric Ailment Fatal to State Political Leader*, NASHVILLE TENNESSEAN, Nov. 19, 1945, at 1. *See also Luke Lea*, FIND-A-GRAVE.COM, https://www.findagrave.com/memorial/6380335/luke-lea (last visited July 1, 2024).

82. *See Who Got Ex-Kaiser's Brass Ash Tray?: Perhaps It Found Its Way to Tennessee; Incident Recalls Further Verification of Col. Lea's Visit to Ex-Kaiser*, CHATTANOOGA NEWS, Apr. 5, 1919, at 5 ("When [Count Godard Bentinck, the owner of the castle and thus the Kaiser's host] found that the ash tray, which was on the library table, was gone, it seems he raised a big howl about it and wanted to know who took it…. It is rumored that the souvenir of the visit landed safely in Tennessee…. The blame is between Capt. McPhail and other officers who were of the [raiding] party"). *See also* Mitchell Yockelson, *The Bizarre Tale of a Kidnapping Attempt, the German Kaiser and a Beloved Ashtray*, WASH. POST, Aug. 14, 2018, https://www.washingtonpost.com/news/retropolis/wp/2018/08/05/the-bizarre-tale-of-a-kidnapping-attempt-the-german-kaiser-and-a-beloved-ashtray/ ("Sitting next to Lea in the Winton's back seat [on the ride back to base], Capt. MacPhail reached into his pocket and said, 'Colonel, I have secured a souvenir for you and the other members of the party.' Without looking down, Lea replied, 'I don't want to hear nor know what I think you have done.'"). For a look at the Kaiser's stay at the castle (which was supposed to be for three days but ended up lasting 18 months), see Sally Marks, *"My Name Is Ozymandias": The Kaiser in Exile*, 16 CENT. EUR. HIST. 122 (1983). Marks discusses Lea's attempt to kidnap the Kaiser *id.* at 135–36. *See also* Luke Lea & William T. Alderson, *The Attempt to Capture the Kaiser*, 23:3 TENN. HIST. Q. 222 (Sept. 1961).

83. *See 30,000 Knoxvillians Greet Heroes of 114th Artillery: Warm Welcome for Overseas Fighters; Glorious Reception Accorded Veterans of St. Mihiel Drive and Argonne Forest Battle—Great Review of Men Unsurpassed Spectacle; Unbridled Enthusiasm and Expressions of Heartfelt Welcome Make Day One Long to Be Remembered in Knoxville*, SUN. J. & TRIB. (Knoxville), Mar. 30, 1919, at 1, 2 ("The remainder of the parade in order of marching was as follows: Battery B, commanded by Capt. L.S. McPhail, of Nashville…").

84. No source explains why MacPhail decided to relocate to Columbus. Certainly, however, Columbus, being a capital city, and having twice the population of Nashville, offered more opportunities for an entrepreneur like MacPhail. For a look at Columbus in the 1920s, see ED LENTZ, COLUMBUS: THE STORY OF A CITY 108–14 (2003).

85. *See Leland Mcphail [sic] in the 1920 United States Federal Census*, ANCESTRY.COM, https://www.ancestry.com/discoveryui-content/view/33526938:6061 (last visited July 1, 2024) (at Line 68).

86. *See* NINE INNINGS, *supra* note 3, at 18; WARFIELD, *supra* note 3, at 24–25; Taylor, *supra* note 27, at 22. *See also* JULES TYGIEL, PAST TIME: BASEBALL AS HISTORY 95–96 (2000).

87. *See, e.g.*, Mark Armour, *Lee MacPhail*, SABR, https://sabr.org/bioproj/person/lee-macphail/ (last visited July 1, 2024) ("When Larry returned home after the war, he opened a law practice in Columbus, Ohio"). In his free time, MacPhail *did* referee Big Ten football games. His son Lee later recalled: "[During my childhood,] I thought that the biggest sporting event in the world was the Ohio State-Michigan football game." *Id.*

88. For the city's baseball history, see JAMES R. TOOLE, BASEBALL IN COLUMBUS (2003).

89. Ralph Berger, *Larry MacPhail*, SABR, https://sabr.org/bioproj/person/larry-macphail/ (last visited July 1, 2024). While running the Red Birds, MacPhail, in addition to being the club's president, was a member of its board of directors. The four other members were Samuel W. "Sam" Breadon (the owner of the Cardinals); Columbus attorney George R. Hedges (1870–1955); Judge Benson W. Hough of the U.S. District Court for the Southern District of

Ohio (1875–1935); and Rickey. For a profile of Hedges, a partner in the law firm of Hedges, Hoover & Tingley, see *George R. Hedges, Columbus Lawyer, Succumbs in Home*, URBANA DAILY CITIZEN (OH), May 27, 1955, at 10. *See also George Robert Hedges*, FIND-A-GRAVE. COM, https://www.findagrave.com/memorial/30014542/george-robert-hedges (last visited July 1, 2024). For a profile of Hough, see *Benson W. Hough, 60, Federal Judge, Dies*, N.Y. TIMES, Nov. 20, 1935, at 23. *See also MG Benson Walker Hough*, FIND-A-GRAVE.COM, https://www.findagrave.com/memorial/11814438/benson-walker-hough (last visited July 1, 2024).

90. Arthur Daley, *When Delay Becomes Disgraceful*, N.Y. TIMES, Feb. 29, 1972, at 43.

91. *See* Jack Ryder, *Redlegs Defeat Phils in Night Game: Big Paul Shoots 'Em Over; Bowman is Shaded in Mound Duel, 2–1; Our Lads Make Four Blows Against Six for Foe—20,422 Attend*, CIN. ENQUIRER, May 25, 1935, at 1. In 1964, MacPhail flipped the script, pushing a ceremonial button that turned on the lights at Shea Stadium, the new home of the New York Mets. *See* Si Burick, *Reds, Larry MacPhail Again Share in Historic Night Baseball Game*, DAYTON DAILY NEWS, May 7, 1964, at 22.

92. For a further discussion, see CHARLIE BEVIS, BASEBALL UNDER THE LIGHTS: THE RISE OF THE NIGHT GAME (2021).

93. *See, e.g.*, Bob Husted, *The Referee*, DAYTON HERALD, Jan. 3, 1936, at 20 ("There was no little criticism poked at MacPhail because he turned the nights games at Crosley Field into extravaganzas with fireworks, band concerts and the like. They said MacPhail was selling … everything but baseball"). This was the beginning of MacPhail's extensive efforts to reinvent the fan experience, which later caused him to gain the nickname "The P.T. Barnum of Baseball." Today, MacPhail shares this nickname with several other people, including William L. "Bill" Veeck, Jr. (the former owner of the Cleveland Indians, St. Louis Browns, and Chicago White Sox) and Charles O. Finley (the former owner of the Kansas City/Oakland A's).

94. *See MacPhail for More Majors, Fewer Night Games; He'd Bet Bums Never Play in 'Ravine,'* ST. LOUIS POST-DISPATCH, Jan. 14, 1958, at 5B. MacPhail offered this opinion at a dinner honoring longtime Dodgers employee Joseph J. "Babe" Hamberger. It was the first time since leaving baseball that MacPhail had publicly spoken about the sport, except for 1951, when he had been required to testify before Congress about baseball's antitrust exemption. *See Study of Monopoly Power: Hearings on H.R. 2820 and S. 719 Before the Subcomm. on Study of Monopoly Power of the H. Comm. on the Judiciary*, 82d Cong., pt. 6, 1060–90 (Oct. 24, 1951) (statement of L. (Larry) S. MacPhail, Bel Air, Md.).

95. *See* Bob Saxton, *MacPhail Quits; Crosley May Take More Active Interest—Red Leader Leaves November 1, Successor to be Named Soon, Director Says; Both Sides Part on Best of Terms—General Manager Here Three Years*, ENQUIRER (Cin.), Sept. 19, 1936, at 13 (quoting MacPhail as saying, "I believe that my work here is about ended and can point with pride to the financial statements of the club over the last three years").

96. *See* BILL MULLIGAN, THE 1940 CINCINNATI REDS: A WORLD CHAMPIONSHIP AND BASEBALL'S ONLY IN-SEASON SUICIDE (2005) (Mulligan's title is a veiled reference to back-up catcher Willard M. Hershberger, who killed himself in August 1940 after performing poorly in two games, both of which the Reds lost).

97. The firm had been founded by C.W., Herman, and MacPhail in January 1936. *See Articles Are Filed by MacPhail Firm*, GRAND RAPIDS PRESS (MI), Jan. 3, 1936, at 22.

98. *See Brooklyn Club Names M'Phail Vice President: Former Cincinnati Reds' Official Given Long-Term Contract*, BROOKLYN CITIZEN, Jan. 19, 1938, at 1. The request "to take over and 'straighten out'" the Dodgers came from the Brooklyn Trust Company, the team's largest creditor, which had to ask MacPhail four times before he finally agreed. *See* Rothe, *supra* note 3, at 376–77.

99. In the 1941 World Series, the Dodgers lost to the Yankees in five games. The series was notable for two reasons: it was the first time the crosstown rivals were meeting in the Fall Classic, and it was the last one to be played before the United States' entry into World War II. For a further discussion, see DOM DIMAGGIO & BILL GILBERT, REAL GRASS, REAL HEROES: BASEBALL'S HISTORIC 1941 SEASON (1990). As DiMaggio and Gilbert point out, 1941 also was the season in which Joseph P. "Joe" DiMaggio (Dom's brother) hit in 56 straight games (a record now considered unbreakable) and Theodore S. "Ted" Williams batted .406 (making him the last player to hit .400 or better for an entire season).

100. *See MacPhail Resigns, Enters Army Sunday*, S.F. EXAMINER, Sept. 24, 1942, at 21 ("MacPhail, who was elevated to the presidency of the club in 1940, was just completing the first year of a new five-year contract under which he reportedly earned approximately $75,000. When he came to the club in 1938 it was a defunct property controlled by the Brooklyn Trust Co., its leading creditor. Under MacPhail the Dodgers have been converted into one of the most valuable properties in baseball"). A few months earlier (Apr. 27, 1942), MacPhail had filled out his draft registration card. On the back of the card he listed his height as 5'10½", his weight as 186 pounds, his complexion as ruddy, his hair as red, and his eyes as blue. *See Leland Stanford Macphail [sic] in the U.S., World War II Draft Registration Cards, 1942*, ANCESTRY.COM, https://www.ancestry.com/discoveryui-content/ view/484640:1002 (last visited July 1, 2024). In contrast to his World War I registration card, see *supra* note 4, this time MacPhail gave his actual birth date (February 3, 1890).

101. *See* Jack Smith & Dick Young, *MacPhail, Topping, Webb Buy Yanks*, DAILY NEWS (NY), Jan. 27, 1945, at 22 ("Against an appropriate background of scotch and soda, Larry MacPhail, flamboyant ex-boss of the Brooklyn Dodgers, came roaring back into the baseball world yesterday. Heading a three-man syndicate which also includes Capt. Dan Topping, owner of the [National Football League's Brooklyn] Tigers, and Del Webb, wealthy Arizona construction magnate, the colorful colonel completed the purchase of 96.88% of the vast New York Yankees baseball empire from the heirs of Col. Jacob H. Ruppert and Edward G. Barrow. The huge deal, MacPhail explained in his formal announcement to reporters at the 21 Club, involved between $2,800,000 and $3,000,000").

102. *See* John Drebinger, *Weiss Appointed General Manager: Former Farm Chief to Direct Yankees, Although Topping Becomes New President—Disputes Precede Shift; Partners Accept Resignation of MacPhail After Buying His One-Third Interest*, N.Y. TIMES, Oct. 8, 1947, at 31. The exact reason for MacPhail's departure is unclear, with there being at least three different theories: 1) MacPhail was frustrated by Topping and Webb's refusal to sell half the team to outside investors (which would have netted MacPhail even more money than the amount he received from the pair); 2) Topping and Webb ousted MacPhail after MacPhail had a drunken meltdown in the Yankees' locker room after Game 7 of the 1947 World Series, which embarrassed both Topping and Webb; and 3) MacPhail had been secretly banned from baseball in 1946 for associating with gamblers but had been given time to dispose of his Yankees' stock, which now was running out. *See id.*

103. *See* Friedman, *supra* note 70 (converting 1947 dollars to 2023 dollars).

104. *See* Frank Fitzpatrick, *Legacy of Shame: '46 Racial Views of Owners Exposed*, PHIL. INQUIRER, June 18, 1997, at E1, E6. Chandler's copy, included among the papers he donated to his law school (the University of Kentucky), has been digitized and can be viewed at Business of Baseball Committee, *League Report, 1946*, SABR, http://research.sabr.org/ business/resources/documents/category/17-other-reports (last visited July 1, 2024).

105. *See* WARFIELD, *supra* note 3, at 207.

106. Richard C. Crepeau, *Book Review*, 15 J. SPORT HIST. 205, 207 (1988).

107. Joseph Durso, *Baseball's Larry MacPhail Dies; Night-Game Pioneer Led Yanks*, N.Y. TIMES, Oct. 2, 1975, at 1. MacPhail purchased Glenangus in 1941 to have a place where he could "get away from baseball." *See* M.H. Cadwalader, *Refuge from the Diamond Dust*, SUN (Balt.), July 12, 1942, § 1, at 3.

108. FRONT OFFICE, *supra* note 3, at 94–95. For two more lawsuits arising from MacPhail's equine activities, see Board of Cnty. Com'rs of Harford Cnty. v. MacPhail, 133 A.2d 96 (Md. Ct. App. 1957) (roadway dispute), and *infra* note 111 (discussing *Sagner v. MacPhail*).

109. *See MacPhail Retiring After Long and Active Career: Horse Breeding Operation Changes Hands*, AEGIS (Bel Air, MD), June 20, 1974, at D9. In his later years, MacPhail increasingly split his time between Glenangus and his home in Key Biscayne, Florida. *See* Samuel Tilghman, *Former Baseball Magnate Larry MacPhail Disposing of Estate in Harford County*, EVENING SUN (Balt.), Nov. 11, 1969, at D4.

110. *See MacPhail's Famed Farm Going on Auction Block: 367 Acres Due to be Sold Wednesday*, AEGIS (Bel Air, MD), June 5, 1975, § 1, at 1; *MacPhail Sells Big Ranch*, DAILY MAIL (Hagerstown, MD), June 13, 1975, at 19.

111. *See Ex-Yank Boss MacPhail Dies*, Miami Herald, Oct. 2, 1975, at 1BW. *See also Leland MacPhail Find-a-Grave Webpage, supra* note 4 (noting that MacPhail is buried in the Elkland Township Cemetery in Cass City). According to one of his biographers,

> MacPhail's last years were sad. The ravages of alcohol and the onset of what is now presumed to be Alzheimer's disease were affecting his once great entrepreneurial mind. He was failing psychologically and physically. His children wanted to [keep] him [in] a private institution, but [at the end] he insisted on going to a veterans hospital, as if he wanted to recapture the past when he was an officer in both World Wars. He was obstreperous with the staff and to the very end true to his nature as the Roaring Redhead.

Berger, *supra* note 89. Another source adds: "MacPhail, who was posthumously elected to baseball's Hall of Fame, died virtually penniless in 1975. Court records indicate that during his later years MacPhail's personal assets had either been tied up in corporate and trust arrangements and mortgages or had been taken over by members of his family." Kimber Matzinger-Vought, *20 Year Old Legal Battle Over Racehorse Nears Finish Line: Principals in Dispute Now All Deceased*, Aegis (Bel Air, MD), July 30, 1981, at A3. (This headline refers to the various lawsuits growing out of MacPhail's unsuccessful effort in 1961 to syndicate a racehorse named Saggy. For a further discussion, see MacPhail v. Sagner, 293 A.2d 257 (Md. Ct. App. 1972). As the newspaper article explains, the subsequent court rulings are unreported.)

112. The award was discontinued after MLB took over minor league baseball in 2020. The last team to win the award was the Lehigh Valley (Pennsylvania) IronPigs, the Triple-A farm team of the Philadelphia Phillies. *See* Tim Housenick, *IronPigs' Office Earns Award*, Morn. Call (Allentown, PA), Oct. 25, 2019, at C6 ("The [IronPigs'] 2019 promotional calendar included unique theme nights like "Jawn" and "IronPugs"—unique, creative in-season marketing campaigns that captured the industry's attention").

113. *See* Gene Spagnoli, *MacPhail Heads Nixon's Lineup of Sports Stars*, Daily News (NY), July 13, 1968, at 7.

114. *See 516 of America's Greatest Athletes are for Dick Nixon*, Aegis (Bel Air, MD), Oct. 24, 1968, at D5. In 1970, Nixon named MacPhail to his Advisory Conference on Physical Fitness and Sports. *See President Names 50 to Fitness Advisory Conference*, President's Council on Physical Fitness and Sports—Newsletter 3 (Oct. 1970).

115. *See MacPhail and Joss are Chosen to Enter Baseball Hall of Fame*, N.Y. Times, Jan. 31, 1978, at 21.

116. *MacPhail HOF Plaque, supra* note 1. In 1970, when Yankees catcher Lawrence P. "Yogi" Berra was preparing to go into the Hall of Fame, MacPhail was asked why he was not enshrined. "Maybe they forgot me," he replied. Frank Eck, *How Can Baseball Forget Larry MacPhail?*, Home News (New Brunswick, NJ), Sept. 29, 1970, at 14. *See also* Daley, *supra* note 90 (asking the same question as Eck).

117. *See* Chris Creamer, *The Birth of Baseball's Batting Helmet*, SportsLogos.net, Apr. 21, 2022, https://news.sportslogos.net/2022/04/21/the-birth-of-baseballs-batting-helmet/baseball/.

118. *See* Tommy Holmes, *'Old Timers' Enjoy Romp at Ebbets Field: Fitzsimmons, Curtis Fit in Nicely with Order of Day as Dodgers Practically Sew Up Second Place*, Brooklyn Daily Eagle, Sept. 23, 1940, at 15.

119. Childs Walker, *Lee MacPhail: Hall of Fame Executive and Member of Baseball Family Helped Lay the Foundation of Orioles' 1966 World Series Champions*, Sun (Balt.), Nov. 10, 2012, at A12. MacPhail's drinking was indeed legendary. In an incident that has become part of baseball lore, MacPhail and Boston Red Sox owner Thomas A. "Tom" Yawkey, after a night of heavy imbibing, agreed to swap stars Joe DiMaggio and Ted Williams in what would have been the biggest trade in baseball history. Yawkey, however, decided not to go forward with the deal after he sobered up. *See* Glenn Stout & Richard A. Johnson, Yankees Century: 100 Years of New York Yankees Baseball 207 (2002).

120. Allan Vought, *Larry McPhail Officially Harford's Number 2 in Hall*, The Aegis (Bel Air, MD), Aug. 1, 2007, at A21. This headline refers to MacPhail being joined in the Hall of Fame by Baltimore Orioles shortstop, and Harford County native, Calvin E. "Cal" Ripken, Jr.

CHAPTER 8

Albert Benjamin "Happy" Chandler, Sr. (1982)

RONALD J. RYCHLAK

Albert Benjamin "Happy" Chandler, Sr. (July 14, 1898–June 15, 1991), was a Kentucky state senator, lieutenant governor, governor, U.S. senator, and the second commissioner of Major League Baseball ("MLB"). In 1921, he entered Harvard University's law school but was forced to leave after a year due to a lack of money. Returning home, he enrolled in the law school at the University of Kentucky ("UK"), where he earned his LL.B. in 1924.

Early Life

Chandler was born in Corydon, Kentucky, the first child of Callie (née Sanders, often misspelled "Saunders") (later Fortune, then Chamberlin) (1880–1954)[1] and Joseph S. Chandler (1870–1959).[2] The pair had married on June 2, 1897, in Gallatin, Illinois.[3]

By the time of Chandler's birth, the family was living on a tenant farm in the Pennroyal section of western Kentucky.[4] Two years later, Callie gave birth to the couple's second child, a son named Robert J. (1900–14).[5] Callie was "vivacious, energetic, and pretty,"[6] but the pressure of raising two young boys in a family of "severely limited means"[7] proved to be too much. As a result, she deserted the family in 1902.[8] Years later, Chandler recalled his father asking his mother: "Do you want to take the children?" When she said she was willing to take only Robert, Joseph replied: "No, if you don't want both, just leave them with me."[9]

Chandler's father Joseph was a "studious man who loved to read, especially works of history[.] [He] lived modestly, farming some and working at various town jobs, and attended the Christian Church."[10] On October 8, 1921, Joseph remarried.[11] His bride was Ruby L. Tapp (1892–1974),[12] with whom he had two children: Dr. Joseph S., Jr. (1923–48),[13] and Mary C. "Katie" (later Bolin) (1925–2017).[14] This gave Chandler a total of five half-siblings, for Callie had had three children with her second husband Walter.[15]

By any standard, Chandler's boyhood was "extremely hard."[16] In addition to helping around the farm, by "the age of seven or eight, [Chandler] virtually supported himself by delivering newspapers, running errands, splitting kindling wood, filling firewood boxes, and whatever other jobs came to hand."[17] In a letter written years later, Chandler's wife revealed:

> [Chandler's] affection for little boys is very genuine not only because of his own 2 little boys but because it brings very vividly to his mind memories of his own unhappy childhood [and] how he was deserted … by his own mother when he was a helpless child of 4. He had a bitter struggle[,] with never enough to eat and never enough clothes to keep him warm. The sight of a small boy selling papers on the street never fails to remind him of his own past.[18]

Despite innumerable hardships, Chandler was unfailingly upbeat, which in later years earned him the nickname "Happy." As a child, however, he was called "Irish," possibly because he reminded people of Andy Burke, the hero of Horatio Alger, Jr.'s 1894 novel *Only an Irish Boy: Or, Andy Burke's Fortunes and Misfortunes*.[19]

College and Law School

Chandler attended Pennroyal's public schools, where he excelled both academically and athletically. At Corydon High School ("CHS"), Chandler was an "apt student"[20] and demonstrated an early taste for politics by being "determined to know everyone 'who counted.'"[21]

Chandler was the captain of the CHS baseball team. He also played basketball; ran track; was a member of the drama club; led the high school choir; and was active in the Livesay Christian Church. When it came time to graduate, the CHS yearbook wrote: "Irish is the 'lark' of our class. He excels in knowledge of History and English. We are certainly proud to have him with us. He goes to Transylvania University next year, and we predict for him the most brilliant future."[22]

In the spring of 1917, Chandler graduated as CHS's valedictorian; in the fall, he matriculated at Transylvania University ("TU") in Lexington, Kentucky. He arrived with "a red sweater, a $5 bill and a smile."[23] Chandler chose TU for three reasons: (1) it was a small school where students enjoyed direct contact with the faculty; (2) it was affiliated with the Disciples of Christ Church, which at the time was Chandler's church; and (3) the school had promised him financial aid.[24]

To help Chandler make ends meet, TU allowed him to live in the basement of the president's house.[25] Having a free room was a plus, but Chandler still needed spending money. To get it, he worked a variety of odd jobs: babysitting, delivering newspapers, doing laundry, washing windows (and other household chores), and serving tables at a nearby boarding house.[26] Despite these jobs, Chandler found time to join a fraternity (Pi Kappa Alpha); captain the baseball and basketball teams; play quarterback on the football team; lead the singing at church services; and, during World War I, train to become a military officer.[27]

Chandler also made money through sports. "My skill and verve in sports had attracted considerable notice among the Lexington high school athletic directors. Henry Clay High School suddenly needed a girls basketball coach. I was offered the position. Naturally I needed the money. It was a part-time job so I could manage to work it into my hectic schedule."[28]

In the classroom, Chandler's interests ran towards English and history. He also enjoyed poetry, memorizing passages that he could still recite years later. After graduating, Chandler never failed to pay homage to TU for providing him with "both [a] formal education and … preparation for life."[29]

TU also is where Chandler acquired the nickname "Happy." During his freshman year, Chandler and a group of friends were walking back from basketball practice. One of the boys turned to Chandler and addressed him as "Happy."[30] The sobriquet stuck, and Chandler later came to view it as a huge political asset, jokingly asking: "Just think. What if he had called me 'Stinky'?"[31]

After earning his Bachelor of Arts degree in 1921 (majoring in both history and political science), Chandler considered becoming a football coach or trying to break into professional baseball. By this time, Chandler had developed close ties with the football program at Centre College, a small liberal arts school in Danville, Kentucky, where he hoped to one day coach.[32] Likewise, in 1919, Chandler had played for the Lexington Reos, a semi-professional baseball team, and had thrown a no-hitter.[33]

In 1920, Dean William T. Lafferty (1856–1922) had offered Chandler a seat in UK's law school, even though Chandler had not yet finished his college studies, an offer Chandler declined.[34] Now, with his bachelor's degree in hand, Chandler decided to enroll in Harvard University's law school. As he later recalled:

> [At some point I decided] I should go to the most prestigious law school in the United States.
> That was a truly frightening decision, and a monumental hurdle to leap. My grades were good enough, I felt, to get in. But going far away from home and financing myself through an Ivy League university might be impractical

and perhaps impossible. But once I had fixed the idea in my mind, I started scratching to try to do it—and scratching hard.[35]

Chandler arrived at Harvard in the fall of 1921. As he described it, "I was wearing my only suit, bought for nineteen dollars in Cincinnati, and carried everything else in one small suitcase. I came to Harvard with only two hundred dollars, borrowed from a fraternity brother, Lexington automobile dealer John Field."[36]

As soon as he got off the train, Chandler was overwhelmed by what he saw:

> Emerging from the South Street station, I was dazzled by my first view of the famous campus, sharply taken aback by the obvious age of everything. Most impressive of all was the walled-in Harvard Yard. I was staggered by the size of my law class, numbering 400 or 500. Lord, that was about twice the size of the whole Transylvania enrollment.[37]

After settling in, Chandler sought out Fred W. Moore, Harvard's athletics director, and asked him for a job. Moore informed Chander that Wellesley Hills High School was looking for a football coach.[38] As a result, on most days during his first semester at Harvard, Chandler would catch a "train for the twenty-five mile ride to Wellesley Hills. My pay was bare-bones, twenty-five dollars a month, but I couldn't have survived without it."[39]

During the season Chandler also served as a scout for the Centre College football team. Chandler's "intelligence" proved crucial, as Centre beat Harvard 6–0.[40] Harvard had gone five years without a loss, and Centre's victory, often referred to as the "Upset of the Century," continues to be a source of local pride.[41]

As Chandler later noted, he enjoyed his first year of law school: "My law school classes were [held during the] mornings. I got on well with my professors. Woodrow Wilson's son-in-law, Francis Bowers Sayre, taught criminal law. He was nice to me. But my most interesting and valuable course at Harvard was six hours on contracts. That helped me immensely in my legal career."[42]

Despite being academically inspired, at the end of his freshman year Chandler decided he had to make a change. "My year at Harvard Law School hadn't worked out. My grades were good. But trying to scrape by in Cambridge on odd jobs was just too rugged. I decided not to remain in New England. Kentucky was home. I decided to transfer to U.K. to finish law."[43]

Once again, one of Chandler's first tasks was to find part-time employment, which he did at Versailles High School ("VHS") (now Woodford County High School).[44] "This job wouldn't make me rich. But I could live on it, and fortunately it would be easy for me to jump back and forth between Versailles High and my law classes in Lexington [15 miles to the east]. An interurban ran about every half hour."[45] In addition to coaching at VHS, Chandler continued to scout football for Centre College.[46]

At the Bar

Chandler fell in love with the town of Versailles, the seat of Woodford County, while coaching at VHS.[47] Thus, when he graduated from UK in 1924, he decided to open his law office in Versailles. He did not, however, quit coaching football. "Naturally I could not afford to abruptly quit my job as coach—my only source of income—to hang out my shingle and plunge exclusively into the practice of law."[48]

Chandler's friendship with Field McLeod (1867–1947), "the most influential lawyer in town," proved quite beneficial: "He offered me rent-free desk space in the law office he shared with Judge [Thomas L.] Edelen [1858–1925]. And he even loaned me a desk! Of course, I was not a member of the law firm, just strictly on my own."[49]

Edelen considered Chandler's nickname to be undignified and advised him to change it:

> "How would you go about getting rid of it?" Chandler asked. "Give me some time," said Judge Edelen, "and I'll let you know." A couple of weeks went by. Finally Judge Edelen called me over and shrugged elaborately. "I've thought about it," he said, "and I don't believe you can do it…. I'd just keep it.'"[50]

Despite Edelen's change of heart, Chandler decided to omit his nickname when he put up his shingle, which read simply: "Albert B. Chandler, Lawyer."[51] In these early years, however, Chandler made more money as a football coach than as a lawyer.[52]

Chandler was admitted to the Kentucky bar on May 13, 1924.[53] The papers from Chandler's time in practice now are housed at UK.[54] As they reveal, Chandler's workload was typical of a small-town attorney: collection cases; divorces; inheritance disputes; insurance matters; real estate contracts; and a little criminal defense work. Chandler also handled a dog bite case and several automobile accidents, including one in which a car ran into a cow. One of the files indicates that Chandler's client was an African American.[55] In another, there is a letter that addresses Chandler as "Coach."[56]

Chandler's first appearance in court involved defending three teenagers accused of stealing an automobile.[57] When he obtained acquittals for two of the boys (the third boy, having escaped from the local jail, did not stand trial),[58] Chandler's practice began to grow. "My pleas to [the] jury, they were listened to, and generally, I think, were reasonably persuasive. The results were good. I enjoyed myself. Very much. Did I make the right choice in going into law? I wouldn't second guess myself about it."[59]

Like other trial attorneys, Chandler prided himself on his ability to pick a jury. In this respect, he had a decided advantage: "I knew them all. I knew everybody in the county nearly. About ten or twelve thousand."[60]

Unfortunately, most of Chandler's cases paid little (if they paid anything at all). "Being a friendly type, I was frequently consulted on small legal questions by friends who considered I was just doing them a favor. That was par for the course. Most of my fees were still little five and ten dollar things, anyhow. Every now and then a good fee would come along."[61] As a result, Chandler continued coaching high school football; started coaching the UK women's basketball team[62]; and joined various fraternal organizations—including the Legionnaires, Masons, Optimists, and Shriners—to try to meet businesspeople who could provide him with more remunerative work.[63]

In one case, Chandler and an attorney named Edward C. O'Rear (1863–1961), who later served on the Kentucky Court of Appeals, represented a woman whose horse and buggy had been struck by an automobile.[64] "We won the trial and collected a fair-sized amount that entitled us to a nice fee."[65] When Chandler proposed that O'Rear, who had much more experience, keep two-thirds of the fee, O'Rear refused and insisted on an equal split.[66] Chandler, who badly needed his full share, was extremely grateful and years later repaid O'Rear with a handsome share of the fee in a lucrative railroad case.[67]

As previously noted, Chandler loved singing, and shortly after law school he joined an amateur theater group in Versailles. There, a young divorcee named Mildred L. Reed (née Watkins) (1899–1995)[68] caught Chandler's eye. The raven-haired beauty, a graduate of Westhampton College (now part of the University of Richmond), had a two-year-old daughter named Marcella V. (later Gregg, then Miller) (1922–2005)[69] and worked as a teacher at a local girls' school. According to Chandler:

> Rarely had I encountered a more confident and self-assured young lady. She was outgoing, full of vim, good spirits and excellent moral judgement. They were just inventing the term "flapper"—but she had already developed that kind of brisk and lively personality as a teenager. Not wild and not bad in that sense. She was a talented and brilliant student. But she confessed that back in her small hometown—Keysville[, Virginia, which] had a population of only 500—she was a sort of tomboy hellion in school.[70]

Although smitten, Chandler worried about his ability to win Mildred's hand:

I was still working myself to death but just scraping by financially. I didn't own a house, a car, any land—not even a horse and buggy. Actually I possessed little more than the clothes on my back. Every now and then I still had to borrow from my friendly banker. Mildred came from a substantial family.... I was afraid the object of my affections might develop misgivings about a husband whose prospects were barely out of the slim and none category.[71]

Mildred, however, was not put off by Chandler's penury, and on November 12, 1925, the couple married in Keysville.[72] Soon, in addition to Marcella, the couple had three more children: Mildred "Mimi" (later Cabel, then Lewis) (1926–2016), a Hollywood actress[73]; Albert B. "Ben" Jr. (1929–2016), a newspaper publisher[74]; and Joseph D. "Dan" (1933–2004), a Las Vegas, Nevada, casino executive.[75]

Mildred and Chandler proved to be an excellent match. An extrovert like Chandler, Mildred played a leading role in Chandler's many political campaigns, and the pair often ended their joint appearances by singing "My Old Kentucky Home," a song that was close to Chandler's heart.[76] After Chandler's election in 1931 as Kentucky's lieutenant governor, Charley Moran, Centre College's former football coach, kiddingly wrote Chandler:

[I]t is [rumored] ... that your wife wrote all your speeches, also has been the brains of the family, and you know it strikes me that there has been a big change in you, as no Shyster Lawyer from a town like Versailles Kentucky could have pulled the wool over the eyes of the Commonwealth of Kentucky without some outside help.[77]

In 1926, the job of head football coach at Centre College became available. Chandler had long coveted this position and thought he had a shot at it. The school, however, hired Harold S. "Hod" Ofstie, a former All-American at the University of Wisconsin. In 1927, Ofstie offered Chandler a spot coaching the team's freshmen. Chandler immediately resigned his coaching position at VHS and started shuttling back and forth to Danville. "There was nothing easy about wearing two or three hats. But I was used to it. I kept plugging away at my law practice, gaining ground all the time. Danville was close to sixty miles away, over some poor, crooked roads. But, like always, I managed."[78]

In 1928, Judge Benjamin G. Williams, Sr. (1859–1930), appointed Chandler to the position of "master commissioner" of the Woodford County Circuit Court.[79] This was a significant office, for its holder handled many duties for the court. It was also very important to the Chandlers because it came with an assured income. As Chandler later wrote, Judge Williams "meant to do a big favor for the Chandlers, and he sure as hell did."[80]

Politics and Baseball

By now, Chandler had been active in the Woodford County Democratic Party for nearly a decade, and in 1929, with its help, he won a seat in the state senate using the campaign slogan, "Be lucky, go Happy!"[81] This would be the start of Chandler's meteoric rise in state politics. In 1931, he was elected lieutenant governor[82]; in 1935, he was elected governor[83]; and in 1939, he was appointed to the U.S. Senate.[84] Along the way, both TU (1936) and UK (1937) awarded Chandler honorary LL.D. degrees.[85]

In 1940, Chandler won a special election to the U.S. Senate, and in 1942 he was elected to his own six-year term.[86] In 1944, Chandler briefly vied to become President Franklin D. Roosevelt's vice-presidential running mate. When the post instead went to Chandler's U.S. Senate colleague Harry S. Truman (D-MO), Chandler good-humoredly told reporters that "all it cost me [to try] was railroad fare [to Chicago, where the Democratic convention was being held]."[87]

On November 25, 1944, Kenesaw Mountain Landis, the subject of Chapter 1 of this book, died. In 1920, Landis had been appointed MLB's first commissioner following the 1919 Black Sox scandal. Landis's death set off a veritable free-for-all—in time, the list of potential successors grew to include former Ohio Governor John W. Bricker, former Postmaster General James A. Farley, National League President Ford C. Frick (who later would become MLB's third commissioner), Democratic National Committee Chairman Robert E. Hannegan, FBI Director J. Edgar Hoover, Ohio Governor Frank J. Lausche, and former U.S. Circuit Court Judge Fred M. Vinson (soon to be named Chief Justice of the United States).[88]

Chandler, however, had the inside track. As World War II had raged on and players had left to join the fight, calls had grown in Washington to shut baseball down. Chandler, an ardent Cincinnati Reds fan, had rejected these calls, arguing that "baseball … should be preserved even during wartime…. We won't win the war by losing our morale. Baseball is a morale-builder, a necessary, helpful, enjoyable athletic competition. We need it. We must have it."[89]

Chandler's support of baseball now was repaid. Leland S. "Larry" MacPhail, Sr., one of the owners of the New York Yankees and the subject of Chapter 7 of this book, pointed out that Chandler's political connections would be helpful in the post-war environment.[90] MacPhail also noted that Chandler's influence on the Hill would be useful in the event that baseball's antitrust exemption was challenged.[91] MacPhail's arguments proved convincing, and on April 24, 1945, Chandler was unanimously elected commissioner.[92] In accepting the job, Chandler remarked, "As baseball commissioner, I'm compelled to spend the winters in Florida and attend baseball games during the summer. If there's a better job than this, I don't know what it is."[93]

On November 1, 1945, Chandler resigned his Senate seat and officially became baseball's second commissioner. As a result, his salary skyrocketed from $10,000 to $50,000 (later increased to $65,000). For the first time in his life, Chandler finally was making real money.[94]

It is not possible here to fully detail Chandler's time as commissioner, which lasted from 1945 until 1951.[95] Among Chandler's major accomplishments as commissioner was his defeat of the Mexican League, whose leaders (the Pasquel brothers) had attempted to raid the majors' rosters by offering U.S. players higher salaries[96]; allowing Wesley Branch Rickey, the co-owner of the Brooklyn Dodgers and the subject of Chapter 6 of this book, to end baseball's color line by hiring Jack R. "Jackie" Robinson[97]; creating MLB's first players' pension fund and helping fund it by selling the radio rights to the All-Star Game and the World Series to the Gillette Safety Razor Company and the Mutual Broadcasting System[98]; and suspending for one year Brooklyn Dodgers manager Leo E. Durocher for associating with suspected gamblers.[99]

Although these achievements made Chandler popular with both the fans and the players, various other actions made Chandler unpopular with the owners:

> [B]aseball club owners were Chandler's employer, [but] he had often asserted his independence [from them], and by midway through his term, the commissioner had made a number of enemies among the owners. For example, he angered Yankees co-owner Del Webb when he voided a trade between the Yankees and White Sox involving outfielder Dick Wakefield, leaving the Yankees on the hook for Wakefield's salary. In 1949, Chandler lost the support of Chicago White Sox boss Chuck Comiskey when he fined and later suspended White Sox general manager Leslie O'Connor for illegally signing a high school player. St. Louis Cardinals owner Fred Saigh disagreed with Chandler's handling of the Mexican League players, while Chandler initiated investigations into Saigh's possible gambling connections, creating another enemy.[100]

In December 1949, Chandler asked the owners to extend his contract, which was set to expire in 1952. This request did not go over well, nor did Chandler's subsequent public campaign for an extension. As a result, the owners decided to defer Chandler's request for a year.

In December 1950, the owners voted 9–7 to keep Chandler.[101] Due to a 1944 rule change, however, Chandler's nine votes were insufficient because 12 votes (a 75 percent super majority) were needed for retention. Chandler later remarked, "It's the first time I ever won a majority but lost an election."[102] Several months later, on July 15, 1951, Chandler stepped down as commissioner.[103]

Life After Baseball

In 1955, Chandler made a triumphant return to Kentucky politics by again being elected governor, beating his Republican opponent (Edwin R. Denney) by more than 16 points (at the time the largest margin of victory in Kentucky's history).[104] "I came back home, hurting, of course. But I couldn't cry about being fired. I just went out again and won the best job I ever had—governor of Kentucky—for the second time."[105]

Unlike other Southern governors, Chandler readily accepted the U.S. Supreme Court's 1954 decision in *Brown v. Board of Education*.[106] "Privately in letters he said he did not know whether he as an individual favored integration, but 'I do not think it is Christian, and I know it is not lawful, to deny any of our fellow citizens equality of opportunity and protection under our laws.'"[107]

During his second term as governor, Chandler increased funding for the state's highways, public schools, and teachers' retirement program and played a leading role in creating UK's medical school and hospital, which he called the greatest achievement of his public life.[108] In 1957, Chandler became one of the first 10 inductees in the Kentucky Sports Hall of Fame.[109]

In October 1959, Chandler was one of the governors "interviewed" by Janice Smiley, a high school student and aspiring reporter who had managed to crash the Southern Governors' Conference in Asheville, North Carolina. The story made national news, with *Life* magazine writing: "Janice started out interviewing 'a jolly little fellow in a bright yellow sweatshirt'—Kentucky Governor Happy Chandler (5 feet 8 inches, 196 pounds)."[110]

In 1960, Chandler sought the Democratic presidential nomination.

Albert B. "Happy" Chandler, Sr. (*c.* 1945) (National Baseball Hall of Fame and Museum).

He insisted that U.S. Senator John F. Kennedy (D-MA), the party's even-
tual nominee, was "too young," argued that Kennedy's religion (Cathol-
icism) was an impossible hindrance, and suggested that Kennedy be his
(Chandler's) running mate.[111] Chandler's candidacy failed to gain any
momentum, however, in large part because of Chandler's inability to
adapt to the new medium of television. This same failing caused him to
lose repeated bids to return to Kentucky's governor's mansion (1963, 1967,
1971).[112]

In March 1965, Chandler became the commissioner of the Continental Football League ("CFL"), a new circuit consisting of 10 franchises that
hoped to become the country's third major professional football league.[113]
In January 1966, after just 10 months on the job, Chandler resigned his
position when the CFL's owners voted to accept optioned players from the
American Football League and the National Football League. In Chandler's view, this decision guaranteed that the CFL would never be more
than a minor league.[114] In 1969, the CFL folded.[115]

In 1968, former Alabama governor George C. Wallace launched a
longshot bid for president, running as the nominee of the recently formed
American Independent Party. Wallace briefly flirted with the idea of having Chandler be his running mate before rejecting him as too liberal and
instead picking U.S. Air Force General Curtis E. LeMay.[116]

Election to the Baseball Hall of Fame

Following his resignation as baseball's commissioner in 1951, Chandler became *persona non grata*. "Neither of his first two successors, Commissioners Ford Frick [and] William Eckert, invited him to All-Star games
or any other functions associated with major league baseball."[117] As Chandler himself later recalled: "They took their revenge by turning me into
baseball's 'forgotten man.' For years I languished in near oblivion, snidely
deprived of my World Series box and given other slights."[118]

In 1969, Bowie K. Kuhn, the subject of Chapter 9 of this book, became
baseball's new commissioner. Like Chandler, Kuhn was a lawyer, and the
two quickly bonded. As Kuhn later explained in his memoirs, "I had the
wit to rescue [Chandler] when I became commissioner in 1969. I consulted
with him, invited him to baseball functions and made frequent references
to him throughout my term."[119]

In 1982, with his place in the sport having been restored, Chandler
was elected to the Baseball Hall of Fame.[120] Chandler proclaimed his election to be "a great moment!"[121] and later explained: "Over my long lifetime I have been fortunate enough to receive recognition and tributes to

satisfy a dozen men. But there was one honor that I thought my due that was very elusive, and I feared it would never come in my lifetime, and perhaps never. That was to be inducted into Baseball's Hall of Fame."[122]

In his induction speech, Chandler referred to the role he had played in desegregating baseball. Recalling Rickey's request for his help, Chandler said: "I'm gonna have to meet my maker someday, and if he asked me why I didn't let this boy play, and I said it was because he was black, that might not be a satisfactory answer. I said [to Rickey], 'you bring him [Jackie Robinson] in, and I'll approve … the transfer of his contract from [the minor league] Montreal [Royals] to [the] Brooklyn [Dodgers],' and I did."[123]

Conclusion

In April 1988, during a meeting of the UK board of trustees, the university's investments in Africa were discussed. Chandler had been a member of the board for decades, and during the exchange he spoke up. While describing the population of Zimbabwe, Chandler, by now 89, used a racially derogatory word.[124] Although the other members of the board let the remark pass, a reporter attending the meeting wrote a story about it that appeared in the next day's *Lexington Herald-Leader*.[125] The news quickly went national,[126] forcing Chandler to issue multiple apologies.[127] In a long piece in the *Woodford Sun*, however, Chandler's wife Mildred placed the blame on the reporter:

> The fact that Governor Chandler used an unfortunate word in a private conversation which was overheard by a reporter was not worth reporting. The fact that it was used by a man known as the best friend our black brothers have in America was enough to make a good reporter discount it. She must have felt that she could use it in a way to gain a little publicity for herself. The net result has been that the *Lexington Herald-Leader* has done the greatest disservice to the state.[128]

Chandler lived out his final years quietly with Mildred in Versailles, dying there on June 15, 1991, of a heart attack at the age of 92.[129] In addition to Mildred, Chandler's survivors included two sons, two daughters, 12 grandchildren, and several great-grandchildren.[130] Chandler's estate—valued at $939,900, the equivalent today of $2.14 million[131]—was left in the first instance to Mildred, with specific stock bequests following her death earmarked for Chandler's half-sister Mary Bolin and Marcella's two daughters and the rest split equally among Chandler's three natural children (Ben, Dan, and Mimi).[132] Chandler's will also specified that Ben was to receive Chandler's Hall of Fame ring as well as his sports memorabilia.[133]

Shortly before her death, Mildred was asked about Chandler. She replied: "He had a most satisfactory life and accomplished many, many things, a lot of things the general public doesn't know about. His mind was always on seeing what he could do to make things equal for those who were considered downtrodden."[134]

NOTES

1. *See Happy's Mother Dies in Florida*, WINCHESTER SUN (KY), Dec. 20, 1954, at 1. Callie does not have a *Find-a-Grave* webpage.

2. For an obituary of Joseph, see *Joseph S. Chandler, 88, Governor's Father, Dies: Hospitalized 10 Days with Kidney Infection, Cerebral Spasms*, HARLAN DAILY ENTERP. (KY), May 25, 1959, at 3. *See also Joseph Sephus "Joe" Chandler*, FIND-A-GRAVE.COM, https://www.findagrave.com/memorial/102874148/joseph-sephus-chandler (last visited July 1, 2024).

3. *See Callie Sanders in the Illinois, U.S., Marriage Index, 1860–1920*, ANCESTRY.COM, https://www.ancestry.com/discoveryui-content/view/1728445:60984 (last visited July 1, 2024). Callie's second husband was Walter H. Fortune (1874–1911), an Evansville, Indiana, barber who accidentally drowned to death. *See 29 Deaths are Reported: Heart Disease Assigned as Cause in Three Cases*, EVANSVILLE J.-NEWS (IN), Oct. 8, 1911, at 8. *See also Walter H. Fortune*, FIND-A-GRAVE.COM, https://www.findagrave.com/memorial/87508013/walter-h.-fortune (last visited July 1, 2024). Callie's third husband was Arthur W. Chamberlin (often misspelled "Chamberlain") (1878–1921), a Jacksonville, Florida, bookkeeper (Arthur and Callie had met while they both living in Indiana). *See "mtevault1954," Arthur Wellington Chamberlin 1878–1921*, ANCESTRY.COM, https://www.ancestry.com/family-tree/person/tree/33040705/person/29581313467/story (last visited July 1, 2024). *See also Arthur W. Chamberlin*, FIND-A-GRAVE.COM, https://www.findagrave.com/memorial/126726436/arthur-w.-chamberlin (last visited July 1, 2024). Arthur died after a long illness. *See Card of Thanks*, SUN. TIMES-UNION (Jacksonville), Dec. 11, 1921, at 22.

4. *See Charles P. Roland, Happy Chandler*, 85 REG. KY. HIST. SOC'Y 138, 138 (1987).

5. *See Robert Jennings Chandler*, FIND-A-GRAVE.COM, https://www.findagrave.com/memorial/102874229/robert_jennings_chandler (last visited July 1, 2024). Robert died after falling out of a cherry tree. *See Robert Chandler*, COURIER-J. (Louisville), June 16, 1914, at 6. Robert's death certificate lists his cause of death as "concussion of [the] brain." *See Callie Saunders [sic] in the Kentucky, U.S., Death Records, 1852–1965*, ANCESTRY.COM, https://www.ancestry.com/discoveryui-content/view/750654699:1222 (last visited July 1, 2024).

6. JEROME HOLTZMAN, THE COMMISSIONERS: BASEBALL'S MIDLIFE CRISIS 47 (1998).

7. Roland, *supra* note 4, at 138.

8. *Id.*

9. HOLTZMAN, *supra* note 6, at 47.

10. *Genetic Chandler Family 4 Thomas Chandler the Younger*, THE CHANDLER FAMILY ASSOCIATION, https://www.chandlerfamilyassociation.org/home/genetic-chandler-families/genetic-chandler-family-group-4/genetic-chandler-family-group-4thomas-chandler-the-younger/ (last visited July 1, 2024).

11. *See Joseph Sweet Chandler in the Indiana, U.S., Select Marriages Index, 1748–1993*, ANCESTRY.COM, https://www.ancestry.com/discoveryui-content/view/518323:60281 (last visited July 1, 2024). No record has been found of Callie and Joseph getting a divorce.

12. For an obituary of Ruby, see *Obituaries: Chandler, Mrs. Rudie [sic] Lee Tapp*, SUN. HERALD-LEADER (Lexington, KY), Oct. 13, 1974, at B17. *See also Ruby Lee Tapp Chandler*, FIND-A-GRAVE.COM, https://www.findagrave.com/memorial/103184102/ruby_lee_chandler (last visited July 1, 2024).

13. For an obituary of Joseph Jr., see *Dr. Joseph Chandler, Happy's Half Brother, Dies After Operation*, PADUCAH SUN-DEMOCRAT (KY), Apr. 5, 1948, at 7. *See also Dr. Joseph*

S. Chandler, Jr., FIND-A-GRAVE.COM, https://www.findagrave.com/memorial/104829824/joseph_s_chandler (last visited July 1, 2024).

14. For an obituary of Mary, see *Obituaries & Memorials: Bolin, Mary Catherine "Katie" Chandler*, LEXINGTON HERALD-LEADER (KY), May 7, 2017, at A6. *See also Mrs Mary Catherine "Katie" Chandler Bolin*, FIND-A-GRAVE.COM, https://www.findagrave.com/memorial/194645452/mary_catherine_bolin (last visited July 1, 2024).

15. These children were Lawrence Fortune (1905–82), William "Billy" Fortune (1909–80), and Mary E. Fortune (later Kelsay, often misspelled "Kelsey") (1909–62). *See Happy Chandler Loses Mother*, MIAMI DAILY NEWS (OH), Dec. 20, 1954, at 10B (listing Callie's children). For an obituary of Lawrence, see *Death Notices: Fortune, Lawrence*, FLA. TIMES-UNION (Jacksonville), Nov. 10, 1982, at B4. *See also Lawerence Fortune*, FIND-A-GRAVE.COM, https://www.findagrave.com/memorial/100163131/lawrence-fortune (last visited July 1, 2024). For an obituary of William, see *Deaths: William Fortune*, TALLAHASSEE DEMOCRAT, Apr. 20, 1980, at 2C. William does not have a *Find-a-Grave* webpage. For an obituary of Mary, see *Funeral Notices—Kelsay*, FLA. TIMES-UNION (Jacksonville), June 1, 1962, at 51. Mary does not have a *Find-a-Grave* webpage. *But see Mary Ellen Kelsay in the Florida, U.S., Death Index, 1877–1998*, ANCESTRY.COM, https://www.ancestry.com/discoveryui-content/view/871120:7338 (last visited July 1, 2024). In 1933, Chandler discovered Callie and her children living in Jacksonville after a long search in which his only clue to his mother's whereabouts was a faded postcard. *See Kentuckian is Reunited Here After 31 Years: Young Lieutenant Governor Finds Mrs. Chamberlin, Also Brother, Sister*, FLA. TIMES-UNION (Jacksonville), Nov. 10, 1933, at 1.

16. Roland, *supra* note 4, at 140.

17. *Id.*

18. *Id.* at 141.

19. *Id.*

20. HOLTZMAN, *supra* note 6, at 47.

21. *Id.*

22. Roland, *supra* note 4, at 142.

23. HOLTZMAN, *supra* note 6, at 2.

24. *See* Roland, *supra* note 4, at 142.

25. *See* Allison Perry, *Ben Chandler III Honors the Legacy of His Grandfather, A.B. "Happy" Chandler*, UK HEALTHCARE, Oct. 12, 2022, https://uknow.uky.edu/uk-healthcare/ben-chandler-iii-honors-legacy-his-grandfather-ab-happy-chandler.

26. *See* Roland, *supra* note 4, at 143.

27. *Id.*; Vincent X. Flaherty, *The Life Story of Albert B. "Happy" Chandler, in* BASEBALL GUIDE AND RECORD BOOK 110, 117 (J.G. Taylor Spink ed., 1946). Chandler had a good voice and briefly considered becoming a professional opera singer. *See* HOLTZMAN, *supra* note 6, at 46.

28. HAPPY CHANDLER WITH VANCE H. TRIMBLE, HEROES, PLAIN FOLKS, AND SKUNKS: THE LIFE AND TIMES OF HAPPY CHANDLER—AN AUTOBIOGRAPHY 29 (1989).

29. Roland, *supra* note 4, at 143.

30. *Id.*

31. *Id.* at 144–45; CHANDLER & TRIMBLE, *supra* note 28, at 22.

32. "His whole goal in life was to be head football coach at Centre College, and he applied for that job, and didn't get it." Perry, *supra* note 25. *See also* CHANDLER & TRIMBLE, *supra* note 28, at 57.

33. *See* HOLTZMAN, *supra* note 6, at 47 (explaining that Earle B. Combs, a future Hall of Famer with the New York Yankees, was a Reos teammate). *See also* Heather C. Watson, *10 Things You Probably Didn't Know About Happy Chandler*, HER KENTUCKY, July 14, 2015, https://www.herkentucky.com/blog1/happy-chandler (showing Chandler in his Reos uniform).

34. *See* Letter from Dean William T. Lafferty, University of Kentucky College of Law, to Albert B. Chandler, dated Sept. 1, 1920 (UK Library, Chandler File, 1920s Series, 39710, Folder 1). For a profile of Lafferty, see Thomas E. King, *Judge William T. Lafferty, the Lawyer*, 11 KY. L.J. 62 (1923). *See also William Thornton Lafferty*, FIND-A-GRAVE.COM, https://

www.findagrave.com/memorial/39060128/william-thornton-lafferty (last visited July 1, 2024).

35. CHANDLER & TRIMBLE, *supra* note 28, at 36.

36. *Id*. at 37–38.

37. *Id*. at 37.

38. *Id*. at 38.

39. *Id*. On Sundays, however, Chandler would attend church services in Harvard Yard: "That remains to this day one of my most memorable Harvard recollections." *Id*. at 39.

40. *See Centre Conquers Harvard, 6 to 0: Kentuckians Hold Crimson Even in First Half; Sweep to Victory in Second*, N.Y. TIMES, Oct. 30, 1921, at 94. Chandler later summarized his efforts by writing: "I took careful notes and diagrammed critical Harvard formations. There is no doubt in my mind that my scouting made significant contributions to the outcome of the Harvard-Centre contest that year." CHANDLER & TRIMBLE, *supra* note 28, at 40.

41. *See* Hayes Gardner, *'C6H0'—Kentucky School Beat Harvard in Major College Football Upset 100 Years Ago Today*, LOUISVILLE COURIER J., Oct. 29, 2021, https://www.courier-journal.com/story/sports/college/football/2021/10/29/centre-college-upset-harvard-100-years-ago-today/8440391002/.

42. CHANDLER & TRIMBLE, *supra* note 28, at 38. Although Chandler does not name him, his contracts professor was the legendary Samuel Williston (1861–1963). It was during this period (1920–22) that Williston was publishing the first edition of his renown work *Treatise on the Law of Contracts*. For a further discussion, see Mark L. Movsesian, *Samuel Williston—Brief Life of a Resilient Legal Scholar: 1861–1963*, HARV. MAG., Jan.–Feb. 2006, https://www.harvardmagazine.com/2006/01/samuel-williston-html. *See also* SAMUEL WILLISTON, LIFE AND LAW: AN AUTOBIOGRAPHY (1940). It is not surprising that Chandler enjoyed Williston's course, for Williston was one of the best-liked professors on the Harvard law faculty. *See* Movsesian, *supra* (explaining that Williston was "a gentle, good-humored teacher who charmed his classes with hypothetical cases involving his horse, Dobbin, and who regularly invited students to dine with his family on Sundays").

43. CHANDLER & TRIMBLE, *supra* note 28, at 46.

44. According to his grandson, Chandler "still has the winningest record as football coach in high school history in Woodford County." Perry, *supra* note 25. Years later, Chandler would play an instrumental role in establishing Kentucky's statewide youth football program. *Id*.

45. CHANDLER & TRIMBLE, *supra* note 28, at 46. Even with public transportation, Chandler's days were long:

> It took a lot of sixteen-hour days but I managed to successfully meld my two careers—law student and football coach. I got up early in the morning and rode the interurban to Lexington. It took more than thirty minutes. I got off at the top of the hill … at the Southern Railway station and walked across the dump to the law school. I stayed until about noon and caught the interurban back to Versailles. I had my first class at the high school at one o'clock and the next at two. Then I went to coaching. And sometimes when the moon came up I was still coaching.

Id. at 47.

46. "[Centre College's coach Charles B. "Charley" Moran] had concluded I was some sort of whiz at [scouting]. Often he would give me a hundred dollars to go study their opponents in some upcoming game." *Id*. at 56.

47. *Id*. at 45. ("I fell in love at first sight with the little Kentucky town of Versailles…. At heart I've always been a country town fellow").

48. *Id*. at 50–51.

49. *Id*. For an obituary of McLeod, see *Field McLeod, Attorney, Dies*, LEXINGTON LEADER (KY), May 12, 1947, at 1. *See also Field McLeod*, FIND-A-GRAVE.COM, https://www.findagrave.com/memorial/132015619/field-mcleod (last visited July 1, 2024). For an obituary of Edelen, see *Edelen, Law Author, Dies: Wrote Standard Reference Book on Kentucky Pleadings*, NEWS-DEMOCRAT (Paducah, KY), Sept. 18, 1925, at 1. *See also Thomas Lewis Edelen*, FIND-A-GRAVE.COM, https://www.findagrave.com/memorial/126510217/thomas-lewis-edelen (last visited July 1, 2024).

50. CHANDLER & TRIMBLE, *supra* note 28, at 51.

51. *Id.*

52. *Id.* at 51.

53. *See Lexington Students Pass State Bar Exams: Thirty-Six Applicants Successful,* T.B. McGregor *Notifies Court of Appeals,* LEXINGTON HERALD (KY), May 14, 1924, at 3 (listing Albert B. Chandler, of Versailles, as among those "licensed and recorded").

54. *See* UK Libraries Special Collections Research Center, *A.B. "Happy" Chandler Papers,* https://exploreuk.uky.edu/fa/findingaid/?id=xt72jm23br0c (last visited July 1, 2024).

55. *See* Letter from Albert B. Chandler, Esq., to Forest Blevins, dated July 2, 1928 (UK Library, Chandler File, 1920s Series, 39710, Folder 4).

56. *See* Letter from Jim Strauss, Kaufman Clothing Company, to Albert B. Chandler, Esq., dated Mar. 29, 1927 (UK Library, Chandler File, 1920s Series, 39710, Folder 3).

57. *See Three Boys Prefer Trial in Louisville,* COURIER-J. (Louisville), Dec. 21, 1924, § 1, at 10.

58. *See Versailles Frees Louisville Boys,* COURIER-J. (Louisville), May 12, 1925, at 11.

59. CHANDLER & TRIMBLE, *supra* note 28, at 64.

60. *Id.*

61. *Id.* at 72.

62. *Id.* at 56 ("My team was pretty good. Not long ago I looked at [an] old picture of those five girls, in their middy blouses and dark scarfs, with me standing in the back row, dark-haired, serious-minded, and with rather visibly large ears. The young lady in the middle, [the team's] captain, and holding the basketball, was Sarah G. Blanding, who went on to become the president of Vassar College").

63. *Id.* at 52. *See also* John Paul Hill, "A. B. 'Happy' Chandler and the Politics of Civil Rights," at 14 (unpublished Ph.D. dissertation, University of Georgia, 2009), https://esploro.libs.uga.edu/esploro/outputs/9949334645202959.

64. For an obituary of O'Rear, see *Death Claims Judge O'Rear: Scholarly Jurist Succumbs at 98,* LEXINGTON HERALD (KY), Sept. 13, 1961, at 1. *See also Judge Edward Clay O'Rear,* FIND-A-GRAVE.COM, https://www.findagrave.com/memorial/84949891/edward-clay-o'rear (last visited July 1, 2024).

65. CHANDLER & TRIMBLE, *supra* note 28, at 72.

66. *Id.* at 72–73.

67. *Id.* at 73.

68. *See Mildred Watkins Chandler,* FIND-A-GRAVE.COM, https://www.findagrave.com/memorial/58794980/mildred_chandler (last visited July 1, 2024). For Mildred's birth certificate, see *Mildred Lucile Watkins in the Virginia, U.S., Birth Records, 1912–2015, Delayed Birth Records, 1721–1920,* ANCESTRY.COM, https://www.ancestry.com/discoveryuicontent/view/8370670:9277 (last visited July 1, 2024). For an obituary of Mildred, see *Mildred W. Chandler, Widow of 'Happy,' Dies,* COURIER-J. (Louisville), Jan. 25, 1995, at B4. As this source indicates, "Throughout most of their married life, Happy Chandler called [Mildred] "Mama"—and it was the last word he spoke before he died in June 1991." *Id.*

69. For an obituary of Marcella, see *Death Notices: Marcella C. Miller,* NEWS & OBSERVER (Raleigh, NC), May 24, 2005, at 8B. *See also Marcella Chandler Miller,* FIND-A-GRAVE.COM, https://www.findagrave.com/memorial/45649025/marcella_miller (last visited July 1, 2024).

70. CHANDLER & TRIMBLE, *supra* note 28, at 57. *See also* Roland, *supra* note 4, at 146 (describing Mildred as "exceptionally bright and exceptionally charming").

71. CHANDLER & TRIMBLE, *supra* note 28, at 59.

72. *See [No Headline in Original],* COURIER-J. (Louisville), Nov. 15, 1925, § 1, at 14. *See also* HOLTZMAN, *supra* note 6, at 47–48 ("They were married for sixty-five years, a joyful union unbroken until [Chandler's] death in 1991"). For Mildred and Chandler's engagement announcement, see *Woodford [Bank Case] Will be Postponed; [Harris] Hurt as Bicycle Hits Truck; A.B. Chandler to Wed Miss Watkins; [YMCA] Music Programme Given,* COURIER-J. (Louisville), May 19, 1925, at 5.

73. For an obituary of Mildred, see *Obituaries & Memorials: Mildred Chandler (Mimi)*

Lewis, Lexington Herald-Leader (KY), Sept. 16, 2016, at 6A. *See also Mimi Chandler Lewis*, Find-a-Grave.com, https://www.findagrave.com/memorial/184350007/mimi-lewis (last visited July 1, 2024).

74. For an obituary of Albert Jr., see Karla Ward, *A.B. Chandler Jr.: 1929–2016, Newspaper Owner, Son of Former Governor, Dies at 87*, Lexington Herald-Leader (KY), Oct. 24, 2016, at 8A. *See also Albert Benjamin "Ben" Chandler*, Find-a-Grave.com, https://www.findagrave.com/memorial/171715093/albert_benjamin_chandler (last visited July 1, 2024).

75. For an obituary of Joseph, see Jennifer Hewlett, *Dan Chandler 1933–2004: 'He Knew All the High Rollers': Son of Former Governor Dies at Versailles Home*, Lexington Herald-Leader (KY), Apr. 28, 2004, at B1. *See also Joseph Daniel "Dan" Chandler Jr.*, Find-a-Grave.com, https://www.findagrave.com/memorial/177326465/joseph_daniel_chandler (last visited July 1, 2024).

76. *See* Emily Bingham, My Old Kentucky Home: The Astonishing Life and Reckoning of an Iconic American Song 156–57 (2022).

77. Roland, *supra* note 4, at 145.

78. Chandler & Trimble, *supra* note 28, at 70.

79. For an obituary of Williams, see *Judge is Called: Ben G. Williams Dies After Three-Day Illness*, Ky. Post (Covington), Apr. 22, 1930, at 1. *See also Judge Benjamin Gardner Williams, Sr.*, Find-a-Grave.com, https://www.findagrave.com/memorial/60325469/benjamin-gardner-williams (last visited July 1, 2024).

80. Chandler & Trimble, *supra* note 28, at 75 (noting that the new position "cut down some on the time I had for keeping tabs on sports").

81. *See* Frank Deford, *Happy Days: In the 90th Baseball Season of His Life, Former Commissioner Happy Chandler is Still at the Top of His Game*, Sports Illus., July 20, 1987, https://vault.si.com/vault/1987/07/20/happy-days-in-the-90th-baseball-season-of-his-life-former-commissioner-happy-chandler-is-still-at-the-top-of-his-game.

82. *See Democratic Majorities Ranged from 70,643 to 74,840 in State Election*, Messenger and Inquirer (Owensboro (KY), Nov. 22, 1931, at 2 (reporting that Chandler beat John C. Worsham, his Republican opponent, 426,247 to 353,573, a margin of 72,674 votes).

83. *See Chandler Victory Kentucky Record: Vote Mounts Toward 100,000 Majority Over His Republican Opponent for Governor—Sales Tax Repeal is Aim—There Will Be 'No High Hats or Striped Pants' at His Inauguration, Winner Says*, N.Y. Times, Nov. 8, 1935, at 2. Chandler ended up beating King Swope, his Republican opponent, 556,262 to 461,104, a margin of 95,158 votes. *See* 2 Malcolm E. Jewell, Kentucky Votes: Gubernatorial Primary and General Elections, 1923–1959, at 19 (1963).

84. Chandler engineered his own appointment to the U.S. Senate. On October 3, 1939, Marvel M. Logan, Kentucky's junior U.S. senator, died in office. Six days later, Chandler resigned as governor, which made Lieutenant Governor Keen Johnson the state's new governor. Johnson then turned around and named Chandler to Logan's seat. In 1938, Chandler had tried to unseat Alben W. Barkley, the state's senior U.S. senator, but had lost in a close race that was tipped by President Franklin D. Roosevelt's support for Barkley. For a further discussion, see *Chandler Resigns, is Named U.S. Senator by Johnson: Pledges Support to FDR, Succeeds Senator Logan—Is Against War; Johnson Takes Office as Governor of Kentucky*, Danville Daily Messenger (KY), Oct. 9, 1939, at 1. For examinations of Kentucky politics during this period, see, e.g., James C. Klotter, Kentucky: Portrait in Paradox, 1900–1950 (1996); John Ed Pearce, Divide and Dissent: Kentucky Politics, 1930–1963 (1987).

85. *See* Harry Heath, *Happy Chandler: Baseball's High Commissioner*, 56 Shield & Diamond (journal of the Pi Kappa Alpha fraternity) 27, 29 (Oct. 1946), http://www.pikearchive.org/wp-content/uploads/2017/11/PKA_SD_1946_OCT.pdf.

86. Roland, *supra* note 4, at 149.

87. Drew Pearson, *Convention Chaff*, Knoxville J., July 22, 1944, at 4.

88. *See* William Marshall, Baseball's Pivotal Era, 1945–1951, at 18–19 (1999) [hereinafter Pivotal Era].

89. J.G. Taylor Spink, *Senator Happy Chandler, Game's Lead-Off Man in Nation's Capital*, Sporting News, May 7, 1942, at 1.

90. *See* Bill Marshall, *Baseball's Most Colorful Commissioner: Happy Chandler*, SABR, https://sabr.org/journal/article/baseballs-most-colorful-commissioner-happy-chandler/ (last visited July 1, 2024).

91. *Id.* Baseball's exemption from the nation's antitrust laws had been recognized in 1922 in an opinion authored by Justice Oliver Wendell Holmes, Jr. *See* Federal Baseball Club v. National League, 259 U.S. 200 (1922). *See further* STUART BANNER, THE BASEBALL TRUST: A HISTORY OF BASEBALL'S ANTITRUST EXEMPTION (2013).

92. *See* Terry Bohn, *Happy Chandler*, SABR, https://sabr.org/bioproj/person/happy-chandler/ (last visited July 1, 2024). As Bohn explains, "When the owners met in Cleveland on April 24, 1945, an informal poll showed that Chandler likely had the support of two-thirds of the 16 major-league team owners needed for election. A second ballot showed he had the necessary [super] majority, and the third vote taken made the choice of Chandler unanimous." *Id.*

93. Deford, *supra* note 81.

94. "No question about it—money was important to me. As a Senator I received $10,000 a year. The [Kentucky] governor's office paid $6,500. I never made any big money in public service. This was a rare opportunity to build up a nest egg for my family. I didn't want to pass it by." CHANDLER & TRIMBLE, *supra* note 28, at 174.

95. For such a recounting, see PIVOTAL ERA, *supra* note 88. During his first year in office, Chandler's executive assistant was Herold D. "Muddy" Ruel. While playing in the majors as a catcher for multiple teams (1915–34), Ruel had earned a law degree from Washington University in St. Louis (1922) and been admitted to the Missouri bar (1923). Ruel left Chandler's staff in November 1946 to become the manager of the St. Louis Browns. For a further discussion, see Robert M. Jarvis, *And Behind the Plate ... Muddy Ruel of the U.S. Supreme Court Bar*, 36 J. SUP. CT. HIST. 1 (2011) (explaining, *id.* at 7, "In November 1945, Happy Chandler hired Ruel to be his executive assistant. For nearly his entire tenure, Landis's chief aide had been a Chicago lawyer named Leslie M. O'Connor. When Landis died, O'Connor left the commissioner's office to become the general manager of the White Sox. In his search for a replacement, Chandler quickly zeroed in on Ruel").

96. To put a stop to the Pasquels' plans, Chandler announced that any player who jumped to the Mexican League would be banned from playing in the United States for five years. In 1949, jumpers Daniel L. "Danny" Gardella, Hubert M. "Max" Lanier, and Fred T. Martin sued MLB, claiming that the ban was preventing them from making a living in the United States. After Chandler permitted the trio to return, the litigation ended. For a further discussion, see G. RICHARD McKELVEY, MEXICAN RAIDERS IN THE MAJOR LEAGUES: THE PASQUEL BROTHERS VS. ORGANIZED BASEBALL, 1946 (2006). *See also* Pasquel v. Owen, 87 F. Supp. 278 (E.D. Mo. 1949), *rev'd*, 186 F.2d 263 (8th Cir. 1950); Brooklyn Nat'l League Baseball Club v. Pasquel, 66 F. Supp. 117 (E.D. Mo. 1946); American League Baseball Club of N.Y. v. Pasquel, 63 N.Y.S.2d 537 (Sup. Ct. 1946).

97. *See* Joe Cox, *Happy Helping? Inside Commissioner Chandler's Role in Jackie Robinson's Great Quest*, SABR, https://sabr.org/journal/article/happy-helping-inside-commissioner-chandlers-role-in-jackie-robinsons-great-quest/ (last visited July 1, 2024).

98. *See* Charlie Bevis, *A Home Run by Any Measure: The Baseball Players' Pension Plan*, SABR, https://sabr.org/research/article/a-home-run-by-any-measure-the-baseball-players-pension-plan/ (last visited July 1, 2024). MLB's pension fund is the oldest among U.S. sports leagues. *See* Maria French, *Major League Baseball's Pension Plan is a Homerun*, NATIONAL PUBLIC PENSION COALITION, May 10, 2023, https://protectpensions.org/2023/05/10/major-league-baseballs-pension-plan-is-a-homerun/.

99. For a further discussion, see David Mandell, *The Suspension of Leo Durocher*, SABR, https://sabr.org/journal/article/the-suspension-of-leo-durocher/ (last visited July 1, 2024).

100. Bohn, *supra* note 92.

101. *See* Nick Klopsis, *1950 Winter Meetings: The Happy Dagger*, SABR, https://sabr.org/journal/article/1950-winter-meetings-the-happy-dagger/ (last visited July 1, 2024) (explaining that there were three votes: 9–7, 8–8, and 9–7, the last one taken at Chandler's insistence).

102. Bohn, *supra* note 92.

103. *See Chandler's Swan Song 'Old Kentucky Home,'* Brooklyn Eagle, July 16, 1951, at 12 (reporting that Chandler's last official act as commissioner was to preside over the opening of a new minor league stadium in Reading, Pennsylvania, where he "warbled his beloved 'My Old Kentucky Home' to 3,000 persons attending [the] dedication[.]").

104. Roland, *supra* note 4, at 155. On the campaign trail, Chandler slyly used the 1929 song *Happy Days Are Here Again. Id.*

105. Chandler & Trimble, *supra* note 28, at 3.

106. 347 U.S. 483 (1954).

107. Lowell H. Harrison & James C. Klotter, A New History of Kentucky 388 (1997).

108. *See* Roland, *supra* note 4, at 159; Hill, *supra* note 63, at 147–48; Perry, *supra* note 25.

109. *See 10 Kentuckians Named for Sports Hall of Fame*, Sun. Herald-Leader (Lexington, KY), Mar. 10, 1957, at 9.

110. *Young Reporter Crashes Conference and Becomes Its Liveliest Guest*, Life, Nov. 2, 1959, at 125.

111. *See* Andy Mead & Jim Warren, *Kentucky's 'Happy' Chandler Dies*, Lexington Herald-Leader (KY), June 16, 1981, at A1; *Kennedy Can't Take Kentucky, Chandler Says*, Bos. Daily Globe, Jan. 13, 1960, at 16.

112. *See* Bohn, *supra* note 92; Hill, *supra* note 63, at 189.

113. *See Continental Grid Circuit Names Happy Chandler as Commissioner at $50,000*, Evening Sentinel (Carlisle, PA), Mar. 18, 1965, at 24.

114. *See Happy Unhappy with Decision; Resigns CFL Commissioner Post*, Lexington Herald-Leader (KY), Jan. 15, 1966, at 10.

115. *See* Sarge Kennedy, *The Continental Football League: A Mini-Tragedy in Five Acts*, 10:5 Coffin Corner (journal of the Professional Football Researchers Association) 1 (1988), https://profootballresearchers.com/coffin-corner-1988.html.

116. *See* Hill, *supra* note 63, at 202–08. Chandler ended up endorsing no one in the election. *See Wallace Gets No Chandler Vote Support*, South Bend Trib. (IN), Oct. 31, 1968, at 40.

117. Bohn, *supra* note 92.

118. Chandler & Trimble, *supra* note 28, at 3–4.

119. Bowie Kuhn, Hardball: The Education of a Baseball Commissioner 27 (rev. ed. 1997) (1987).

120. *See* Joseph Durso, *Chandler, Jackson to Join Hall*, N.Y. Times, Mar. 11, 1982, at B18 (describing Chandler as a "surprise choice"). *See also Happy Chandler*, National Baseball Hall of Fame and Museum, https://baseballhall.org/hall-of-famers/chandler-happy (last visited July 1, 2024). Chandler's Hall of Fame plaque reads in part: "Iron-willed and honest, he was known as a 'player's commissioner' because of his broad concern for all phases of the game." *Id.*

121. Chandler & Trimble, *supra* note 28, at 4.

122. *Id.* at 279.

123. *See* Hill, *supra* note 63, at 131 (noting that Chandler often told this story in slightly different ways). To view Chandler's induction speech, see *Happy Chandler 1982 Hall of Fame Induction Speech*, YouTube.com, https://www.youtube.com/watch?v=a5rDbTldtCs (last visited July 1, 2024).

124. *See* Bohn, *supra* note 92 (explaining that Chandler said: "You all know Zimbabwe is all nigger now. There aren't any whites").

125. *See* Jamie Lucke, *Chandler Denounces Education Advocate*, Lexington Herald-Leader (KY), Apr. 6, 1988, at A10.

126. *See, e.g., Racial Remark by 'Happy' Chandler Stirs Up Students*, L.A. Times, Apr. 7, 1988, pt. III, at 4.

127. It has been suggested that Chandler was suffering from dementia when he made his remark and may have reverted to a past time when the N-word was acceptable due to a series of mini-strokes. *See* Hill, *supra* note 63, at 221–22.

128. Mrs. A.B. Chandler, *Opinions and Personals*, Woodford Sun (KY), Apr. 14, 1988, at 5.

129. *See* Robert McG. Thomas, Jr., *A.B. (Happy) Chandler, 92, Dies; Led Baseball During Integration*, N.Y. Times, June 16, 1991, at 26. *See also Albert Benjamin "Happy" Chandler*, Find-a-Grave.com, https://www.findagrave.com/memorial/2397/albert-benjamin-chandler (last visited July 1, 2024) (reporting that Chandler is buried in the Pisgah Presbyterian Church Cemetery in Pisgah, Kentucky).

130. *See* Thomas, *supra* note 129.

131. *See* S. Morgan Friedman, *The Inflation Calculator*, https://westegg.com/inflation/ (last visited July 1, 2024) (converting 1991 dollars to 2023 dollars).

132. *See* Al Cross, *Happy Chandler Left Most of Estate Worth Almost $1 Million to Widow*, Courier-J. (Louisville), July 25, 1991, at B4.

133. *Id.*

134. Bohn, *supra* note 92.

CHAPTER 9

Bowie Kent Kuhn (2008)

ELIZABETH MANRIQUEZ

From 1969 to 1984, Bowie Kent Kuhn (October 28, 1926–March 15, 2007) served as the fifth commissioner of Major League Baseball ("MLB").[1] Prior to becoming commissioner, Kuhn had been a partner in the New York City law firm of Willkie Farr & Gallagher. Because the firm represented the National League, Kuhn began the job of commissioner better prepared than any of his predecessors. Yet as matters turned out, Kuhn was ill-equipped for his new position. By the time he was shown the door, he had become one of the most polarizing figures in baseball history.

Growing Up a Senators Fan

Kuhn was born in Takoma Park, Maryland (a Washington, D.C., suburb), the third child of Alice W. (née Roberts) (1898–1988)[2] and Louis C. Kuhn, Sr. (1893–1980).[3] Louis, an executive with the Petroleum Heat and Power Company, was a native of Ebenhausen (a city in Bavaria, Germany), while Alice was a direct descendant of Leonard Calvert, Maryland's first colonial governor (1634–47).[4] Alice and Louis had married in Nashville, Tennessee, on May 20, 1920,[5] and had three children: Louis C., Jr., an insurance company executive (1921–84)[6]; Alice R. (later McKinley), a librarian (1923–2017)[7]; and Kuhn (1926–2007).[8]

Kuhn grew up in Washington, D.C., and graduated from the Alexander R. Shepherd Elementary School (1938), the Edward Paul Junior High School (1941), and the Theodore Roosevelt High School (1944).[9] As a teenager, Kuhn spent his summer months working at Griffith Stadium, the home of the Washington Senators baseball team.[10] Kuhn (like his mother) was a diehard Senators fan,[11] and Kuhn later remarked: "I have had only a few jobs in my life, but the best was scoreboard boy at Griffith Stadium.... I never spent an unhappy day there."[12]

Following his graduation from high school, Kuhn entered the U.S. Navy's V-12 program, which trained reserve officers.[13] Kuhn spent two years in the program, first at Franklin and Marshall College in Lancaster, Pennsylvania (16 months), and then at Princeton University in Princeton, New Jersey (eight months).[14]

Throughout his youth, Kuhn was a terrible athlete. Describing his time at Franklin and Marshall, for example, Kuhn wrote in his autobiography:

> My sixteen months at Franklin and Marshall ... were highlighted by my failing to make the basketball team [despite being 6′5″]..., failing to make the baseball team as a pitcher for want of shoes big enough for my size 13 feet (I suspect [this] reason was [given out of] politeness), [and] failing to make the football team as an end....[15]

Law School

After being discharged from the V-12 program, Kuhn returned to Princeton and in 1947 graduated with an honors A.B. in economics.[16] Kuhn then enrolled in the law school at the University of Virginia ("UVA") in Charlottesville, where he became a member of Minor Inn, UVA's chapter of the national legal fraternity Phi Delta Phi.[17] In his junior year, Kuhn was elected to the law review,[18] and in his senior year he became the review's associate decisions editor.[19] He also published a 23-page note on reporter "shield laws."[20] After reviewing the common law (which required a reporter to divulge his or her sources), and the subsequent passage in 12 states of shield laws designed to reverse the common law, Kuhn concluded that such statutes were neither necessary nor desirable:

> Broad public policy grounds, moreover, indicate that the newspaper confidence statutes are undesirable. The present tendency toward the indiscriminate privileging of occupational groups is unhealthy. The existing power of a judicial officer to order a witness to answer a proper question under threat of contempt should be jealously guarded against encroachment. At a time when the soundness of a number of the oldest existing privileges may be fairly questioned, it seems unwise to extend further protection to the newsman. Privilege to refrain from answering proper questions cannot be extended too far before the administration of justice becomes seriously impaired.
>
> For the foregoing reasons the writer does not believe that newspaper confidence statutes are warranted or justifiable. Conceding that situations may from time to time arise in which the public interest would be best subserved by permitting the newsman to remain silent, still legislation is not the proper method of achieving the desired result. It must be for the presiding official of each forum where a newsman may appear to reach the just result in a

particular instance by a judicious exercise of the discretionary power to treat a witness in contempt.[21]

As would be the case so often in his later life, Kuhn turned out to be on the wrong side of history—today, every U.S. jurisdiction except Wyoming has a reporter's shield law (40 states and the District of Columbia by legislative enactment and the rest by judicial pronouncement).[22]

Working at Willkie

In June 1950, Kuhn graduated from UVA with an LL.B.[23] In September 1950, having passed the New York bar exam,[24] Kuhn went to work for the Wall Street law firm of Willkie, Owen, Farr, Gallagher & Walton at a starting salary of $4,000 (the equivalent today of $51,000).[25] The firm had been founded in 1888 as Hornblower & Byrne and quickly became counsel to a roster of blue chip clients, including the New York Life Insurance Company, the Otis Elevator Company, the United States Shipbuilding Company, and the famed inventor Thomas A. Edison.[26]

In 1906, future U.S. Supreme Court justice Felix Frankfurter began his legal career at the firm (by now known as Hornblower, Byrne, Miller & Potter).[27] In 1931, the firm merged with Miller, Otis & Farr and became Hornblower, Miller, Miller & Boston.[28] (With 12 partners and 24 associates, the firm was one of the largest law firms in New York City.) In 1935, the firm became Miller, Boston & Owen.[29]

In 1940, Wendell L. Willkie (1892–1944), a 1916 graduate of Indiana University's law school, became the Republican candidate for president.[30] With President Franklin D. Roosevelt running for an unprecedented third term, Willkie used the baseball-themed slogan "Out at Third" to try to persuade voters to make a change.[31] Despite its clever word play, the motto did not work: Roosevelt buried Willkie, winning 54.7 percent of the popular vote and 84.5 percent of the Electoral College vote.[32]

In April 1941, Willkie agreed to become a partner in what, by now, was the law firm of Miller, Owen, Otis & Bailly, causing the firm to change its name to Willkie, Owen, Otis & Bailly.[33] A year later, the firm's name became Willkie, Owen, Otis, Farr & Gallagher.[34] By the time Kuhn became an associate, Otis's name had been dropped and Walton's name had been added.[35]

In his autobiography, Kuhn gave two reasons for wanting to join the firm: Willkie had been one of his heroes, and since 1933 the firm had represented the National League.[36] Two months after joining the firm, Kuhn approached Louis F. Carroll (1905–71), the partner in charge of the

National League's account, and asked to be allowed "to work on base-ball"—Carroll replied that he would keep Kuhn's request in mind.[37] Carroll soon made good on his promise by assigning Kuhn to a case that was making its way up to the U.S. Supreme Court: *Toolson v. New York Yankees, Inc.*,[38] an unsuccessful challenge to baseball's longstanding exemption from the nation's antitrust laws.[39] Although Carroll and Kuhn stayed mostly on the sidelines in *Toolson* (due to the fact that the action involved the American League's Yankees), the lawsuit did bring Kuhn "into contact with Commissioner Ford Frick and the League presidents, Warren Giles of the National League and Will Harridge of the American League."[40]

Following the *Toolson* case, Carroll began having Kuhn work on more and more baseball matters, including two that resulted in published opinions.[41] As a result, in January 1956 the *Princeton Alumni Weekly* reported "that *Bowie K. Kuhn* is the best informed member of the Class on baseball; Bowie is a Wall Street lawyer with Willkie, Owen et al."[42]

On October 20, 1956, Kuhn got married.[43] His bride was Louise M. "Luisa" Degener (née Hegeler) (1930–2023),[44] a widow with two small children (George L. Degener IV, born 1952, and Paul H. Degener, born 1956) he had met in Quogue, Long Island.[45] Later, the couple would welcome two more children: Alexandra R. "Alix" Kuhn (later Bower), born 1959, and Stephen B. Kuhn, born 1961.[46] For the first eight years of their marriage, Luisa and Kuhn lived in Luisa's house in Tuxedo Park, New York.[47]

In 1961, Kuhn was elevated to partner at what, by now, was the law firm of Willkie, Farr, Gallagher, Walton & FitzGibbon.[48] By this point, Kuhn was spending much of his time working on cases involving the Continental Can Company ("CCC"),[49] including one that made it to the U.S. Supreme Court.

In 1956, CCC had acquired the Ahzel-Atlas Glass Company, putting CCC squarely in the federal government's antitrust crosshairs. Although the firm successfully defended CCC in the district court,[50] in June 1964 the U.S. Supreme Court reversed the district court:

> A merger between the second and sixth largest competitors in a gigantic line of commerce is significant not only for its intrinsic effect on competition but also for its tendency to endanger [sic—should probably be engender] a much broader anticompetitive effect by triggering other mergers by companies seeking the same competitive advantages sought by Continental in this case.[51]

By the time the Court ruled, Luisa and Kuhn had moved from Luisa's house in Tuxedo Park to a brand-new home in Ridgewood, New Jersey.[52]

In addition to CCC, Kuhn was spending significant amounts of time on "the corporate activities of the International Minerals and Metals Company and the Hygrade Food Products Corporation."[53] Soon, however, a development halfway across the country would push Kuhn to the center of the baseball world.

In October 1964, the Milwaukee Braves decided to move to a new stadium being built in Atlanta, Georgia.[54] In August 1965, the State of Wisconsin filed a civil lawsuit in Milwaukee County Circuit Court against the National League and its 10 clubs, arguing that the move violated Wisconsin's state antitrust laws.[55] For the next year, Kuhn, assisted by Carroll and other Willkie lawyers, and together with a bevy of lawyers from the Chicago law firm of Winston, Strawn, Smith & Patterson (now Winston & Strawn), who had been hired to represent the Braves, threw himself into the case.[56]

On April 14, 1966, after an exhausting five-week bench trial in which Kuhn not only gave the opening statement but also cross-examined various witnesses, including Allan H. "Bud" Selig (a wealthy local businessman who was both working to keep the Braves in Milwaukee and, at the same time, seeking a National League expansion team if they left), Circuit Judge Elmer W. Roller ruled in favor of the state.[57] Three months later, however, after an expedited oral argument, the Wisconsin Supreme Court reversed Roller by a vote of 4–3 because of baseball's exemption from the federal antitrust laws:

> [A]pplication and enforcement of a state antitrust law to decisions of the [National League] as to the location of franchises and membership in the league would conflict with … national policy.… We deem it unrealistic to interpret [the] decisions of the supreme court of the United States [i.e., Federal Baseball and Toolson] plus the silence of Congress as creating a … vacuum in national policy, leaving the states free to regulate the membership of the baseball leagues.[58]

Commissioner of Baseball

In November 1965, former U.S. Air Force Lieutenant General William D. Eckert was unanimously elected baseball's fourth commissioner.[59] Eckert quickly lost the support of the sport's owners, however, and in December 1968 was dismissed.[60]

For a time, it looked like Eckert's replacement would be either New York Yankees president E. Michael Burke or San Francisco Giants vice president Charles S. "Chub" Feeney. When neither man was able to muster enough votes to win the job, John J. McHale, the president of the expansion Montreal Expos, emerged as a compromise candidate. McHale, however, took himself out of the running after speaking with Kuhn, who convinced him (perhaps self-servingly or perhaps not—the question of

Kuhn's intentions remains a subject of speculation to this day) that he had both a moral and a legal obligation to stay with the Expos.[61]

In February 1969, with the position still unfilled, the owners decided to offer Kuhn a one-year term as "interim commissioner" at a salary of $100,000—$35,000 more than Eckert had been making but $100,000 less than what Kuhn was earning at what, by now, was the firm of Willkie, Farr & Gallagher.[62] Despite the pay cut and the lack of any assurances about the future, Kuhn accepted the offer.[63] At 42, Kuhn was the youngest commissioner in baseball history.

In reporting on Kuhn's selection, the Associated Press wrote:

> Kuhn, a six-foot, five-inch, 230-pound lawyer, was the surprise unanimous choice of 24 club owners who gave him a mandate to restructure the game in a year.... Francis Dale, president of [the] Cincinnati Reds, who announced Kuhn's election, said a planning committee of the majors will make a report within a year "which might say that we do not need the office of a commissioner."[64]

As matters turned out, Kuhn remained in the job for the next 15 years, during which time baseball's economic pie grew rapidly, even as football overtook baseball as America's favorite sport.[65] Yet Kuhn's tenure was a tumultuous one, wracked by unceasing litigation and ever-increasing hostility and suspicion between the sport's owners and players.

It is not possible here to provide a complete recounting of Kuhn's long tenure as commissioner.[66] The following incidents, however, provide a good sense of the chaos that Kuhn was forced to deal with (and often created[67]):

- In April 1969, baseball added four new teams (the Kansas City Royals, Montreal Expos, San Diego Padres, and Seattle Pilots) and divided the American and National Leagues into divisions (dubbed "East" and "West"), heralding the start of baseball's playoff era.[68] A week before the start of the 1970 season, Bud Selig (who Kuhn had cross-examined during the 1966 Braves relocation lawsuit) purchased the Pilots out of bankruptcy and moved them to Milwaukee, where he renamed them the Brewers.[69] In 1977, the American League added two more expansion teams (the National League, rejecting Kuhn's pleas, decided to stand pat): the Seattle Mariners and the Toronto Blue Jays, bringing the total number of major league teams to 26.[70]

- In December 1969, the U.S. District Court for the Southern District of New York reaffirmed baseball's exemption from the nation's antitrust laws in a lawsuit brought by two American League umpires who had been fired for trying to unionize their fellow umpires.[71]

Bowie K. Kuhn (*c.* 1969) (National Baseball Hall of Fame and Museum).

- In January 1970, St. Louis Cardinals center fielder Curtis C. "Curt" Flood, Sr., sued Kuhn and MLB after he was traded to the Philadelphia Phillies, a team he did not want to play for, claiming that baseball's reserve clause violated the 13th Amendment's prohibition on involuntary servitude. In June 1972, the U.S. Supreme Court ruled against Flood and reaffirmed baseball's immunity from the nation's antitrust laws.[72]
- In February 1970, Kuhn indefinitely suspended Detroit Tigers pitcher Dennis D. "Denny" McLain, MLB's last 30-game winner, due to his involvement with bookmakers during the 1967 season.[73] In April 1970, Kuhn decided to reinstate McLain as of July 1 after concluding that McLain had been a victim of a confidence scheme,[74] but suspended McLain again in September 1970 for insubordination and carrying an unlicensed gun on a road trip.[75] In October 1970, Kuhn lifted the suspension so that McLain could

be traded to the Washington Senators (a deal Kuhn thought the Tigers got the better of).[76]

- In June 1970, Houston Astros pitcher James A. "Jim" Bouton released *Ball Four: My Life and Hard Times Throwing the Knuckleball in the Big Leagues*, a no-holds-barred look at baseball's seamy underbelly, including its players' prolific womanizing and abuse of alcohol and drugs (particularly amphetamines, colloquially referred to as "greenies").[77] Kuhn quickly called Bouton and his editor, sportswriter Leonard Shecter, on the carpet and warned them not to write any more exposés about baseball.[78] Today, *Ball Four* is considered one of the greatest sports books ever published.[79]

- In December 1971, the U.S. District Court for the District of Oregon rejected a lawsuit by the Portland Beavers of the Class AAA Pacific Coast League seeking compensation for MLB's expansion into San Diego and Seattle.[80]

- In April 1972, the first work stoppage in MLB history took place (players' strike—April 1 to April 13–86 games lost). Further disruptions occurred in 1973 (owners' lockout—February 8 to February 25—spring training delayed); 1976 (owners' lockout—March 1 to March 17—spring training delayed); 1980 (players' strike—April 1 to April 8—last eight days of spring training cancelled); and 1981 (players' strike—June 12 to August 9–713 games lost).[81]

- In April 1974, Kuhn angered many fans when he ordered the Atlanta Braves to play Henry L. "Hank" Aaron on the road, instead of letting him sit so that he could hit his 714th and 715th home runs (tying and breaking George H. "Babe" Ruth's record) in Atlanta. As a result, Aaron hit his 714th home run in Cincinnati. To make matters worse, when the Braves came home Kuhn was not in the stands to see Aaron hit his 715th home run.[82]

- In November 1974, Kuhn suspended New York Yankees owner George M. Steinbrenner III for two years (later reduced to 15 months) after Steinbrenner pled guilty to federal campaign finance violations stemming from his use of "cutouts" to funnel money to CREEP, President Richard M. Nixon's 1972 re-election organization.[83]

- In December 1975, arbitrator Peter Seitz struck down baseball's reserve clause in a case brought by pitchers David A. "Dave" McNally of the Montreal Expos and John A. "Andy" Messersmith of the Los Angeles Dodgers. When Seitz's decision was upheld by the courts,[84] free agency became a part of baseball for the first time since the 1890 Players League (also spelled Players' League).[85]

- In June 1976, Kuhn blocked Oakland A's owner Charles O. Finley from selling three of his best players—Joe Rudi and Rollie Fingers to the Boston Red Sox and Vida Blue to the New York Yankees—because the sales were "not in the best interests of baseball." Upon learning of Kuhn's decision, Finley called Kuhn "the village idiot."[86] In March 1977, the U.S. District Court for the Northern District of Illinois sided with Kuhn.[87]
- In May 1977, the U.S. District Court for the Northern District of Georgia upheld Kuhn's one-year suspension of Atlanta Braves owner Robert E. "Ted" Turner III for attempting to tamper with the contract of San Francisco Giants left fielder Gary N. Matthews, Sr.[88]
- In September 1977, the Boise (Idaho) A's, a team in the Class A Northwest League, filed a $1.3 million lawsuit claiming that the decision to place an expansion team in Seattle had harmed them.[89] In December 1980, the U.S. Court of Appeals for the Ninth Circuit affirmed the district court's dismissal of the case.[90]
- In September 1978, the U.S. District Court for the Southern District of New York, on equal protection grounds, struck down Kuhn's order barring female reporters from baseball's locker rooms.[91]
- In August 1979, Kuhn levied a $100,000 fine on Raymond A. "Ray" Kroc, the owner of the San Diego Padres (as well as the owner of the hamburger chain McDonald's), for tampering with the contracts of Cincinnati Reds second baseman Joe L. Morgan and New York Yankees third baseman Graig Nettles. In response, Kroc announced that he was turning control of the Padres over to his son-in-law Ballard F. Smith because he had become "disillusioned" with baseball and felt there was "a lot more future in hamburgers than in baseball."[92]
- In October 1979, Kuhn banned retired New York Mets center fielder Willie H. Mays, Jr., from baseball after Mays became a goodwill ambassador for the Park Place Hotel and Casino in Atlantic City.[93] In February 1983, Kuhn banned retired New York Yankees center fielder Mickey C. Mantle when Mantle took a similar position with the Claridge Hotel and Casino in Atlantic City.[94] In February 1985, both bans were lifted by Commissioner Peter V. Ueberroth, Kuhn's successor.[95]
- In December 1980, the Florida corporate owner of the Rocky Mount (North Carolina) Pines of the Class A Carolina League filed a $5 million antitrust case against Kuhn and various other parties.[96] In December 1982, the U.S. Court of Appeals for the Eleventh Circuit affirmed the district court's dismissal of the lawsuit.[97]

In August 1969, Kuhn had been elected to a full seven-year term as commissioner even though his term as interim commissioner still had six months to run.[98] In July 1975, Kuhn had been narrowly re-elected to a new seven-year term despite a determined effort by Charles Finley of the A's to oust him.[99] In 1982, Kuhn was eager for a third term, but by now he had made too many enemies among the owners; as a result, his request for a new contract was rejected in November 1982.[100] Nevertheless, he kept running for re-election until August 1983, when he finally bowed out.[101]

In March 1984, Peter Ueberroth was elected Kuhn's successor.[102] Because Ueberroth would not be available until October 1, 1984 (after he finished running the 1984 Summer Olympics in Los Angeles), Kuhn agreed to stay on until September 30, 1984.[103] Years later, Ueberroth described the mess Kuhn left him:

> The institution (baseball) ... was a disaster in all ways when I arrived. It was a disaster in (terms of) goodwill. The owners wouldn't even talk to each other.... It (baseball) was a scandal-ridden, drug-ridden thing. And every labor negotiation had a labor stoppage, a huge stoppage.[104]

Myerson & Kuhn

Following the end of his commissionership, Kuhn returned to Willkie, Farr & Gallagher as a non-equity partner[105] and wrote his autobiography, appropriately titled, "Hardball: The Education of a Baseball Commissioner."[106] It soon became obvious to everyone at the firm, however, that Kuhn was

> a man long on ceremony but short on work[, and therefore it] was expected that he'd probably transition into some kind of foundation role[. Instead, on January 4, 1988,] he formed a new law firm with Harvey [D.] Myerson, a famed New York trial lawyer whose clients had included Donald Trump in his [United States Football League antitrust] lawsuit against the NFL.[107]

Looking back, it is impossible to understand how a strait-laced patrician like Kuhn (who often was described as a "stuffed shirt"[108]) could have ended up becoming partners with a crook like Myerson (1940–2015).[109] A short time earlier, Myerson's previous law firm—Finley, Kumble, Wagner, Heine, Underberg, Manley, Myerson & Casey (founded 1968)—had imploded after it was discovered that the firm, which Myerson, as managing partner, was in charge of, had fueled its meteoric growth by vastly overbilling its clients.[110] Yet in an interview in May 1988, Kuhn expressed no concerns about Myerson, even as Myerson was putting in place the same practices at Myerson & Kuhn that had sunk Finley, Kumble:

Finley grew sort of topsy turvy—largeness seemed to become a predominant theme. We still have some filling in to do here and there, some additions to make to the roster, but I don't think any of us here are particularly interested in being large just for the sake of being large. If, in time, our success makes us a lot larger, I imagine we can't escape the inevitabilities of that. But we're not starting out to build numbers just because we think numbers are impressive to people.[111]

With Kuhn unaware of what was going on, it did not take long for Myerson & Kuhn to fail:

In December 1989, Myerson & Kuhn filed for bankruptcy, and the following spring, the *New York Times* noted that Kuhn was in [Ponte Vedra,] Florida— but not for spring training. He had sold his home in New Jersey and moved to the Sunshine State, which protected residences from being seized in bankruptcy proceedings. Kuhn was on the hook for at least $3.1 million in debts; Myerson was ultimately convicted of fraud in 1992.[112]

Following the demise of Myerson & Kuhn, Kuhn

remained in Florida, where he founded a [sports and financial] consulting firm [called the Kent Group Inc.] and served as … a lay minister for his Catholic faith. In October 2004, he had heart surgery, repairing a valve as well as a double bypass.… Kuhn died March 15, 2007, at the age of 80, at St. Luke's Hospital in Ponte Vedra Beach, Florida, where he had been hospitalized for several weeks with pneumonia.[113]

In addition to his religious work,[114] in his later years Kuhn was active in Republican politics[115]; served on the board of trustees of the Ave Maria School of Law (at the time located in Ann Arbor, Michigan)[116]; and regularly made the 20-minute drive from his home to watch the Class AA Southern League Jacksonville (Florida) Suns. Following Kuhn's death, Suns president Peter D. Bragan, Jr., told a reporter:

[Kuhn] brought a formality and dignity to the commissioner's office that nobody before or since could match. He knew how to act like a commissioner because he was a lawyer who had been around enough judges. He brought a presence to that office. Bowie was always in a $600 suit at a time when a $600 suit was [a] pretty big [deal].[117]

Conclusion

On December 3, 2007, less than nine months after his death, Kuhn was elected to Baseball's Hall of Fame.[118] A short time later, on July 27, 2008, Kuhn was formally enshrined in the Hall.[119] In a long piece in the *New York Times*, several Hall voters explained why they had voted for Kuhn.

While one pointed to Kuhn's love for the game, a second noted Kuhn's longevity as commissioner and a third emphasized Kuhn's efforts to do what he thought was best for baseball.[120] These sentiments are reflected in the wording of Kuhn's Hall of Fame plaque, which reads in full as follows:

> Baseball's fifth commissioner who presided over astounding growth in the game's popularity, with a proactive and inventive administration. Under his leadership, tripled major league attendance, extended postseason with creation of the league championship series and introduced night-time baseball to the World Series. Expanded television coverage with dual network broadcasts and a variety of baseball programming. Known as a tough disciplinarian, also as a strong supporter of amateur baseball. Instrumental in the Hall of Fame's 1971 decision to induct Negro League players.[121]

Not everyone, however, agrees with this depiction of Kuhn. In a long piece penned shortly after Kuhn's death, for example, *New York Times* reporter Murray Chass disputed the praise of Kuhn's tenure as baseball commissioner that was appearing in obituaries, writing that he was

> at the heart of the poor relationship between the owners and the players. He liked to portray himself as the commissioner of the owners and the players, but that notion didn't fool anyone....
>
> Kuhn was the commissioner when baseball's oppressive reserve system ended—not that he did anything to contribute to changing the system. Kuhn rejected Curt Flood's objection to a 1969 trade and forced him to sue to gain rights to movement that baseball denied players. Then Kuhn testified against Flood.
>
> Several years later, Kuhn fought against free agency, arguing that it would create an elite class of teams to the detriment of others. He had a golden opportunity in 1975 to influence change in the system, but he instead joined the hard-line owners who opposed compromise with the players.

Chass pointed out that attendance at major league games rose nearly 40 percent in the three years after free agency began following the 1976 season and questioned whether Kuhn deserved the credit he was receiving for two other MLB developments seen as positive: team expansion and the growth of player salaries (which "rose in spite of him, not because of him").

Chass quoted from a telephone interview with sports economist and author Andrew Zimbalist, who pronounced of Kuhn, "He never did anything enlightening; he never did anything that anticipated the future." In a previous interview with the *Boston Globe*, Zimbalist said that Kuhn "established a pattern of antagonism and acrimony and distrust between the owners and players ... that took baseball 25-plus years to work through."[122]

NOTES

1. For Kuhn's autobiography, see BOWIE KUHN, HARDBALL: THE EDUCATION OF A BASEBALL COMMISSIONER (rev. ed 1997) (1987) [hereinafter EDUCATION]. For shorter works about Kuhn, see, e.g., JEROME HOLTZMAN, THE COMMISSIONERS: BASEBALL'S MID-LIFE CRISIS 133–207 (1998); *Bowie Kuhn, in* JONATHAN FRASER LIGHT, THE CULTURAL ENCYCLOPEDIA OF BASEBALL 222 (2d ed. 2005); Vince Guerrieri, *Bowie Kuhn*, SABR, https://sabr.org/bioproj/person/bowie-kuhn/ (last visited July 1, 2024); Richard C. Crepeau, *Bowie Kuhn*, ON SPORT AND SOCIETY, May 13, 2007, https://stars.library.ucf.edu/onsportandsociety/759/; *Bowie Kent Kuhn, Fifth Commissioner of Baseball—Elected: 1969–1984*, MAJOR LEAGUE BASEBALL, https://www.mlb.com/official-information/about-mlb/commissioners/bowie-kuhn (last visited July 1, 2024).

2. For an obituary of Alice, see *Kuhn's Mother is Dead at 90*, MIAMI HERALD, Nov. 30, 1988, at 2D ("A native of Marlboro, Md., Mrs. Kuhn had lived in St. Augustine since 1958. She died in Regency Health Care Center, a local nursing home"). *See also Alice Waring Roberts Kuhn*, FIND-A-GRAVE.COM, https://www.findagrave.com/memorial/45239975/alice-waring-kuhn (last visited July 1, 2024).

3. For an obituary of Louis, see *Kuhn's Father Dies*, PHIL. INQUIRER, Oct. 14, 1980, at 2B (reporting that Louis, 87, "had been ill for some time" and that Kuhn "will miss the first two games of the World Series in Philadelphia"). *See also Louis Charles Kuhn, Sr.*, FIND-A-GRAVE.COM, https://www.findagrave.com/memorial/45240022/louis_charles_kuhn (last visited July 1, 2024).

4. *See* EDUCATION, *supra* note 1, at 12–13. For a history of the Calverts, see JOHN D. KRUGLER, ENGLISH AND CATHOLIC: THE LORDS BALTIMORE IN THE SEVENTEENTH CENTURY (2004). In his autobiography, Kuhn claimed to be a distant relative of James "Jim" Bowie, the inventor of the Bowie knife and one of the heroes of the Alamo. *See* EDUCATION, *supra* note 1, at 13.

5. *See* EDUCATION, *supra* note 1, at 13.

6. *See* Tylen Darling, *Louis Charles Kuhn Jr 1921–1984*, ANCESTRY.COM, https://www.ancestry.com/family-tree/person/tree/11480390/person/282027325889/story (last visited July 1, 2024). An obituary for Louis has not been found. He also does not have a *Find-a-Grave* webpage.

7. For an obituary of Alice, see *Alice Roberts McKinley, 93*, DUXBURY CLIPPER (MA), Nov. 15, 2017, https://www.duxburyclipper.com/articles/alice-roberts-mckinley-93/. *See also Alice Roberts Kuhn McKinley*, FIND-A-GRAVE.COM, https://www.findagrave.com/memorial/186554824/alice_roberts_mckinley (last visited July 1, 2024).

8. For an obituary of Kuhn, see Richard Goldstein, *Bowie Kuhn, 80, Former Baseball Commissioner, is Dead*, N.Y. TIMES, Mar. 16, 2007, at C10. *See also Bowie Kuhn*, FIND-A-GRAVE.COM, https://www.findagrave.com/memorial/18422891/bowie-kuhn (last visited July 1, 2024).

9. *See Roosevelt Student Wins Lanier Essay Prize*, EVENING STAR (DC), Sept. 7, 1942, at B5 (reporting on Kuhn winning $5 in a writing contest sponsored by the United Daughters of the Confederacy).

10. Griffith Stadium, named after Senators owner Clark C. Griffith (1869–1955), served as the Senators' home from 1911 to 1960. Following the Senators' relocation to Minnesota after the 1960 season (where they became the Twins), an expansion team, also called the Senators, played at Griffith Stadium during the 1961 season. In 1962, these Senators moved into a new ballpark called District of Columbia Stadium (later renamed Robert F. Kennedy Memorial Stadium). As a result, in 1965 Griffith Stadium was torn down. The site now is the home of Howard University's hospital. For a further look at Griffith Stadium, see John Schleppi, *Griffith Stadium (Washington, DC)*, SABR, https://sabr.org/bioproj/park/griffith-stadium-washington-dc/ (last visited July 1, 2024). As Schleppi notes, "The location of home plate is marked inside the hospital entrance. A plaque along Georgia Avenue notes the historic ballpark and notable moments in its history."

11. *See* EDUCATION, *supra* note 1, at 15. Kuhn later claimed that his earliest memory was of the Senators winning the pennant in 1933, the last time the Senators would

capture the American League pennant prior to moving to Minnesota. *Id.* For a further discussion, see GARY A. SARNOFF, THE WRECKING CREW OF '33: THE WASHINGTON SENATORS' LAST PENNANT (2009) (explaining that the Senators lost the World Series in five games to the New York Giants). The city would not see another pennant winner until 2019, when the National League's Washington Nationals (previously the Montreal Expos, and the successor to the expansion Senators, who in 1972 moved to Dallas-Fort Worth and became the Texas Rangers) won the World Series. *See* JESSEY DOUGHETY, BUZZ SAW: THE IMPROBABLE STORY OF HOW THE WASHINGTON NATIONALS WON THE WORLD SERIES (2020).

12. *See* EDUCATION, *supra* note 1, at 15. Kuhn was paid $1 a game to sit in the scoreboard in the right center field wall and turn numbers. *Id.*

13. The V-12 Navy College Training Program operated from July 1943 to June 1946. Established to increase the number of commissioned officers available for wartime service, the program eventually grew to 125,000 participants at 131 colleges and universities. For a further look at the program, see HENRY C. HERGE, NAVY V-12 (1996). *See also* U.S. BUREAU OF NAVAL PERSONNEL, THE NAVY COLLEGE TRAINING PROGRAM V-12: CURRICULA—SCHEDULES—COURSE DESCRIPTIONS (1943).

14. *See* EDUCATION, *supra* note 1, at 16.

15. *Id.*

16. *See Princeton Gives Sheepskins to 19 Area Graduates*, TIMES-HERALD (DC), June 10, 1947, at 5 (listing "Bowie K. Kuhn, 7704 Alaska Ave., N.W." as among the graduates).

17. *See* PHI DELTA PHI ALUMNI DIRECTORY 214 (1980).

18. *See Editorial Board*, 35 VA. L. REV. 335, 335 (1949) ("The Review takes pleasure in announcing the election to the Editorial Board of the following members: … Bowie K. Kuhn…").

19. *See Editorial Board*, 36 VA. L. REV. 59, 59 (1950) (listing Edward M. Selfe, Jr., as the decisions editor and Kuhn as the associate decisions editor).

20. *See* B.K.K., Note, *The Right of a Newsman to Refrain from Divulging the Sources of His Information*, 36 VA. L. REV. 61 (1950).

21. *Id.* at 83.

22. *See* Reporters Committee for Freedom of the Press, *Reporter's Privilege Compendium*, https://www.rcfp.org/reporters-privilege/ (last visited July 1, 2024).

23. *See University of Virginia Confers 936 Degrees*, EVENING STAR (DC), June 13, 1950, at A2 (listing "Kuhn, Bowie Kent" as among the graduates).

24. After being approved by the character committee, Kuhn was admitted to the New York bar on June 27, 1951. *See* New York State Unified Court System, *Attorney Search*, https://iapps.courts.state.ny.us/attorneyservices/search (last visited July 1, 2024) (under Kuhn, Bowie K.) (listing Kuhn's admission date and giving his bar registration number as 2086759).

25. *See* EDUCATION, *supra* note 1, at 16–17. *See also* S. Morgan Friedman, *The Inflation Calculation*, https://westegg.com/inflation/ (last visited July 1, 2024) (converting 1950 dollars to 2023 dollars).

26. *See Willkie Farr & Gallagher LLP*, 95 INTERNATIONAL DIRECTORY OF COMPANY HISTORIES 450, 450 (Jay P. Pederson ed., 2008). For a further history of the firm, see JOHN OLLER, "ONE FIRM": A SHORT HISTORY OF WILLKIE FARR & GALLAGHER, 1888— (2004). *See also* JOHN OLLER, WHITE SHOE: HOW A NEW BREED OF WALL STREET LAWYERS CHANGED BIG BUSINESS AND THE AMERICAN CENTURY 5 (2019).

27. Frankfurter did not stay long at the firm, for he soon was recruited by Harry L. Stimson, the U.S. Attorney for the Southern District of New York, to join the government. *See* Royal C. Gilkey, *Felix Frankfurter's Years of Preparation: From Immigrant Status to Service with Stimson*, 32 UMKC L. REV. 322, 328 (1964).

28. Pederson, *supra* note 26, at 451.

29. *Id.*

30. Willkie, a dark horse candidate, was chosen during a raucous five-day convention that rejected the party's three leading candidates: District Attorney Thomas E. Dewey (New York), Senator Robert A. Taft (Ohio), and Senator Arthur H. Vandenberg (Michigan).

See CHARLES PETERS, FIVE DAYS IN PHILADELPHIA: THE AMAZING "WE WANT WILKIE!" CONVENTION OF 1940 AND HOW IT FREED FDR TO SAVE THE WESTERN WORLD (2005) (explaining that the convention's delegates turned to Willkie, an internationalist, after rejecting Dewey, Taft, and Vandenberg because of their isolationist views). For a profile of Willkie, see JAMES H. MADISON, WENDELL WILLKIE: HOOSIER INTERNATIONALIST (1992).

    31. *See* JOHN W. JEFFRIES, A THIRD TERM FOR FDR: THE ELECTION OF 1940, at 169 (2017) ("Among the GOP campaign buttons and signs in 1940 were those saying 'Out at Third'—or, with more asperity, 'Out Stealing Third.'"). One particularly popular button showed a cartoon baseball player, labelled "Willkie," applying a tag at third base to another cartoon baseball player, labelled "Roosevelt," with the capitol dome in the background and the words "F.D.R. Y'R 'Out' at Third" encircling the scene. *See* Heritage Auctions, *Wendell Willkie: Highly Sought-After "Out at Third" Cartoon Pin*, Sept. 14, 2020, https://perma. cc/RG8E-9NXD.

    32. For a further look at the election, see, e.g., SUSAN DUNN, 1940: FDR, WILLKIE, LINDBERGH, HITLER—THE ELECTION AMID THE STORM (2013).

    33. Pederson, *supra* note 26, at 451.

    34. *Id.*

    35. *Id.*

    36. *See* Education, *supra* note 1, at 16–17.

    37. *Id.* at 18–19. For a profile of Carroll, see *Louis F. Carroll, 66, a Lawyer for Professional Baseball, Dies*, N.Y. TIMES, Oct. 26, 1971, at 45. Carroll does not have a *Find-a-Grave* webpage. A 1930 graduate of the University of Iowa's law school, Carroll had joined the firm after law school and had begun representing the National League in 1936. In 1938, Carroll successfully handled his first major assignment from the league, obtaining an injunction on behalf of the Pittsburgh Pirates against a local radio station that was illegally broadcasting accounts of the team's games. *See* Pittsburgh Athletic Co. v. KQV Broadcasting Co., 24 F. Supp. 490 (W.D. Pa. 1938). For a further look at the case, see *Unfair Competition—Unauthorized Broadcasts of Baseball Games*, 37 MICH. L. REV. 988 (1939) (praising the decision as providing a means with which to go after "unscrupulous competitors").

    38. *See* Toolson v. New York Yankees, Inc., 101 F. Supp. 93 (S.D. Cal. 1951), *aff'd*, 200 F.2d 198 (9th Cir. 1952), *cert. granted*, 345 U.S. 963, *judgment aff'd*, 346 U.S. 356, *reh'g denied*, 346 U.S. 917 (1953).

    39. *See* Ed Edmonds, *Remembering Earl—Not George—Toolson: The Plaintiff Who Took the New York Yankees to the U.S. Supreme Court*, SABR, https://sabr.org/journal/article/remembering-earl-not-george-toolson-the-plaintiff-who-took-the-new-york-yankees-to-the-us-supreme-court/ (last visited July 1, 2024). As Edmonds explains:

> On November 9, 1953, the United States Supreme Court issued a one paragraph opinion in *Toolson v. New York Yankees, Inc.* The decision affirmed three lower federal court decisions that turned aside lawsuits challenging the Court's 1922 ruling regarding the application of the nation's antitrust laws to Organized Baseball. The concluding sentence succinctly declared that "without re-examination of the underlying issues, the judgments below are affirmed on the authority of *Federal Baseball Club of Baltimore v. National League of Professional Baseball Clubs* … so far as that decision determines that Congress had no intention of including the business of baseball within the scope of the federal antitrust laws." Although the majority opinion was challenged by a much lengthier and strenuously argued dissent by Justices Harold H. Burton and Stanley Reed, the *Toolson* decision reinforced baseball's exemption from antitrust challenge.

Id. (footnotes omitted). The Court's 1922 *Federal Baseball* decision was the handiwork of Justice Oliver Wendell Holmes, Jr. *See* Federal Baseball Club of Balt., Inc. v. National League of Prof'l Baseball Clubs, 259 U.S. 200 (1922). Although widely criticized, the decision has managed to hold on by virtue of the principle of *stare decisis*. For a further discussion, see STUART BANNER, THE BASEBALL TRUST: A HISTORY OF BASEBALL'S ANTITRUST EXEMPTION (2013). *See also* Samuel A. Alito, Jr., *The Origin of the Baseball Antitrust Exemption: Federal Baseball Club of Baltimore, Inc. v. National League of Professional Baseball Clubs*, 34 J. SUP. CT. HIST. 183 (2009).

40. EDUCATION, *supra* note 1, at 19.

41. *See* Pendergast v. Syracuse Baseball Club, Inc., 157 N.Y.S.2d 324, 325 (Sup. Ct. 1956) (listing Carroll and Kuhn as co-counsel in a case in which they defended Commissioner Ford C. Frick against a reserve clause lawsuit filed by a minor league player); National Exhibition Co. v. Fass, 143 N.Y.S.2d 767, 768 (Sup. Ct. 1955) (listing Carroll and Kuhn as co-counsel in a case in which they obtained an injunction on behalf of the New York Giants against an unauthorized radio re-broadcaster).

42. Robert K. Heimann, *Class Notes*, PRINCETON ALUMNI WKLY., Jan. 27, 1956, at 25 (italics as in original).

43. *See Louise H Hegeler in the New York State, Marriage Index, 1881–1967*, ANCESTRY. COM, https://www.ancestry.com/discoveryui-content/view/3225222:61632 (last visited July 1, 2024); *Bowie K Kuhn in the New York State, Marriage Index, 1881–1967*, ANCESTRY.COM, https://www.ancestry.com/discoveryui-content/view/3237312:61632 (last visited July 1, 2024). *See also Weddings: Kuhn-Degener*, EVENING STAR (DC), Oct. 22, 1956, at B7 (reporting that the wedding took place at St. Patrick's Roman Catholic Church in Millstone, New York).

44. For an obituary of Luisa, see *Louise H. Kuhn, November 25, 1930—August 11, 2023, Ponta Vedra Beach*, QUINN-SHALZ FAMILY FUNERAL HOME, https://www.quinn-shalz. com/obituaries/louise-kuhn (last visited July 1, 2024) [hereinafter *Louise Kuhn Obituary*]. *See also Louise "Luisa" Hegeler Kuhn*, FIND-A-GRAVE.COM, https://www.findagrave. com/memorial/258063935/louise_kuhn (last visited July 1, 2024). Luisa's first husband had been George L. Degener III (1926–55), a wealthy stockbroker who had been killed in a car accident. *See Socialite, 29, Killed in Park Ave. Crash*, SUN. NEWS (NY), Sept. 18, 1955, at 5. *See also George Ludwig Degener III*, FIND-A-GRAVE.COM, https://www.findagrave.com/ memorial/43832762/george-l-degener (last visited July 1, 2024).

45. *See Louise Kuhn Obituary, supra* note 44.

46. *Id.*

47. *See Weddings: Kuhn-Degener, supra* note 43. *See also infra* note 52 and accompanying text.

48. *See* 2 MARTINDALE-HUBBELL LAW DIRECTORY 4130 (94th ed. 1962) (first listing of Kuhn as a member of the firm).

49. *See* EDUCATION, *supra* note 1, at 20.

50. *See* United States v. Continental Can Co., 217 F. Supp. 761 (S.D.N.Y. 1963) (dismissing the government's lawsuit at the close of the government's case).

51. United States v. Continental Can Co., 378 U.S. 441, 464 (1964).

52. *See* SUN. NEWS (Ridgewood, NJ), Mar. 8, 1964, at 46 ("Harold E. Clark, Realtor, is pleased to announce the sale of this new Williamsburg Colonial at 230 Heights Road, Ridgewood; constructed by James A. Ten Kate. Mr. and Mrs. Bowie K. Kuhn and family, formerly of Tuxedo Park, N.Y., will soon be occupying their new home here. The sale was negotiated by Beatrice Clark Peterman of the Clark office").

53. EDUCATION, *supra* note 1, at 20. In 1957, Hygrade had become the exclusive supplier of hot dogs to the Detroit Tigers; in 1959, Hygrade renamed them "Ball Park Franks," a name that quickly caught on with fans everywhere. *See further* CLYDE RILEY & DORON LEVIN, SPEAKING FRANKLY: A SOUTHERN BOY'S JOURNEY FROM SLAUGHTERHOUSE TO CREATION OF THE WORLD'S TOP HOT DOG BRAND 47–53 (2014).

54. *See Braves Will Ask League Today for Permission to Shift: Board's Decision Made in Chicago—Statement Given Out Amid Confusion—Giles Calls Owners to Meeting Here*, N.Y. TIMES, Oct. 22, 1964, at 28. The Braves' request was granted two weeks later, effective for the 1966 season. *See League Refuses to Allow Braves to Move Till '66; Team to Stay in Milwaukee Next Season, But May Go to Atlanta Thereafter*, N.Y. TIMES, Nov. 8, 1964, at 1 (Sports). The Braves are the oldest existing MLB franchise, having been founded in Boston as the Red Stockings in 1871. For a history of the team, see BRADSHER HAYES, 150 YEARS OF THE BRAVES: FROM BOSTON TO MILWAUKEE TO ATLANTA (2022).

55. The county acted first. *See Milwaukee County Files Antitrust Suit*, GREEN BAY PRESS-GAZ. (WI), Aug. 3, 1965, at 9. Four days later, the state filed its own antitrust lawsuit. *See Wisconsin Hits NL with Antitrust Suit*, DAILY NEWS (NY), Aug. 7, 1965, at 22C. Thereafter, the State took the lead in the litigation.

56. In his autobiography, Kuhn made it clear that while he had pursued the case vigorously, he was deeply unhappy having to defend the Braves' decision to move: "My heart and my responsibilities were not in the same place. I have always seen franchise movement as an absolute last resort. I hoped and expected that Milwaukee interests would come forward to purchase the Braves. It never happened." EDUCATION, *supra* note 1, at 21. Publicly, however, Kuhn applauded the Braves' planned moved to Atlanta, telling reporters that the National League was "making the game truly national in scope" by "carrying the big league gospel into the Southeast." Red Smith, *Veeck Becomes Braves' Scapegoat*, PHIL. INQUIRER, Dec. 24, 1965, at 25.

57. *See Wisconsin Court Orders Braves Back Unless League Expands*, N.Y. TIMES, Apr. 14, 1966, at 1. *See also National League to Appeal Wisconsin Ruling on Braves: Baseball to Cite Trust Immunity—1922 Supreme Court Ruling Exempting Sport to Be Used in Its Appeal*, N.Y. TIMES, Apr. 15, 1966, at 25. In his autobiography, Kuhn described Roller as a kind and decent man. *See* EDUCATION, *supra* note 1, at 21. During the trial, however, Kuhn and Roller clashed repeatedly, especially when Roller permitted a fan-turned-amateur-schedule-maker to testify that giving Milwaukee an expansion team was both possible and feasible. *See* Ken Hartnett, *Baseball Charges Judge Applies Double Standard in Court Room*, TERRE HAUTE STAR (IN), Apr. 2, 1966, at 9 ("'I respectfully submit, your honor, that a double standard is being applied in this court,' complained Bowie Kuhn, attorney for the National League, as the trial neared its close.... Kuhn said Roller was allowing the state to present its 'opinion' witnesses while denying the same right to the defense").

58. State v. Milwaukee Braves, Inc., 144 N.W.2d 1, 17–18 (Wis.), *cert. denied*, 385 U.S. 990 (1966), *reh'g denied*, 385 U.S. 1044 (1967). *See also Baseball Called Legal Monopoly: Court, by 4-to-3 Vote, Rules That State Cannot Order Club Back to Milwaukee*, N.Y. TIMES, July 28, 1966, at 25. In his autobiography, Kuhn claimed the lion's share of the credit for the appeal's outcome: "[I]n the summer of 1966 I argued the antitrust issue on which the court ruled in our favor and vacated Judge Roller's injunction." EDUCATION, *supra* note 1, at 22. It later was estimated that the litigation had cost the parties a combined $1.5 million (the equivalent today of $14.3 million), with the Atlanta Stadium Authority paying Kuhn's fees. *See* Wilt Browning, *Braves Celebrate Court Victory: Verdict May Cost $1.5 Million*, ATLANTA J., Dec. 13, 1966, at 33; Friedman, *supra* note 25 (converting 1966 dollars to 2023 dollars).

59. *See Former AF General Eckert Elected Czar of Baseball*, MIAMI HERALD, Nov. 18, 1965, at 1D. For a profile of Eckert, see Brian McKenna, *William Eckert*, SABR, https://sabr.org/bioproj/person/william-eckert/ (last visited July 1, 2024). *See also* HOLTZMAN, *supra* note 1, at 121–32.

60. *See* Joseph Durso, *Eckert Dismissed by Owners as Commissioner of Baseball*, N.Y. TIMES, Dec. 7, 1968, at 1.

61. *See* Rory Costello, *John McHale*, SABR, https://sabr.org/bioproj/person/john-mchale/ (last visited July 1, 2024).

62. In 1968, the firm had decided to stop adding and subtracting partner names and had voted to be known as "Willkie, Farr & Gallagher." *See* Pederson, *supra* note 26, at 452. *See also* Mickey Porter, *Potpourri*, AKRON BEACON J., Mar. 7, 1969, at B1 (reporting on Kuhn's 1968 salary at Willkie, Farr & Gallagher); *Baseball Barrister: Kuhn Surprised by Selection; New "Czar" Hired for One Season*, HARTFORD COURANT, Feb. 5, 1969, at 33 (reporting on Eckert's 1968 salary).

63. *See* Leonard Koppett, *Bowie Kuhn, Wall St. Lawyer, Named Commissioner Pro Tem of Baseball: $100,000 Contract to Run for a Year—Choice of National League Lawyer Ends Deadlock Over Burke and Feeney*, N.Y. TIMES, Feb. 5, 1969, at 29. With Kuhn gone, Louis L. Hoynes, Jr., another Willkie partner, inherited the National League's account. *See* Murray Chass, *Nederlander Gets Owners' Approval*, N.Y. TIMES, Sept. 13, 1990, at B15.

64. *Unknown Lawyer Selected as Baseball Commissioner*, OTTAWA CITIZEN (Can.), Feb. 5, 1969, at 30.

65. *See* Jeffrey M. Jones, *Football Retains Dominant Position as Favorite U.S. Sport*, GALLUP, Feb. 7, 2024, https://news.gallup.com/poll/610046/football-retains-dominant-position-favorite-sport.aspx ("When Gallup first asked Americans to name their favorite

spectator sport in 1937, 34% named baseball and 23% football. Baseball continued to rank first in subsequent surveys conducted in 1948 and 1960, before football gained the top spot in 1972. Since then, no less than 28% of U.S. adults have ranked football as their favorite sport, with the percentages closer to 40% in polls taken over the past two decades. Baseball and basketball have generally vied for second place since 1995").

66. For such examinations, see, e.g., PAUL HENSLER, GATHERING CROWDS: CATCHING BASEBALL FEVER IN THE NEW ERA OF FREE AGENCY (2021); JOSEPH G. PRESTON, MAJOR LEAGUE BASEBALL IN THE 1970S: A MODERN GAME EMERGES (2004); CHARLES P. KORR, THE END OF BASEBALL AS WE KNEW IT: THE PLAYERS UNION, 1960–81 (2002).

67. In April 1978, when Ford C. Frick, baseball's third commissioner, died, Kuhn, in a rare moment of self-introspection, eulogized Frick by saying that Frick "brought the game [of baseball] integrity, dedication and a happy tranquility far removed from the turbulence of today." *A World He Improved Pays Tribute to Frick*, DAILY NEWS (NY), Apr. 10, 1978, at 54.

68. *See* TIME FOR EXPANSION BASEBALL 141–252 (Maxwell Kates & Bill Nowlin eds., 2018).

69. For a look at the Pilots, see KENNETH HOGAN, THE 1969 SEATTLE PILOTS: MAJOR LEAGUE BASEBALL'S ONE-YEAR TEAM (2006). For a look at the Brewers, see DAVID ELL-MANN, BIG LEAGUE AGAIN: THE 1970 MILWAUKEE BREWERS (2020). Selig served as the Brewers' owner from 1970 until 1998, when he became baseball's ninth commissioner (1998–2015). In 2017, he was elected to the Baseball Hall of Fame. For a further look at Selig, see CHRIS ZANTOW, BUILDING THE BREWERS: BUD SELIG AND THE RETURN OF MAJOR LEAGUE BASEBALL TO MILWAUKEE (2019); ANDREW ZIMBALIST, IN THE BEST INTERESTS OF BASEBALL? THE REVOLUTIONARY REIGN OF BUD SELIG (2006). For Selig's autobiography, see BUD SELIG & PHIL ROGERS, FOR THE GOOD OF THE GAME: THE INSIDE STORY OF THE SUR-PRISING AND DRAMATIC TRANSFORMATION OF MAJOR LEAGUE BASEBALL (2019).

70. *See* Kates & Nowlin, *supra* note 68, at 253–311. Today, baseball has 30 teams, having added the Colorado Rockies (1993), Florida Marlins (1993—now Miami Marlins), Arizona Diamondbacks (1998), and Tampa Bay Devil Rays (1998—now Tampa Bay Rays). *See id.* at 312–423. It is expected that baseball will add two more teams sometime in the next decade. *See* Jeff Passan, *MLB Expansion: History, Teams, Potential Cities and Hurdles*, ESPN, Feb. 20, 2024, https://www.espn.com/mlb/insider/story/_/id/39533275/mlb-expansion-32-teams-line-cities-nashville-montreal-portland-salt-lake-city-orlando-charlotte.

71. *See* Salerno v. American League of Prof'l Baseball Clubs, 310 F. Supp. 729 (S.D.N.Y. 1969), *aff'd*, 429 F.2d 1003 (2d Cir. 1970), *cert. denied sub nom.* Salerno v. Kuhn, 400 U.S. 1001 (1971). For a profile of Salerno, see Mark Armour, *Al Salerno*, SABR, https://sabr.org/bioproj/person/al-salerno/ (last visited July 1, 2024). For a profile of Salerno's co-plaintiff, see Mark Armour, *Bill Valentine*, SABR, https://sabr.org/bioproj/person/Bill-Valentine/ (last visited July 1, 2024). For more about their lawsuit, see Mark Armour, *Salerno/Valentine Case*, SABR, https://sabr.org/bioproj/topic/salerno-valentine-case/ (last visited July 1, 2024).

72. *See* Flood v. Kuhn, 309 F. Supp. 793 (S.D.N.Y.) (denying plaintiff's request for a pre-liminary injunction), *later proceedings at* 312 F. Supp. 404 (S.D.N.Y.) (denying plaintiff's request for injunctive relief), *later proceedings at* 316 F. Supp. 271 (S.D.N.Y. 1970) (entering judgment for defendants), *aff'd*, 443 F.2d 264 (2d Cir.), *cert. granted*, 404 U.S. 880 (1971), *judgment aff'd*, 407 U.S. 258 (1972). For a detailed look at the case, see BRAD SNYDER, A WELL-PAID SLAVE: CURT FLOOD'S FIGHT FOR FREE AGENCY IN PROFESSIONAL SPORTS (2006). Prior to suing, Flood had begged Kuhn to make him a free agent, but Kuhn had rejected his plea. *See* Joe Trimble, *Kuhn Nixes Curt's Request to Make Him a Free Agent*, DAILY NEWS (NY), Dec. 31, 1969, at 46.

73. *See* George Vecsey, *Baseball Suspends McLain for Ties to Gambling*, N.Y. TIMES, Feb. 20, 1970, at 1.

74. *See* Leonard Koppett, *Kuhn to Lift McLain's Suspension on July 1; Pitcher Glad Ten-sion is Over: Tiger Ace Called 'Victim of Scheme'—Kuhn Says McLain Never was Bookmak-ing Partner After Investing $5,700*, N.Y. TIMES, Apr. 2, 1970, at 62.

75. *See* Al Harvin, *Decision Reached in 3-Hour Meeting: Reasons for Suspension Not Connected with 2 Previous Cases, Kuhn Declares*, N.Y. TIMES, Sept. 10, 1970, at 64.

76. *See* Leonard Koppett, *Probation Order Stays in Effect: Tigers Obtain Rodriguez, Brinkman, Two Pitchers*, N.Y. TIMES, Oct. 10, 1970, at 32. *See also* EDUCATION, *supra* note 1, at 72 (discussing the trade).

77. *See* Robert Lipsyte, *Crack in the Clubhouse Wall*, N.Y. TIMES, June 1, 1970, at 43.

78. *See Bouton is Warned by Kuhn on Content of His Writings*, N.Y. TIMES, June 2, 1970, at 47.

79. For a further discussion, see Mark Armour, *Ball Four*, SABR, https://sabr.org/bioproj/topic/ball-four/ (last visited July 1, 2024).

80. *See* Portland Baseball Club, Inc. v. Kuhn, 368 F. Supp. 1004 (D. Or. 1971), *aff'd*, 491 F.2d 1101 (9th Cir. 1974). *See also Judge Rules Against Bevos in Attempt to Get Damages*, CAP. J. (Salem, OR), Dec. 29, 1971, § 4, at 40 (explaining that although MLB awarded the Pacific Coast League $540,000 as compensation for losing the San Diego and Seattle markets, the Beavers, believing that this figure was too low, sued for an additional $8 million).

81. For a further look at these work stoppages, see G. RICHARD MCKELVEY, FOR IT'S ONE, TWO, THREE, FOUR STRIKES YOU'RE OUT AT THE OWNERS' BALL GAME: PLAYERS VERSUS MANAGEMENT IN BASEBALL 72–128 (2001).

82. *See Kuhn Has No Comment About Booing in Atlanta*, BOS. EVENING GLOBE, Apr. 9, 1974, at 34 (reporting that Kuhn had skipped the game to be able to attend a baseball dinner in Cleveland).

83. *See* Joseph Durso, *Steinbrenner Suspended for 2 Years*, N.Y. TIMES, Nov. 28, 1974, at 49. *See also* Murray Chass, *Yankees Owner Is Reinstated by Kuhn*, N.Y. TIMES, Mar. 2, 1976, at 48. For a further discussion, see Vince Guerrieri, *George Steinbrenner*, SABR, https://sabr.org/bioproj/person/george-steinbrenner/ (last visited July 1, 2024) (speculating that Kuhn ended the suspension early so that Steinbrenner could help open Yankee Stadium II).

84. *See* Kansas City Royal Baseball Corp. v. Major League Baseball Players Ass'n, 409 F. Supp. 233 (W.D. Mo.), *aff'd*, 532 F.2d 615 (8th Cir. 1976).

85. For a further discussion, see KORR, *supra* note 66. *See also* ROBERT B. ROSS, THE GREAT BASEBALL REVOLT: THE RISE AND FALL OF THE 1890 PLAYERS LEAGUE (2016) (explaining that the Players League had been formed to do away with the reserve clause).

86. *See* Roger Williams, *Kuhn Blocks A's Sales; Finley Sues*, S.F. EXAM'R, June 18, 1976, at 49.

87. *See Kuhn Beats the Rap in Finley's Lawsuit*, DET. FREE PRESS, Mar. 18, 1977, at 1D. On appeal, the Seventh Circuit affirmed. *See* Charles O. Finley & Co., Inc. v. Kuhn, 569 F.2d 527 (7th Cir.), *cert. denied*, 439 U.S. 876 (1978). Kuhn's edict prevented Finley from sending relief pitcher Roland G. "Rollie" Fingers and left fielder Joseph O. "Joe" Rudi to the Boston Red Sox for $2 million and starting pitcher Vida R. Blue, Jr., to the New York Yankees for $1.5 million. For a further discussion, see John Hickey, *12 Days That Shook MLB: Finley Sells Fingers, Rudi, Blue Only to be Overruled by Kuhn*, SPORTS ILLUS., June 15, 2020, https://www.si.com/mlb/athletics/news/12-days-that-shook-mlb-finley-sells-fingers-rudi-blue-only-to-be-overruled-by-kuhn.

88. *See* Atlanta Nat'l League Baseball Club, Inc. v. Kuhn, 423 F. Supp. 1213 (N.D. Ga. 1977). For a further discussion, see J. Scott Shaffer & Millard Fisher, *Ted Turner*, SABR, https://sabr.org/bioproj/person/ted-turner/#_edn26 (last visited July 1, 2024).

89. *See Minors Sue Majors*, CAP. J. (Salem, OR), Sept. 16, 1977, at 4D.

90. *See* Boise Baseball Club, Inc. v. Kuhn, 636 F.2d 1226 (9th Cir. 1980), *cert. denied*, 451 U.S. 971 (1981). *See also Appeals Court Backs Mariners*, SPOKESMAN-REV. (Spokane, WA), Dec. 13, 1980, at 22.

91. *See* Ludtke v. Kuhn, 461 F. Supp. 86 (S.D.N.Y. 1978). For a further discussion, see MELISSA LUDTKE, LOCKER ROOM TALK: A WOMAN'S STRUGGLE TO GET INSIDE (2024).

92. *See* Murray Chass, *Kroc, Citing $100,000 Fine, Gives Up Control of Padres*, N.Y. TIMES, Aug. 25, 1979, at 11

93. *See* James Tuite, *Mays Leaving Baseball*, N.Y. TIMES, Oct. 30, 1979, at B15.

94. *See* Joseph Durso, *Mantle Takes $100,000 Jersey Casino Job: Kuhn Orders Him to Sever Yankee Ties*, N.Y. TIMES, Feb. 9, 1983, at B15.

95. *See* Michael Martinez, *Mays and Mantle Reinstated: New Rules to be Set on Casino Ties*, N.Y. TIMES, Feb. 9, 1985, at B7.

96. *See* Saravette Trotter, *Pines Team Sues Baseball League*, Nashville Graphic, Dec. 2, 1980, at 1.

97. *See* Professional Baseball Schools and Clubs, Inc. v. Kuhn, 693 F.2d 1085 (11th Cir. 1982).

98. *See* Leonard Koppett, *Kuhn Calls Tune and Receives 7-Year Pact Worth $1-Million*, N.Y. Times, Aug. 14, 1969, at 39.

99. *See* Joseph Durso, *Owners Re-elect Kuhn as Finley's Coup Fails*, N.Y. Times, July 18, 1975, at 48.

100. *See* Joseph Durso, *Kuhn is Voted Out as Baseball Commissioner*, N.Y. Times, Nov. 2, 1982, at A1.

101. *See* Murray Chass, *Bowie Kuhn Steps Aside to Put an End to Acrimony: Surprising Decision 'Is Final,'* N.Y. Times, Aug. 4, 1983, at A1.

102. *See* Joseph Durso, *Baseball Names Ueberroth to Replace Kuhn Oct. 1*, N.Y. Times, Mar. 4, 1984, at 1 (Sports) [hereinafter *Baseball Names Ueberroth*]. For a profile of Ueberroth, *see* Zac Petrillo, *Peter Ueberroth*, SABR, https://sabr.org/bioproj/person/peter-ueberroth/ (last visited July 1, 2024).

103. *See Baseball Names Ueberroth, supra* note 102.

104. Dave Nightingale, *Ueberroth a 1-Term Commissioner: Support for His Reelection Simply Not There, He Says*, Sporting News, Dec. 21, 1987, at 44.

105. *See* Murray Chass, *Kuhn's Descent from Commissioner to Legal Outcast*, N.Y. Times, May 12, 1991, § 8, at 3 [hereinafter *Kuhn's Decent*] ("At the time Kuhn returned to Willkie Farr, people in baseball knew and talked privately about how the firm didn't really want him back, but had no choice. He was rehired not as a full partner but as a contract partner, making $175,000 a year, substantially less than the full partners").

106. *See supra* note 1.

107. Guerrieri, *supra* note 1 (footnote omitted).

108. In his autobiography, Kuhn rejected the notion that he was a stuffed shirt, although he admitted that many people viewed him as one. *See* Education, *supra* note 1, at 12. Following Kuhn's death, one of his biographers wrote:

> Bowie Kuhn always seemed out of place around baseball. He was someone who seemed to belong more to the sport of polo, even though much of his life was spent in baseball. There was an upper-class arrogance, a haughtiness about him, that was not overbearing, but always [was] part of his persona. Bowie Kuhn seemed to be uncomfortable with ordinary people, people not of his class.

Crepeau, *supra* note 1, at 1–2.

109. The pair were brought together by a mutual friend, former U.S. Secretary of the Treasury William E. Simon, who suggested that the two men form a law firm. *See* Jeffrey H. Lieberman, *Esq.*, 16:9 Stud. Law. 34, 34 (May 1988). Kuhn later explained that he jumped at the chance to start his own law firm as well as Myerson's promise to increase his pay to $500,000. *See Kuhn's Descent, supra* note 105. Myerson, on the other hand, explained that he needed Kuhn's name and pedigree. *Id.*

110. For a further look at Finley, Kumble (later wickedly nicknamed "Finley, Crumble" by its detractors), *see* Kim Isaac Eisler, Shark Tank: Greed, Politics, and the Collapse of Finley Kumble, One of America's Largest Law Firms (1990). *See also* Steven J. Kumble & Kevin J. Lahart, Conduct Unbecoming: The Rise and Ruin of Finley, Kumble (1990).

111. Lieberman, *supra* note 109, at 35.

112. Guerrieri, *supra* note 1. *See also* Robert M. Jarvis, Florida Constitutional Law in a Nutshell 235 (2020) (explaining Florida's unlimited homestead protection rules and Kuhn and Myerson's efforts to take advantage of them); David Margolick, *Bowie Kuhn is Said to Be in Hiding*, N.Y. Times, Feb. 9, 1990, at D1 (same). For more about Myerson & Kuhn's bankruptcy, see In re Myerson & Kuhn, 121 B.R. 145 (Bankr. S.D.N.Y. 1990). For more about Myerson's fraud conviction, see United States v. Myerson, 18 F.3d 153 (2d Cir.), *cert. denied*, 513 U.S. 855 (1994). For Myerson's disbarments due to his fraud conviction, see Matter of Myerson, 679 N.Y.S.2d 136 (App. Div. 1998) (loss of New York State law license); In the Matter of Disbarment of Myerson, 525 U.S. 1119 (1999) (loss of U.S.

Supreme Court license). For additional details about Myerson's life, see Partridge v. Myerson, 556 N.Y.S.2d 707 (App. Div. 1990), *appeal denied*, 564 N.E.2d 671 (N.Y. 1990) (action by Myerson's former wife for unpaid maintenance and child support). For Myerson's obituary, see Brian Baxter, *A Quiet Death for a Legendary Lawyer Who Fell from Grace*, AM. LAW., Nov. 15, 2015, https://www.law.com/americanlawyer/almID/1202742442627/. Myerson does not have a *Find-a-Grave* webpage.

113. Guerrieri, *supra* note 1. Kuhn is buried in the Quogue Cemetery in Quogue, New York. *See Bowie Kuhn Find-a-Grave Webpage, supra* note 8. There is no public reporting regarding how much of an estate Kuhn left at his death. *But see* Mark Woods, *You'll Learn Lots Touring Estate Sales*, FLA. TIMES-UNION (Jacksonville), Aug. 16, 2009, https://www.jacksonville.com/story/news/2009/08/16/youll-learn-lots-touring-estate-sales/15976063007/ (describing the three-day estate sale held in 2009 to clear out Kuhn's Florida home).

114. In July 2001, Kuhn detailed the role that his Catholic faith had played in his life and work during an hour-long television interview. *See Bowie Kuhn: Former Cultural Catholic—The Journey Home Program*, YOUTUBE.COM, https://www.youtube.com/watch?v=YHm8WP9GSTc (last visited July 1, 2024). Luisa likewise was very religious. *See Louise Kuhn Obituary, supra* note 44. The Catholic executive peer group Legatus now annually presents the "Bowie Kuhn Award for Evangelization" to a business leader who has successfully spread the gospel. *See, e.g.*, *Legatus Honors Mario Costabile with 2020 Bowie Kuhn Award for Evangelization*, STANDARD NEWSWIRE, Oct. 12, 2021, http://www.standardnewswire.com/news/8443417844.html (profiling media executive Mario V. Costabile).

115. *See Bowie Kuhn Obituary*, LEGACY.COM, https://www.legacy.com/us/obituaries/washingtonpost/name/bowie-kuhn-obituary?id=5584908 (last visited July 1, 2024) ("A lifelong Republican, Kuhn served on the election committees of the 2000 Bush/Cheney campaign, the 1988 and 1992 Bush/Quayle campaigns and the 1996 Dole campaign").

116. *Id.* The law school moved to Naples, Florida, in the summer of 2009. *See* Dave Breitenstein, *Law School Ready for Debut: Ave Maria Set to Begin Classes in North Naples*, NEWS-PRESS (Fort Myers, FL), Aug. 6, 2009, at B1 (explaining that the school originally opened in Ann Arbor in 2000 and moved following a zoning dispute).

117. Gene Frenette, *Bowie Kuhn: 1926–2007; Commissioner Led Baseball Through Best, Worst of Times; His Time at the Top Saw More Interest in the Game, as well as Strikes and Bans*, FLA. TIMES-UNION (Jacksonville), Mar. 16, 2007, at A1.

118. *See* Joe Lapointe, *Hall Opens Its Doors to Kuhn, Not Miller*, N.Y. TIMES, Dec. 4, 2007, at D5. This headline refers to the fact that Marvin J. Miller, the executive director of the players' union and Kuhn's nemesis during his commissionership, had been snubbed. Upon hearing that Kuhn had made it but Miller had not, Jim Bouton remarked, "That's like putting Wile E. Coyote in the Hall of Fame instead of the Road Runner." Guerrieri, *supra* note 1. In 2019, Miller finally was recognized. *See Veterans Committee Elects Two Hall of Famers*, N.Y. TIMES, Dec. 9, 2019, at D5.

119. *See* Richard Sandomir, *O'Malley and Kuhn Enter Hall, Forever Linked by Bold Moves*, N.Y. TIMES, July 27, 2008, at 2 (Sports). This headline refers to the fact that during Kuhn's commissionership, the most powerful team owner was Walter F. O'Malley of the Los Angeles Dodgers, the subject of Chapter 10 of this book. In his autobiography, Kuhn denied that he had been O'Malley's puppet while serving as commissioner:

> Did Walter O'Malley control Bowie Kuhn, as was often charged by the press during the decade before O'Malley's death in 1979? I imagine the fair answer is that I have always been too mulish to be controlled by anyone. By training, personal philosophy and nature, I believe I have always had good manners, which means I try, not with invariable success, to treat other people with respect. So it was with Walter. Old enough to be my father, he had not only my respect but my admiration and affection as well.

EDUCATION, *supra* note 1, at 23.

120. *See* Sandomir, *supra* note 119.

121. *Bowie Kuhn*, NATIONAL BASEBALL HALL OF FAME AND MUSEUM, https://baseball hall.org/hall-of-famers/kuhn-bowie (last visited July 1, 2024).

122. Murray Chass, *Kuhn's Legacy is Not All That It Seems*, N.Y. Times, Mar. 20, 2007, at D5. Many years earlier, Southern California sportswriter Walter "Bud" Tucker had been both blunter and more succinct: "An empty cab recently pulled up at a New York hotel and baseball commissioner Bowie Kuhn stepped out." Bud Tucker, ... *Of Ships, Shoes and Sealing Wax*, Indep. Press-Telegram (Long Beach, CA), Apr. 9, 1972, at S4. For a further discussion, see Emma Span, *Let's Talk About How Wrong Bowie Kuhn Was About Basically Everything*, OldTimeFamilyBaseball.com, Jan. 19, 2014, https://oldtimefamilybaseball. com/post/73886697009/everything-bowie-kuhn-wrong.s

CHAPTER 10

Walter Francis O'Malley (2008)

ROBERT M. JARVIS

In 1957, after being a borough fixture for 75 seasons, the Brooklyn Dodgers moved to Los Angeles, California.[1] Fans of the team, furious at having been betrayed, knew exactly whom to blame: owner Walter Francis O'Malley (October 9, 1903–August 9, 1979).[2] O'Malley's decision was met with such ire that the following joke soon began making the rounds:

Q: Who are the three most hated persons of the 20th century?
A: Adolf Hitler, Joseph Stalin, and Walter O'Malley.
Q: If a Brooklyn man is in a room with Hitler, Stalin, and O'Malley, but has only two bullets in his gun, what should he do?
A: Shoot O'Malley twice.[3]

Long before he had amassed enough power to move the Dodgers across the country, however, O'Malley, who was inducted into baseball's Hall of Fame in 2008,[4] was just another Depression Era lawyer hustling to make a living.

Birth, Baseball, and the Boy Scouts

Walter F. O'Malley was born on October 9, 1903, in the South Bronx, the only child of Alma C. (née Feltner) (1883–1940)[5] and Edwin J. O'Malley (1881–1953).[6] Alma's ancestry was German, while Edwin's family was from County Mayo, Ireland.[7] Both were raised in large households—Alma had seven siblings while Edwin had 13.[8] Government records indicate that the couple married in New Jersey in 1903 but do not give the date or place.[9] At the time of O'Malley's birth, Edwin was working as a dry goods salesman.[10]

As a child, O'Malley was introduced to baseball by his uncle Clarence

G. Feltner (1891–1960) (Alma's brother), and the pair often attended games together.[11] Like other Bronxites, Clarence and O'Malley rooted for the National League's New York Giants, who played at the Polo Grounds in northern Manhattan.[12] During this period, the Giants, led by future Hall of Famers Christopher "Christy" Mathewson and John J. McGraw, were the toast of both boroughs, having won the pennant in 1904 and the World Series in 1905.[13] Manhattan's other professional baseball team—the American League's New York Highlanders, who played at Hilltop Park, a mere 10 blocks to the west of the Polo Grounds—were still years away from being renamed the Yankees (1913), moving to the Bronx (1923), and featuring a pair of sluggers named George H. "Babe" Ruth and Henry L. "Lou" Gehrig (1925).[14]

In 1910, the O'Malleys left the Bronx for Hollis, a rural neighborhood in southeast Queens,[15] where an increasingly affluent Edwin became increasingly involved in land deals and Democratic politics.[16] As for O'Malley, he became a student at Hollis's Public School 35, where he "worked hard at his studies, but equally liked many activities outside of school, including swimming, fishing and boating. He also thoroughly enjoyed his experience as a Boy Scout, where he first went camping, hunting and 'learned how to cook and make a bed.'"[17] As a member of Hollis Boy Scouts Troop 2, O'Malley earned 32 merit badges; reached the rank of "Life scout" (the organization's second highest rank, just below "Eagle scout"); formed his own unit (the "Pine Tree Patrol"); and attended and later helped run Camp Matinecock, the Boy Scouts' summer camp at Bear Mountain in upstate New York.[18]

A Scandalous Father

In March 1918, Edwin was appointed deputy commissioner of the city's Department of Public Markets ("DPM"),[19] an important government post that came with a $5,000 salary (the equivalent today of $103,000[20]). In October 1919, Dr. Jonathan C. Day, Edwin's boss, fired Edwin after Edwin was accused of arranging to have the city sell surplus food (obtained from the U.S. Navy) to hungry New Yorkers at inflated prices.[21] Just one month later, however, Edwin was named the city's new Deputy Commissioner of Charities, a position that also carried a salary of $5,000.[22] Then, in a truly remarkable turn of events, in December 1919 Edwin was given Day's job after Day was fired.[23] Edwin owed his good fortune to Mayor John F. Hylan, who, like Edwin, was a member of Tammany Hall, the city's powerful political machine.[24]

Edwin's tenure as the head of the DPM got off to a rocky start—on

December 31, 1919, "a near riot" occurred when Edwin "distributed 10,000 pounds of sugar to city employees ... at 12 cents a pound ... [and] many sugar hungry workers attempted to make purchases."[25] A short time later, Fiorello H. La Guardia, the president of the city's Board of Alderman, introduced a resolution calling for an investigation into the October 1919 surplus food scandal that had gotten Edwin fired. Hylan, however, was able to block La Guardia's resolution,[26] and the public eventually moved on from the affair, but not before several other politicians lost their jobs.[27]

Matters again became dire for Edwin in April 1921, when the New York State Legislature, having already created the Lockwood Committee to investigate graft in the city's housing industry,[28] established the Meyer Committee to examine corruption in the city's government.[29]

On August 31, 1921, Edwin appeared before the Meyer Committee, which was meeting in City Hall's ornate Council Room. After taking the stand and spending two hours talking without saying anything of substance (and without answering any of the committee's questions), Edwin got up and left while being cheered wildly by the audience.[30]

In June 1922, the Meyer Committee issued its findings. Taking direct aim at Edwin, the committee accused him of allowing the DPM to become a "vehicle for the collection of graft."[31] Even more bad news was just around the corner. In July 1922, New York State Supreme Court Justice James C. Cropsey found that DPM employees were extorting the city's pushcart peddlers. Speaking from the bench, Cropsey called the scheme a "nice plunder for somebody."[32]

In the end, nothing happened to Edwin. How this occurred is unknown. What is known is that Edwin remained the head of the DPM until December 31, 1925, when Hylan's second term as mayor ended.[33]

College, Law School, Marriage, and Children

While Edwin fought for his political life, O'Malley, who previously had been a student at the city's Jamaica High School (1918–20), was far away. In August 1920, over O'Malley's vehement protests, Alma and Edwin had shipped O'Malley, by now 16 years old, to the Culver Military Academy ("CMA") in Culver, Indiana.[34] In addition to wanting to shield O'Malley from news about Edwin's political struggles, the couple felt that CMA, which doubled as an elite finishing school, would help O'Malley make connections that would assist him in the future.[35]

At CMA, O'Malley wrote a column for *The Vedette*, CMA's student newspaper; managed the baseball and tennis teams; and was a member of the Bible Discipline Committee, the debate team, the Hospital Visitation

Committee, and the local YMCA.[36] O'Malley also tried out for the CMA baseball team, an endeavor that ended after a hard-hit ball broke his nose:

> "I went to Culver and graduated there in 1922," said O'Malley. "It was there that I thought I might become a ballplayer—I tried out at first base...."
>
> [O'Malley's] fairly short baseball playing career ended at Culver when he was hit on the nose by a ball. A hot grounder to him at first base caromed off his nose, breaking it, [and] leading doctors to advise him not to play without wearing his glasses, something that wasn't in vogue at the time.
>
> "Yes, they banged my nose open and I was also handicapped by the fact that I wore glasses and, at that time, there weren't many players who wore glasses," said O'Malley.[37]

As his graduation from CMA neared, O'Malley had hopes of attending Princeton University in New Jersey, but his grades were not good enough to get in.[38] Alma wanted O'Malley to go to West Point (as a CMA graduate, O'Malley automatically received a commission as a second lieutenant in the U.S. Army Reserve[39]), but three senior CMA faculty members nixed the idea after deciding that O'Malley was not "West Point material."[40] With both schools off the table, Alma and Edwin urged O'Malley to go to Cornell University in Ithaca, New York, but after visiting the campus O'Malley refused: "Since my return from Culver, [O'Malley wrote a friend,] family sentiment is strongly bent towards Cornell—so there I went to 'inspect' the college. I am really disappointed! Cornell is too large!"[41] O'Malley finally decided to enroll in the University of Pennsylvania ("UP") in Philadelphia, where neither his poor grades, nor his lack of foreign language proficiency (French had been a problem), were obstacles to his being admitted.[42]

O'Malley entered UP in 1922 and immediately thrived. He joined a fraternity (Theta Delta Chi, eventually becoming chapter president); led both the freshmen (1923) and the sophomores (1924) to victories in the Penniman Bowl (a kind of Olympics games between the two classes); served on the Vigilance Committee (an organization of sophomores tasked with keeping freshmen in line); and was an active member of the Scabbard and Blade military honor society.[43] In the words of one of his biographers, "As a campus wheel O'Malley was at the heart of [UP's] social activities."[44]

In October 1924, O'Malley was elected president of the junior class[45]; in May 1925, he was elected president of the senior class.[46] In winning these posts (an unprecedented achievement in UP's history), O'Malley benefited considerably from the large number of CMA alumni attending UP.[47]

In March 1926, O'Malley was named "Spoon Man," the senior class's highest honor.[48] In reporting on his election, UP's student newspaper wrote:

Walter F. O'Malley is president of the Senior Class. He hails from Amityville, N.Y. [a reference to Alma and Edwin's summer home], and prepared at the Culver Military Academy. He was also president of the Junior Class, and is distinguished by having succeeded himself in office. He is, by virtue of his position as president of the Senior Class, chairman of the Undergraduate Council, a member of the Council on Welfare and Student Activities, and is on the Council of Athletics. He is claimed by the Friars Senior Society and the Theta Delta Chi Fraternity. O'Malley has been closely associated with class affairs, and his election as Spoon Man comes as a fitting climax of four years' activity at the University.[49]

In June 1926, O'Malley graduated from UP with an A.B.[50] As a graduation gift, Alma and Edwin gave O'Malley a 42-foot cabin cruiser.[51]

As has been explained elsewhere, in later years O'Malley "changed" his major and embellished other aspects of his UP academic record:

> Despite telling one newspaper reporter he had graduated first in his class, O'Malley had a mixed academic career.... Overall, he mostly got "pass" grades, the equivalent of Cs in Pennsylvania's system.... Of the 72.5 units O'Malley took at Penn, only 9 rated the grade of "distinguished," the equivalent of today's As.
>
> Undoubtedly, the most interesting thing about Walter O'Malley's college transcript is what it does not show. Over the years O'Malley would many times tell of studying engineering at Pennsylvania, occasionally describing it as his major. His transcript contains no engineering courses. It contains no science courses, and it shows two of his three mathematics courses were cause for probation. What Walter O'Malley concentrated on was psychology, a relatively new and highly trendy discipline in the 1920s....[52]

In the fall of 1926, O'Malley enrolled in the law school at Columbia University ("CULS"). In what has become a common error in works about O'Malley, it often is reported that O'Malley dropped out of CULS after the stock market crashed and Edwin lost all his money. The story then continues that O'Malley enrolled in Fordham University's law school ("FULS"), where he was able to obtain his degree in 1930 after attending classes at night while working during the day.[53] As is obvious, this story cannot possibly be true—as a 1926 matriculant, O'Malley would have finished at CULS in June 1929, months before the stock market crashed in October 1929.

More astute biographers have realized that O'Malley dropped out of CULS because Edwin became destitute in 1927, with O'Malley merely changing the year to 1929 (presumably to avoid questions about what caused Edwin's penury):

> [In a *New York Post* article, Maury Allen quoted O'Malley as saying:] "The crash ruined my father's business as it did a lot of other people's. He never really recovered financially or emotionally." But a close look at the timeline of

young Walter O'Malley shows that something had blighted Edwin O'Malley's finances before 1929....

[After graduating from UP,] Dad enrolled [O'Malley] at Columbia. And it was during or just after that first year there that the money ran out, for Walter had to leave [CULS's] Morningside Heights [campus] and head downtown to less expensive Fordham Law, housed then in the Woolworth Building, where he was able to take night classes and pay his way with [his own] wages....[54]

Andy McCue, O'Malley's principal biographer, believes Edwin's inability to keep O'Malley at CULS was due to Edwin's loss of his DPM job and its $5,000 salary, coupled with a possible downturn in his real estate dealings:

It is clear that at some point [Edwin] switched [from the dry goods business] to the real estate business and that he had a severe reduction in income around the spring of 1927. But beyond that nothing is very clear....

Others have tied Edwin's financial straits to the stock market crash that precipitated the Great Depression, but Walter dropped out of Columbia two years before Black Thursday.

It ... seems significant that Edwin's financial straits hit just over a year after he left public office. The opportunities of running the Public Markets Department were no longer available, and perhaps some investments went bad. Whatever happened, Walter O'Malley withdrew from Columbia's law school in June 1927.[55]

McCue's euphemistic phrase—"The opportunities of running the Public Markets Department were no longer available"—gets to the real cause of Edwin's financial problems. Because he no longer was DPM commissioner, Edwin could not shake down food suppliers and vendors. And with his graft spigot turned off, his pocketbook developed a hole he could not fill except by cutting back on his expenses.

Edwin still had enough political clout, however, to get O'Malley a job—as a result, at the end of June 1927, O'Malley began working for the city's Board of Transportation ("BOT"), earning $130 a month.[56] As McCue reports, "The secretary of the board was Francis J. Sinnott, a Brooklyn politician whose younger brother was the secretary and son-in-law of Edwin's patron, former Mayor John Hylan."[57]

In September 1927, O'Malley enrolled as a night student at FULS.[58] At this time, FULS's night law program required three years of study.[59] Because it took O'Malley three years to graduate from FULS, it appears that FULS did not give O'Malley any credit for his time at CULS. This suggests that O'Malley withdrew from CULS before he had a chance to take his first-year final examinations.

In September 1929, O'Malley left the BOT. During his two years at the BOT, O'Malley had been an "engineering assistant."[60] McCue believes that it was during this period that O'Malley began claiming that he had studied engineering at UP to cover up his lack of qualifications.[61]

Soon after leaving the BOT, O'Malley got a job at the Riley Drilling Company ("RDC"). Six weeks later, RDC "was part of a group that won a $2 million contract for geologic and other preliminary work on the Queens Midtown Tunnel. The contract was overseen by the [BOT]."[62]

In June 1930, O'Malley graduated from FULS with an LL.B.[63] By now, he had been seeing Katharina E. "Kay" Hanson (1907–79) for approximately six years.[64] Kay, who also was known as "Kay Kay," was the daughter of Elizabeth G. (1877–1965)[65] and Peter B. Hanson (1877–1965).[66] Peter, originally from Sweden, was a graduate of New York Law School (1900) and had been appointed to a seat on the Brooklyn Children's Court (later renamed the Domestic Relations Court) in 1927.[67] During his senior year at FULS, "O'Malley gained valuable experience working in the offices of Judge Hanson."[68]

O'Malley had met Kay (and her younger sister Helen) after O'Malley's parents purchased their summer home in Amityville (1922).[69] As O'Malley later explained, "Kay's folks lived in the house next to ours in Amityville, Long Island. We were on the Great South Bay and we liked fishing and boating. I saw her grow up—she's younger than I [am], of course. Gradually, it led into romance."[70]

In July 1930, O'Malley took Kay, his parents, and various friends on a moonlight cruise (despite Edwin's money troubles, O'Malley had been able to hold on to his cabin cruiser).[71] A year later, the pair married,[72] but not before Edwin tried to convince O'Malley to dump Kay because she was "damaged goods." In 1927, Kay had been diagnosed with cancer and had her larynx removed during what was, at the time, experimental surgery. Although the operation was a success, "her voice box was permanently impaired, leaving her to speak … [in] a barely audible whisper for the remainder of her life."[73] In rejecting Edwin's entreaties, O'Malley told his father, "She's the same girl I fell in love with."[74]

On May 16, 1933, Kay and O'Malley had their first child, a daughter named Therese A. "Terry" (later Seidler).[75] On December 12, 1937, the couple had a son named Peter.[76] As has been explained elsewhere, "Kay graduated from [the] College of New Rochelle and attended St. John's Law School. But she set aside her plans to become an attorney in order to marry Walter in 1931 and later raise [their] two children…."[77]

Hanging Up a Shingle

In March 1931, O'Malley took the New York bar examination; in May 1931, he learned that he had passed.[78] It would be nearly two years, however, before O'Malley completed the clerkship required of all successful bar takers and was able to formally apply for admission.[79] Finally, however, on April 10, 1933, O'Malley was sworn into the New York bar.[80]

While waiting to be admitted, O'Malley found multiple ways to make money:

> [Working out of an office in] the Lincoln Building located at 60 E. 42nd Street[,] O'Malley founded, published and was editor of "Sub-Contractors Register [and Bulletin]," an important directory listing personnel and services for contractors…. He quickly became President of the Society of Allied Building Trades, working on correcting troubles of labor. O'Malley also wrote an impressive and popular law guide to explain the New York City Building Code….[81]

According to McCue, O'Malley had time to engage in these enterprises because he was skirting the clerkship rules: "[Y]oung lawyers were supposed to complete their training by working under an experienced lawyer for at least six months. But that was not Walter O'Malley's way. Instead, he gave an experienced but officeless lawyer space in [his office] and used this as his clerkship."[82]

Following his admission to the bar, O'Malley closed his other businesses and hung out his shingle. Initially, O'Malley got much of his work from judges, who would appoint O'Malley to serve as a referee overseeing foreclosure sales.[83] It seems a safe assumption that O'Malley landed these lucrative patronage positions by relying on Edwin, who continued to be able to call on his old political allies for favors.

O'Malley & Wilson

With the boost provided by his referee appointments, O'Malley soon developed a thriving practice focusing on bankruptcies, reorganizations, and workouts—what lawyers during this time called "grave dancing."[84] In later years, O'Malley would claim that the practice grew until he was the senior partner of a 20-lawyer firm.[85] As usual, however, he was embellishing.[86]

Initially, O'Malley worked as a sole practitioner.[87] In 1935, however, O'Malley formed a partnership—dubbed O'Malley & Wilson—with a lawyer named Raymond F. Wilson.[88] Unfortunately, little is known about Wilson, his prior relationship with O'Malley, or how the pair came to be partners. What records do exist indicate that Wilson was born in 1900,[89] went to Stuyvesant High School in Manhattan,[90] graduated from St. Lawrence University's law school (now Brooklyn Law School),[91] became a member of the New York bar in 1927,[92] and died in 1948.[93] According to one source, Wilson "had significant associations with insurance and indemnity corporations."[94]

A 1934 newspaper story mentions that at a party celebrating the end of Long Island's summer season, Kay and O'Malley's guests included "Mr. and Mrs. Raymond Wilson."[95] This suggests that O'Malley and Wilson were social companions before they decided to become law partners. Additionally, a 1937 newspaper story identifies both Flora (Wilson's wife) and Kay as being alumna of the College of New Rochelle.[96] This suggests that O'Malley and Wilson met through their wives.

Although O'Malley & Wilson prospered, the firm did not reach the heights O'Malley later claimed it did. The firm's 1940 letterhead,[97] for example, lists just seven lawyers: O'Malley; Wilson; Nicholas P. Callaghan (1902–58)[98]; George O. Lehmann (1901–89)[99]; Ruth F. Sturm (1911–96)[100]; Aloysius J. (James) Melia (1915–2002)[101]; and Charles H. McAuliffe (1914–57).[102] Except for Wilson and Sturm, all were graduates of FULS.

From the available evidence, it appears that O'Malley and Wilson ended their partnership in late 1941 or early 1942.[103] During its brief existence, the firm had been counsel in numerous cases, a good number of which resulted in published opinions.[104] Although O'Malley had brought many of these cases to the firm, as a lawyer he left much to be desired. As attorney William A. Shea, who later would become the namesake of New York City's Shea Stadium, remarked: "He [O'Malley] was one lousy lawyer. O'Malley was the most brilliant businessman I've ever met, but we were talking about law here, weren't we? I wouldn't have let O'Malley plead a parking ticket for me."[105]

Exactly why O'Malley & Wilson closed is unclear, although World War II certainly played a part.[106] In any event, O'Malley's attention was about to shift to baseball.

O'Malley and the Dodgers

In 1890, Charles H. Ebbets, Sr., a Brooklyn bookkeeper, began buying stock in the Brooklyn Bridegrooms. By 1898, he owned 80 percent of the team (soon to be renamed the Superbas).[107] In 1912, Ebbets began building Ebbets Field, which opened in 1913.[108] To finance the stadium, Ebbets arranged for Edward J. McKeever and his brother Stephen W. McKeever, two Brooklyn construction moguls, to buy half the team (Ebbets retained the other half).[109]

In 1925, Ebbets and Edward McKeever died within 11 days of each (ironically, McKeever passed away after catching a cold at Ebbets' funeral).[110] Ebbets and McKeever's deaths led to unrelenting acrimony among their heirs. The Great Depression only made things worse, and by 1934 the team effectively was bankrupt.

The interests of the heirs were overseen by the Brooklyn Trust Company ("BTC") (acting as trustee—the bank also was the team's biggest creditor, being owed $700,000, the equivalent today of $16.2 million[111]). In 1937, George V. McLaughlin, BTC's president,[112] convinced the heirs to hire turnaround specialist Leland S. "Larry" MacPhail, Sr., the subject of the seventh essay of this book, as the team's new executive vice president and general manager.[113] MacPhail, living up to his reputation, quickly made the team a winner on and off the field but resigned in September 1942 to enlist in the Army.[114] As a result, in October 1942 McLaughlin convinced the heirs to replace MacPhail with Wesley Branch Rickey, the subject of Chapter 6 of this book.[115]

As one of his first acts, Rickey fired the team's longtime law firm (Willkie, Owen, Otis, Farr & Gallagher), which he felt had a conflict of interest because it also represented the National League. (In 1950, Bowie K. Kuhn, the subject of the ninth essay of this book, opted to begin his legal career at the firm *because* it represented the National League.) Following the firing, Rickey turned to McLaughlin, who suggested that Rickey hire O'Malley, BTC's outside counsel. (McLaughlin and O'Malley's ties ran deep—McLaughlin knew O'Malley's father Edwin and had gone to UP baseball games with O'Malley while O'Malley was a UP student.[116]) As a result, O'Malley became the Dodgers' lawyer in 1943.[117]

In 1944, O'Malley, Rickey, and John L. Smith, the longtime vice president of Charles Pfizer and Company (the pharmaceutical giant), purchased the 25 percent of the team that was owned by Edward McKeever's heirs.[118] In 1945, the trio purchased the 50 percent of the team that was owned by Ebbets' heirs.[119] "At McLaughlin's insistence, the 75 percent owned by the [trio] had to be voted as a block, to prevent the kind of 50–50 splits that had plagued the team during the 1930s."[120] The remaining 25 percent, which had belonged to Stephen McKeever, was in the hands of Elizabeth M. "Dearie" Mulvey, Stephen's daughter. She had inherited her father's shares following his death in 1938.[121]

At first, O'Malley and Rickey got along well as co-owners. As time went on, however, the pair began to clash over Rickey's salary (which O'Malley felt was excessive) and Rickey's penchant for spending money to improve the team's farm system and spring training facilities (which O'Malley thought was unnecessary). The pair also argued over Rickey's decision to invest in a football team (the Brooklyn Dodgers of the fledgling All-America Football Conference). O'Malley likewise appears to have been less than enthusiastic regarding Rickey's plan to break baseball's color line, although commentators remain divided on just where O'Malley stood on the question of integration and the extent to which he helped or hindered Rickey in signing Jack R. "Jackie" Robinson, who in 1947 became the first African American in 60 years to play in the major leagues.

O'Malley and Rickey also clashed on a personal level. O'Malley was a Democrat, while Rickey was a Republican. O'Malley was Catholic, while Rickey was a Methodist. O'Malley liked to drink; Rickey was a teetotaler. O'Malley enjoyed telling jokes and giving people a slap on the back; Rickey was more reserved. And while O'Malley was a brash New Yorker, Rickey was still, in many ways, an Ohio farm boy.

Matters finally came to a head in the fall of 1950. With Rickey's five-year contract as the team's president and general manager set to expire, O'Malley offered to buy Rickey's 25 percent for $346,000, the same amount that Rickey had paid for his shares. A short time earlier, Smith had died, and O'Malley had convinced Smith's widow to place his shares with BTC. As BTC's general counsel, O'Malley was authorized to vote these shares, thereby giving him control of the team.

Unwilling to work for O'Malley, Rickey demanded $1 million for his 25 percent. Knowing that Rickey, who always lived beyond his means,

had margined his Dodgers stock and fully leveraged his life insurance policy, O'Malley held firm, believing that Rickey would cave. Rickey, however, arranged for one of his Delta Tau Delta fraternity brothers—William Zeckendorf, Sr., a prominent New York City real estate developer—to offer him $1 million for his shares. Zeckendorf's offer, which may or may not have been sincere, triggered a clause in the O'Malley-Rickey-Smith partnership agreement that required O'Malley to match Zeckendorf's offer (and pay Zeckendorf $50,000 as "compensation") if O'Malley wanted Rickey's shares. Having

Walter F. O'Malley (c. 1951) (National Baseball Hall of Fame and Museum).

been outmaneuvered by Rickey, O'Malley grudgingly paid the $1,050,000 (the equivalent today of $13,525,000[122])—as a further comeuppance, Zeckendorf later gave the $50,000 he received from O'Malley to Rickey.[123]

Conclusion

With Rickey gone,[124] O'Malley gave up what remained of his law practice and became a full-time baseball executive.[125] In this role, his chief priority was getting a new stadium built to replace Ebbets Field, which had become cramped, outdated, and increasingly inconvenient for the team's fans, who were moving in droves to the suburbs. After considering various alternatives, O'Malley picked a plot of land at the corner of Atlantic and Flatbush Avenues in Brooklyn.[126] Not only did this site have plenty of room for parking, it was serviced by nine subway lines and the Long Island Rail Road. O'Malley also hired (Richard) Buckminster Fuller, the noted architect, to design an enormous plastic dome that would cover the entire facility, thereby allowing games to be played regardless of the weather.[127]

In the end, however, O'Malley's plans came to naught. For cost reasons, O'Malley needed the city to use its eminent domain powers to condemn the land on which the stadium would sit. Robert Moses, the city's chief urban planner, refused O'Malley's request and attempted to convince O'Malley to accept a site in Queens called Flushing Meadows (the home of the 1939 World's Fair).[128] Deeming this idea unacceptable, O'Malley agreed to move the Dodgers to Los Angeles, where the local politicians *were* willing to use their eminent domain powers to acquire a large tract of land known as Chavez Ravine.[129]

On April 18, 1958, the Dodgers played their first game in the Los Angeles Memorial Coliseum, their temporary home from 1958 to 1961, attracting a crowd of 78,672.[130] Ten days later, *Time* magazine put O'Malley on its cover. Over his left shoulder a Brooklyn bum (the club's former mascot) could be seen playing catch with an angel, a clever representation of the team's past and future.[131]

In 1962, O'Malley opened Dodger Stadium (still the team's home today) at Chavez Ravine.[132] In 1970, O'Malley turned the daily running of the club over to his son Peter.[133] In 1975, O'Malley finally acquired Dearie Mulvey's stock from her heirs, giving him complete ownership of the Dodgers.[134]

On August 9, 1979, O'Malley died at the Mayo Clinic in Rochester, Minnesota, less than a month after Kay had died at their home in Los Angeles.[135] For years, O'Malley had been baseball's "godfather," and his passing left a considerable void atop the sport.[136] No subsequent owner has had the kind of power that O'Malley exercised.

O'Malley's will left his entire estate, estimated at $60 million, to his children Peter (50%) and Therese (50%).[137] The Dodgers accounted for half of O'Malley's wealth; the rest came from real estate holdings.[138] In 1998, Peter and Therese sold the Dodgers to media mogul (Keith) Rupert Murdoch for $311 million.[139]

NOTES

1. *See* NEIL J. SULLIVAN, THE DODGERS MOVE WEST (1987) (explaining, *id.* at 5, that the Dodgers were founded in 1883; played in the American Association from 1884 to 1889; jumped to the National League in 1890, and used various names before finally becoming the Dodgers in 1932–33). Brooklyn (officially "Kings") is one of New York City's five boroughs (*i.e.*, counties)—the other four are the Bronx, New York (Manhattan), Queens, and Richmond (Staten Island). The quintet consolidated as the City of New York in 1898. *See The New City Ushered In: Big Parade and Brilliant Display at the Birth of Greater New York; Bad Weather Disregarded—The City's Flag Raised Over the City Hall Upon a Signal from the Mayor of San Francisco, 3,700 Miles Away*, N.Y. TIMES, Jan. 1, 1898, at 1. For a further discussion, see EDWIN G. BURROWS & MIKE WALLACE, GOTHAM: A HISTORY OF NEW YORK CITY TO 1898, at 1219–36 (1999).

2. *See, e.g.*, Dick Young, *Lust for More $ Killed Brooks*, DAILY NEWS (NY), Oct. 9, 1957, at 95, 98 ("Walter O'Malley ... leaves Brooklyn a rich ... and ... despised man"). In Los Angeles, on the other hand, O'Malley was hailed as a hero for bringing major league baseball to the West Coast. On October 23, 1957, two weeks after announcing that he had decided to move the Dodgers, O'Malley visited Los Angeles. When his airplane, bearing the freshly painted words "Los Angeles Dodgers" on its fuselage, touched down at Los Angeles International Airport, O'Malley was given a "rousing welcome [by] a crowd estimated by police at several thousand persons ... [and] was crushed for almost 45 minutes [by] the ... throng...." *Dodgers Begin L.A. Honeymoon*, INDEP. (Pasadena, CA), Oct. 24, 1957, at 1.

3. Daniel Wyatt, *Understanding Mr. O'Malley*, SABR, https://sabr.org/latest/wyatt-understanding-mr-omalley/ (last visited July 1, 2024). There are many variations of this joke. *See, e.g.*, Matthew Lysiak, *Evil O'Malley is in the Hall*, BROOKLYN PAPER, Dec. 8, 2007, https://www.brooklynpaper.com/evil-omalley-is-in-the-hall/ ("If Stalin, Hitler and O'Malley are in a room and you only have two bullets, who do you kill? Answer: You shoot O'Malley twice, just to make sure he's dead!"). *See also* Joe Dowd, *The Ghost of Walter O'Malley*, L.I. BUS. NEWS, Jan. 14, 2016, https://libn.com/2016/01/14/joe-dowd-the-ghost-of-walter-omalley/ ("In Brooklyn, the joke went like this. Question: Who are the three people you are guaranteed to meet in Hell? Answer: Hitler, Stalin and Walter (expletive deleted) O'Malley").

4. *See Known for Move to L.A.*, *O'Malley Moves into Hall*, STAR (Ventura County, CA), July 28, 2008, at C5. For O'Malley's Hall of Fame plaque, see *Walter O'Malley*, NATIONAL BASEBALL HALL OF FAME AND MUSEUM, https://baseballhall.org/hall-of-famers/omalley-walter (last visited July 1, 2024).

5. For an obituary of Alma, see *Mrs. E.J. O'Malley, Wife of Hylan Aide*, BROOKLYN EAGLE, June 4, 1940, at 11. *See also Alma Feltner O'Malley*, FIND-A-GRAVE.COM, https://www.findagrave.com/memorial/139568809/alma_o'malley (last visited July 1, 2024).

6. For an obituary of Edwin, see *Edwin J. O'Malley Dies; Father of Dodger Prexy*, BROOKLYN EAGLE, Apr. 12, 1953, at 23. *See also Edwin Joseph O'Malley*, FIND-A-GRAVE.COM, https://www.findagrave.com/memorial/7768604/edwin_joseph_o'malley (last visited July 1, 2024).

7. *See* BOB MCGEE, THE GREATEST BALLPARK EVER: EBBETS FIELD AND THE STORY OF THE BROOKLYN DODGERS 174 (2005).

8. *See* Brent Shyer, *Walter O'Malley: The Early Years*, WALTEROMALLEY.COM, https://www.walteromalley.com/biographies/walter-omalley-reference-biography/the-early-years/ (last visited July 1, 2024) [hereinafter *Early Years*].

9. *See Alma Feltner in the New Jersey, U.S., Marriage Index, 1901–2016*, ANCESTRY.COM, https://www.ancestry.com/discoveryui-content/view/102008:61253 (last visited July 1, 2024); *Edwin Omalley in the New Jersey, U.S., Marriage Index, 1901–2016*, ANCESTRY.COM, https://www.ancestry.com/discoveryui-content/view/900102008:61253 (last visited July 1, 2024).

10. *See* Andy McCue, *Walter O'Malley, in* THE TEAM THAT FOREVER CHANGED BASEBALL AND AMERICA: THE 1947 BROOKLYN DODGERS 276, 279 (Lyle Spatz ed., 2012). *See also Edwin J O'Malley in the New York, U.S., State Census, 1905*, ANCESTRY.COM, https://www.ancestry.com/discoveryui-content/view/1997321:7364 (last visited July 1, 2024) (listing Edwin, at Line 28, Box 10, as a "salesman").

11. *See Early Years, supra* note 8. For an obituary of Clarence, see *Clarence Feltner Services Conducted*, POUGHKEEPSIE J. (NY), Aug. 31, 1960, at 46. *See also Clarence George Feltner*, FIND-A-GRAVE.COM, https://www.findagrave.com/memorial/166940937/clarence_george_feltner (last visited July 1, 2024).

12. This Polo Grounds was Polo Grounds III, which opened in April 1890 (replacing Polo Grounds II) and burned to the ground in April 1911. *See* CHRIS EPTING, THE EARLY POLO GROUNDS (2009). The more famous Polo Grounds IV, which served as the Giants' final home in New York City, opened in June 1911. For a further discussion, see THE POLO GROUNDS: ESSAYS AND MEMORIES OF NEW YORK CITY'S HISTORIC BALLPARK, 1880–1963 (Stew Thornley ed., 2019).

13. *See* FRANK DEFORD, THE OLD BALL GAME: HOW JOHN MCGRAW, CHRISTY MATHEWSON, AND THE NEW YORK GIANTS CREATED MODERN BASEBALL (2005). O'Malley later revealed that his favorite Giant was neither Mathewson nor McGraw but Edward T. "Eddie" Brannick, one of the team's front office workers:

> I used to walk along a railroad trestle, up at Morrisania [in the South Bronx], with an uncle of mine, Clarence Feltner, to watch the Giants. We lived in the Bronx then and the Giants were my team and the most wonderful guy in the world was Eddie Brannick. Eddie was terrific to us kids. He'd see we got a seat if we got into the park—and there were ways. Ho, ho, there were ways.

Robert Shaplen, *O'Malley and the Angels: A Man's Struggle with a Sport a Business*, SPORTS ILLUS., Mar. 24, 1958, at 62. For a profile of Brannick, who worked for the Giants from 1905 to 1971, rising from "gofer" to club secretary, see R.J. Lesch, *Eddie Brannick*, SABR, https://sabr.org/journal/article/eddie-brannick/ (last visited July 1, 2024). As Lesch mentions, when the Giants held a banquet in 1955 at the Waldorf-Astoria hotel to mark Brannick's 50th year with the team, O'Malley was present. *Id.*

14. For a further discussion, see JIM REISLER, BEFORE THEY WERE THE BOMBERS: THE NEW YORK YANKEES' EARLY YEARS, 1903–1919 (2002). *See also* GARY A. SARNOFF, THE FIRST YANKEES DYNASTY: BABE RUTH, MILLER HUGGINS AND THE BRONX BOMBERS OF THE 1920S (2014).

15. *See Early Years, supra* note 8. Due to a quirk of geography, Hollis sometimes is described as "Hollis, Long Island." Long Island, the largest island in the contiguous United States, comprises four counties: Brooklyn, Nassau, Queens, and Suffolk. Thus, while Hollis is *on* Long Island, it is *in* Queens. In 1910, Hollis had just 130 homes and primarily was farmland; by 1920, a residential building boom had increased its population to 4,000. For a further discussion, see CLAUDIA GRYVATZ COPQUIN, THE NEIGHBORHOODS OF QUEENS 81–84 (2007).

16. *See, e.g., Connolly Favors Lowering of Tracks: Residents of Hollis and Queens Applaud Message from Borough President*, BROOKLYN TIMES, July 9, 1913, at 8 (listing Edwin as a member of the Hollis Improvement Association); *Thespian at Cards: Proceeds Will Be Given to the Jamaica Hospital*, BROOKLYN TIMES, Nov. 18, 1913, at 9 (listing Edwin as a member of the Hollis Dramatic Club); *League Begins District Work: Business Men Begin Organization in Every Assembly District for Mayoralty Candidate*, BROOKLYN DAILY TIMES, Mar. 5, 1917, at 3 (listing Edwin as a member of the Business Men's League); *Fire Chief Re-Elected: Edwin J. O'Malley Again Heads the Hollis Company*, BROOKLYN DAILY TIMES, July 27, 1917, at 6 (listing Edwin as the head of the Hollis Volunteer Fire Department).

17. *Early Years, supra* note 8.

18. *See To Reward Hollis Scouts*, BROOKLYN DAILY EAGLE, Oct. 21, 1917, at 7 (O'Malley

receiving service *emblem* for selling Liberty Loan bonds); *Medals for Scouts in Jamaica Drive: To be Presented at Loan Rally Held Tonight*, BROOKLYN DAILY EAGLE, Apr. 15, 1918, at 4 (O'Malley receiving service *medal* for selling Liberty Loan bonds); *Will Talk to Boy Scouts About the American Indian*, BROOKLYN DAILY TIMES, Apr. 28, 1919, at 9 (O'Malley receiving assorted merit badges and being promoted to life scout); *Camp Matinecock Season Brings Record Enrollment*, BROOKLYN DAILY EAGLE, Sept. 7, 1919, at 4 (O'Malley attending Camp Matinecock); *Queen Lad Wins Eagle Scout Rank: William H. Carr Jr., of Flushing, Receives Award—Special Classes Announced—Troop News*, BROOKLYN DAILY EAGLE, Mar. 28, 1920, at 2 (O'Malley appointed senior patrol leader of Hollis Troop 2); *Queens Adopts Troop Plan in Choosing Trip Winners*, BROOKLYN DAILY EAGLE, May 2, 1920, at 11 (O'Malley forming Pine Tree Patrol); *New Mess Hall Greets Queens Boys at Camp Matinecock's Opening*, BROOKLYN DAILY EAGLE, July 11, 1920, at 6 (O'Malley helping to run Camp Matinecock). *See also Scout Council Honors Boss of Dodgers*, L.A. TIMES, Dec. 17, 1964, pt. III, at 10 ("The Los Angeles Council of the Boy Scouts Wednesday celebrated the record registration of 50,000 boys in 1964 with a luncheon honoring that old assistant camp-master, Walter O'Malley. The Dodger boss headed the spring recruiting drive. Before a luncheon at the California Club he recalled winning 32 merit badges as a member of a Long Island troop and helping run a camp on Bear Mountain").

19. *See Hollis Man Gets $5,000 Job*, BROOKLYN DAILY EAGLE, Mar. 25, 1918, at 8.

20. *See* S. Morgan Friedman, *The Inflation Calculator*, https://westegg.com/inflation/ (last visited July 1, 2024) (converting 1918 dollars to 2023 dollars).

21. *See Price List Errors for Navy's Goods Made by O'Malley: City's Profit Increased One Cent Per Unit—His Dismissal Resulted*, BROOKLYN DAILY EAGLE, Oct. 19, 1919, at 8 (reporting that Edwin was fired after he sent out lists offering U.S. Navy surplus food for sale "at a margin of three cents per unit [even though] the agreement between the Navy ... and the city ... allowed [the city] a margin of [no more than] 2 cents per unit"). Food had become scarce in New York City during World War I, and the end of the conflict had done little to ease the crisis. For a further discussion, see ROSS J. WILSON, NEW YORK AND THE FIRST WORLD WAR: SHAPING AN AMERICAN CITY 17, 82–85, 144–49, 162, 178 (2016).

22. *See O'Malley in Job Under Coler Now: Ousted from Markets Department by Day, He is Named Deputy Charities Commissioner*, BROOKLYN DAILY EAGLE, Nov. 29, 1919, at 2.

23. *See Pick O'Malley for Day's Job: Mayor Tells Ousted Commissioner to Go to District Attorney*, BROOKLYN DAILY CITIZEN, Dec. 3, 1919, at 10.

24. Hylan (1868–1936) served as mayor of New York City from 1918 to 1925. Originally from the Catskills, Hylan moved to Brooklyn in 1887 and became a railroad worker. After graduating from New York Law School in 1897, he opened his own law firm in Brooklyn and became an acolyte of Tammany Hall. For a further look at Hylan, see AUTOBIOGRAPHY OF JOHN FRANCIS HYLAN: MAYOR OF NEW YORK CITY (1922). *See also John Francis Hylan*, FIND-A-GRAVE.COM, https://www.findagrave.com/memorial/7100035/john-francis-hylan (last visited July 1, 2024). For a further look at Tammany Hall, see TERRY GOLWAY, MACHINE MADE: TAMMANY HALL AND THE CREATION OF MODERN AMERICAN POLITICS (2014).

25. *See Cuban Sugar to Retail Here at 17 Cents a Pound: Wholesalers Will Receive Margin of Half a Cent on Crop of 1920*, N.Y. TRIB., Jan. 1, 1920, at 12.

26. *See Halts La Guardia's Food Sale Inquiry: Hylan Shelves His Resolution Pending Other Action*, SUN (NY), Jan. 24, 1920, at 5.

27. *See Mulry Latest Victim in Markets Warfare: Brooklyn Democratic Chief Admits Resignation from Hylan's Stormy Department Formerly Dominated by Jonathan C. Day—Widespread Gossip of an Impending "Explosion" in Bureau Which Had Charge of Army Food Sales and Now Has $300,000 Surplus Fund*, STANDARD UNION (Brooklyn), Feb. 15, 1920, at 1.

28. The Lockwood Committee, formally known as the Joint Legislative Committee on Housing, was created in May 1919 and was chaired by Senator Charles C. Lockwood (R-Brooklyn). *See Housing Probers Will Hear Mayor: New Group of Albany Investigators Start After Rent Profiteers—Hearing Next Thursday—Senator Lockwood Formally Chosen as Chairman*, BROOKLYN STANDARD UNION, May 11, 1919, at 3. The committee's investigation, which culminated in a series of new laws that became the subject of prolonged litigation, is described in ROBERT M. FOGELSON, THE GREAT RENT WARS: NEW YORK, 1917–1929 (2013).

29. The Meyer Committee, formally known as the Joint Legislative Committee to Investigate the Affairs of the City of New York, was chaired by Senator Schuyler M. Meyer (R-Manhattan). *See Meyer Will Lead City Inquiry Board: Local Senator Selected Over Opposition Which Favored Walton of Kingston—Others to be Named Today; Theodore Douglas Robinson, Clayton R. Lusk and James J. Walker Head the List,* N.Y. TIMES, Apr. 29, 1921, at 17.

30. *See O'Malley in Rage Quits as Witness; Case Up to Swann: Meyer Committee Sends Graft Testimony Involving Commissioner to Prosecutor—His Resignation Expected; Hylan Reported Ready to Remove Market Chief Unless He Voluntarily Retires; He Denies All Charges—Talks Two Hours Uninterrupted, Then Leaves Stand When Cross Examination Begins,* N.Y. TIMES, Sept. 1, 1921, at 1. *See also* MICHAEL D'ANTONIO, FOREVER BLUE: THE TRUE STORY OF WALTER O'MALLEY, BASEBALL'S MOST CONTROVERSIAL OWNER, AND THE DODGERS OF BROOKLYN AND LOS ANGELES 5–8 (2009).

31. *See Meyer Committee Report Criticizes Hylan and Enright: Four City Departments Accused; Kings County Hospital Heating Contract Attacked,* BROOKLYN DAILY EAGLE, June 12, 1922, at 20.

32. *See "Nice Plunder," Says Cropsey of Money Paid by Peddlers: $500,000 Collected in Six Months, but Nothing for City,* BROOKLYN DAILY EAGLE, July 13, 1922, at 1.

33. *See* D'ANTONIO, *supra* note 30, at 8–9.

34. *See Long Island News—Hollis and Queens,* BROOKLYN DAILY TIMES, Oct. 2, 1920, at 7. *See also* D'ANTONIO, *supra* note 30, at 9–10.

35. *See* D'ANTONIO, *supra* note 30, at 9–10.

36. *See* MICHAEL SHAPIRO, THE LAST GOOD SEASON: BROOKLYN, THE DODGERS AND THEIR FINAL PENNANT RACE TOGETHER 22 (2003).

37. *Early Years, supra* note 8.

38. *See* D'ANTONIO, *supra* note 30, at 13–14.

39. *See Early Years, supra* note 8.

40. *See* D'ANTONIO, *supra* note 30, at 14.

41. ANDY MCCUE, MOVER AND SHAKER: WALTER O'MALLEY, THE DODGERS, AND BASEBALL'S WESTWARD EXPANSION 14 (2014) [hereinafter WESTWARD EXPANSION].

42. *Id.*

43. *See Early Years, supra* note 8.

44. WESTWARD EXPANSION, *supra* note 41, at 15.

45. *See Commissioner's Son is Made Class Head: Walter O'Malley, Son of Market Official, Honored at University of Pennsylvania,* BROOKLYN CITIZEN, Oct. 23, 1924, at 2.

46. *See O'Malley's Son Heads Senior Class at Penn,* BROOKLYN DAILY TIMES, May 7, 1925, at 8.

47. *See Culver Club Will Meet at Initial Monthly Luncheon,* DAILY PENNSYLVANIAN (student newspaper of the University of Pennsylvania), Dec. 11, 1923, at 1 (listing O'Malley as the club's vice president); *Culver Club Enrolls Thirty New Members,* DAILY PENNSYLVANIAN, Oct. 2, 1925, at 6 (listing O'Malley as the club's president).

48. *See O'Malley, Robinson, Eichelberger and Morine Chosen Senior Honor Men at General Elections: Four Selected Have Distinguished Themselves in Many and Varied Student Activities,* DAILY PENNSYLVANIAN, Mar. 10, 1926, at 1.

49. *Id.*

50. *See 33 Boro-L.I. Boys Get Penn Degrees: Walter F. O'Malley of Amityville was President—The List,* BROOKLYN DAILY TIMES, June 16, 1926, at 5.

51. *See* WESTWARD EXPANSION, *supra* note 41, at 16.

52. *Id.* at 15–16 (footnotes omitted).

53. For an example of this erroneous tale, see BURTON A. BOXERMAN & BENITA W. BOXERMAN, EBBETS TO VEECK TO BUSCH: EIGHT OWNERS WHO SHAPED BASEBALL (2003):

> After graduation from Pennsylvania, O'Malley attended Columbia University Law School until the stock market crash wiped out the O'Malley family's finances. Walter switched to night classes at Fordham University Law School while working during the day. He received his law degree from Fordham in 1930.

Id. at 99.

54. Robert Murphy, After Many a Summer: The Passing of the Giants and Dodgers and a Golden Age in New York Baseball 43 (2009).

55. Westward Expansion, *supra* note 41, at 17–18.

56. *Id.* at 18. Although this amounts to $1,560 a year, O'Malley later nearly doubled the figure. *See* Penelope McMillan, *Fighter, 'Gambler': O'Malley's Life: Variety, Vision*, L.A. Times, Aug. 10, 1979, pt. I, at 1, 30 ("I was a junior engineer for the city of New York Board of Transportation. That paid $3,019 a year—[I] always remember the odd numbers").

57. Westward Expansion, *supra* note 41, at 18.

58. *Id.*

59. *See* Robert J. Kaczorowski, Fordham University School of Law: A History 123 (2012). Night students had classes Monday through Friday and were required to take a total of 18 courses, as follows:

> First Year: Agency, Contracts, Crimes, Jurisprudence, Property, Torts
> Second Year: Bankruptcy, Corporations, Equity, Evidence, Sales, Wills
> Third Year: Conflict of Laws, Practice Courses, Insurance, Quasi-Contracts, Suretyship, Trusts

Fordham University School of Law—Woolworth Building, New York, *Schedule of Lecture Periods for the Second Half of the Academic Year 1929–1930*, at 2 (1929), https://ir.lawnet.fordham.edu/cgi/viewcontent.cgi?article=1002&context=academics_miscellanea (last visited July 1, 2024).

60. *See* Westward Expansion, *supra* note 41, at 18. Once again, O'Malley later gave himself a promotion, claiming he had been a junior engineer. *See supra* note 56.

61. *See* Westward Expansion, *supra* note 41, at 18.

62. *Id.*

63. *Id.*

64. For an obituary of Kay, see Austin Scott, *Kay O'Malley, 72, Wife of Dodgers Owner, Dies*, L.A. Times, July 14, 1979, pt. II, at 8. *See also Katharina Elizabeth Hanson O'Malley*, Find-a-Grave.com, https://www.findagrave.com/memorial/7804176/katharina_elizabeth_o'malley (last visited July 1, 2024).

65. For an obituary of Elizabeth, see *Dodger Officials' Kin Dies at 87*, L.A. Times, Feb. 25, 1965, pt. III, at 4. *See also Mrs Elizabeth G. Geyer Hanson*, Find-a-Grave.com, https://www.findagrave.com/memorial/177947034/elizabeth_g_hanson (last visited July 1, 2024).

66. For an obituary of Peter, see *Obituary*, Daily News (NY), Apr. 16, 1965, at 34. *See also Peter B. Hanson*, Find-a-Grave.com, https://www.findagrave.com/memorial/177947032/peter_b_hanson (last visited July 1, 2024).

67. *See Peter B. Hanson Named to Take Wilkin's Place: Women's Organizations Express Disappointment at Selection of Mayor Walker*, Brooklyn Citizen, Dec. 14, 1927, at 2. In November 1937, with his 10-year term nearly up, Hanson retired from the bench. *See Justice Hanson Applies for Retirement Pension: His Term Ends Dec. 12—M'Dermott, Director of Budget, McCann and Ward Take Same Step*, Brooklyn Daily Eagle, Nov. 18, 1937, at 1; *Retirement Petitions Granted*, Brooklyn Daily Eagle, Nov. 19, 1937, at 1.

68. *Early Years, supra* note 8.

69. *See* Westward Expansion, *supra* note 41, at 19.

70. *Early Years, supra* note 8.

71. *See Amityville News*, Brooklyn Daily Times, July 15, 1930, at 5 (explaining that by this time the vessel had been named the *Alamo*). Following the outbreak of World War II, O'Malley donated the boat to the U.S. Coast Guard. *See Early Years, supra* note 8.

72. The wedding took place on September 5, 1931, at St. Malachy's (better known as "The Actors' Chapel") in Manhattan (O'Malley's parents did not attend). The marriage was not publicly announced until three months later (due to Edwin's objection to the union). *See Miss Kay Hanson's Marriage Announced to Walter O'Malley*, Brooklyn Daily Times, Dec. 5, 1931, at 3.

73. Brent Shyer, *Walter O'Malley: Entering the Business World*, WalterOMalley. com, https://www.walteromalley.com/biographies/walter-omalley-reference-biography/entering-the-business-world/ (last visited July 1, 2024) [hereinafter *Business World*].

Because of her condition, friends and family learned to read lips to be able to communicate with Kay. *Id.*

74. *Id.*

75. *See Daughter to Mrs. W.F. O'Malley*, N.Y. TIMES, May 24, 1933, at 18.

76. *See Son Born to Walter O'Malleys*, N.Y. TIMES, Dec. 25, 1937, at 7.

77. *Kay O'Malley, First Lady of the Dodgers*, WALTEROMALLEY.COM, https://www.walter omalley.com/biographies/kay-omalley-first-lady-of-the-dodgers/ (last visited July 1, 2024).

78. *See 633 Students Pass Law Examination: Only One-Third of Would-Be Lawyers in This State Were Successful in March Test—Must Now Serve as Clerks; Will Also Have to Face Board on Character and Fitness Before Admission to Bar*, N.Y. TIMES, May 16, 1931, at 19 (listing O'Malley as one of the successful test takers).

79. *See Admission to Bar is Sought by 119: Character Committee Seeks Data on Applicants Called for Examination Tuesday; Six Women on the List—Appellate Division Clerk Will Compile Information on Group Asking Permits to Practice*, N.Y. TIMES, Mar. 16, 1933, at 24 (listing O'Malley as one of the petitioners).

80. *See Business World, supra* note 73 (explaining that O'Malley, who by this time was living at 2 Beekman Place in midtown Manhattan, was sworn in by the First Department of the Appellate Division of the New York State Supreme Court).

81. *Id.*

82. WESTWARD EXPANSION, *supra* note 41, at 19.

83. *See, e.g., Williamsburgh Sav. Bank v. Kallman*, BROOKLYN TIMES UNION, May 13, 1933, at 9; *Fulton Sav. Bank v. Bushwick Improvement Co.*, BROOKLYN DAILY EAGLE, May 24, 1933, at 26; *Prudential Sav. Bank v. People*, BROOKLYN TIMES UNION, June 14, 1933, at 11; *East N.Y. Sav. Bank v. Behr*, BROOKLYN DAILY EAGLE, Aug. 15, 1933, at 22; *Dime Sav. Bank of Brooklyn v. Lane*, BROOKLYN TIMES UNION, Sept. 29, 1933, at 10; *Equitable Life Assurance Soc'y of the U.S. v. Lynn*, BROOKLYN TIMES UNION, Sept. 30, 1933, at 9; *Mayer v. Kaufman*, BROOKLYN CITIZEN, Oct. 26, 1933, at 2; *Bushwick Sav. Bank v. Kenney*, BROOKLYN TIMES UNION, Nov. 28, 1933, at 10; *Strauss v. Solomon*, BROOKLYN TIMES UNION, Dec. 12, 1933, at 8. *See also Boro Business Records—Bankruptcy Proceedings [in the] Eastern District*, BROOKLYN TIMES UNION, Aug. 21, 1933, at 18 (reporting that in In re Max D. Miller, "Judge Campbell has appointed Walter F. O'Malley, 60 42d St., Manhattan, receiver…").

84. *See* SHAPIRO, *supra* note 36, at 24. O'Malley, however, later insisted that he got his start when a priest called him:

> Long after he became a wealthy man, [O'Malley] liked to tell the story of his start in the law. It was a wonderful and useful yarn, folksy, and impossible to confirm: one day, just after he opened his practice, he took a call from a man with a thick Irish brogue. "D'you do wills?" the man asked. O'Malley could not tell if the man said "wills" or "wells." Still, he took the man's address and arrived on East Fourteenth Street in Manhattan at the door of a Catholic church. It was the priest who had called; a wealthy parishioner was dying. The fellow had land and needed to settle his estate. "Tell me, Father," O'Malley asked, "how did you come to pick me? I only opened my law practice yesterday." "I just looked at the lawyer's directory till I found a name that looked like it came from County Mayo," replied the priest.

Id.

85. *Id. See also Business World, supra* note 73 (quoting O'Malley as saying, "Our law firm had 18 lawyers in the second year of my practice").

86. As McCue points out, in later years O'Malley embellished his *Who's Who* listings to the point that almost nothing (except his birth) was accurately reported. *See* WESTWARD EXPANSION, *supra* note 41, at 24–25.

87. *See, e.g.,* 1 THE MARTINDALE-HUBBELL LAW DIRECTORY 1380 (67th ed., Jan. 1935) (listing O'Malley as a sole practitioner at 60 East 42nd Street).

88. *See, e.g.,* 1 THE MARTINDALE-HUBBELL LAW DIRECTORY 1426 (69th ed., Jan. 1937) (listing the law firm of O'Malley & Wilson and giving its address as 60 East 42nd Street).

89. *See Raymond Wilson in the U.S., World War I Draft Registration Cards, 1917–1918*, ANCESTRY.COM, https://www.ancestry.com/discoveryui-content/view/8952585:6482 (last visited July 1, 2024) (listing Wilson's birth date as January 22, 1900).

90. *Id.* (describing Wilson as a student at Stuyvesant High School and a part-time employee at the American Railway Express company).

91. *See* 1 THE MARTINDALE-HUBBELL LAW DIRECTORY 1446 (72d ed., 1940) [hereinafter 1940 MARTINDALE-HUBBELL] (listing Wilson's law school but not his graduation year). St. Lawrence University's law school existed from 1903 to 1943, when the university and the law school separated; following the dissolution, the law school became known as Brooklyn Law School. *See Law School Here to be Independent: Brooklyn Institution Pays $167,000 to End Ties with St. Lawrence University*, N.Y. TIMES, Dec. 31, 1943, at 17. For a further discussion, see JEFFREY BRANDON MORRIS, BROOKLYN LAW SCHOOL: THE FIRST HUNDRED YEARS (2001).

92. *See* 1940 MARTINDALE-HUBBELL, *supra* note 91, at 1446 (listing Wilson's bar admission year).

93. *See Death Notices*, DAILY NEWS (NY), July 11, 1948, at 69 (giving Wilson's date of death as July 10, 1948, and listing his survivors as his wife Flora, his mother Ellen, and his brother Edward). Wilson does not have a *Find-a-Grave* webpage. Flora and Wilson married in Manhattan on July 2, 1933. *See Flora F Spaulding in the New York, New York, U.S., Extracted Marriage Index, 1866–1937*, ANCESTRY.COM, https://www.ancestry.com/discoveryui-content/view/5013040:9105 (last visited July 1, 2024); *Raymond F Wilson in the New York, New York, U.S., Extracted Marriage Index, 1866–1937*, ANCESTRY.COM, https://www.ancestry.com/discoveryui-content/view/4316844:9105 (last visited July 1, 2024).

94. *Business World, supra* note 73.

95. *See Society*, BROOKLYN DAILY EAGLE, Nov. 7, 1934, at 21.

96. *See Initial List of Patronesses for New Rochelle Bridge Given*, BROOKLYN DAILY EAGLE, Feb. 28, 1937, at 2B.

97. For a copy of the firm's letterhead, see https://www.walteromalley.com/biographies/walter-omalley/#gallery-9 (last visited July 1, 2024).

98. Callaghan had studied at the City College of New York ("CCNY"), where he had been a member of Theta Delta Chi (the same fraternity O'Malley had joined at CMA), and was a 1926 graduate of FULS. *See Charge Letters*, 36:1 THE SHIELD (national magazine of Theta Delta Chi Fraternity) 364–65 (Oct. 1919) (listing Callaghan as a Theta Delta Chi pledge at CCNY); Fordham University, *The School of Law of Fordham University: Announcement, 1927–1928*, at 14 (1927) (listing Callaghan as a 1926 graduate of FULS and indicating that he did not have a college degree). Callaghan later moved to Vero Beach, Florida, where he died. *See Public Notices*, VERO BEACH PRESS-J., June 19, 1958, at 2C. *See also Nicholas P. Callaghan*, FIND-A-GRAVE.COM, https://www.findagrave.com/memorial/119429003/nicholas-p.-callaghan (last visited July 1, 2024). At the time of his death, Callaghan was seeking admission to the Florida bar and was working for the Fort Pierce, Florida, law firm of Brown & Cooksey. *See Associations and Partnerships*, 31:9 FLA. B.J. 539 (Nov. 1957); *List of Current Applicants for Admission to The Florida Bar*, 32:1 FLA. B.J. 28–29 (Jan. 1958).

99. Lehmann was a 1925 graduate of FULS. *See* Fordham University, *The School of Law of Fordham University: Announcement, 1926–1927*, at 15 (1926) (listing Lehmann as a 1925 graduate of FULS and indicating that he did not have a college degree). No further information has been found for Lehmann.

100. Sturm was a 1932 graduate of Vassar College (where she was elected to Phi Beta Kappa) and a 1935 graduate of CULS. She was with O'Malley & Wilson from 1936 to 1942, when she left the firm to become a law clerk for Judge Albert Conway of the New York State Court of Appeals. In 1944, she joined the U.S. Customs Court as a permanent law clerk, retiring in 1976. In 1974, she published the first edition of her highly regarded treatise *Customs Law and Administration*. *See* Ruth F. Sturm, *Customs: Past, Present, and Future*, 37:3 FED. B. NEWS & J. 151 (Mar./Apr. 1990) (at biographical footnote). For an obituary of Sturm, see *Ruth Foster Sturm: Retired Attorney*, DAILY ITEM (Port Chester, NY), May 30, 1996, at 8A. *See also Ruth F. Sturm*, FIND-A-GRAVE.COM, https://www.findagrave.com/memorial/58041870/ruth-f-sturm (last visited July 1, 2024).

101. Melia, whose first and middle names often were transposed, was a 1935 graduate of Fordham University and a 1938 graduate of FULS. After working for O'Malley & Wilson from 1939 to 1941, he left the firm to become an assistant district attorney. He later became a judge on the New York City Criminal Court (1968–71) and then the New York

State Supreme Court (1971–80). For an obituary of Melia, see *Death Notices—James Aloy-sius Melia*, POUGHKEEPSIE J. (NY), Nov. 8, 2002, at 4B. *See also Aloysius J. Melia*, FIND-A-GRAVE.COM, https://www.findagrave.com/memorial/104307928/aloysius-j.-melia (last vis-ited July 1, 2024).

102. McAuliffe was a 1937 graduate of Fordham University and a 1940 graduate of FULS. *See* Fordham University, BULLETIN OF FORDHAM UNIVERSITY: ANNOUNCEMENT OF THE SCHOOL OF LAW 1941–1942, at 21 (1941). At the time of his death, he was a partner in the New York City law firm of Clark, Carr & Ellis. *See Charles H. McAuliffe, Brother of Res-ident*, STANDARD-STAR (New Rochelle, NY), Nov. 26, 1957, at 2. McAuliffe does not have a *Find-a-Grave* webpage.

103. On his World War II draft registration card, dated February 15, 1942, O'Malley listed his employer as "Own business—attorney." That he did not instead write "O'Mal-ley & Wilson" supports the idea that the firm dissolved sometime in late 1941 or early 1942. *See Walter F O'Malley in the U.S., World War II Draft Cards Young Men, 1940–1947*, ANCESTRY.COM, https://www.ancestry.com/discoveryui-content/view/193989896:2238 (last visited July 1, 2024). On the back of the card, O'Malley provided additional details about himself: he listed his height as 5'10½", his weight as 200 pounds, his complexion as light, and his eyes and hair as brown. *Id.*

104. *See, e.g.*, Brooklyn Trust Co. v. Rembaugh, 110 F.2d 838 (2d Cir. 1940); In re 31 West 72nd Street Corp., 20 F. Supp. 971 (S.D.N.Y. 1937), *aff'd*, 94 F.2d 584 (2d Cir. 1938); McMeekan v. B/G Sandwich Shops, Inc., 6 N.Y.S.2d 66 (App. T. 1938); Christal v. Fifty-Five Columbus Corp., 5 N.Y.S.2d 227 (App. T. 1938); In re Bond & Mortgage Guarantee Co., 39 N.Y.S.2d 760 (Sup. Ct. 1942); In re 24–52 Forty-Fourth St., Long Island City, 26 N.Y.S.2d 265 (Sup. Ct. 1941); Shulsky v. Title Guarantee & Trust Co., 23 N.Y.S.2d 827 (Sup. Ct.), *aff'd*, 23 N.Y.S.2d 844 (App. Div. 1940); In re N.Y. Title & Mortgage Co., 9 N.Y.S.2d 994 (Sup. Ct. 1939); In re Lawyers Mortgage Co. (8910 35th Avenue, Jackson Heights), 2 N.Y.S.2d 79 (Sup. Ct. 1937); In re Lawyers Mortgage Co. (83–12 35th Avenue, Jackson Heights), 3 N.Y.S.2d 475 (Sup. Ct. 1937); In re Lawyers Title & Guar. Co. (Guar. No. 223,743), 283 N.Y.S. 57 (Sup. Ct. 1935); In re N.Y. Title & Mortgage Co., 282 N.Y.S. 598 (Sup Ct. 1935); In re N.Y. Title & Mortgage Co. (Series N-109), 279 N.Y.S. 525 (Sup. Ct. 1935); In re Evans' Estate, 65 N.Y.S.2d 723 (Surr. Ct. 1940); In re Ryan's Estate, 48 N.Y.S.2d 522 (Surr. Ct. 1940), *aff'd*, 34 N.Y.S.2d 49 (App. Div.), *appeal granted*, 35 N.Y.S.2d 267 (App. Div. 1942), *aff'd*, 52 N.E.2d 909 (N.Y. 1943); In re Lindewall's Estate, 15 N.Y.S.2d 274 (Surr. Ct. 1939), *rev'd*, 18 N.Y.S.2d 281 (App. Div.), *appeal granted*, 22 N.Y.S.2d 522 (App. Div. 1940), *rev'd*, 39 N.E.2d 907 (N.Y. 1942); In re Hossan's Estate, 294 N.Y.S. 516 (Surr. Ct. 1937).

105. WESTWARD EXPANSION, *supra* note 41, at 24.

106. *See, e.g., Raymond F Wilson in the U.S., World War II Draft Cards Young Men, 1940–1947*, ANCESTRY.COM, https://www.ancestry.com/discoveryui-content/view/193314631:2238 (last visited July 1, 2024) (dated Feb. 16, 1942) (listing Wilson, now with a business address of 16 Court Street in Brooklyn, as working as an "attorney for [the] U.S. govern-ment"). *See also Miss Eileen Schmitt is Married at Bogota to James A. Melia of New York*, BER-GEN EVENING REC. (NJ), June 7, 1941, at 19 ("Immediately after the ceremony, the couple left for La Porte, Ind., where the bridegroom will serve as legal representative at the Kingsbury Ordnance Plant. He is a graduate of Fordham University and Fordham Law School…").

107. *See Councilman Ebbets by Purchase and Option the New Owner*, N.Y. TIMES, Jan. 2, 1898, at 2.

108. *See To Lift Lid on New York Baseball Fans: Yankees and Superbas to Open New Ebbets Field in Brooklyn To-day [in Exhibition Game]*, N.Y. TIMES, Apr. 5, 1913, at 16.

109. *See Ebbets Takes in Partners: McKeever Brothers Buy Shares in Brooklyn Baseball Club*, N.Y. TIMES, Aug. 30, 1912, at 7. Although Stephen McKeever often was called "Judge," he was neither a lawyer nor a judge. *See Stephen W. McKeever*, FIND-A-GRAVE.COM, https://www.findagrave.com/memorial/112148689/stephen-w.-mckeever (last visited July 1, 2024) (explaining that the nickname was a corruption of the word "jedge").

110. *See C.H. Ebbets Dies of Heart Disease: Confined to Room Since Return from Brook-lyn Training Camp 2 Weeks Ago; Called Dean of Baseball—All National League Games Called Off for Tuesday, Day of Funeral*, N.Y. TIMES, Apr. 19, 1925, at 26; *Death Takes Second*

Owner of the Robins: E.J. McKeever Dies Following Charles H. Ebbets, Whom He Succeeded on April 18—Caught Cold at Funeral—Stephen McKeever, 71, is Only Surviving Partner of the Brooklyn Baseball Club, N.Y. TIMES, Apr. 30, 1925, at 1. ("Robins" was the team's principal nickname from 1914 to 1931).

111. *See* Friedman, *supra* note 20 (converting 1934 dollars to 2023 dollars).

112. For a profile of McLaughlin, see *George McLaughlin, Banker, 80, Dies*, N.Y. TIMES, Dec. 8, 1967, at 42.

113. Following lengthy negotiations, MacPhail officially accepted the Dodgers' offer in January 1938. *See Brooklyn Club Names M'Phail Vice President: Former Cincinnati Reds' Official Given Long-Term Contract*, BROOKLYN CITIZEN, Jan. 19, 1938, at 1.

114. *See MacPhail Resigns, Enters Army Sunday*, S.F. EXAMINER, Sept. 24, 1942, at 21.

115. *See Rickey Will be Dodgers' President-General Manager for 5 Years: Former Card "Brain" in Town to Formally Accept Brooklyn Post*, BROOKLYN CITIZEN, Oct. 29, 1942, at 6. By this time, Rickey had been in baseball for nearly 40 years, first as a player, then as a manager, and most recently as an executive with the St. Louis Cardinals. For a further look at Rickey's career, see, e.g., LEE LOWENFISH, BRANCH RICKEY: BASEBALL'S FEROCIOUS GENTLEMAN (2007); MURRAY POLNER, BRANCH RICKEY: A BIOGRAPHY (1982); ARTHUR MANN, BRANCH RICKEY: AMERICAN IN ACTION (1957).

116. *See* WESTWARD EXPANSION, *supra* note 41, at 23.

117. *See* Richard Vanderveld, *How Tenant O'Malley Became a Landlord*, L.A. TIMES, Apr. 8, 1962, § I (Outlook), at 1, 5 ("[O'Malley's] entrée [to the Dodgers] was as an attorney for a Brooklyn trust company.... He supplanted the late Wendell Willkie as the team's attorney in 1943"). In addition to his new club duties, O'Malley, with the help of Callaghan and Lehmann, continued to handle BTC's legal affairs. *See, e.g.*, Brooklyn Trust Co. v. R.A. Security Holdings, Inc., 134 F.2d 164 (2d Cir. 1943); In re Bond & Mortgage Guaranty Co. (Guar. No. 186,129), 68 N.E.2d 52 (N.Y. 1946); Public Operating Corp. v. Brooklyn Trust Co., 50 N.E.2d 295 (N.Y. 1943); Brooklyn Trust Co. v. Ravenna Court Jackson Heights, Inc., 59 N.Y.S.2d 160 (App. Div. 1945); Zellner v. Brooklyn Trust Co., 70 N.Y.S.2d 114 (Sup. Ct. 1947), *order modified*, 77 N.Y.S.2d 347 (App. Div. 1948), *and order modified*, 86 N.E.2d 657 (N.Y. 1949).

118. *See* Joe Trimble, *Rickey, 2 Others Buy 25% of Dodger Stock*, DAILY NEWS (NY), Nov. 2, 1944, at 48.

119. *See* Harold C. Burr, *Penicillin Maker Gives Rickey, Club Financial 'Shot': John L. Smith, Angel of Deal, Hands Branch Full Control of Dodgers—Stars May Stride on Block Now*, BROOKLYN EAGLE, Aug. 14, 1945, at 11.

120. Andy McCue, *Walter O'Malley*, SABR, https://sabr.org/bioproj/person/walter-omalley/ (last visited July 1, 2024).

121. *See Mrs. James A. Mulvey, 70, Dies: Heiress to Share of the Dodgers*, N.Y. TIMES, Nov. 25, 1968, at 47.

122. *See* Friedman, *supra* note 20 (converting 1950 dollars to 2023 dollars).

123. *See* PETER GOLENBOCK, BUMS: AN ORAL HISTORY OF THE BROOKLYN DODGERS 251 (1984).

124. Rickey quickly landed on his feet, becoming the general manager of the Pittsburgh Pirates. *See* ANDREW O'TOOLE, BRANCH RICKEY IN PITTSBURGH: BASEBALL'S TRAILBLAZING GENERAL MANAGER FOR THE PIRATES, 1950–1955 (2000).

125. At times, however, O'Malley and the law still collided. In October 1954, for example, Dr. Samuel Shenkman performed successful surgery on catcher Roy Campanella's left hand. Incredibly, both Campanella and the Dodgers then refused to pay the $9,500 bill (each claimed the other was responsible). During a press conference about the matter, O'Malley insisted that the surgery had been unnecessary and said, "It appears that he [Shenkman] thought he was operating on Roy's bankroll." This caused Shenkman to sue O'Malley for slander. After the courts rejected O'Malley's defense of "fair comment," see Shenkman v. O'Malley, 147 N.Y.S.2d 87 (Sup. Ct. 1955), *aff'd as modified*, 157 N.Y.S.2d 290 (App. Div. 1956), and set the case for trial, O'Malley agreed to pay Shenkman $15,000 (plus $5,000 on the original bill). *See* Dick Young, *Losing Streak*, DAILY NEWS (NY), Nov. 22, 1957, at B7 (explaining that the $5,000 had been awarded by a prior jury that had heard Shenkman's bill collection lawsuit).

126. *See* G. Scott Thomas, A Brand New Ballgame: Branch Rickey, Bill Veeck, Walter O'Malley and the Transformation of Baseball, 1945–1962, at 155 (2021).

127. For a further discussion, see Brent Shyer, *The O'Malley-Fuller Connection*, WalterOMalley.com, https://www.walteromalley.com/dodger-history/the-omalley-fuller-connection/ (last visited July 1, 2024) (explaining that Fuller designed the dome while he was in residence at Princeton University). Although many people mocked O'Malley's idea, in 1965 the Houston Astros opened baseball's first domed stadium. *See* Robert Lipsyte, *[President] Johnson Attends Opening of Houston's Astrodome*, N.Y. Times, Apr. 10, 1965, at 1.

128. For a profile of Moses, see Robert A. Caro, The Power Broker: Robert Moses and the Fall of New York (1974). *See also* Sullivan, *supra* note 1.

129. *See* City of L.A. v. Superior Ct. of L.A. Cnty., 333 P.2d 745 (Cal. 1959) (upholding Los Angeles's use of its eminent domain powers to benefit the Dodgers). *See also* Eric Nusbaum, Stealing Home: Los Angeles, the Dodgers, and the Lives Caught in Between (2020). Ironically, just a few years later Flushing Meadows became (and remains) the home of the National League's New York Mets (Shea Stadium, 1964–2008; Citi Field, 2009–present), the expansion team that replaced the Dodgers (and the New York Giants, who had been convinced by O'Malley to also head west and play in San Francisco). *See* Jason A. Winfree & Mark S. Roentraub, Sports Finance and Management: Real Estate, Entertainment, and the Remaking of the Business 117 (2012). Even more ironically, since 2012 the site at Atlantic and Flatbush Avenues that O'Malley coveted has been the location of the Barclays Center, the home arena of the National Basketball Association's Brooklyn Nets. *Id.*

130. *See* Paul Zimmerman, *78,672 See Dodgers Win; City Gives Team Big Welcome—L.A. Beats Giants 6–5 in Opener*, L.A. Times, Apr. 19, 1958, pt. I, at 1.

131. The cover, drawn by famed illustrator Boris Chaliapin, can be viewed at https://content.time.com/time/magazine/0,9263,7601580428,00.html (last visited July 1, 2024). The accompanying story, titled "Walter in Wonderland," can be read at https://time.com/archive/6806026/sport-walter-in-wonderland/ (last visited July 1, 2024).

132. *See* Paul Zimmerman, *Stadium Opener Lost by Dodgers: 52,564 Fans See Cincinnati Win Chavez Ravine Inaugural, 6–3*, L.A. Times, Apr. 11, 1962, pt. I, at 1.

133. *See O'Malley Son to Head Dodgers: Peter, 32, Replaces Father, Now Chairman of the Board*, N.Y. Times, Mar. 17, 1970, at 50.

134. *See* Andy McCue, *Los Angeles/Brooklyn Dodgers Team Ownership History*, SABR, https://sabr.org/bioproj/topic/los-angeles-brooklyn-dodgers-team-ownership-history/ (last visited July 1, 2024). By the time she died in 1968, Mulvey owned 33.33.% of the Dodgers—in 1958, her stake had increased from the 25% left to her by her father when John L. Smith's widow sold her shares to Mulvey and O'Malley (whose stake increased to 66.67%).

135. *See Walter F. O'Malley, Leader of Dodgers' Move to Los Angeles, Dies at 75*, N.Y. Times, Aug. 10, 1979, at A1 (explaining that O'Malley, although being treated for cancer, died of congestive heart failure). *See also Walter O'Malley*, Find-a-Grave.com, https://www.findagrave.com/memorial/5262/walter-o'malley (last visited July 1, 2024). As their respective *Find-a-Grave* webpages explain, see *supra* note 64 and this note, Kay and O'Malley are buried together in Holy Cross Cemetery in Culver City, California.

136. *See* Neil MacCarl, *Baseball Lacking a Godfather: But Ever-Changing Owners are Powerful Figures in Their Own Right*, Toronto Star, June 17, 1981, at D2 ("There is no single figure who stands above the rest, not even the high-profile George Steinbrenner. There is no godfather, as the late Walter O'Malley was with the Los Angeles Dodgers. He could either get it for you, or make it impossible for you except by getting a favor from him. Even baseball commissioner Bowie Kuhn did not relish a confrontation. In fact, Kuhn was well aware of … O'Malley's feelings on anything").

137. *See O'Malley Leaves Estate in Trust for 2 Children*, L.A. Times, Aug. 23, 1979, pt. II, at 2 [hereinafter *O'Malley Estate*]. Today, O'Malley's estate would be worth $255.74 million. *See* Friedman, *supra* note 20 (converting 1979 dollars to 2023 dollars).

138. *See O'Malley Estate*, *supra* note 137.

139. *See* Murray Chass, *A Family Circle Breaks: Murdoch Owns Dodgers*, N.Y. Times, Mar. 20, 1998, at C8.

CHAPTER 11

Anthony "Tony"
La Russa, Jr. (2014)

LOUIS H. SCHIFF

On July 27, 2014, Anthony "Tony" La Russa, Jr.[1] (born October 4, 1944), was inducted into baseball's Hall of Fame.[2] At the time of his induction, La Russa was a former manager of the Chicago White Sox (1979–86), Oakland A's (1986–95), and St. Louis Cardinals (1996–2011), and his Hall of Fame plaque summarized his accomplishments as follows:

> Master of maneuvering lineups and managing bullpens. Guided teams to 2,728 wins, third-most ever. Led clubs to three World Series championships (1989, 2006, 2011) and six pennants, including three straight with Oakland from 1988–90. Four-time Manager of the Year, became first skipper to win All-Star Game in both leagues and second to win World Series in both circuits. His Game 6 direction in 2011 Series propelled Cardinals to improbable comeback. Managed 5,097 games, becoming second skipper of 5,000 or more contests in American pro sports history.[3]

Omitted from this long recitation is the fact that just a year before becoming the manager of the White Sox, La Russa had earned his J.D., with honors, at Florida State University ("FSU") (1978).[4] La Russa is one of just eight lawyers to ever serve as a major league manager—of this group, six have been enshrined in Cooperstown.[5]

A Naturally Gifted Athlete

La Russa's parents were Oliva (née Cuervo) (1913–98)[6] and Anthony "Tony" LaRussa, Sr. (1911–2002) (hereinafter "Tony Sr.").[7] The pair were from Ybor City, Florida,[8] and had met while working at the Perfecto Garcia & Bros. cigar factory.[9] Oliva's family was from Spain, while Tony Sr.'s family was from Italy.[10] On December 22, 1937, the couple married.[11]

208

In 1942, Oliva and Tony Sr. welcomed their first child, a daughter named Eva.[12] Two years later, La Russa was born.[13] By the time La Russa was five, Tony Sr. was working as an ice deliveryman.[14] Later, Tony Sr. got a job driving a truck for a dairy, which allowed the family to move to West Tampa and buy their first home.[15]

La Russa grew up attending Tampa's public schools: V.M. [Vicente Martinez] Ybor Elementary School (named for the founder of Ybor City); West Tampa Junior High School; and Thomas Jefferson High School. Encouraged by Tony Sr. (a former sandlot catcher and a lifelong baseball fan), La Russa began playing baseball when he was six years old.[16] As La Russa later remarked, "I loved baseball as a kid."[17]

La Russa, a naturally gifted athlete, quickly excelled as a middle infielder. As he climbed the ranks of amateur baseball (playing first on city park teams, then in the Pony League, then in the Colt League, and finally for Post 248 of the American Legion), he attracted increasing attention for his excellent glove and bat.[18] By the time La Russa was a senior in high school (where he captained the baseball team, known as the Dragons), 17 major league teams were jockeying to sign him—only the Los Angeles Dodgers and the expansion Houston Colt .45s (later Astros) and Los Angeles Angels failed to express an interest in him.[19]

On June 7, 1962, two days after his graduation from high school, La Russa agreed to a contract worth $100,000—the equivalent today of $1,025,000—with the Kansas City (later Oakland) Athletics.[20] Although La Russa's favorite team was the New York Yankees,[21] the Athletics had pressed harder to sign La Russa than any other club: not only had owner Charles O. Finley and his wife Shirley flown to Tampa to meet with La Russa,[22] the Athletics agreed to give La Russa a $50,000 signing bonus; a new car (a white Pontiac Bonneville with black leather seats); and, at the insistence of La Russa's parents, $8,000 for college.[23] In 1969, La Russa graduated from the University of South Florida ("USF") in Tampa with a B.A. in industrial management.[24] Asked how he had found the motivation to keep returning to school off-season after off-season, La Russa replied, "I promised my mom I would get an education."[25]

Professional Playing Career

After being inked by the Athletics, La Russa, standing 6'1" and weighing 175 pounds, spent 16 seasons (1962–77) playing professional baseball.[26] Although primarily used as a second baseman, La Russa ended up spending time at every position except catcher. By the time he was done, La Russa had appeared in 132 major league games (122 with the Athletics, nine with the Atlanta Braves, and one with the Chicago Cubs) and hit .199. He also had appeared in 1,295 minor league games with 15 different teams and hit .265.[27] Throughout his career, La Russa often was sidelined with injuries or played hurt[28]—had he been healthy, things likely would have turned out differently.

From 1962 to 1971, La Russa split his time between the Athletics (with whom he played in 1963 as a "bonus baby" signee[29]) and nine of its farm teams: the Daytona Beach (Florida) Islanders of the Class D Florida State League (1962); the Binghamton (New York) Triplets of the Class A Eastern League (1962); the Lewiston (Idaho) Broncs of the Class A Northwest League (1964); the Birmingham (Alabama) Barons of the Class AA Southern League (1965); the Modesto Reds of the Class A California League and the Mobile (Alabama) A's of the Class AA Southern League (1966); the Birmingham (Alabama) A's (previously the Barons) of the Class AA Southern League (1967); the Vancouver Mounties of the Class AAA Pacific League (1968); and the Iowa (Des Moines) Oaks of the Class AAA American Association (1969–71).

In August 1971, the Atlanta Braves purchased La Russa's contract from the Athletics.[30] In nine games with the team, La Russa hit .286. Despite this impressive performance, he spent 1972 playing for the Class AAA Richmond (Virginia) Braves of the International League, hitting .309 but not getting a call-up.[31] In October 1972, the Braves traded La Russa to the Chicago Cubs for former Baltimore Orioles pitching ace Thomas H.S. "Tom" Phoebus.[32]

On April 6, 1973 (Opening Day versus the Montreal Expos), La Russa got into a game with the Cubs as a pinch runner.[33] This appearance marked the end of La Russa's major league career. He continued to play in the minors until 1977, however, spending time with the Wichita Aeros of the Class AAA American Association (a Chicago Cubs farm team) (1973); the Charleston (West Virginia) Charlies of the Class AAA International League (a Pittsburgh Pirates farm team) (1974); the Denver Bears (1975) and Iowa Oaks (1976) of the Class AAA American Association (both farm teams of the Chicago White Sox); and the New Orleans Pelicans of the Class AAA American Association (a St. Louis Cardinals farm team) (1977). La Russa later explained that he continued playing during this time to earn the money he needed for his law school tuition and books.[34]

Law School

Following his superb 1972 season with the Richmond Braves, La Russa had had an even better 1973 season with the Wichita Aeros, hitting

.314. Once again, however, he failed to get a call-up. "'That's when I began to see the handwriting on the wall,' [La Russa told a reporter]. 'I was getting to the end of my career, [I was] not making very much money, and [I was stuck] in AAA (minor league) ball.'"[35]

After considering his options, La Russa decided to take the Law School Admission Test ("LSAT"): "I've always read a lot. And things like contract disputes and labor problems always interested me. Also, I have a lot of friends who are lawyers and we talked a lot. So I just decided to do it, although I didn't know how I'd do."[36] When he "did well" on the LSAT,[37] La Russa applied to, and was accepted by, all of Florida's law schools.[38] He ended up picking FSU because it was the only one that was willing to accommodate his baseball schedule, allowing him to attend classes during the Fall and Winter quarters (which began in late September and ended in early March) and take off the Spring and Summer quarters.[39] Thus, in the Fall of 1973, La Russa enrolled in FSU and began what turned out to be a five-year grind to acquire his law degree.[40]

Law school presented La Russa with multiple challenges. "I had to dig in to prove that I belonged.... I was competing for grades five winters and two quarters at a time[.]"[41] Despite being pulled in different directions, La Russa proved to be a dedicated law student and quickly garnered a reputation for refusing to let anyone "outwork him."[42] As a result, La Russa earned grades that placed him near the top of the class.[43] As La Russa later wrote in his autobiography, "'[I] wasn't ... a brilliant student, but because I was competitive [and went] to law school with a couple of friends who started with better grades than me.... I studied harder.'"[44]

While in law school, La Russa became friendly with Professor Charles W. Ehrhardt.[45] In early 1977, Ehrhardt arranged for La Russa to clerk for the U.S. Court of Appeals for the Fifth Circuit in New Orleans while La Russa played for the New Orleans Pelicans.[46] Logistical obstacles, however, prevented the plan from coming to fruition.

In September 1977, with La Russa's graduation from FSU quickly approaching, Ehrhardt asked La Russa: "What are you going to do after you graduate? Whatever you do, make sure you take the bar exam to preserve [your] option to practice [law]."[47] A short time later, La Russa sent a letter to every major league team seeking employment.[48] Because of his long years in the minors, La Russa received several positive replies, including one from William L. "Bill" Veeck, Jr., the unconventional owner of the Chicago White Sox,[49] who hired La Russa to be the manager of the Knoxville (Tennessee) Sox ("K-Sox") of the Class AA Southern League.[50] Veeck's son Michael (also a baseball executive) believes that his father was intrigued by the fact that La Russa was a law student.[51]

In March 1978, La Russa finished his last class at FSU and turned his attention to the K-Sox.[52] From the beginning, things went swimmingly, and on June 13, 1978, the K-Sox won the league's Western Division first-half pennant.[53] Indeed, the only down note was the fact that La Russa had been forced to miss his law school graduation a few days earlier due to the K-Sox's schedule.[54] For his stellar work, La Russa was given a promotion three weeks later, becoming the first base coach of the Chicago White Sox,[55] a position he would hold for the rest of the season.

Following the end of the 1978 season, Bill Veeck offered La Russa a choice: he could remain the White Sox's first base coach or he could become the new manager of the Iowa Oaks in Des Moines, the White Sox's farm team in the Class AAA American Association.[56] La Russa, wanting to gain more managerial experience, took the job with the Oaks.

Passing the Florida Bar Examination

When Bill Veeck hired La Russa to manage the K-Sox in January 1978, Veeck made La Russa promise that he would become a licensed attorney.[57] Thus, in February 1979, just before heading off to Des Moines to manage the Oaks, La Russa took and passed two parts of Florida's bar examination (the national Multistate Bar Examination and Florida's professional responsibility examination).[58]

In August 1979, Donald E. "Don" Kessinger, the White Sox's player-manager (he had come to the White Sox in August 1977 via a trade with the St. Louis Cardinals and been given the added responsibility of manager in October 1978), unexpectedly resigned. With the White Sox mired in fifth place with a 46–60 record (.434), La Russa was brought up from Des Moines to finish out the season.[59] At 35, La Russa became the youngest manager in the major leagues. In a remarkable turnaround, La Russa guided the White Sox to a 27–27 record (.500) in their final 54 games. As a result, in October 1979 La Russa was hired for the 1980 season.[60] Later that month, La Russa took and passed the Florida bar examination's remaining part (the "local" portion, testing on Florida law).[61]

Admission to the Florida Bar

On the afternoon of August 22, 1980, La Russa was sworn into the Florida Bar[62] by U.S. Senior District Judge Abraham Lincoln Marovitz of the Northern District of Illinois.[63] The ceremony had been arranged by Bill Veeck (who knew Marovitz because Marovitz was a longtime White Sox season ticketholder) and took place in Marovitz's chambers in Chicago.[64]

U.S. District Judge Abraham Lincoln Marovitz (left) shaking hands with Anthony "Tony" La Russa, Jr., after swearing La Russa into the Florida Bar (1980) (Getty Images Sport/Ron Vesely).

That night, just before the start of the White Sox's game against the Toronto Blue Jays at Comiskey Park (a 2–0 White Sox home victory), La Russa did an on-field interview with White Sox television announcer Harry C. Caray. Unsurprisingly (given his reputation for verbal blunders), Caray completely botched the description of the ceremony, telling listeners that La Russa "got his law degree today right here in Chicago."[65] La Russa ignored the mistake (or possibly did not hear it because of the crowd noise) and instead thanked Veeck, praised Marovitz, and finished by saying "it's an honor to be sworn in by a federal judge."[66]

Conley and Dooley

Due to his meteoric rise from the K-Sox to the White Sox,[67] La Russa had no time to practice law.[68] For approximately 15 years (1979–94), however, La Russa was affiliated with a Sarasota, Florida, law firm called Conley and Dooley (later known as Thorp, Reed, Conley and Dooley).[69] In a 1985 interview, La Russa described his role at the firm:

In January of 1979, I started talking to firms in Sarasota (Florida)[,] my winter home. I found a young, five[-]man firm, Conley and Dooley, that I thought was perfect. They understood my baseball obligation and that I wanted to keep the (legal) interest alive during the winter. I joined them and I've been there ever since.

We eventually merged with a large firm out of Pittsburgh [Thorp Reed & Armstrong] that's been around since the 1800s [1895]. Now we're Thorp, Reed, Conley and Dooley. The firm handles most everything. The office in Florida does mostly commercial law and real estate.

I don't practice law, because managing is such a full-time job. The White Sox run me around a lot during the winter. I still have an office and during the winter I go in a couple of times a week and talk with the guys, but I don't do any legal work. That's on a continuing basis and I just can't be there.

In baseball I get asked for advice all the time because I'm an attorney. I feel very comfortable referring the guys to Bill Dooley or Roger Conley with the firm and they get expert treatment.[70]

Very early in his tenure at the firm, however, La Russa did work on one case involving an elderly woman whose children were attempting to have her declared mentally incompetent. La Russa both interviewed the woman and researched Florida's laws regarding competency. Although La Russa had to leave for Spring Training before the case could be heard, when it finally did get to court the woman was declared competent.[71]

Years later, when asked what type of law he would have practiced if he had not become a manager, La Russa replied: "I would have become a trial lawyer. [The] [c]ourtroom is competition."[72] When asked what lessons he had learned in law school that had helped him as a manager, La Russa replied: "You can't shoot from the hip as you must value preparation and you must always pay attention to detail. Winning or losing a case, or winning or losing a ballgame, starts with preparation and [paying attention to] each detail of what you need to accomplish."[73]

Conclusion

Given his remarkable success as a major league manager,[74] La Russa continues to attract attention. In 2024, two new books about his career were published: Joann A. Bennett's *Tony La Russa: The Playbook of a Baseball Genius*[75] and William A. Lewis's *Tony La Russa Biography: A Diamond Mind in Baseball's Hall of Fame*.[76] Both books include chapters on La Russa's support of charitable causes,[77] which in recent years have focused on animal welfare and assisting injured veterans.[78]

As the only living lawyer member of baseball's Hall of Fame, La Russa has shown a particular willingness to help law students and would-be law students. In 1985, for example, when first-year University of San Diego law student Michael V. Saverino asked La Russa if he could interview him for his law school newspaper, La Russa went out of his way to make time for Saverino: "A major league manager leads a busy life. His time is valuable. Tony La Russa shared fifteen minutes with me in the visitor's dugout of Anaheim Stadium during a late September [1985] visit by his ball club, the Chicago White Sox."[79]

In 1988, Robin F. Fuson (born 1958), a journeyman minor league pitcher who was taking one last shot at breaking into the major leagues,[80] had a chance to meet La Russa during spring training. During their encounter, Fuson mentioned that he was finishing his criminology degree at USF and was contemplating going to law school after his baseball career was done. La Russa encouraged Fuson, telling him: "It never hurts, you can use your law degree for a lot of things."[81] Inspired by La Russa's advice, Fuson enrolled in Stetson University's law school and graduated in 1993.[82] In 2018, after 25 years as a Tampa criminal defense lawyer, Fuson was elected to the Hillsborough County circuit court bench.[83]

More recently, on April 10, 2024, La Russa spent the day at Elon University's law school in Greensboro, North Carolina. During his visit, La Russa "met with Elon Law students for a roundtable classroom conversation[,] answered questions about his law school experiences[,] and … autographed books, posed for photos, and offered encouragement in their continued pursuit of excellence."[84]

La Russa's most significant contribution to the public good, however, may be how he single-handedly changed social media for the better:

> Former White Sox manager Tony La Russa sued Twitter back in 2009 after an account bearing his name and likeness was sending out tweets.
> La Russa claimed the account gave the false impression that the comments came from him and that they were derogatory and damaged his brand.
> Twitter responded to the lawsuit by unveiling [a] verified seal so users could distinguish between real people and imposters.
> Four years later in 2013, Twitter refined its verification process, expanding to distinguish legitimate sources of information.[85]

NOTES

1. La Russa's actual family name is "LaRussa." It is not clear when sportswriters first began inserting a space—the earliest example I have found is a 1968 Associated Press wire story. *See Oakland Dumped in Home Opener,* HAWAII TRIB.-HERALD (Hilo), Apr. 18, 1968, at 21 ("McNally held the Athletics hitless until Rick Monday homered leading off the sixth and after that the only Oakland hit was Tony La Russa's single in the ninth. He was promptly erased in a double play"). In any event, "La Russa" now is the accepted spelling. Accordingly, in this essay "La Russa" is used except when quoting sources that use "LaRussa."

2. *See* Joey Johnston, *Pride of Tampa: Tony La Russa Enters Hall of Fame; La Russa's Playing Career Didn't Go as Planned, But He's Appreciative of His Success as a Major-League Manager*, TAMPA TRIB., July 27, 2014, at 1 (Sports).

3. *Tony La Russa*, NATIONAL BASEBALL HALL OF FAME AND MUSEUM, https://baseballhall.org/hall-of-famers/la-russa-tony (last visited July 1, 2024). After stepping down as the manager of the Cardinals in 2011, La Russa spent two years working for Major League Baseball Commissioner Allan H. "Bud" Selig (2012–14) and then spent six years in the front offices of the Arizona Diamondbacks (2014–17), Boston Red Sox (2018–19), and Los Angeles Angels (2020). In 2021, La Russa again became the manager of the White Sox, a post he held for two years (2021–22) before becoming a special advisor to team owner Jerry M. Reinsdorf. As a result, La Russa's updated managerial record stands at 2,884–2,499 (.536), which makes him second in managerial wins (at the time of La Russa's Hall of Fame induction, John J. McGraw was second with 2,763 wins). For La Russa's managerial statistics, see *Tony La Russa*, BASEBALL-REFERENCE.COM, https://www.baseball-reference.com/managers/larusto01.shtml (last visited July 1, 2024). For La Russa's managerial decision-making process, see TONY LA RUSSA, TONY LA RUSSA TALKS BASEBALL STRATEGY WITH JOE BUCK (2002). La Russa's 5,387 games as a manager are second only to Cornelius McGillicuddy, better known as Connie Mack, who managed 7,755 games while helming the Pittsburgh Pirates (1894–96) and the Philadelphia Athletics (1901–50). During his time in the dugout, Mack compiled a record of 3,731–3,948 (.486) and led the Athletics to six pennants and five World Series championships (1910–11, 1913, 1929–30). For a profile of Mack, see TED DAVIS, CONNIE MACK: A LIFE IN BASEBALL (2000).

4. *See* Bob Cohn, *A Clubhouse Lawyer with All the Credentials*, TALLAHASSEE DEMO-CRAT, Apr. 11, 1978, at 4B ("Tony LaRussa, at 33 the first-year manager of the AA Knoxville White Sox of the Southern League, has just received a juris doctor degree from the Florida State University law school").

5. Major League Baseball's six Hall of Fame lawyer-managers are Hugh A. "Hughie" Jennings (the subject of Chapter 2 of this book); James H. "Jim" O'Rourke (the subject of Chapter 3 of this book); Miller J. "Hug" Huggins (the subject of Chapter 4 of this book); John Montgomery "Monte" Ward (the subject of Chapter 5 of this book); Wesley Branch Rickey (the subject of Chapter 6 of this book); and La Russa. The two lawyer-managers who are not in the Hall of Fame are John C. "Jack" Hendricks, who managed the St. Louis Cardinals (1918) and the Cincinnati Reds (1924–29) and was a graduate of the Kent College of Law (now Chicago-Kent) (1895), and Herold D. "Muddy" Ruel, who managed the St. Louis Browns (1947) and was a graduate of Washington University in St. Louis's law school (1922). For a biography of Hendricks, see Robert M. Jarvis, *John C. "Jack" Hendricks: Major League Baseball's Forgotten Lawyer-Manager*, 33 NINE: J. BASEBALL HIST. & CULTURE 39 (2024). For a biography of Ruel, see Robert M. Jarvis, *And Behind the Plate ... Muddy Ruel of the U.S. Supreme Court Bar*, 36 J. SUP. CT. HIST. 1 (2011).

6. For an obituary of Oliva, see *Oliva LaRussa, 84, Mother of Cardinals Team Manager*, ST. PETERSBURG TIMES (FL), Sept. 5, 1998, at 7B. Oliva does not have a *Find-a-Grave* webpage.

7. For an obituary of Tony Sr., see *LaRussa, Tony Sr.*, TAMPA TRIB., Apr. 13, 2002, at 9 (Metro). Tony Sr. does not have a *Find-a-Grave* webpage.

8. Ybor City is a historic neighborhood just to the northeast of downtown Tampa. Originally a separate community, it was annexed by Tampa in 1887. From the 1890s to the 1930s, Ybor City was the cigar manufacturing capital of the world. For a further discussion, see Durward Long, *Historical Beginnings of Ybor City and Modern Tampa*, 45 FLA. HIST. Q. 31 (1966).

9. *See* BOB RAINS, TONY LA RUSSA: MAN ON A MISSION 2 (2009). The Perfecto Garcia & Bros. factory was built in 1914 and opened in 1917. As has been explained elsewhere:

> In its heyday, Perfecto Garcia [&] Bros. made many fine cigars, including the Perla Del Mar. Started by four Garcia brothers, the company grew tobacco on their farms in Cuba, hand crafted cigars in Ybor City ... and marketed them mainly in Chicago, where it owned [more than] fifteen cigar stores. One brother [later] returned to Spain; two ran the Chicago interests; and Perfecto, a colorful community leader

and a member of the Centro Austuriano social club located on the outskirts of Ybor City, ran the factory....

A Philadelphia company purchased Perfecto Garcia [&] Bros. for its brand, ignoring the building and property. Closed since 1982, the venerable factory building is in sad despair, surrounded by chain-link fences.

Ask Margaret, Tampa Bay Mag., July/Aug. 2005, at 67. After many false starts, the factory now is being turned into private residences. *See Ybor's Century Old Perfecto Garcia Cigar Factory Being Converted to Apartments*, Cigar Public, Feb. 18, 2023, https://cigarpublic. com/2023/02/18/ybors-century-old-perfecto-garcia-cigar-factory-being-converted-to-apartments/.

10. Many years later, while discussing his heritage, La Russa recalled: "Spanish was my first language. I had to learn English to go to school. I was raised in a Latin American, Italian American community with a bunch of people who really loved baseball." Lawrence Baldassaro, *Tony La Russa*, SABR, https://sabr.org/bioproj/person/tony-la-russa/ (last visited July 1, 2024).

11. *See Marriage Licenses*, Tampa Morn. Trib., Dec. 22, 1937, at 14.

12. *See* Joey Johnston, *La Russa Was Destined to Lead—and Succeed*, Tampa Trib., Oct. 2, 1990, https://joeyjohnstoncommunications.com/la-russa-was-destined-to-lead-and-succeed/.

13. *See On the Record: Births*, Tampa Daily Times, Oct. 5, 1944, at 15 ("At Centro Asturiano, Oct. 4—Mr. and Mrs. Tony LaRussa, 1305 17th Ave., son"). During this period, the Centro Asturiano was Ybor City's primary hospital for Spanish immigrants. The facility closed in 1990. *See Centro Asturiano Hospital is Closed*, Tampa Bay Times, Aug. 25, 1990, https://www.tampabay.com/archive/1990/08/25/centro-asturiano-hospital-is-closed/.

14. *See Tony Larussa in the 1950 United States Federal Census*, Ancestry.com, https://www.ancestry.com/discoveryui-content/view/81457963:62308 (last visited July 1, 2024) (at Line 2).

15. *See* Rains, *supra* note 9, at 5.

16. *Id.* at 3.

17. Author's interview with Anthony "Tony" La Russa, Jr. (Mar. 24, 2024) [hereinafter La Russa Interview].

18. *See, e.g., City District Champs Named, Finals Next Week*, Tampa Daily Times, Aug. 11, 1955, at 14, 15; *Ybor Loop Stars on Havana Trip*, Tampa Daily Times, Aug. 26, 1955, at 15; *Here Are Tampa's Playground Baseball Champs*, Tampa Daily Times, Oct. 4, 1957, at 14; *North Palomino All-Stars*, Tampa Trib., July 10, 1958, at 3B; *Rock-A-Bye Wins Pony Loop Title*, Tampa Trib., Aug. 30, 1959, at 3C; *Tampa's Colts World Series Finalists*, Tampa Times, Aug. 20, 1960, at 6; *Legion Stars Awarded*, Tampa Trib., Sept. 13, 1960, at 20; *Dragons Score 13th Win in a Row—LaRussa Stars*, Tampa Trib., Apr. 14, 1961, at 2C; *All-Star Baseball Club Set*, Tampa Times, May 19, 1961, at 15A; *LaRussa Leads Post 248 Win*, Tampa Times, July 8, 1961, at 8.

19. *See* Tom McEwen, *It Started in California*, Tampa Trib., June 7, 1962, at 1D. Because major league baseball did not yet have a draft, La Russa was free to sign with the team of his choice. For a further discussion, see John Manuel, *The History and Future of the Amateur Draft*, SABR, https://sabr.org/journal/article/the-history-and-future-of-the-amateur-draft/ (last visited July 1, 2024) (explaining that in 1965 baseball finally instituted an amateur draft to cut down on the amount of bonus money being paid to amateur players—as Manuel explains, "In 1964, led by the $205,000 bonus the Angels gave to Wisconsin outfielder Rick Reichardt, major-league clubs paid more than $7 million to amateur players—more than [the entire amount] spent on major-league salaries").

20. *See* Jim Selman, *LaRussa to Join Athletics Tonight*, Tampa Trib., June 8, 1962, at 1C [hereinafter *Join*]. *See also* S. Morgan Friedman, *The Inflation Calculator*, https://westegg.com/inflation/ (last visited July 1, 2024) (converting 1962 dollars to 2023 dollars). In 1968, the Athletics moved from Kansas City to Oakland. *See* David M. Jordan, The A's: A Baseball History (2014) (explaining that the team was founded in Philadelphia in 1901 and moved to Kansas City in 1954). In 2025, the team will temporarily move to Sacramento; in 2028, it expects to open its new ballpark in Las Vegas. *See* Sophie Austin, *Oakland A's to*

Play in Sacramento for Three Seasons Before Vegas Move, KEARNEY HUB (NE), Apr. 6, 2024, at B7.

21. *See* McEwen, *supra* note 19.

22. *See* Jim Selman, *A's Head Visits LaRussa,* TAMPA TRIB., June 5, 1962, at 1C. During the visit, Tony Sr. asked Finley if the rumors that he planned to move the team to Texas were true. When questioned about Finley's response, Tony Sr. told reporters that Finley had dismissed the idea with a laugh. *Id.*

23. *See* Marc Topkin, *Tampa Bred a Legend: Tony La Russa Began a Hall of Fame Path as a Baseball Rat on Area Playgrounds,* TAMPA BAY TIMES, July 27, 2014, at 1C, 3C; *Join, supra* note 20.

24. *See* Baldassaro, *supra* note 10 ("In the 1962 offseason, La Russa first enrolled at the University of South Florida. Seven years later he received his degree in industrial management").

25. La Russa Interview, *supra* note 17. La Russa began college at the University of Tampa but after two semesters transferred to USF. *See Anthony La Russa Jr in the U.S.,* Baseball *Questionnaires, 1945–2005,* ANCESTRY.COM, https://www.ancestry.com/discoveryui-content/view/93961:61599 (last visited July 1, 2024).

26. It was during these years that La Russa got married (1965), had two children, got divorced (1973), got married again (to a different woman) (1973), and had two more children. Author's follow-up interview with Anthony "Tony" La Russa, Jr. (Feb. 15, 2025).

27. For La Russa's playing statistics, see *Tony La Russa,* BASEBALL-REFERENCE.COM, https://www.baseball-reference.com/players/l/larusto01.shtml (last visited July 1, 2024). In 1963, La Russa also played 45 games in the Florida Instructional League, an unclassified winter rookie league. *See id.*

28. During the 1962–63 off-season, La Russa hurt his right arm playing softball with his friends and reported to spring training in a sling. *See A's Tampa Bonus Player Lame,* TAMPA TRIB., Mar. 7, 1963, at 1B. La Russa never fully recovered from this injury and subsequently suffered a host of other medical setbacks, including tearing the ligaments in his left knee and injuring his back. *See* Jim Selman, *'Healthy LaRussa' Bids for A's Role,* TAMPA TRIB., Mar. 22, 1968, at 3C (reporting that "LaRussa's career reads like a hospital disaster report").

29. Between 1947 and 1965, a major league team that gave a player a signing bonus exceeding $4,000 had to keep that player on their roster for two full seasons (reduced in 1962 to one full season). The rule was designed to prevent wealthier clubs from signing young players and then stashing them in the minor leagues. Thus, to comply with the rule, La Russa spent the 1963 season on the Athletics' roster, even though he was hurt and only able to play in 34 games. For more about the bonus rule, see Wynn Montgomery, *Georgia's 1948 Phenoms and the Bonus Rule,* SABR, https://sabr.org/journal/article/georgias-1948-phenoms-and-the-bonus-rule/ (last visited July 1, 2024). *See also* Steve Treder, *Cash in the Cradle: The Bonus Babies,* HARDBALL TIMES, Nov. 1, 2004, https://tht.fangraphs.com/cash-in-the-cradle-the-bonus-babies/.

30. *See Braves Purchase LaRussa,* TAMPA TRIB.-TIMES, Aug. 15, 1971, at 9D.

31. La Russa's failure to be called up came as a shock to local observers and left La Russa feeling depressed:

> The Atlanta Braves have decided to promote four Richmond farmhands, and the intriguing part is not who was selected, but who wasn't.
>
> Jimmy Freeman, Larry Jaster, Tom House and Bob Didier got the good news yesterday. They're going up [to the majors]....
>
> There was nothing surprising about Atlanta naming the above quartet. Freeman is the local club's biggest winner (12–9). Didier handled the brunt of the catching chores with dispatch. Jaster and House have been standouts in relief....
>
> Conspicuous by their absence on the list of promotions were Tony LaRussa and Andy Thornton, both of whom figured to deserve at least a look based on their season's performance.
>
> The R-Braves' leading hitter, LaRussa has maintained a .300-plus average since assuming a regular's role in mid-May. He's currently batting .307.

Yesterday's announcement, LaRussa said, "was very disappointing. I think I feel as low as I have at any time in my career, and I think it showed in my game tonight. I don't think this is fair, but I know I've got to pull myself together. I've had a good year, and I'll try to work hard the last nine days." Jerry Lindquist, *Tidewater Outlasts R-Braves*, RICHMOND TIMES-DISPATCH (VA), Aug. 27, 1972, at E1, E6.

32. *See Braves Deal LaRussa; Get Cub Pitcher*, RICHMOND TIMES-DISPATCH (VA), Oct. 20, 1972, at C1.

33. *See* Al Yellon, *Today in Cubs History: Tony La Russa's Single Cubs Appearance: The Longtime MLB Manager was a Cub ... for One Game*, BLEEDCUBBIEBLUE.COM, Apr. 6, 2023, https://www.bleedcubbieblue.com/2023/4/6/23389717/today-cubs-history-tony-la-russa-single-cubs-appearance. In an odd coincidence, La Russa got into his first major league game (May 10, 1963, versus the Minnesota Twins) and his last major league game as a pinch runner. Although La Russa was a good runner and stole 120 bases in the minor leagues, he did not attempt to steal a base as a major leaguer. *See supra* note 27.

34. *See* Jerry Lindquist, *This Clubhouse Lawyer Has a Degree*, RICHMOND TIMES-DISPATCH (VA), Jan. 6, 1980, at B5 [hereinafter *Clubhouse Lawyer*].

35. Cohn, *supra* note 4.

36. *Id.*

37. Mike Lupica, *Tony LaRussa Finally Making It Big in Bigs*, DAILY NEWS (NY), Apr. 27, 1980, at 8 (Sports).

38. *See* Cohn, *supra* note 4. During this time, Florida had four law schools: FSU (founded 1966); Stetson University in Gulfport (1900); the University of Florida in Gainesville (1909); and the University of Miami in Coral Gables (1926). *See Florida's Law Schools*, FLA. B. NEWS, Sept. 1, 2011, https://www.floridabar.org/the-florida-bar-news/cooley-to-open-tampa-campus/.

39. La Russa Interview, *supra* note 17. FSU also allowed La Russa to miss class as necessary and take his final exams early. Author's interview with Scott K. Tozian (one of La Russa's law school classmates) (Mar. 25, 2024) [hereinafter Tozian Interview]. *See also* Author's interview with Michael "Mike" Veeck (May 6, 2024) [hereinafter Mike Veeck Interview].

40. La Russa Interview, *supra* note 17.

41. *Id.*

42. Tozian Interview, *supra* note 39.

43. La Russa Interview, *supra* note 17. *See also* TONY LA RUSSA & RICK HUMMEL, ONE LAST STRIKE: FIFTY YEARS IN BASEBALL, TEN AND A HALF GAMES BACK, AND ONE FINAL CHAMPIONSHIP SEASON 281 (2012) ("I don't think anybody knows this, but I graduated with honors from law school").

44. LA RUSSA & HUMMEL, *supra* note 43, at 282.

45. For a profile of Ehrhardt (born 1940), see Christi N. Morgan, *Celebrating Professor Ehrhardt*, FLORIDA STATE LAW ALUMNI MAGAZINE 2 (2018), https://law.fsu.edu/sites/g/files/upcbnu1581/files/2018-florida-state-law-magazine.pdf (explaining that Ehrhardt, an evidence expert, joined FSU in 1967 as the law school's fourth faculty member).

46. *See* E-mail to the author from Professor Charles W. Ehrhardt, dated Mar. 25, 2024 (copy on file with the author). *See also* LA RUSSA & HUMMEL, *supra* note 43, at 282.

47. E-mail to the author from Professor Charles W. Ehrhardt, dated July 11, 2022 (copy on file with the author). Many years later, when Ehrhardt was spending a week teaching at the National Judicial College in Reno, Nevada, La Russa arranged for field passes for Ehrhardt and his family to a California Angels-Oakland A's game (a 7–6 A's victory). When Ehrhardt stepped onto the field before the game, reporters rushed over to him after La Russa mentioned that Ehrhardt had been his professor. Asked about La Russa, Ehrhardt replied: "He couldn't make up his mind whether to be a minor-league manager or a lawyer.... He said that if he was offered a Class A job, he'd become a lawyer [but if he was offered a Class AA job, which is what he got, he'd become a manager]. He could have been a good lawyer...."). Bob Burns, *A's Update*, MODESTO BEE (CA), July 24, 1990, at C3.

48. *See* La Russa Interview, *supra* note 17.

49. From 1940 to 1945, Veeck was the owner of the minor league Milwaukee Brewers.

Subsequently, he became the owner of the Cleveland Indians (1946–48), St. Louis Browns (1951–53), and White Sox (1959–61). In 1975, Veeck repurchased the White Sox but in 1981 sold the team to broadcasting executive Edward M. "Eddie" Einhorn and attorney Jerry M. Reinsdorf for $20 million. Veeck died in 1986; in 1991, he was posthumously inducted into baseball's Hall of Fame. To stimulate attendance, Veeck engaged in numerous unorthodox promotions, such as having a little person (3'7" Edward C. "Eddie" Gaedel) take a turn at bat while wearing the number "⅛" (1951—unable to adjust for Gaedel's small size, Detroit Tigers pitcher Robert M. "Bob" Cain walked Gaedel on four straight pitches—after reaching first base, Gaedel was lifted for a pinch runner and never again appeared in a major league game) and staging a "Disco Demolition Night" during which a crate of disco records was blown up between games of a twi-night doubleheader (1979—following the detonation fans spontaneously left their seats and ran onto the field—the ensuing riot caused the White Sox to forfeit the game to the Tigers). For a further look at Veeck's life, see PAUL DICKSON, BILL VEECK: BASEBALL'S GREATEST MAVERICK (2012).

50. *See* Nick Gates, *K-Sox' LaRussa a Big Hit*, KNOXVILLE NEWS-SENTINEL, Jan. 2, 1978, at D3.

51. *See* Mike Veeck Interview, *supra* note 39 ("My dad signed Tony on a hunch, feeling that his commitment to the study of law would make him a detail-oriented manager. He found that Tony was an intellect").

52. *See* La Russa Interview, *supra* note 17.

53. *See* Harold Harris, *K-Sox Wrap Up SL West, 3–0, 4–2—Manager Charts Second-Half Course: 'There'll Be No Playoff,' Says Tony LaRussa*, KNOXVILLE NEWS-SENTINEL, June 14, 1978, at D3.

54. La Russa Interview, *supra* note 17. FSU's law school graduation was held on the afternoon of June 10, 1978. *See* James Cramer, *Graduation '78: A Time When Everyone Comes Up a Winner*, TALLAHASSEE DEMOCRAT, June 11, 1978, at 10A (explaining that the keynote speaker was U.S. District Judge William H. Stafford, Jr., of the Northern District of Florida). That night, the K-Sox played a home game and beat the Savannah Braves. *See* Nick Gates, *4th-Inning Burst Powers Sox, 5–4*, KNOXVILLE NEWS-SENTINEL, June 11, 1978, at D3. With the K-Sox having not yet clinched the first-half pennant, and knowing that he could not make it back to Knoxville from Tallahassee (a trip of 480 miles) in time to manage the game, La Russa opted to stay in Knoxville. Many years later, La Russa was able to attend the May 2014 commencement program at Washington University in St. Louis, where he was awarded an honorary doctor of humanities degree. *See* Leslie Gibson McCarthy, *'Earn Your Own Respect,' La Russa Tells Graduates: Hall of Fame Baseball Manager Delivers Commencement Address to Class of 2014*, THE SOURCE, May 16, 2014, https://source.wustl.edu/2014/05/earn-your-own-respect-la-russa-tells-graduates/. La Russa's speech can be viewed at https://www.youtube.com/watch?v=aUXWYi4ymrU (last visited July 1, 2024).

55. *See Sox 'Promote' Minoso*, CHI. TRIB., July 4, 1978, § 4, at 1 ("First-base coach Minnie Minoso was 'promoted laterally' to the team's public relations department and Knoxville Manager Tony LaRussa was summoned as Minoso's replacement.... LaRussa, 33, earned promotion by directing Knoxville to a runaway victory in the first-half standings of the Class AA Southern League.... LaRussa was replaced at Knoxville by Joe Jones..."). *See also* Bob Cohn, *LaRussa Makes Move to Big Club*, TALLAHASSEE DEMOCRAT, July 8, 1978, at 3B.

56. *See Clubhouse Lawyer*, *supra* note 34.

57. *See* La Russa Interview, *supra* note 17.

58. *Id. See also Beware, Umps: LaRussa Has Degree in Arguing*, PALM BEACH POST-TIMES, Aug. 11, 1979, at B4.

59. *See Tampa's LaRussa Gets Shot at Managing in the Majors*, TAMPA TIMES, Aug. 3, 1979, at 1C.

60. *See LaRussa New White Sox Manager*, PITT. POST-GAZ., Oct. 9, 1979, at 14.

61. *See* La Russa Interview, *supra* note 17. *See also* Lupica, *supra* note 37.

62. The Florida Bar's web site, however, lists La Russa's admission date as July 30, 1980. *See* The Florida Bar, *Find a Lawyer*, https://www.floridabar.org/directories/find-mbr/ (last visited July 1, 2024) (under "Anthony La Russa, Jr."). La Russa's bar admission number is 300756. *Id.*

63. Under Florida's bar rules, any person authorized to administer oaths can swear in a new attorney. *See* Florida Board of Bar Examiners, *Frequently Asked Questions*, https://www.floridabarexam.org/web/website.nsf/faq.xsp (last visited July 1, 2024) (under "How can I execute my Oath of Attorney?"). For an obituary of Marovitz (1905–2001), see Rick Kogan & Noah Isackson, *Abraham Lincoln Marovitz, 1905–2001: Veteran Jurist Beloved for Feisty Spirit, Compassion*, Chi. Trib., Mar. 18, 2001, § 1, at 1. Despite his name, Marovitz was not related to President Abraham Lincoln—Marovitz's mother Rachel, a Lithuanian immigrant, mistakenly thought that Lincoln was a Jew and that she was naming her son after an American Jewish hero. *Id.* at 16. For a further look at Marovitz, see *Judge Abraham Lincoln Marovitz*, Find-a-Grave.com, https://www.findagrave.com/memorial/128631977/abraham-lincoln-marovitz (last visited July 1, 2024).

64. *See Attorney at Law—Tony LaRussa*, J. & Courier (Lafayette, IN), Aug. 23, 1980, at B3.

65. *See 1980 08 22 Blue Jays at White Sox*, YouTube.com, https://www.youtube.com/watch?v=lAlYrj1F9ZA&t=127s (at 0:50).

66. *Id.* (at 2:09). For a profile of Caray, see Don Zminda, The Legendary Harry Caray: Baseball's Greatest Salesman (2019).

67. On more than one occasion, La Russa expressed surprise at how quickly he had been able to jump from AA ball to the majors: "I'm not sure as a player I got a whole lot of breaks. But I've gotten a lot of breaks since I've been managing. I've had just about every break you can get." Lupica, *supra* note 37. Many years later, La Russa caught an even bigger break when, after being charged with DUI in March 2007 (near the end of spring training), his Florida attorneys (Douglas N. Duncan and David L. Roth) were able to reach a plea deal with prosecutors. *See* Susan Spencer-Wendel, *La Russa Pleads Guilty in DUI Case*, Palm Beach Post, Nov. 29, 2007, at 3C. Afterwards, La Russa released a statement in which he "accept[ed] full responsibility … and assure[d] everyone that I have learned a very valuable lesson and that this will never occur again." *Id.* In 2020, however, La Russa again was charged with DUI after he ran his car into a curb in Phoenix just after the start of spring training. *See White Sox Manager Tony La Russa Charged with DUI Again*, Associated Press, Nov. 9, 2020, https://apnews.com/article/tony-la-russa-charged-dui-white-sox-44e952343d703449fd4876620c071da7. In December 2020, La Russa pled guilty to a lesser charge (reckless driving). *See Chicago White Sox's Tony La Russa Resolves DUI, Pleads to Lesser Charge*, ESPN, Dec. 21, 2020, https://www.espn.com/mlb/story/_/id/30573665/chicago-white-sox-tony-la-russa-resolves-dui-pleads-lesser-charge.

68. However, when Bill Veeck sold the White Sox to Einhorn and Reinsdorf in 1981, see *supra* note 49, Veeck told La Russa to get ready to start practicing law because there was no guarantee that La Russa would be kept on as the team's manager. Reinsdorf, however, quickly made it clear that La Russa's position was safe. *See* Mike Veeck Interview, *supra* note 39.

69. *See* Author's Interview with William A. Dooley (May 31, 2024) [hereinafter Dooley Interview].

70. Mike Saverino, *Tony La Russa: White Sox Lawyer-Manager is a Baseball Man at Heart*, 26:3 The Woolsack (student newspaper of the University of San Diego School of Law) 11 (Oct. 24, 1985), https://digital.sandiego.edu/cgi/viewcontent.cgi?article=1162&context=woolsack. *See also* Tracy Ringelsby, *The Trials of Baseball: A's Manager La Russa Just Couldn't Stay Away*, Austin American-Statesman (TX), Sept. 20, 1986, at C2 ("La Russa … [is] an associate of the law firm of Thorp, Reed, Conley and Dooley…. 'What I've done the last few years (in the law firm) is walk in the office and say, Hi…. If anybody wants to talk to me about serious law business, I refer them to a lawyer in the firm.'"). In 2013, Thorp Reed merged with the Detroit law firm of Clark Hill to form Clark Hill Thorp & Reed. In 2014, the firm became known as Clark Hill. *See* Patty Tascarella, *Clark Hill Dropping Thorp Reed from Name in Pittsburgh*, Pitt. Bus. Times, May 30, 2014, https://www.bizjournals.com/pittsburgh/news/2014/05/30/clark-hill-drops-thorp-reed-name.html. *See also* https://www.clarkhill.com/ (last visited July 1, 2024).

71. *See* La Russa Interview, *supra* note 17; Dooley Interview, *supra* note 69.

72. La Russa Interview, *supra* note 17.

73. *Id.*

74. *See supra* notes 2–3 and accompanying text. *But see supra* note 67 (discussing La Russa's drunk driving arrests while managing the Cardinals and the White Sox). *See also* Steve Kornacki, *Baseball's Animal-Crazed, Tea Party-Liking Manager: Tony La Russa is a Fan of Arizona's Immigration Law and the Tea Party Movement*, SALON, July 1, 2010, https://www.salon.com/2010/07/01/tony_la_russa_tea_party/ (taking La Russa, a lifelong Democrat, to task for his public support of a harsh new Arizona law targeting immigrants that had been condemned by the Major League Baseball Players Association).

75. *See* JOANN A. BENNETT, TONY LA RUSSA: THE PLAYBOOK OF A BASEBALL GENIUS (2024).

76. *See* WILLIAM A. LEWIS, TONY LA RUSSA BIOGRAPHY: A DIAMOND MIND IN BASEBALL'S HALL OF FAME (2024).

77. *See* BENNETT, *supra* note 75, at Chapter 11 ("Humanitarian Efforts"); LEWIS, *supra* note 76, at Chapter 6 ("Out of the Field").

78. *See* Eric Townsend, *A Home Run Talk on Leadership, Law School, and Baseball*, TODAY AT ELON, Apr. 16, 2024, https://www.elon.edu/u/news/2024/04/16/a-home-run-talk-on-leadership-law-school-and-baseball/.

79. Saverino, *supra* note 70.

80. For Fuson's career statistics, see *Robin Fuson*, BASEBALL-REFERENCE.COM, https://www.baseball-reference.com/register/player.fcgi?id=fuson-001rob (last visited July 1, 2024). As this source indicates, Fuson was drafted out of Valencia Community College in Orlando, Florida, by the Cleveland Indians in the fourth round of the January 1978 draft. Between 1978 and 1986, Fuson played for multiple minor league teams at the Class A, AA, and AAA level. After starring for Tecolotes de los Dos Laredos in the Mexican League in 1987, where he won the best pitcher award, Fuson in 1988 tried to make the majors one last time. When he failed, he hung up his spikes. *See* Rocco Constantino, *Robin Fuson*, BALLNINE.COM, Nov. 4, 2022, https://ballnine.com/2022/11/04/robin-fuson/.

81. Author's interview with Robin F. Fuson (May 7, 2024).

82. *Id.*

83. *See Area Judicial Races: Lopsided Outcomes Point to Victors*, TAMPA BAY TIMES, Nov. 7, 2018, at 8B.

84. Townsend, *supra* note 78.

85. Marshall Harris, *A Former White Sox Manager's Connection to Twitter's Verification Check Mark History*, CBSNEWS.COM, Apr. 20, 2023, https://www.cbsnews.com/chicago/news/white-sox-twitter-check/. The lawsuit, titled *La Russa v. Twitter, Inc.*, initially was filed in California Superior Court in San Francisco (CGC-09-488101); subsequently, it was removed to the U.S. District Court for the Northern District of California (3:09-cv-02503-EMC). For more about the case, see *La Russa v. Twitter, Inc.*, DIGITAL MEDIA LAW PROJECT, Sept. 10, 2023, https://www.dmlp.org/threats/la-russa-v-twitter-inc#node-legal-threat-full-group-description. *See also* Jillian Bluestone, Comment, *La Russa's Loophole: Trademark Infringement Lawsuits and Social Networks*, 17 VILL. SPORTS & ENT. L.J. 573 (2010).

Appendix 1: "Vital Statistics"

To aid readers, the "vital statistics" of each inductee are presented below.

(1) Name; (2) Boyhood Team; (3) Hall of Fame Admission Year and Reason; (4) Birth Year; (5) Birth Place; (6) Parents' Occupations; (7) Number of Siblings (including half-siblings); (8) Height; (9) Weight; (10) Religion; (11) Military Service; (12) Political Affiliation; (13) College; (14) Law School; (15) Bar and Admission Date; (16) Legal Career; (17) Spouse; (18) Place and Year of Marriage; (19) Children; (20) Death Year; (21) Place of Death; (22) Cause of Death; (23) Burial Site; (24) Value of Estate at Death; (25) Modern Day Value of Estate

(1) **KENESAW MOUNTAIN LANDIS**; (2) None (later rooted for Chicago Cubs and Chicago White Sox); (3) 1944—served as the first Commissioner of Baseball (1921–44); (4) 1866; (5) Millville, OH; (6) Physician (father), homemaker (mother); (7) 6; (8) 5'6"; (9) 130 pounds; (10) Atheist; (11) None; (12) Republican; (13) None; (14a) Cincinnati College (attended 1889–90); (14b) Northwestern University (LL.B., 1891); (15a) Indiana (1888); (15b) Illinois (1891); (16) Sole practitioner, 1888–89, 1891–93, 1895–97, 1897–1905; Partner, Uhl, Jones & Landis, 1897; U.S. District Judge, 1905–22; (17) Winifred (1872–1947); (18) Ottawa, IL, 1895; (19a) Reed (1896–1975); (19b) Susanne (1898–1977); (20) 1944; (21) Chicago, IL; (22) Heart attack; (23) Chicago, IL; (24) $100,000; (25) $1.76 million

(1) **HUGH AMBROSE "HUGHIE" JENNINGS**; (2) None; (3) 1945—star shortstop of the National League's championship Baltimore Orioles (1893–99); (4) 1869; (5) Pittston, PA; (6) Miner (father), homemaker (mother); (7) 9; (8) 5'8"; (9) 165 pounds; (10) Catholic; (11) None; (12) Democrat; (13) St. Bonaventure College (attended 1895–97); (14) Cornell University (attended 1901–04); (15a) Maryland (1905); (15b) Pennsylvania (1908); (16) Associate, Willis, Homer, France & Smith, 1905; Partner, Jennings & Jennings, 1907–22; (17a) Elizabeth (1871–98); (17b) Nora (1883–1943); (18a) Avoca, PA,

1897; (18b) Scranton, PA, 1911; (19a) Grace (1898–1964); (19b) Amelia (1911–12); (20) 1928; (21) Scranton, PA; (22) Meningitis; (23) Moscow, PA; (24) $87,000; (25) $1.58 million

(1) JAMES HENRY "JIM" O'ROURKE; (2) None; (3) 1945—collected the first hit in National League history (1876) and played in his final major league game when he was 54 (1904); (4) 1850; (5) Bridgeport, CT; (6) Farmer (father), homemaker (mother); (7) 3; (8) 5'8"; (9) 185 pounds; (10) Catholic; (11) None; (12) Democrat; (13) None; (14) Yale University (B.C.L., 1887); (15) Connecticut (1887); (16) Sole practitioner, 1887–1919; (17) Anna (1854–1910); (18) Bridgeport, CT, 1872; (19a) Sarah (1873–1941); (19b) Anna (1874–83); (19c) Agnes (1879–1968); (19d) James (1880–1955); (19e) Ida (1883–1959); (19f) Lillian (1885–1977); (19g) Irene (1886–1968); (19h) Edith (1889–1979); (20) 1919; (21) Bridgeport, CT; (22) Pneumonia; (23) Stratford, CT; (24) $75,000 (est.); (25) $1.35 million

(1) MILLER JAMES "HUG" HUGGINS; (2) Cincinnati Reds; (3) 1964—piloted the New York Yankees to six pennants and three World Series titles (1923, 1927, 1928); (4) 1878; (5) Cincinnati, OH; (6) Grocer (father), homemaker (mother); (7) 3; (8) 5'2"; (9) 120 pounds; (10) Methodist; (11) None; (12) Republican; (13) University of Cincinnati (attended 1897–99); (14) University of Cincinnati (LL.B., 1902); (15) Ohio (1902); (16) None; (17) None; (18) N/A; (19) None; (20) 1929; (21) New York, NY; (22) Influenza and pyaemia; (23) Cincinnati, OH; (24) $250,000; (25) $4.53 million

(1) JOHN MONTGOMERY "MONTE" WARD; (2) None; (3) 1964—founded the first baseball players union (1885) and later founded the Players League (1890); (4) 1860; (5) Bellefonte, PA; (6) Farm equipment dealer (father), school teacher (mother); (7) 4; (8) 5'9"; (9) 165 pounds; (10) Presbyterian; (11) None; (12) Republican; (13) Columbia University (Ph.B., 1886); (14) Columbia University (LL.B., 1885); (15) New York (1895); (16) Sole practitioner, 1895–1900, 1906–25; Partner, Baldwin & Ward, 1900–03; Partner, Ward & Martyn, 1903–06; (17a) Helen (1859–1923); (17b) Katherine (1877–1966); (18a) New York, NY, 1887 (divorced 1893); (18b) Brookyln, NY, 1903; (19) None; (20) 1925; (21) Augusta, GA; (22) Pneumonia; (23) Uniondale, NY; (24) $58,122; (25) $1.03 million

(1) WESLEY BRANCH RICKEY; (2) Cincinnati Reds; (3) 1967—invented baseball's farm system and engineered the breaking of baseball's color line (1947); (4) 1881; (5) Portsmouth, OH; (6) Farmer (father), homemaker (mother); (7) 3; (8) 5'9"; (9) 175 pounds; (10) Methodist; (11) U.S. Army (1918); (12) Republican; (13) Ohio Wesleyan University (B. Litt., 1904; B.A., 1906); (14) University of Michigan (J.D., 1911); (15) Idaho (1911); (16) Partner, Rickey, Crow & Ebbert, 1911–12; (17) Jane (1882–1971); (18) Lucasville,

OH, 1906; (19a) Unnamed baby girl (1909–09); (19b) Mary (1913–2005); 19c) Branch, Jr. (1914–61); (19d) Jane (1916–2004); (19e) Mabel (1918–96); (19f) Sue (1923–83); (19g) Elizabeth (1924–2009); (20) 1965; (21) Columbia, MO; (22) Heart failure; (23) Rushtown, OH; (24) $379,475; (25) $3.03 million

(1) **LELAND STANFORD "LARRY" MACPHAIL, SR.**; (2) None; (3) 1978— credited with numerous innovations, including night baseball (1935); (4) 1890; (5) Cass City, MI; (6) Banker (father), homemaker (mother); (7) 3; (8) 5'10½"; (9) 186 pounds; (10) Episcopalian; (11) U.S. Army (1917–19, 1942– 45); (12) Republican; (13) Beloit College (attended 1906–07); (14a) University of Michigan (attended 1907–08); (14b) George Washington University (LL.B., 1910); (15a) Illinois (1910); (15b) Michigan (1911); (16) Partner, Fowler, McDonnell, Rosenberg & MacPhail, 1911–12; (17a) Inez (1890– 1965); (17b) Jean (1910–97); (18a) Chicago, IL, 1910 (divorced 1945); (18b) Baltimore, MD, 1945; (19a) Marian (1912–93); (19b) Leland, Jr. (1917–2012); (19c) William (1920–96); (19d) Jean (born 1946); (20) 1975; (21) Miami, FL; (22) Pneumonia; (23) Cass City, MI; (24) $0; (25) $0

(1) **ALBERT BENJAMIN "HAPPY" CHANDLER, SR.**; (2) Cincinnati Reds; (3) 1982—served as the second Commissioner of Baseball (1945–51); (4) 1898; (5) Corydon, KY; (6) Farmer (father), homemaker (mother); (7) 6; (8) 5'8"; (9) 196 pounds; (10) Presbyterian; (11) U.S. Army (1918) (student corps); (12) Democrat; (13) Transylvania University (B.A., 1921); (14a) Harvard University (attended 1921–22); (14b) University of Kentucky (LL.B., 1924); (15) Kentucky (1924); (16) Sole practitioner, 1924–31; (17) Mildred (1899–1995); (18) Keysville, VA, 1925; (19a) Marcella (1922–2005, adopted); (19b) Mildred (1926–2016); (19c) Albert, Jr. (1929–2016); (19d) Joseph (1933– 2004); (20) 1991; (21) Versailles, KY; (22) Heart attack; (23) Pisgah, KY; (24) $939,900; (25) $2.14 million

(1) **BOWIE KENT KUHN**; (2) Washington Senators; (3) 2008—served as the fifth Commissioner of Baseball (1969–84); (4) 1926; (5) Takoma Park, MD; (6) Energy company executive (father), homemaker (mother); (7) 2; (8) 6'5"; (9) 230 pounds; (10) Catholic; (11) U.S. Navy (1944–46) (student corps); (12) Republican; (13a) Franklin and Marshall College (attended 1944–45); (13b) Princeton University (A.B., 1947); (14) University of Virginia (LL.B., 1950); (15) New York (1951); (16) Associate and then Partner, Willkie, Farr & Gallagher (and predecessors), 1950–69 and 1984–87; Partner, Myerson & Kuhn, 1988–89; (17) Louise (1930–2023); (18) Millstone, NY, 1956; (19a) George (born 1952, adopted); (19b) Paul (born 1956, adopted); (19c) Alexandra (born 1959); (19d) Stephen (born 1961); (20) 2007; (21) Ponte Vedra, FL; (22) Pneumonia; (23) Quogue, NY; (24) Unknown; (25) Unknown

(1) **WALTER FRANCIS O'MALLEY**; (2) New York Giants; (3) 2008—brought major league baseball to the West Coast (1958); (4) 1903; (5) Bronx, NY; (6) Salesman, later municipal official (father), homemaker (mother); (7) None; (8) 5'10½"; (9) 200 pounds; (10) Catholic; (11) None; (12) Democrat; (13) University of Pennsylvania (A.B., 1926); (14a) Columbia University (attended 1926–27); (14b) Fordham University (LL.B., 1930); (15) New York (1933); (16) Sole practitioner, 1933–1935, 1942–50; Partner, O'Malley & Wilson, 1935–41; (17) Katharina (1907–79); (18) New York, NY, 1931; (19a) Therese (born 1933); (19b) Peter (born 1937); (20) 1979; (21) Rochester, MN; (22) Congestive heart failure; (23) Culver City, CA; (24) $60 million (est.); (25) $255.74 million

(1) **ANTHONY "TONY" LA RUSSA, JR.**; (2) New York Yankees; (3) 2014—named "Manager of the Year" four times and piloted both the American League Oakland A's (1989) and the National League St. Louis Cardinals (2006, 2011) to World Series titles; (4) 1944; (5) Ybor City, FL; (6) Truck driver (father), homemaker (mother); (7) 1; (8) 6'1"; (9) 175 pounds; (10) Catholic; (11) None; (12) Democrat; (13a) University of Tampa (two semesters); (13b) University of South Florida (B.A., 1969); (14) Florida State University (J.D., 1978); (15) Florida (1980); (16) Part-time associate, Conley and Dooley (later Thorp, Reed, Conley and Dooley), 1979–94; (17a) First wife (details withheld upon request); (17b) Second wife (details withheld upon request); (18a) First marriage (1965–73); (18b) Second marriage (1973–present); (19a) First child (details withheld upon request); (19b) Second child (details withheld upon request); (19c) Third child (details withheld upon request); (19d) Fourth child (details withheld upon request); (20) N/A; (21) N/A; (22) N/A; (23) N/A; (24) N/A; (25) N/A

Appendix 2:
Non–Hall of Famers

Although this book focuses on the 11 lawyers who are in the Baseball Hall of Fame, there are many other lawyers who have been associated with the National Pastime.

Indeed, if one wanted to, one could put together a highly competitive team consisting of lawyers who are not in the Hall of Fame but who played professionally. The lineup card, filled out by manager John C. "Jack" Hendricks (1875–1943) (IIT-Chicago Kent College of Law, 1895) (manager of the St. Louis Cardinals, 1918, and Cincinnati Reds, 1924–29),[1] might read as follows:

1. **Edward L. "Eddie" Grant, 3b** (1883–1918) (Harvard University Law School, 1909) (Cleveland Naps, 1905; Philadelphia Phillies, 1907–10; Cincinnati Reds, 1911–13; New York Giants, 1913–15)—In 10 big league seasons, Grant compiled a .249 batting average but was better known for his fielding and baserunning. Following his retirement from baseball in 1915, Grant began practicing law in New York City. In April 1917, Grant became one of the first Americans to enlist in World War I. Grant was killed in France on October 5, 1918, while leading a search party looking for the "Lost Battalion," the first major leaguer killed in battle. In 1921, during a Memorial Day service at the Polo Grounds, the Giants unveiled a five-foot tall monument in centerfield paying tribute to Grant's heroism. Commissioner Kenesaw Mountain Landis later spent years advocating, without success, for Grant's enshrinement in the Baseball Hall of Fame.[2]

2. **Harry L. Taylor, 1b** (1866–1955) (Cornell University Law School, 1893) (Louisville Colonels, 1890–92; Baltimore Orioles, 1893)—Although Taylor played for only four years, he compiled a .286 career batting average and hit .306 during his rookie season (1890). He thus could have been a standout player had he not given up baseball for a legal career in Buffalo, New York. In 1906, he was elected to the county

bench, beginning a 30-year judicial career that saw him elevated to the Supreme Court in 1913 and to the Appellate Division in 1924. In 1936, he was forced to step down due to the state's mandatory retirement rules. Taylor additionally was a lecturer at the University of Buffalo's law school from 1907 to 1915.[3]

3. **David L. "Dave" Fultz, cf** (1875–1959) (New York Law School, 1904) (Philadelphia Phillies, 1898–99; Baltimore Orioles, 1899; Philadelphia Athletics, 1901–02; New York Highlanders, 1903–05)—In his seven-year career, Fultz batted .271, although during his best season (1902) he hit .302, led the American League with 109 runs, and stole 44 bases. During the second inning of a game against the Detroit Tigers on September 4, 1902, Fultz incredibly stole second base, third base, and home plate. In 1912, Fultz organized and became president of the Players Fraternity, baseball's second players' union. The organization's vice presidents included Hall of Famers Tyrus R. "Ty" Cobb and Christopher "Christy" Mathewson.[4]

4. **Donn A. Clendenon, dh** (1935–2005) (Duquesne University School of Law, 1978) (Pittsburgh Pirates, 1961–68; Montreal Expos, 1969; New York Mets, 1969–71; St. Louis Cardinals, 1972)—During his time in the majors, Clendenon was used as a first baseman. Today, however, the powerful slugger (.274 lifetime batting average) likely also would have been a designated hitter. While Clendenon spent most of his career with the Pirates, where he played alongside Hall of Famers Roberto E. Clemente and Wilver D. "Willie" Stargell, Clendenon now is best remembered as the leader of the 1969 "Amazin' Mets." For his efforts in helping New York beat the heavily favored Baltimore Orioles in five games, he was named the 1969 World Series MVP.[5]

5. **Sumner S. Bowman, lf** (1867–1954) (University of Pennsylvania Law School, 1891) (Philadelphia Phillies, 1890; Pittsburgh Alleghenies, 1890; Philadelphia Athletics, 1891)—Although he gained more fame as a pitcher, Bowman also was an excellent outfielder, hitting .266 during his two-year career. The son of a lawyer, Bowman left baseball after graduating from law school and practiced for 17 years in New York City. He later returned to Pennsylvania and had a long career in Harrisburg. In World War I, he served as a major in the Judge Advocate General's Department.[6]

6. **Morris "Moe" Berg, c** (1902–72) (Columbia University Law School, 1930) (Brooklyn Robins, 1923; Chicago White Sox, 1926–30; Cleveland Indians, 1931; Washington Senators, 1932–34; Cleveland Indians, 1934; Boston Red Sox, 1935–39)—Berg today is known as having been the brainiest individual to ever play in the major leagues. A graduate of both Princeton University and Columbia University, Berg

spoke 10 languages and eventually became a partner in the Wall Street law firm of Satterlee & Canfield, where he specialized in international contract law. Berg began his career in the majors as a shortstop but later transitioned to catcher. During World War II, Berg worked for the Office of Strategic Services (the forerunner of the Central Intelligence Agency) and was awarded the Medal of Freedom for his still-classified contributions. A lifetime .243 hitter, Berg accompanied Hall of Famers George H. "Babe" Ruth, Henry L. "Lou" Gehrig, Jr., and James E. "Jimmie" Foxx on Major League Baseball's famous 1934 Goodwill Tour of Japan, serving as an interpreter.[7]

7. **Fred H. Brown, rf** (1879–1955) (Boston University School of Law, 1906) (Boston Beaneaters, 1901–02)—Brown played only two seasons in the majors and batted a mere .200. After leaving baseball, however, Brown found much greater success in the political arena, serving as the U.S. Attorney for the District of New Hampshire (1914–22); New Hampshire's governor (1923–25); New Hampshire's U.S. Senator (1933–39); the second U.S. Comptroller General (1939–40); and as a member of the U.S. Tariff Commission (1940–41).[8]

8. **Clarence E. "King" Lehr, ss** (1886–1948) (University of Michigan Law School, 1914) (Philadelphia Phillies, 1911)—After playing in the majors for one season, during which he hit .148, Lehr decided to enroll in law school. Following graduation, Lehr became a lawyer in Detroit, Michigan. In 1933, when the Michigan legislature legalized horse racing, Lehr organized and became the president of the Detroit Racing Association. Lehr continued to head the organization until his death in 1948. In 1940, Lehr made headlines when he hired his former Phillies teammate, Grover Cleveland Alexander, to be a racetrack ticket taker after the Hall of Fame pitcher fell on hard times.[9]

9. **Newell O. "Bud" Morse, Jr., 2b** (1904–87) (Oakland College of Law, 1933) (Philadelphia Athletics, 1929)—In June 1929, after a standout collegiate career at the University of California–Berkeley and the University of Michigan, Morse was signed by the San Francisco Mission Reds of the Class AA Pacific Coast League. Sold two weeks later to the Des Moines (Iowa) Demons of the Class A Western League, Morse hit .302 while playing a superb second base. As a result, in August 1929 his contract was purchased by the Philadelphia A's. Morse found it difficult to crack the A's lineup, however, which was led by future Hall of Famers Gordon S. "Mickey" Cochrane, James E. "Jimmie" Foxx, and Aloysius H. "Al" Simmons. As a result, Morse got into only eight games and hit just .074. Following the season, the A's sent Morse back to Des Moines. After retiring from baseball in 1930, Morse entered law school and later worked as an attorney for the Veterans Administration. In November

1957, Morse disarmed Elza W. Eaton, a former security guard at the VA hospital in Reno, Nevada, after Eaton entered the facility with a shotgun and a revolver and killed two people and injured a third person. Nevada Governor Charles H. Russell subsequently presented Morse with a gold medal for his exceptional heroism.[10]

    10. **William P. "Bill" Bray, p** (born 1983) (William & Mary Law School, 2018) (Washington Nationals, 2006; Cincinnati Reds, 2006–12)—During his six years in the majors, Bray compiled a 13–12 record with a 3.74 earned run average in 68 games. In the 2010 National League Division Series against the Philadelphia Phillies, Bray appeared in two games and pitched a scoreless 1.2 innings. Today, Bray is a partner in the Williamsburg, Virginia, law firm of Bray Knicely, PLLC (https://brayknicelylaw.com/), where he focuses on corporate law.[11]

The foregoing names, it should be pointed out, do not begin to exhaust the list of lawyers who have played in the major leagues.[12]

The list grows further if one includes baseball executives, such as Richard L. "Sandy" Alderson (born 1947) (Harvard University Law School, 1976), the former general manager of the Oakland A's (1983–97) and New York Mets (2011–18) and the former chief executive officer of the San Diego Padres (2005–09)[13]; Theodore N. "Theo" Epstein (born 1973) (University of San Diego School of Law, 2000), the former general manager of the Boston Red Sox (2002–05) and former president of the Chicago Cubs (2011–20)[14]; Stan Kasten (born 1952) (Columbia University Law School, 1976), the former president of the Atlanta Braves (1986–2003) and Washington Nationals (2006–10) and the current president of the Los Angeles Dodgers (since 2012)[15]; Randy L. Levine (born 1955) (Hofstra University School of Law, 1980), the president of the New York Yankees (since 2000)[16]; Lawrence "Larry" Lucchino (1945–2024) (Yale University Law School, 1971), the former president of the Baltimore Orioles (1988–93), San Diego Padres (1995–2001), and Boston Red Sox (2002–15)[17]; Robert D. "Rob" Manfred (born 1958) (Harvard University Law School, 1983), baseball's current commissioner (since 2015)[18]; David P. Samson (born 1968) (Yeshiva University School of Law, 1993), the former president of the Florida (later Miami) Marlins (2002–17)[19]; and Fay T. Vincent, Jr. (born 1938) (Yale University Law School, 1963), baseball's eighth commissioner (1989–92).[20]

One can keep expanding the list by including team owners, such as Peter G. Angelos (1929–2024) (University of Baltimore School of Law, 1960), the former owner of the Baltimore Orioles (1993–2024)[21]; Mark L. Attansio (born 1957) (Columbia University Law School, 1982), the owner of the Milwaukee Brewers (since 2005)[22]; Emil E. "Judge" Fuchs (1878–1961) (New York University School of Law, 1901), the former owner of the

Boston Braves (1922–35)[23]; Francis J. "Frank" Navin (1871–1935) (Detroit College of Law, now Michigan State University College of Law, 1897), the former owner of the Detroit Tigers (1908–35)[24]; and Jerry M. Reinsdorf (born 1936) (Northwestern University School of Law, 1960), the owner of the Chicago White Sox (since 1981).[25]

Even more names can be added if one goes deeper into the history books.[26] The most obvious example, of course, is William A. Shea (1907–91) (Georgetown University Law Center, 1931), who in 1964 became the namesake of the New York Mets' second home (William A. Shea Municipal Stadium, better known as Shea Stadium, 1964–2008) in recognition of his efforts to bring the National League back to New York City following the departure of the Brooklyn Dodgers and the New York Giants in 1957.[27] Similarly, U.S. Supreme Court Justice Sonia M. Sotomayor (born 1954) (Yale University Law School, 1979) is known as the "woman who saved baseball" for her decision that ended the 1994–95 players' strike.[28]

NOTES

1. For a profile of Hendricks, see Robert M. Jarvis, *John C. "Jack" Hendricks: Major League Baseball's Forgotten Lawyer-Manager*, 33:1 NINE: J. BASEBALL HIST. & CULTURE 39 (2024).

2. For a further look at Grant's career, see Tom Simon, *Eddie Grant*, SABR, https://sabr.org/bioproj/person/eddie-grant/ (last visited July 1, 2024).

3. For a further look at Taylor's career, see Charlie Bevis, *Harry L. Taylor*, SABR, https://sabr.org/bioproj/person/harry-taylor-3/ (last visited July 1, 2024).

4. For a further look at Fultz's career, see Brian McKenna, *Dave Fultz*, SABR, https://sabr.org/bioproj/person/dave-fultz/ (last visited July 1, 2024).

5. For a further look at Clendenon's career, see Ed Hoyt, *Donn Clendenon*, SABR, https://sabr.org/bioproj/person/donn-clendenon/ (last visited July 1, 2024).

6. A SABR biography is planned but does not currently exist for Bowman. *See Sumner Bowman*, SABR, https://sabr.org/bioproj/person/sumner-bowman/ (last visited July 1, 2024). Similarly, Bowman's Baseball-Reference.com page is all but empty. *See Sumner Bowman*, BASEBALL-REFERENCE.COM, https://www.baseball-reference.com/bullpen/Sumner_Bowman (last visited July 1, 2024). For a profile of Bowman, see *Sumner Sallade Bowman, 1867–1954*, PENN LIBRARIES, https://archives.upenn.edu/exhibits/penn-people/biography/sumner-sallade-bowman/ (last visited July 1, 2024).

7. For a further look at Berg's career, see Ralph Berger, *Moe Berg*, SABR, https://sabr.org/bioproj/person/moe-berg/ (last visited July 1, 2024).

8. For a further look at Brown's career, see Bill Lamb, *Fred Brown*, SABR, https://sabr.org/bioproj/person/fred-brown/ (last visited July 1, 2024).

9. A SABR biography is planned but does not currently exist for Lehr. *See Clarence Lehr*, SABR, https://sabr.org/bioproj/person/clarence-lehr/ (last visited July 1, 2024). Similarly, Lehr's Baseball-Reference.com page is all but empty. *See Clarence Lehr*, BASEBALL-REFERENCE.COM, https://www.baseball-reference.com/bullpen/Clarence_Lehr (last visited July 1, 2024). For a profile of Lehr, see *Sports Figures of the Boston-Edison Historic District: Clarence E. Lehr*, HISTORIC BOSTON-EDISON, https://historicbostonedison.org/Sports-Figures-of-BE (last visited July 1, 2024). (Boston-Edison was an early 20th century neighborhood located in the heart of Detroit—its name was derived from the fact that its northern border ended at Boston Boulevard while its southern border ended at Edison Avenue.)

10. A SABR biography is planned but does not currently exist for Morse. *See Bud*

Morse, SABR, https://sabr.org/bioproj/person/bud-morse/ (last visited July 1, 2024). Similarly, Morse's Baseball-Reference.com page is all but empty. *See Bud Morse*, BASEBALL-REFERENCE.COM, https://www.baseball-reference.com/bullpen/Bud_Morse (last visited July 1, 2024). Morse does have a surprisingly robust Wikipedia page, although it incorrectly refers to him as "Sr." rather than "Jr." and wrongly lists his law school as UC-Berkeley instead of the Oakland College of Law ("OCL"). *See Bud Morse*, WIKIPEDIA: THE FREE ENCYCLOPEDIA, https://en.wikipedia.org/wiki/Bud_Morse (last visited July 1, 2024). For proof that Morse was a "Jr." and graduated from OCL, see *13 Will Get Law Diplomas*, OAKLAND TRIB., May 30, 1933, at 5.

11. A SABR biography is planned but does not currently exist for Bray. *See* Paul Boren, *Bill Bray*, SABR, https://sabr.org/bioproj/person/bill-bray/ (last visited July 1, 2024). For a profile of Bray, see *Paul Bray*, BASEBALL-REFERENCE.COM, https://www.baseball-reference.com/bullpen/Paul_Bray (last visited July 1, 2024).

12. Although they did not play in the majors, also worthy of mention are players like John G. "Gabby" Shackelford (1905–64), who played in the Negro Leagues (Birmingham Black Barons, Chicago American Giants, Cleveland Browns, and Harrisburg Giants, 1924–30), and then earned a law degree from the University of Michigan (1931), and Patricia I. Brown (1931–2012), who played in the All-American Girls Professional Baseball League (Battle Creek Belles and Chicago Colleens, 1950–51) and then earned a law degree at Suffolk University Law School (1965). For a profile of Shackelford, see *John Shackelford*, ARKANSAS BASEBALL ENCYCLOPEDIA, https://arkbaseball.com/tiki-index.php?page=John+Shackelford (last visited July 1, 2024). For a profile of Brown, see *Patricia Brown*, ALL-AMERICAN GIRLS PROFESSIONAL BASEBALL LEAGUE, https://www.aagpbl.org/profiles/patricia-brown-pat/219 (last visited July 1, 2024).

13. A SABR biography is planned but does not currently exist for Alderson. *See Sandy Alderson*, SABR, https://sabr.org/bioproj/person/sandy-alderson/ (last visited July 1, 2024). For a profile of Alderson, see *Sandy Alderson*, BASEBALL-REFERENCE.COM, https://www.baseball-reference.com/bullpen/Sandy_Alderson (last visited July 1, 2024).

14. Epstein does not have a SABR biography. For a profile of Epstein, see *Theo Epstein*, BASEBALL-REFERENCE.COM, https://www.baseball-reference.com/bullpen/Theo_Epstein (last visited July 1, 2024).

15. For a further look at Kasten's career, see Bob Webster, *Stan Kasten*, SABR, https://sabr.org/bioproj/person/stan-kasten/ (last visited July 1, 2024).

16. Levine does not have a SABR biography. For a profile of Levine, see *Randy Levine*, BASEBALL-REFERENCE.COM, https://www.baseball-reference.com/bullpen/Randy_Levine (last visited July 1, 2024).

17. A SABR biography is planned but does not currently exist for Lucchino. *See Larry Lucchino*, SABR, https://sabr.org/bioproj/person/larry-lucchino/ (last visited July 1, 2024). For a profile of Lucchino, see *Larry Lucchino*, BASEBALL-REFERENCE.COM, https://www.baseball-reference.com/bullpen/Larry_Lucchino (last visited July 1, 2024).

18. Manfred does not have a SABR biography. For a profile of Manfred, see *Rob Manfred*, BASEBALL-REFERENCE.COM, https://www.baseball-reference.com/bullpen/Rob_Manfred (last visited July 1, 2024).

19. Samson does not have a SABR biography. For a profile of Samson, see *David Samson*, BASEBALL-REFERENCE.COM, https://www.baseball-reference.com/bullpen/David_Samson (last visited July 1, 2024).

20. For a further look at Vincent's career, see Rory Costello, *Fay Vincent*, SABR, https://sabr.org/bioproj/person/fay-vincent/ (last visited July 1, 2024).

21. Angelos does not have a SABR biography. For a profile of Angelos, see *Peter Angelos*, BASEBALL-REFERENCE.COM, https://www.baseball-reference.com/bullpen/Peter_Angelos (last visited July 1, 2024).

22. Attansio does not have a SABR biography. Similarly, Attansio's Baseball-Reference.com page is empty. *See Mark Attansio*, BASEBALL-REFERENCE.COM, https://www.baseball-reference.com/bullpen/Mark_Attansio (last visited July 1, 2024). For a profile of Attansio, see *Mark Attansio*, MILWAUKEE BREWERS, https://www.mlb.com/brewers/team/front-office/mark-attanasio (last visited July 1, 2024).

23. For a further look at Fuchs's career, see Bob LeMoine, *Judge Emil Fuchs*, SABR, https://sabr.org/bioproj/person/judge-emil-fuchs/ (last visited July 1, 2024).

24. For a further look at Navin's career, see David Jones & Marc Okkonen, *Frank Navin*, SABR, https://sabr.org/bioproj/person/frank-navin/ (last visited July 1, 2024).

25. Reinsdorf does not have a SABR biography. For a profile of Reinsdorf, see *Jerry Reinsdorf*, BASEBALL-REFERENCE.COM, https://www.baseball-reference.com/bullpen/Jerry_Reinsdorf (last visited July 1, 2024).

26. A good place to start is with the list that appears at ED EDMONDS & FRANK G. HOUDEK, BASEBALL MEETS THE LAW: A CHRONOLOGY OF DECISIONS, STATUTES AND OTHER LEGAL EVENTS 173–98 (2017).

27. For a further look at Shea's career, see Rory Costello, *William Shea*, SABR, https://sabr.org/bioproj/person/william-shea/ (last visited July 1, 2024).

28. *See* Silverman v. Major League Baseball Player Relations Comm., Inc., 880 F. Supp. 246 (S.D.N.Y.), *aff'd*, 67 F.3d 1054 (2d Cir. 1995). *See also* Richard Sandomir, *Sotomayor's Baseball Ruling Lingers, 14 Years Later*, N.Y. TIMES, May 26, 2009, https://www.nytimes.com/2009/05/27/sports/baseball/27sandomir.html.

Selected Bibliography

Chapter 1: Kenesaw Mountain Landis (1944)

Books:

McNutt, Randy, Kenesaw Mountain Landis: The Man Who Banned Shoeless Joe (2017)

Pietrusza, David, Judge and Jury: The Life and Times of Judge Kenesaw Mountain Landis (1998)

Spink, J.G. Taylor, Judge Landis and 25 Years of Baseball (1947)

Surdam, David George & Michael J. Haupert, The Age of Ruth and Landis: The Economics of Baseball During the Roaring Twenties (2018)

Articles:

Busby, Dan, *Kenesaw Mountain Landis*, Society for American Baseball Research, https://sabr.org/bioproj/person/kenesaw-landis/ (last visited July 1, 2024)

Henderson, John, "The Most Interesting Man in America": Folk Logic and First Principles in the Early Career of Judge Kenesaw Mountain Landis (unpublished Ph.D. dissertation, University of Florida, 1995), https://archive.org/details/mostinterestingm00hend/

Jacobowitz, Jan L., *Baseball, Kenesaw Mountain Landis, and the Judicial Strike Zone—Home Run or Foul on the Play?*, 13:1 Journal of the Texas Supreme Court Historical Society 9 (2023)

Sigman, Shayna M., *The Jurisprudence of Judge Kenesaw Mountain Landis*, 15 Marquette Sports Law Review 277 (2005)

Miscellany:

Judge Landis Dies; Baseball Czar, 78: Commissioner for 24 Years—Barred Eight Players for 'Throwing' 1919 Series—Freed 'Slave' Athletes—On Bench, Fined Standard Oil $29,240,000—Presided in Haywood, Berger Cases, New York Times, November 26, 1944, at 56

Kenesaw Mountain Landis, Find-a-Grave.com, https://www.findagrave.com/memorial/600/kenesaw_mountain_landis (last visited July 1, 2024)

Kenesaw Mountain Landis, National Baseball Hall of Fame and Museum, https://baseballhall.org/hall-of-famers/landis-kenesaw (last visited July 1, 2024)

Chapter 2: Hugh Ambrose "Hughie" Jennings (1945)

Books:

Smiles, Jack, "Ee-Yah": The Life and Times of Hughie Jennings, Baseball Hall of Famer (2005)

Solomon, Burt, Where They Ain't: The Fabled Life and Untimely Death of the

ORIGINAL BALTIMORE ORIOLES, THE TEAM THAT GAVE BIRTH TO MODERN BASEBALL (1999)

Articles:

Rogers, III, C. Paul, *Hughie Jennings*, SOCIETY FOR AMERICAN BASEBALL RESEARCH, https://sabr.org/bioproj/person/hughie-jennings/ (last visited July 1, 2024)

Miscellany:

Hugh Jennings Dies After Long Illness: Famous Baseball Veteran, Ailing for Three Years, Succumbs in Scranton—Was Picturesque Figure—Captained Old Orioles, Won Three Pennants for Detroit and Helped Giants Take Four, NEW YORK TIMES, February 1, 1928, at 1
Hugh Jennings, FIND-A-GRAVE.COM, https://www.findagrave.com/memorial/3696/hugh_jennings (last visited July 1, 2024)
Hughie Jennings, NATIONAL BASEBALL HALL OF FAME AND MUSEUM, https://baseballhall.org/hall-of-famers/jennings-hughie (last visited July 1, 2024)

Chapter 3: James Henry "Jim" O'Rourke (1945)

Books:

CROWLEY, BERNARD J., THE REMARKABLE LIFE OF JAMES HENRY O'ROURKE: A CONNECTICUT FARM BOY'S JOURNEY TO BASEBALL'S HALL OF FAME (2022)
ROER, MIKE, ORATOR O'ROURKE: THE LIFE OF A BASEBALL RADICAL (2005)

Articles:

Lamb, Bill, *Jim O'Rourke*, SOCIETY FOR AMERICAN BASEBALL RESEARCH, https://sabr.org/bioproj/person/jim-orourke-2/ (last visited July 1, 2024)

Miscellany:

Old Giant Player Dies: Jim O'Rourke Played with New York from 1885 to 1889, NEW YORK TIMES, January 9, 1919, at 8
James Henry "Orator Jim" O'Rourke, FIND-A-GRAVE.COM, https://www.findagrave.com/memorial/21216/james-henry-o'rourke (last visited July 1, 2024)
Jim O'Rourke, NATIONAL BASEBALL HALL OF FAME AND MUSEUM, https://baseballhall.org/hall-of-famers/orourke-jim (last visited July 1, 2024)

Chapter 4: Miller James "Hug" Huggins (1964)

Books:

SARNOFF, GARY A., THE FIRST YANKEES DYNASTY: BABE RUTH, MILLER HUGGINS AND THE BRONX BOMBERS OF THE 1920s (2014)
STEINBERG, STEVE & LYLE SPATZ, THE COLONEL AND HUG: THE PARTNERSHIP THAT TRANSFORMED THE NEW YORK YANKEES (2015)

Articles:

Steinberg, Steve, *Miller Huggins*, SOCIETY FOR AMERICAN BASEBALL RESEARCH, https://sabr.org/bioproj/person/miller-huggins/ (last visited July 1, 2024)

Miscellany:

Miller Huggins Dies; Many Pay Tribute: Manager of Yankees' Baseball Team for 12 Seasons is a Victim of Blood Poisoning—League's Games Today Off—Group He Led to Three World Championships Will Attend the Funeral Here Tomorrow, NEW YORK TIMES, September 26, 1929, at 1

Miller James Huggins, Find-a-Grave.com, https://www.findagrave.com/memorial/2038/miller_james_huggins (last visited July 1, 2024)

Miller Huggins, National Baseball Hall of Fame and Museum, https://baseballhall.org/hall-of-famers/huggins-miller (last visited July 1, 2024)

Chapter 5: John Montgomery "Monte" Ward (1964)

Books:

Di Salvatore, Bryan, A Clever Base-Ballist: The Life and Times of John Montgomery Ward (1999)

Hawking, James, Strikeout: Baseball, Broadway and the Brotherhood in the 19th Century (2012)

Ross, Robert B., The Great Baseball Revolt: The Rise and Fall of the 1890 Players League (2016)

Stevens, David, Baseball's Radical for All Seasons: A Biography of John Montgomery Ward (1998)

Ward, John Montgomery, Base-Ball: How to Become a Player, with the Origin, History and Explanation of the Game (1888)

Articles:

Lamb, Bill, *John Montgomery Ward*, Society for American Baseball Research, https://sabr.org/bioproj/person/john-montgomery-ward/ (last visited July 1, 2024)

Miscellany:

John M. Ward Dies Suddenly in South: Famous Baseball Player and Noted Golfer Succumbs Suddenly in Georgia Hospital: Was with Giants in '80s: Led Them to Two World's Titles—Organized Players' League to Fight National—Friends Shocked, New York Times, March 5, 1925, at 17

John Montgomery Ward, Find-a-Grave.com, https://www.findagrave.com/memorial/6169/john_montgomery_ward (last visited July 1, 2024)

John Ward, National Baseball Hall of Fame and Museum, https://baseballhall.org/hall-of-famers/ward-john (last visited July 1, 2024)

Chapter 6: Wesley Branch Rickey (1967)

Books:

Breslin, Jimmy, Branch Rickey (2011)

Chalberg, John C., Rickey and Robinson: The Preacher, the Player, and America's Game (2000)

Frommer, Harvey, Rickey and Robinson: The Men Who Broke Baseball's Color Barrier (1982)

Kahn, Roger, Rickey & Robinson: The True, Untold Story of the Integration of Baseball (2014)

Lipman, David, Mr. Baseball: The Story of Branch Rickey (1966)

Lowenfish, Lee, Branch Rickey: Baseball's Ferocious Gentleman (2007)

Mann, Arthur, Branch Rickey: American in Action (1957)

O'Toole, Andrew, Branch Rickey in Pittsburgh: Baseball's Trailblazing General Manager for the Pirates, 1950–1955 (2000)

Polner, Murray, Branch Rickey: A Biography (1982)

Rickey, Branch, with Robert Riger, The American Diamond: A Documentary of the Game of Baseball (1965)

Shapiro, Michael, Bottom of the Ninth: Branch Rickey, Casey Stengel, and the Daring Scheme to Save Baseball from Itself (2009)

THOMAS, G. SCOTT, A BRAND NEW BALLGAME: BRANCH RICKEY, BILL VEECK, WALTER O'MALLEY AND THE TRANSFORMATION OF BASEBALL, 1945–1962 (2021)

Articles:

McCue, Andy, *Branch Rickey*, SOCIETY FOR AMERICAN BASEBALL RESEARCH, https://sabr.org/bioproj/person/branch-rickey/ (last visited July 1, 2024)

Miscellany:

Branch Rickey, 83, Dies in Missouri: A Leading Baseball Figure—Helped Break Color Bar, NEW YORK TIMES, December 10, 1965, at 1
Branch Rickey, FIND-A-GRAVE.COM, https://www.findagrave.com/memorial/6644/branch_rickey (last visited July 1, 2024).
Branch Rickey, NATIONAL BASEBALL HALL OF FAME AND MUSEUM, https://baseballhall.org/hall-of-famers/rickey-branch (last visited July 1, 2024)

Chapter 7: Leland Stanford "Larry" MacPhail, Sr. (1978)

Books:

MacPhail, Lee, MY NINE INNINGS: AN AUTOBIOGRAPHY OF 50 YEARS IN BASEBALL (1989)
McKelvey, G. RICHARD, THE MACPHAILS: BASEBALL'S FIRST FAMILY OF THE FRONT OFFICE (2000)
WARFIELD, DON, THE ROARING REDHEAD: LARRY MACPHAIL—BASEBALL'S GREAT INNOVATOR (1987)

Articles:

Berger, Ralph, *Larry MacPhail*, SOCIETY FOR AMERICAN BASEBALL RESEARCH, https://sabr.org/bioproj/person/larry-macphail/ (last visited July 1, 2024)

Miscellany:

Durso, Joseph, *Baseball's Larry MacPhail Dies; Night-Game Pioneer Led Yanks*, NEW YORK TIMES, October 2, 1975, at 1
Leland MacPhail, FIND-A-GRAVE.COM, https://www.findagrave.com/memorial/5860525/leland_macphail (last visited July 1, 2024)
Larry MacPhail, NATIONAL BASEBALL HALL OF FAME AND MUSEUM, https://baseballhall.org/hall-of-famers/macphail-larry (last visited July 1, 2024)

Chapter 8: Albert Benjamin "Happy" Chandler, Sr. (1982)

Books:

CHANDLER, HAPPY, WITH VANCE H. TRIMBLE, HEROES, PLAIN FOLKS, AND SKUNKS: THE LIFE AND TIMES OF HAPPY CHANDLER—AN AUTOBIOGRAPHY (1989)
MARSHALL, WILLIAM, BASEBALL'S PIVOTAL ERA, 1945–1951 (1999)

Articles:

Bohn, Terry, *Happy Chandler*, SOCIETY FOR AMERICAN BASEBALL RESEARCH, https://sabr.org/bioproj/person/happy-chandler/ (last visited July 1, 2024)
Marshall, Bill, *Baseball's Most Colorful Commissioner: Happy Chandler*, SOCIETY FOR AMERICAN BASEBALL RESEARCH, https://sabr.org/journal/article/baseballs-most-colorful-commissioner-happy-chandler/ (last visited July 1, 2024)

Miscellany:

Thomas, Jr., Robert McG., *A.B. (Happy) Chandler, 92, Dies; Led Baseball During Integration*, NEW YORK TIMES, June 16, 1991, at 26

Albert Benjamin "Happy" Chandler, Find-a-Grave.com, https://www.findagrave.com/memorial/2397/albert-benjamin-chandler (last visited July 1, 2024)

Happy Chandler, National Baseball Hall of Fame and Museum, https://baseballhall.org/hall-of-famers/chandler-happy (last visited July 1, 2024)

Chapter 9: Bowie Kent Kuhn (2008)

Books:

Kuhn, Bowie, Hardball: The Education of a Baseball Commissioner (rev. ed 1997)

Ludtke, Melissa, Locker Room Talk: A Woman's Struggle to Get Inside (2024)

Preston, Joseph G., Major League Baseball in the 1970s: A Modern Game Emerges (2004)

Articles:

Guerrieri, Vince, *Bowie Kuhn*, Society for American Baseball Research, https://sabr.org/bioproj/person/bowie-kuhn/ (last visited July 1, 2024)

Miscellany:

Goldstein, Richard, *Bowie Kuhn, 80, Former Baseball Commissioner, is Dead*, New York Times, March 16, 2007, at C10

Bowie Kuhn, Find-a-Grave.com, https://www.findagrave.com/memorial/18422891/bowie-kuhn (last visited July 1, 2024)

Bowie Kuhn, National Baseball Hall of Fame and Museum, https://baseballhall.org/hall-of-famers/kuhn-bowie (last visited July 1, 2024)

Chapter 10: Walter Francis O'Malley (2008)

Books:

McCue, Andy, Mover and Shaker: Walter O'Malley, the Dodgers, and Baseball's Westward Expansion (2014)

Nusbaum, Eric, Stealing Home: Los Angeles, the Dodgers, and the Lives Caught in Between (2020)

Sullivan, Neil J., The Dodgers Move West (1987)

Articles:

McCue, Andy, *Walter O'Malley*, Society for American Baseball Research, https://sabr.org/bioproj/person/walter-omalley/ (last visited July 1, 2024)

WalterOMalley.com, https://www.walteromalley.com/ (last visited July 1, 2024)

Miscellany:

Walter F. O'Malley, Leader of Dodgers' Move to Los Angeles, Dies at 75, New York Times, August 10, 1979, at A1

Walter O'Malley, Find-a-Grave.com, https://www.findagrave.com/memorial/5262/walter-o'malley (last visited July 1, 2024)

Walter O'Malley, National Baseball Hall of Fame and Museum, https://baseballhall.org/hall-of-famers/omalley-walter (last visited July 1, 2024)

Chapter 11: Anthony "Tony" La Russa, Jr. (2014)

Books:

Bennett, Joann A., Tony La Russa: The Playbook of a Baseball Genius (2024)

La Russa, Tony, Tony La Russa Talks Baseball Strategy with Joe Buck (2002)
La Russa, Tony & Rick Hummel, One Last Strike: Fifty Years in Baseball, Ten and a Half Games Back, and One Final Championship Season (2012)
Lewis, William A., Tony La Russa Biography: A Diamond Mind in Baseball's Hall of Fame (2024)
Rains, Bob, Tony La Russa: Man on a Mission (2009)

Articles:

Baldassaro, Lawrence, *Tony La Russa*, Society for American Baseball Research, https://sabr.org/bioproj/person/tony-la-russa/ (last visited July 1, 2024)
Bluestone, Jill, Comment, *La Russa's Loophole: Trademark Infringement Lawsuits and Social Networks*, 17 Villanova Sports & Entertainment Law Journal 573 (2010)

Miscellany:

Tony La Russa, National Baseball Hall of Fame and Museum, https://baseballhall.org/hall-of-famers/la-russa-tony (last visited July 1, 2024)

General Resources

Books:

National Baseball Hall of Fame and Museum, The National Baseball Hall of Fame Almanac: 2022 (2022)
Reisler, Jim, A Great Day in Cooperstown: The Improbable Birth of Baseball's Hall of Fame (2007)

Articles:

Brill, Christian H. & Howard W. Brill, *Lawyers in the Baseball Hall of Fame*, 34 Marquette Sports Law Review 137 (2023)
Kosin, Phil, *Diamond Classics: Baseball Lawyers Make Mark*, 71:10 American Bar Association Journal 34 (October 1985)

Miscellany:

Ancestry.com, https://www.ancestry.com/ (last visited July 1, 2024)
Baseball-Reference.com, https://www.baseball-reference.com/ (last visited July 1, 2024)
Find-a-Grave.com, https://www.findagrave.com/ (last visited July 1, 2024)
National Baseball Hall of Fame and Museum, https://baseballhall.org/ (last visited July 1, 2024)
Newspapers.com, https://www.newspapers.com/ (last visited July 1, 2024)

About the Contributors

Walter T. **Champion**, Jr. (walter.champion@tmslaw.tsu.edu) is a professor of law at Texas Southern University (Houston). His numerous books include *Baseball and the Law: Cases and Comments* (Cognella Academic Publishing, 2016); *Fundamentals of Sports Law* (Thomson Reuters, 2d ed., 2022); and *Sports Law in a Nutshell* (West Academic Publishing, 6th ed., 2022). He holds a B.A. from St. Joseph's University, an M.A. from Western Illinois University, an M.S.L.S. from Drexel University, and a J.D. from Temple University. He roots for the Philadelphia Phillies.

Edmund P. **Edmonds** (edmonds.7@nd.edu) is a professor emeritus of law at the University of Notre Dame (Indiana). He is the co-author of *Baseball Meets the Law: A Chronology of Decisions, Statutes and Other Legal Events* (McFarland & Company, 2017) and the author of numerous shorter works about baseball. He holds a B.A. from the University of Notre Dame, an M.L.S. from the University of Maryland, and a J.D. from the University of Toledo. He roots for the Cincinnati Reds.

Richard D. **Friedman** (rdfrdman@umich.edu) is the Alene and Allan F. Smith Professor of Law at the University of Michigan (Ann Arbor). A co-founder of the emerging field of sports and games as legal systems, he is the co-author of *The Jurisprudence of Sport: Sports and Games as Legal Systems* (West Academic Publishing, 2021). He holds a D. Phil. from the University of Oxford and a B.A. and a J.D. from Harvard University. He roots for the Philadelphia Phillies. He thanks Christopher E. Miller, UM Law Class of 2008, for his superb research assistance.

Robert M. **Jarvis** (jarvisb@nova.edu) is a professor of law at Nova Southeastern University (Fort Lauderdale, Florida). He is the co-author of *Baseball and the Law: Cases and Materials* (Carolina Academic Press, 2016) (recipient of the 2017 SABR Baseball Research Award) and the lead co-author of *Sports Law: Cases and Materials* (West Group, 1999). He holds a B.A. from Northwestern University, a J.D. from the University of Pennsylvania, and an LL.M. from New York University. He roots for the New York Yankees.

Elizabeth **Manriquez** (elizabeth.manriquez@wisc.edu) is the head of reference and scholarly support at the law library of the University of Wisconsin–Madison. Her campus research guides include *Play Ball! Resources on Sports Law* (2022). She holds a B.A. from DePaul University, an M.L.I.S. from the University of Washington, and a J.D. from the IIT Chicago-Kent College of Law. She roots for the Chicago White Sox.

Stephanie Hunter **McMahon** (stephanie.mcmahon@uc.edu) is a professor of law at the University of Cincinnati (Ohio). A tax law expert, she is the author of *Principles of Tax Policy* (West Academic Publishing, 3d ed., 2023) and has published shorter works in such periodicals as the *Florida Tax Review*, *Northwestern Law Review*, and *The Tax Lawyer*. She holds a B.A. from Oglethorpe University, an M.A. and a Ph.D. from the University of Virginia, and a J.D. from Harvard University. She roots for the New York Yankees.

Savanna L. **Nolan** (savnolan@uga.edu) is an instruction and faculty services librarian at the Alexander Campbell King Law Library at the University of Georgia (Athens). Her writings include "Inside Baseball: Justice Blackmun and the Summer of '72," 2020 *The Green Bag Almanac & Reader* 351. She holds a B.A. from the University of Southern California, an M.S.L.I.S. from the Catholic University of America, and a J.D. from the University of Georgia. She roots for the Atlanta Braves.

Geoffrey Christopher **Rapp** (geoffrey.rapp@utoledo.edu) is the senior associate dean for academic affairs and the Harold A. Anderson Professor of Law and Values at the University of Toledo (Ohio). He is the co-author of *Careers in Sports Law* (American Bar Association, 2015) and the author of articles in the *DePaul Journal of Sports Law*, *Marquette Sports Law Review*, and *Texas Review of Entertainment & Sports Law*. He holds an A.B. from Harvard University and a J.D. from Yale University. He roots for the Detroit Tigers.

Ronald J. **Rychlak** (rrychlak@olemiss.edu) is Distinguished Professor of Law, Jamie L. Whitten Chair of Law and Government, and faculty athletics representative at the University of Mississippi (Oxford). He is a contributor to *Courting the Yankees: Legal Essays on the Bronx Bombers* (Carolina Academic Press, 2003) and the author of "Pete Rose, Bart Giamatti, and the Dowd Report," 68 *Mississippi Law Journal* 889 (1999). He holds a B.A. from Wabash College and a J.D. from Vanderbilt University. He roots for the St. Louis Cardinals. He thanks Albert B. Chandler III and the staff at the University of Kentucky Libraries Special Collections Research Center for their assistance.

Louis H. **Schiff** (schiff@baseballandthelaw.org) is a retired judge (Broward County Court—Seventeenth Judicial Circuit of Florida) and an adjunct professor of law at the Mitchell Hamline School of Law (Saint Paul, Minnesota). He also is the lead co-author of *Baseball and the Law: Cases and Materials* (Carolina Academic Press, 2016) (recipient of the 2017 SABR Baseball Research Award). He holds a B.S. from the University of Florida and a J.D. from Hamline University. He roots for the Miami Marlins. He thanks William A. Dooley, Charles W. Ehrhardt, Robin F. Fuson, Anthony "Tony" La Russa, Jr., Scott K. Tozian, and Michael Veeck for sharing their insights with him. He also thanks Ben Meyer, of the MH Law Class of 2024, for his research assistance. Lastly, he thanks his wife Leslee for her support and encouragement.

Index

Numbers in *bold italics* indicate pages with illustrations